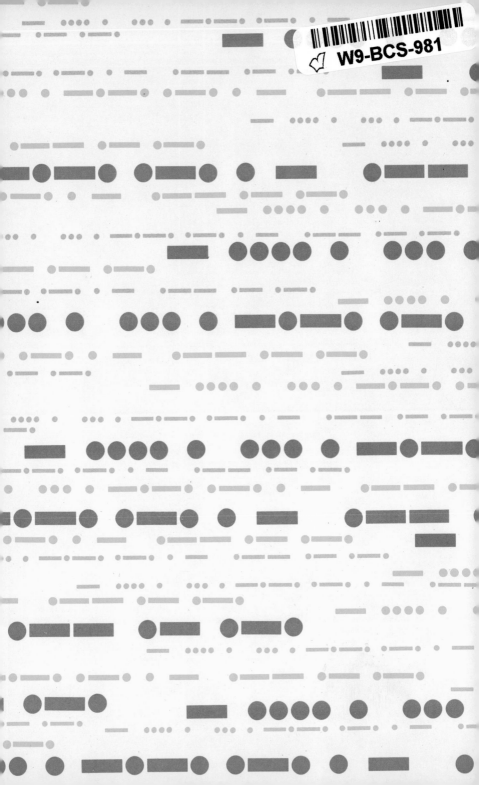

terrible attrition, the Alliance endured until the survivors were saved by the Liberation, the Allied victory they had done so much to bring about. The book is a tonic reminder of the great courage some of the French mustered in the face of a murderous enemy—and of the appalling level of brutality reached by the police and military of a Germany gone mad under a maniacal dictator.

The extraordinary author of *Noah's Ark*, Marie-Madeleine Fourcade, was one of the network's chief organizers and for long periods its principal leader. She was also, with her own courage and iron will, its inspiration. Brought up in privilege, the beautiful daughter of a wealthy shipping family, she hesitated hardly a moment after France's 1940 defeat to begin fighting with all her power for the invaders' defeat. Perpetually dodging hostile police, making a succession of hairbreadth escapes, assuming half a dozen aliases and many disguises as she traveled all over France helping direct Alliance cells, she was finally caught by the Gestapo—and miraculously escaped by wriggling her slight body through the iron bars of her cell.

Having survived years of this terrifying existence, this heroine of France—she was made a Commander of the Legion of Honor and awarded the Croix de Guerre—continued after the War to battle with formidable energy for what she believed in. She was a fervent supporter of General Charles De Gaulle, who she felt had kept alive the spirit of France during the dreadful days of the Occupation, and was a founder of De Gaulle's Union for the New Republic. She was a passionate enemy of all forms of totalitarianism, becoming a leader of both the Committee for the Defense of Human Rights and the League Against Racism and Anti-Semitism. She also spent much time helping survivors of the Resistance and the widows and orphans of Resistance fighters who were killed. Only weeks before her death at age 79 in 1989, she was still active, helping refugees from revolution-torn Lebanon.

—THE EDITORS

This volume, like every book in Classics of World War II: The Secret War, has been reproduced photographically from an original edition. It thus preserves the authenticity of the original, including typographical errors and printing irregularities.

TIME
LIFE

TIME-LIFE BOOKS INC., ALEXANDRIA, VIRGINIA 22314

CLASSICS OF WORLD WAR II

Noah's Ark is a vivid and moving account written by a wholly extraordinary woman of what was surely one of the most perilous, and important, intelligence operations of World War II. This was the French "Alliance," a huge underground organization made up of hundreds of Gallic patriots who gathered vast amounts of information about the Nazi occupiers of their country and beamed it by radio to British intelligence agencies in London.

Separate from the armed French Resistance—and little known to non-Frenchmen—the Alliance was astonishingly active and farflung. Alliance members worked under such evocative aliases as Eagle, Tiger, Cricket, and Mandrill, the animal code names that prompted the Germans to dub the organization "Noah's Ark" and thus gave this book its title. At any one time, two dozen or more clandestine radios were in place in various parts of France, ready to send out their Morse code messages. Members on France's Atlantic coast kept the Royal Navy informed of U-boat sailings. Spies in Marseilles reported on Mediterranean shipping. A couple of particularly daring agents in northern France pinpointed the launching pads for Hitler's supposedly secret weapons, the V-1 and V-2 rockets that threatened to level London. From every corner of the nation, Alliance members reported on the movements of German troops and supplies. In all they dispatched literally thousands of reports, many so valuable to the Allies that they helped turn the tide of the war.

The book is a story of triumph, but also of tragedy. Using traitors and turncoats, German counterintelligence agencies, especially the dreaded Gestapo, caught and crushed one Alliance cell after another, arresting and then torturing and killing many of the network's bravest men and women. Hundreds of them perished in prisons and before firing squads, including most of the leaders whom the reader comes to know and admire. Somehow, despite the

NOAH'S ARK

NOAH'S ARK

by Marie-Madeleine Fourcade O.B.E.

Translated from the French by Kenneth Morgan

Preface by Commander Kenneth Cohen, C.B., C.M.G., R.N.

New York

E. P. Dutton & Company, Inc.

1974

CONTENTS

ILLUSTRATIONS

Photographs 1 through 8 follow page 128

PREFACE

by Commander Kenneth Cohen c.b., c.m.g., r.n.

'The Germans may take Paris but they will not stop my going on with the war. We will fight on the Loire, we will fight on the Garonne, we will even fight on the Pyrenees. And at last, if we are driven off the Pyrenees, we will continue the war at sea—but ask for peace—never!'

From Sir David Thompson, *Democracy in France*. Statement attributed to Clemenceau.

I did not meet the author of this deeply moving book till 1943, although the origin of her 3,000 strong network goes back to the disastrous late summer of 1940. I had, however, made contact with her predecessor, the redoubtable Commandant Loustaunau-Lacau (alias Navarre) in clandestine circumstances at Lisbon in 1941. Even a bitter political enemy described him as *'un grand Monsieur'*. There, after a *'reniflement mutuel'* (Marie-Madeleine's canine expression for mutual assessment), we worked out together a joint war-plan. The principal objective was to ensure that the results of the Commandant's promising intelligence organization in France (The 'Alliance'), then virtually unexploited, should be speedily available to the British (and later American) General Staffs. The Alliance's potentialities were, on the whole, quickly recognized by the British. The author, however, is at times over-generous to her supporters (including the writer of this preface). There is a suggestion that only a discreet whisper in the Prime Minister's ear was needed to bring supplies parachuting down to them from the air. Would that this had been the case!

These brave French men and women, who constituted the Alliance network, served the allies with great fortitude and skill and eventually became an integral part of the *Forces Françaises Combattantes*. Some 500 of them were to die in the struggle, many of them first suffering torture and captivity in appalling circumstances.

Loustaunau-Lacau was early betrayed, but miraculously survived the torment of Mauthausen concentration camp. He was replaced by a woman, of whom we (the British) then knew little beyond her code name, 'Poz 55'. She first made contact with the outside world when she emerged, paralysed with cold and cramp, from a sealed diplomatic bag. This had been carried in the boot of a car to Madrid by a compliant Vichy courier, who had crossed the Pyrenees in mid-winter. Reports to London that her Nefertiti-like beauty and charm (she was then thirty-two, mother of two children) were equalled by her total dedication and executive capacity proved unexaggerated. Fact had out-paced fiction in producing the copybook 'beautiful spy'. This was Marie-Madeleine.

It was not till twenty years after the liberation of France that the author started on this Homeric saga of her *réseau's* 'daily life' under German occupation. She tells of their desperate anxieties, their suffering, their elation, their disasters, their interminable waiting for 'the landings', and of their final freedom. The various characters of whom she quickly became established as the chosen leader range, as will be seen, from the magnificent but totally aggressive 'Eagle', to the highly disciplined wireless operator 'Magpie'; from Dukes and Duchesses to *concierges* (where would 'intelligence' be without these latter?); from politicians to policemen. She allows the characters to speak for themselves and these, alas, include a traitor who was sent to her with disastrous results. This blunder did not dim her loyalty to the British alliance, and was perhaps later appropriately redeemed by the splendid record of 'Magpie', another British subject and clandestine wireless operator.

Marie-Madeleine's ability at this distance of time to recount with such evocative detail the lives of her fellow helpers is a tribute to her intellectual powers and her human comprehension. This is perhaps, in part, an explanation of her success as a resistance leader. That she did not take this success for granted is shown by her self-questioning at the time of her 'accession': '*Vont ils m'obéir?*' As a digression it might be added that on one of the two or three occasions known to the writer, when Churchill gave personal attention to the affairs of the Alliance, the qualities of a '*Grand chef*' were defined to him by a French officer. They were: (1) *Courage*, (2) *Connaissance de son métier*, (3) *Compréhension des hommes*. These qualities, in maximum or minimum degree, were then assigned to General de Gaulle, but (with a different 'mix') could readily have been ascribed to Marie-Madeleine.

With a Tolstoyan inevitability she tells of the ebb of the national spirit as the armies disintegrated in the summer of 1940, and then of the very slow turn of the tide as a permanent German hegemony became less certain. But only a minute elite (who became known to us as 'vintage 1940') were ready at that time to risk their all. Amongst these few were, of course, Loustaunau-Lacau, the founder of the network '*Oui nous les refoulerons.* . . . *Il (Hitler) fonce comme une brute avec des moyens puissants, certes, mais pas infaillibles ni éternels. Il faut prévoir la gaffe que l'Allemand commet inévitablement tôt ou tard et en attendant—tenir*'.[1]

They started their work appropriately enough in Loustaunau's beloved Pyrenees. A vivid picture of his own tumultuous life there (and elsewhere) can be found in his well-named book, *Mémoires d'un Français rebelle*. His successor's, Marie-Madeleine's, attitude was more personal (and feminine?): '*Qu'est-ce que la patience? ruminais-je. Une vertu idiote faite pour les gens sans nerfs comme Diogène et Socrate . . . des ânes qui n'exige point de vengeance. Je*

---

[1] 'We'll drive them back. Hitler will batter his way in but his resources are neither infallible nor everlasting. Sooner or later we can expect the inevitable German blunder. Until then—hold on!'

m'examinais. Mon ressentiment ne cédait pas et je bouillais du désir de me venger.'[1]

But such personal feelings in no way diminished Marie-Madeleine's capacity to lead her 3,000 followers without any of the aids which a field commander would take for granted at his relatively safe headquarters. Her attitude towards the enemy was accompanied by a shrewd appreciation of what was 'worthwhile' in the way of information, both from the point of view of her agents' opportunities and the criteria of the Service Staffs for whom it was destined. But for her, *me venger* meant more than that, and to the dismay of her subordinates, of the British Staffs concerned, to say nothing of her immediate family, she would insist on plunging into the fray in the first person. This brought about her arrest by the Vichy police and her subsequent escape (admittedly, in this case, with some rather light-hearted collusion), her smuggled appearance in Madrid, a visit to London by a clandestine air operation, and finally a further arrest by the Gestapo, with a desperate escape to follow. Thus she stoutly combined the role of fighter and strategist.

No single French network can claim the monopoly of intelligence-gathering from occupied territory (soon to include the whole of France), but this writer would maintain that the Alliance survivors and their 500 dead had particularly well served the allied services with their emphasis on information concerning German submarine bases and, in 1944, rocket sites. Many of their sources had begun their flow in 1941, when resistance was confined to the few. Moreover, reporting of intelligence had none of the glamour or the 'instant results' of sabotage, which was, together with organizing escapes, the other principal opportunity of resistance open to French patriots. Their remarkable exploits included, incidentally, as described in the book, the organizing of the escape of General Giraud on the eve of the North African landings. Although Giraud's subsequent performance proved something of an anticlimax, General Eisenhower, it should be noted, at the time attached great importance to this delicate operation.

Marie-Madeleine describes with telling pathos the capture and eventual execution of her splendid second-in-command, Commandant Faye, and his last wishes, later found hidden in his cell, might serve as a requiem for the Alliance's sacrifices. *'Fermez les prisons, chassez les bourreaux . . . Plus tard les historiens jugeront. Pour l'instant il s'agit d'union et non de représailles, de travail et non de désordre, c'est mon dernier voeu.'*[2]

I will add only a short personal postscript concerning Loustaunau-Lacau, the network's founder, and the author, his successor. As might

---

[1] 'And patience, I reflected? An absurd virtue fit for a thin-blooded Diogenes or Socrates; for an ass that seeks no vengeance. I looked into my heart. My hostility remained undiminished and I boiled with a desire for revenge.'

[2] 'Close down the prisons, throw out the executioners . . . later the historians will give their verdict. Now we need unity, not reprisals, work and not chaos. These are my last wishes.'

be expected, it is not of a 'they lived happily ever after' character. With his unbelievable stamina, Loustaunau-Lacau survived three years in the hands of the Gestapo, coming back to Paris the merest skeleton of his normally bull-like frame, and, as it happened, at the height of the Pétain trial. He had been Pétain's personal assistant during the pre-war years, but this had not prevented his former chief from allowing him to be handed over by Vichy to the Gestapo. The prosecuting counsel, not knowing their man, rashly brought him forward as a promising witness. Certainly his evidence hit the headlines. Like Faye, he felt this was no time for fostering enmities and questioned in no uncertain terms whether the judges' and prosecution's own records justified their pursuing the trial: '*Vous n'allez pas refiler à ce vieillard l'ardoise de vos erreurs . . .*!'[1] He was not recalled to the witness box! In the few years remaining to him after his war time sufferings, this formidable man of the Right, but inveterate rebel, was to serve as an independent deputy. There he eagerly pursued the possibility of reconciliation behind the Iron Curtain—an attitude much ahead of the politics of the day.

Marie-Madeleine—like Faye—never lost faith in the regeneration of France, and I remember this attitude of hers being expressed with characteristic vividness on the evening of D-Day, when she and the acting head of the Free French special services dined in London with my wife and myself. (Owing to Gestapo raids on her *réseau* it was only some days later that she was allowed by the British authorities to return to her dangerous task in occupied France.) She was exultant over the prospective liberation, but our other guest thought more of the ravaged and embittered state of his country, as our conversation was punctuated by the detonations of occasional V.2s. '*Voyons donc*,' expostulated Marie-Madeleine, '*dans les accouchements, ce sont les femmes qui sont vaillantes*'.[2]

Since the armistice she has devoted her time and immense energy to the well-being of her wartime comrades. She has also played an important part (mainly behind the scenes) in Gaullist politics, combining this with a crusade to unmask any signs of Nazi or Fascist resurgence in Europe or the Middle East. She has, however, retained in an enchantingly mundane manner her enjoyment of the good things of this world, and most particularly so when they are to be had in her husband's and her estate in the Camargue.

K.C.

---

[1] 'Don't pile on this old man the weight of your own faults . . . !'
[2] 'You see! In confinements only the women are brave.'

London
October 1972

NOAH'S ARK

INTRODUCTION

Fight in the armour of Light (St Paul)

On 19 August 1944, Lucien Berne and an English comrade were taken at dead of night from Avignon prison, where for weeks they had awaited the sentence of the Third Reich. Chained together, they were driven to the banks of the Rhone. The men of the Gestapo pushed them ahead to a deserted spot.

Lucien Berne heard the whistle of the bullet that struck his companion in the back of the neck. Instinctively he fell to the ground at the very moment that the shot intended for him flashed past. The Nazis came up. They bent over their victims, who sprawled face downwards, and fired the *coups de grâce*. Lucien's left lung was pierced by the bullet. A gush of blood poured from his mouth.

Was this—the cool sensation of the stream that covered, penetrated, cleansed and consumed his unconscious body—the sensation of dying? Suddenly Lucien's mind regained awareness and he realized that he was in the Rhone, with the swift current sweeping him back towards the bank where his executioners still stood. Then, without surfacing, with his good arm, he began to swim. In spite of the choking blood and mud, he fought the current tirelessly to gain the island of La Barthelasse. Finally a bush caught him and he plunged, exhausted, into a thick bed of reeds.

The Gestapo agents had seen nothing. Of the two corpses that they had dumped in the river there remained only the handcuffs. They wiped these methodically before returning to further vile tasks, to other victims who would pay with their lives for the collapse of the 'thousand-year Reich'.

The Englishman's body was found, but no-one ever discovered his name. He was buried at Avignon as the Alliance Network's Unknown Soldier. Lucien Berne is its living corpse.

The years have passed, my friends have died, but their spirit is still alive. They rejected the invader, the occupier, the profaners of our liberties, and their fight weighs heavily on my conscience.

Who were the men and women who risked and often lost their lives to resist Nazi domination? They were the members of a military intelligence network that waged a relentless and unremitting fight in France from her fall in 1940 until her liberation in 1945. Soon people will no longer know what they did nor why they did it, nor even if it was necessary to do it: indeed, they will be pitied for dying for nothing. I should like to know that they will not be forgotten, that the divine flame that burned in their hearts will be understood.

This book is not a diary of the course of events. An eye-witness account is not that of a historian. As the only survivor left to recall the entire tragedy, I have had to limit myself to describing the people whom I knew best. Those whom I have not been able to name will forgive me. They will meet one another again through their brothers-in-arms in the Alliance Intelligence Service, that army of three thousand shadows who shifted and succeeded one another and changed places like images in a film, fading and being replaced by others to ensure continuity.

I often let my companions live again under their underground aliases. Indeed, we rarely knew one another's real names. At the beginning we described ourselves by groups of letters and numbers, by symbols: KSI 42, KIF 141, ASO 43. Later, as the war went on, we adopted the names of animals: Eagle, Humming Bird, Tiger, Ermine. . . .

The Germans called us 'Noah's Ark'.

THE CRUSADE

*Time seems long to those who are going
to undertake something great*

Winston Churchill

1 THE FLOOD

Paris, in June 1940, was a city veiled in black. Thick clouds of soot from burning petrol dumps masked the blinding summer sky. Houses disgorged their contents into all kinds of vehicles; furniture, possessions and people were huddled under pyramids of mattresses. Dogs were killed to save food. It was a case of every man for himself, with whatever he could salvage in all its sadness. Farm tractors lumbered forward to the slow clank of their caterpillar treads, constantly endangering the handcarts. Old people, piled into perambulators, were pushed along by weeping women, the children trailing after them, stupefied by the heat.

Push on, and on, and then on again. Those were the orders. Where to? The authorities had left for Bordeaux; one after another the ministries were moving; the tradesmen were shutting their shops. It was all over. There was already a sense of armistice about the abandonment of Paris. You hoped for an earthquake that you might escape the shame; you were glad of the pall of soot veiling the long lines of vehicles, four abreast, that suddenly blocked the great arteries leading to the south.

Since 1937 I had been the general secretary of a magazine publishing group inspired by Commandant Georges Loustaunau-Lacau. A brilliant scholar and a daring man of action, he described himself as a total rebel against the corrupt political practices that were dooming his country to dismemberment. He was convinced that war would break out and that France was in no fit state to win. This hero of World War I, a product of Saint Cyr, who was the first of his year in the Ecole Supérieure de Guerre, with a fluent command of five languages, had one obsessive interest—the secret services. He believed the secrets only if he dug them out himself and trusted the services only if he ran them himself. So he was obliged to create them. From that time onwards we began to build up an intelligence network against the Nazis.

In 1938 and 1939 the battle order of Hitler's land, sea and air forces appeared in our journal, *L'Ordre National*. It had been compiled by a Jew, Bertold Jacob, a sort of intelligence wizard who had been keeping careful track of the advance of Nazism from its beginnings. The forces of the Greater German Reich increased in defiance of every treaty. Deliberately willed by the Führer, war emerged from these reports as a certainty. It was obvious that people fed on a diet of guns rather than butter would spit fire.

This threat soon became reality, and after general mobilization in September 1939 I found myself running the paper practically single-handed, except for the help of a very young assistant editor, Jean-Philippe Salmson, who was itching to fight. But its title, *L'Ordre National*, seemed so ridiculous in the circumstances of the 'phoney war' that we no longer really knew what to put in it. An extensive tour in a zone where our armies were bottled up made me realize that our information about the enemy positions, gathered over many years, on the terrain itself, were assuming an halucinatory character. I saw that the activities of our little group could perhaps take other channels than writing. That gave me courage to wait for the inevitable to happen and so, when I got back from my trip, I closed the paper down.

Once Loustaunau-Lacau had personally experienced the phoney front he could see for himself the truth of his gloomy prophecies. Naturally he did not mince his words, but accused the high command of high treason. His conduct earned him imprisonment and his friends had to alert Parliament and public opinion to save him from the firing squad. Then, on 10 May 1940, an intelligent examining magistrate confirmed the validity of the evidence that 'Navarre'—Georges Loustaunau-Lacau's pseudonym, which we had fallen into the habit of using—had vainly asked should be considered before it was too late.

That morning, while we were at the Palais de Justice with my young colleague, Jean-Philippe, and his parents Georges and Geneviève Salmson, waiting for Navarre to be released, the tanks of the Wehrmacht were tearing the French army to shreds and beginning to fan out through the gaps in our unimaginative defences. Loustaunau-Lacau, freed and unembittered, immediately asked for a new command. Leaving on 9 June to join a Zouave battalion to which he had been assigned somewhere in eastern France, he had warned us:

'It's absolutely hopeless. There *is* a possible solution: to establish circular positions, stick to the towns, let Hitler's wave sweep past, and cut its lines of communication. I'm going to see what I can do in the ranks. Your best way to escape the Germans would be to take the roads that run down through central France. Rendezvous ultimately at my place in Oloron-Sainte-Marie in the Pyrenees.'

That same day, a Sunday, the 'Sawdust Caesar', Mussolini, declared war on France. Belgium had cracked. The British had re-embarked for home. The units in Bertold Jacob's order of battle were rushing towards Paris. An ocean of misery was submerging us.

The Salmsons and I had left Paris on 11 June, in full flight, not knowing how we were going to be able to hold on but determined not to yield to brute force, and having the incredible presumption to believe that amid all this shambles we stood for something.

It was like a strange sort of country outing! Whole towns were out in the fields. My car was forced to halt against the side of the road. 'Let's get out and stretch our legs,' I said to my maid, a Norman hot-head with a quick tongue who had insisted on accompanying me. I called to the Salmsons, whose cars I could see wedged between two vans a little further ahead.

'At this rate it'll take us twelve hours to get as far as Fontainebleau,' Georges reckoned, in the depths of despair.

Georges Salmson was a member of the automobile manufacturing family of that name and for the moment regretted that he had ever supported the rise of such an industry. I asked: 'Shall we turn round and follow those Red Cross cars? They're getting through as though by magic!'

'You can't really mean that, Marie-Madeleine!' exclaimed Genevieve Salmson in her usual lively way. 'What about our rendezvous with Navarre?'

In the distance the drone of aircraft and dull explosions could be heard. For the first time I experienced the abominable relief that you feel when a bomb falls on a neighbour instead of on yourself.

Our rendezvous with Navarre seemed to belong to the world of dreams.

I jammed my foot down on the accelerator, swallowing up a few miles of clear road. Now I felt sure that nothing would halt the enemy before the Pyrenees. This was the fall of France. Grief, fraught with humiliation and impotent rage, possessed me. The night and then a long day passed and we plunged into the province of Berry, the very heart of France.

I remembered a friend who used to spend her summers there, George Sand's grand-daughter. As luck would have it, her charming smile welcomed us as though this were nothing more than a surprise visit. 'There are too many of you to be put up here,' she said, 'but go and make yourself at home in the Château de Nohant.'

A few more miles and we found ourselves at the historic abode of George Sand and Alfred de Musset. I chose to sleep in Chopin's bed. Lying there in a rather overwrought state, I imagined I was playing the popular *Lorelei Ballade*, which merged with the rustling of the leaves in the park—the same rustling that the idol of my youth had transposed for the piano at my side. I fingered the keys, but it was the *Etude Revolutionnaire* that thundered out, and at last I understood to the full the depth of its shattering vision.

Then we dashed through central France, travelling only by night, with all our lights out. As we lay low by day, concealed in sunken roads or sprawling on the soft earth amid the undergrowth, I had a strong feeling that our days were numbered. The orders we were able to glean from the regional authorities were contradictory. The wave of refugees from the north was now running into those fleeing from the Italians in the south.

Encouraged by the radio, the idea of an armistice was uppermost in people's minds. When Marshal Pétain's bleating voice uttered the fatal words, they did not surprise us. On that lovely summer Sunday the imminence of the armistice burst into our consciousness. Uniforms were whisked away. Women smiled. People kissed one another. In the cafés the crowds drank the health of the old Marshal.

Hitler's raving, in *Mein Kampf*, 'I will separate the men from the women and this race will cease', arose in my memory to cancel out the instinctive feeling of relief that I, like everyone else, felt at the first news of the cease fire. An immense wave of anguish swept over me: it was disaster now and uncertainty in the future. I turned towards my companions, whose faces expressed the same suffering.

Salmson (the 'Knight' we called him) was the first to recover. He told me he had managed to store away some cans of petrol which the troops had been selling him on the sly. It meant we could make a dash for Dax, down towards the Pyrenees.

A good room at Dax was our reward for the last few nights in the vineyards. My maid busied herself with my crumpled clothes. I was getting out of a bath, almost relaxed, when I looked out of the window and suddenly I saw *them*.

With fifes playing at the head of their column, the Germans came marching over the bridge across the Adour. A few locals caught in the middle of the bridge stood gazing down at the water in embarrassment.

It was a very fine division, whose officers could speak Basque and even the dialect of the Landes. They knew every inch, every twist and turn in the town, and without asking the petrified inhabitants a single question they led their men to the billets that had already been fixed back in Berlin. I had never expected anything like this. The conventional way they marched and took over the town made it seem even more cruel than I had ever imagined.

'The bastards! To think they've come all that way and look so fresh,' fumed my maid. 'We'll be killed off like rats!'

This dreadful possibility came as a rude shock. I rushed out to meet Georges Salmson, who was coming back from the town hall. He had details of the armistice terms. Relying on the Nazis' sense of honour, Pétain had initialled the map that dismembered and enslaved the country. Dispensing with any sort of peace treaty, Alsace and Lorraine and the rich northern areas were annexed by the German Reich under the guise of forbidden zones. The remaining *départements* were occupied by Hitler's troops, except for a southern zone, described as unoccupied. But we were soon to see it invaded by armistice commissions that would rob it as well. I stood bewildered and speechless.

'So that's that,' the Knight said. 'Where d'you want to go now?'

'It seems to me that we must try to keep our rendezvous with Navarre, even if nothing comes of it,' I replied, pulling myself together.

The demarcation line between the two zones was already a fact but it was only weakly guarded by polite SS men who were not yet searching vehicles. We crossed without any trouble.

At Oloron-Sainte-Marie, Navarre's wife and children had no news of him. They sent us to the Spanish consular agent, a warm and friendly man who welcomed us in a very generous way. He told us what was happening in the world and we spent the evenings discussing the birth of Vichyism and Gaullism.

Pétain had set up his regime at Vichy and called it a 'National Revolution'. In London, in lone defiance, one Frenchman was proclaiming that the war was not lost and calling on his compatriots to continue the fight. That man was Charles de Gaulle, who wanted to restore to France her soul by giving her fresh hope. I had been privileged to make the acquaintance of General de Gaulle four years earlier at a party that my brother-in-law, Commandant Georges-Picot, had given for army men, including Commandant Loustaunau-Lacau and Colonel de Gaulle (as he was at that time). The three of them were haunted by the same fear—the increasing interference of a demagogic policy in national defence matters. And now, within four weeks, five and a half million Frenchmen under arms had been defeated by a half million of Hitler's soldiers. After erecting forts like card houses, were we going to owe our salvation to a mere ditch—the English Channel?

But the youth of France was hesitant to answer de Gaulle's call. Families were divided against one another by painful debates. Only too glad to have some of their sons saved from the vast harvest of prisoners, parents forbade them to make the slightest gesture of revolt. People genuinely believed that they could live under the Nazi jackboot. 'The Germans will go back home as soon as they've beaten the British. It's only a matter of months,' the know-alls insisted.

The situation was desperate. At Mers-el-Kébir, France's naval base in Algeria, the fleet had been attacked by the Royal Navy. The *Bretagne*, the *Provence*, the *Mogador* and the *Dunkerque* were sunk or crippled. The death roll was 1,297. This struggle with Britain, our ally in 1914–1918 and 1939–1940, and now the last bastion of the free world, was difficult to believe. Was there not still in France one single clear-sighted politician to save us from the Nazi flood?

We learned that Navarre had been seriously wounded and was a prisoner in a Nazi military hospital in the eastern part of occupied France. The Oloron rendezvous was turning sour on us. I was, however, happy to know that my family was safe and sound. My mother had been able to join my children, whom I had sent several months earlier to the island of Noirmoutier for safety. My brother had managed to slip through the enemy lines and get back to our property at Mougins on the Riviera. I wrote and told them not to move until I was clear about the next step.

A few gleams of hope nevertheless relieved the uncertainty. Certain units had fought desperately, proving that the will to fight was still alive in France. So the secret meetings we held at night took on a more definite purpose. The consul knew his region like the back of his hand. 'They seem to be settling in for life. They are bringing in large quantities of men and *matériel*,' he said, referring to the SS divisions stationed in the extreme south-west.

'These concentrations seem to me to be more than just occupation troops,' I remarked. 'Can we be of any use to those who are carrying on the struggle by letting them know what we see?'

'You mean warn the British?' The old Franco-fighter bristled: 'Don't give it a thought. They're finished, anyway.'

One evening we were joined by Philippe Le Couteux, a friend of the Salmsons. He was a man of Florentine charm and so we called him 'Valori' after the Tuscan family founded by Valore. Like us, he believed any sort of collaboration was out of the question, and we were scheming to leave without having any definite plans in mind when the glorious news of Navarre's escape broke. Slithering from one train to another like a snake, he had slipped across the demarcation line on 20 August. Exhausted and in great pain because of his unhealed wound, he had lost forty pounds and it was a miracle that he could still stand. His presence was an inspiration, for here was someone who would make vital decisions and tell us what to do.

We bombarded him with questions. How could we recreate an army in a country swarming with conquerors, in towns full of fifth columnists? How could a conquered people help?

'We must act quickly,' I put in. 'Shall we go to England?'

'It's not a practical proposition for forty million Frenchmen to cross the mountains and the sea. We shall have to get ourselves sorted out and show what we can do for help to come from outside,' said Navarre. 'For the moment Hitler controls France, with Marshal Pétain at the head of affairs. He's fed up with our concerns. It's just what we need to get a foothold in Vichy.'

'Vichy?' I asked, disgusted. 'The place has become a phoney capital.'

'Of course, Vichy. Marie-Madeleine, you'll have to get into the habit of deceiving people. If you want to get information you *must* go to the source of power, and to act you *must* make outside contacts. Quite apart from being the source of power, Vichy is the diplomatic centre, the place where the foreign embassies are. It is only when we know all the facts that we'll be able to persuade other people to act.'

'To gather information and act is obviously a practical programme, but what means can we use?' I asked.

'Our own will do for a start,' he concluded in a tone of voice that clinched the matter. 'From today we are Crusaders. Back to Vichy!'

The journey back along the road that we had travelled in such despair a few weeks before, now clear of all traffic, moved us even more profoundly than it had then. From that moment we understood how pleasant it is to walk on one's native soil, how sweet to gaze on the countryside, how dear are the faces that one cannot forget.

Almost all the plots which finally led to the emergence of La France Combattante were hatched as early as September 1940 in Vichy, in hotel rooms originally planned and built for French colonials suffering from liver complaints. The weather was glorious and there was a holiday atmosphere in the air. A dense, mixed crowd of people fought to obtain even the meanest little room; endless queues stood outside the restaurants watching for the first free table. Who of those who were received at the Hôtel du Parc, Marshal Pétain's headquarters, can claim that they did not experience at the time a feeling of satisfaction and pride at getting into the den of the prophets of doom? The monarchists regarded the Marshal as the stepping stone to the return of the French King; the best industrial brains were members of the Cabinet; the intellectuals rushed to pursue educational, sporting and racist aims. Those people were the aristocracy of defeat. Anyone who was not a member was treated as a pariah. The enemy, apparently, was careful not to interfere.

'The Marshal's terrific,' said his aide-de-camp, Bonhomme, a sort of light-skinned Mameluke. 'Nothing puts him out.'

'So he wouldn't be put out if I went and offered him my services?' barked Navarre, sounding like an artillery officer giving the order to fire.

'Have you got a plan?' Bonhomme asked anxiously.

'Yes, in a vague sort of way. In the twenty-four hours I've been wandering around Vichy I've met a lot of first-class men, fellows who've been demobilized or escaped or come from Paris to see how the land lies. None of the poor devils could get a look in; every door was closed. I'd like to set up a sort of reception centre here. We'd cheer up some of them, we'd give others a fresh start. It's all very pleasant for your bright bunch, the admirals and technical experts, but what are the men who did the fighting going to think?'

'Yes,' Bonhomme replied doubtfully, 'You're right, but you know how it is with the Old Man. He doesn't like people to tell him his business.'

'I'm not telling him his business,' insisted Navarre, strangely calm. 'I didn't escape just for the fun of it. I've taken a hotel, the Hotel des Sports, where I'm going to set up my . . . rehabilitation centre, if you like. I need money and help—support, a sort of official sanction. The Old Man can certainly afford to do that for me.'

That was how the Hôtel des Sports came into being, and at his own request Loustaunau-Lacau was appointed general delegate of the Légion des Combattants.

'What a reservoir!' he exclaimed when he came back from the Hotel du Parc. 'I'm going to pick out the best elements, the ones who want to put up a fight. This Légion will make it possible to set up patrols throughout France. In the meantime *you*,' he said, pointing his cigarette at me, '*you* will organize the underground side.'

'But Navarre, I'm only a woman!' I exclaimed, taken completely aback.

'That's another good reason! Who will ever suspect a woman? For the next few months I'm going to let myself be seen among that bunch of ninnies, see the Marshal in order to do what the old hypocrite has asked me to do, let him know what is happening to his "dear old soldiers". I must be absolutely above suspicion. So I'll leave you to do all the secret stuff. It'll be a tough job. Poor Marie-Madeleine, you have every right to give it all up. You won't be the only one,' he added sarcastically, fixing me with a piercing look.

'Yes, I'm very afraid I won't be able to live up to what you expect of me, Navarre. This job is terrifying. I'm hardly thirty and you're asking me to command hardened old campaigners like yourself. I know your friends; they aren't easy. I'd rather serve in the ranks.'

There was a long silence. He stopped walking round the room, sat down at the table and put his glasses on. Before picking up his pen he said: 'If you haven't the strength to take the job on I won't give it to anyone at all. I'll do it by myself. I've been betrayed so many times. I must make a clean sweep and start again from scratch.'

His pen sped across the blue-tinted paper. On the back of his neck I could see the still unhealed scar at the top of the wound that zigzagged down the whole length of his back from the bullet that had struck him during the battle on the Meuse. I thought of the other battles that he had taken on single-handed, deliberately and unmindful of the damage he might do to his brilliant career.

'You don't think that someone else . . . ?'

'No, I can't trust anyone.'

'Thank you. I'll try not to let you down. I accept.'

He wrote a few more sentences, then handed me the paper. 'These are my intentions and your orders. Learn them by heart. I told you before France fell that the means at Hitler's disposal are neither infallible nor eternal. We're going to nibble them away.'

2 THE HOTEL DES SPORTS

All sorts of strange customers flocked to the aptly-named Hôtel des Sports. 'Everyone coming here must think of it as a house of glass. Those we wish to keep must be able to stay right out of sight,' Navarre had said.

By day the residents behaved with the utmost circumspection; at night they at last came to life, slipping skilfully from floor to floor or from room to room to establish the contacts necessary to an incipient underground movement. Meals were served by Mme Salmson, acting as hostess at little tables where groups of like-minded old comrades gathered as though they were new friends, solid fellows wearing new Vichy-State uniforms that made them look like Snow White's seven dwarfs. They discussed the organizations Pétain had created to occupy the rising generation: the Chantiers de Jeunesse, Compagnons de France, and Groupes de Protection. Genuine escapers appeared, their eyes still haunted by the experience of the Stalags. There were bogus escapers, too, easily recognized by their discreetly martial bearing. Among them a character who might have stepped straight out of a Tolstoy novel intrigued me because of his habit of looking out of the corner of his eye and the strange, over-elaborate way in which he adjusted a leather jacket with abnormally large pockets.

My greatest joy was to be visited by friends who came from the occupied zone in the hope of carrying on the fight. One was Paul Bernard, an administrator in an important colonial company; and there was Jean Sainteny, son-in-law of a former Minister of the Interior.

'Our visitors have a spontaneous and natural flair for action and intelligence,' was Navarre's opinion. 'You can see that they're in contact with the Boches.'

Thanks to their information, the German occupation became for me more real. It was like being fascinated by a snake. There were the plans for adapting the Renault workshops to repair Hitler's tanks; and a depressing report on economic annexation. France was even going to help the Nazis wage their war: our Atlantic ports were becoming U-boat nests.

'We must bomb here, sabotage there,' commented Navarre.

'How? What with?' I inquired in astonishment.

'I already have two channels for passing on the information we get. The first is the man in the leather jacket. He's Captain Fourcaud, the first of General de Gaulle's special envoys.'

'That Tolstoy character? The arrival of General de Gaulle himself couldn't be more of a bombshell!'

'"Bombshell"! Thanks. That's just the alias I was looking for. Among ourselves we'll never call him anything else. I'm just arranging for him to return to London through Spain with the assistance of what is left of the Army Intelligence Service. My second channel is a remarkably brave Canadian diplomat whom the British have sent officially to sound out the Hôtel du Parc. He quickly summed up the situation and agreed to carry my messages. But I also ought to have a personal ambassador. In secret service affairs missions must always be duplicated several times over.'

'How about my brother? I'm expecting him any day.'

'Put it to him as soon as he arrives. But there's something much more urgent. Make sure you find a job for the three boys hanging around in the small lounge.'

'The ones who spun a yarn about escaping?'

'They've just been demobilized. I recruited them at the Légion des Combattants meeting.'

I knew my orders by heart: 'First, divide the so-called unoccupied zone into sectors. Each one of these sectors must allow you both to observe the enemy in the unoccupied zone and to move our couriers in every direction.' The south-west sector was already functioning, with crossing points established along the demarcation line, and channels of communication down to Spain were in course of preparation. Still to be created were the patrols to operate to Switzerland and Italy and one in Marseilles for keeping a watch on the Mediterranean, with extensions in North Africa.

'Secondly, divide up the occupied zone, create patrols with extensions in forbidden zones. . . .' We bent over the map of France. Navarre marked the sectors selected for subversive activity in red pencil, in order of priority.

I was seized with panic. Would they obey me?

The three young men greeted me with a scowl and the words: 'We didn't come here to twiddle our thumbs.' They too were wearing leather jackets.

'So all we need to do is round up the leather jackets, and we shall have found the men who want to fight,' I said in an attempt to assert myself.

'Who are you exactly?'

'We're Blue-White-Red.'

Concealing my surprise, I ordered them to explain what they meant. Then Maurice Coustenoble spoke. He said they had been in the Air Force—he was in the reserve; Lieutenant Lenoir, known as 'White', was a regular; and 'Red' was in the gliders. They had met in 1939 at an aerobatics school and had stuck together ever since. Hence 'Blue, White and Red'.

'You're the leader?'

'Yes. I'm "Blue".' His carefully slicked-down hair, his little freshly-waxed moustache and his big dark eyes produced a curious effect on me.

What could he be in civilian life? Some little clerk? But I was immediately won over by his sincerity and his directness.

'When I was forced down near Bordeaux with an empty fuel tank, before I set fire to my crate I yanked the joystick out and swore I'd fight any way I could until I found another.' He had then wandered around with his friends until their savings were exhausted, rallying to their colours not only Air Force comrades but also any chance acquaintances they happened to make in bars and during interminable waits in station buffets. To prove the truth of what they said they pulled out of their pockets scraps of paper scribbled all over with addresses.

I would have to teach them to train their memories and to burn their notes, I thought in alarm, but first I must find out how they got them. 'How can you be sure of these people?'

Coustenoble extracted from his briefcase an even more crumpled piece of paper and handed it to me with a mysterious smile. Dog-eared, yellow, dirty, it must have been folded and unfolded hundreds of times. In amazement I read:

'*The Prophecy of Saint Odile*'
'Listen, oh my brothers, for I have seen the terror of the forests and the mountains . . .
'Horror has numbed the peoples . . .
'The time has come when Germania will be called "the most warlike nation on earth" . . .
'Nevertheless, the conqueror will have reached the height of his triumph towards the middle of the sixth month of the second year of the war . . .
'The third period will be short. It will be called the period of invasion for, by a just reversal of fortune, the conqueror's country will be invaded from all quarters . . .'

'It's our tract. The Germans have banned it in the occupied zone. We start off by moaning about what is happening and then we produce Saint Odile's prophecy. That sets people talking. We can see in a flash those who think they're finished for ever. We're only interested in the others. We tell them to copy out the prophecy and circulate it and that we shall come back to put them in the picture.'

'That's marvellous; but what picture?'

Lenoir raised his arms like a sniper taking aim. 'There are lots of weapons that have been hidden all over the place, and stocks of ammunition.'

'Take up arms again now? You must be out of your mind. That won't be for ages. The Commandant reckons it will last as long as the "14 war".'

They looked at me in despair. 'Five years! We can't go on being occupied for five years.'

I could not dash their splendid optimism. These young men had guts. They must be given active jobs at once. 'Since you're used to working together,' I said, 'you'll form the Blue-White-Red patrol and help to get new sectors organized and operating. But first, in Vichy itself, you will hunt out other men, who, because of their jobs as railwaymen, truck drivers or commercial travellers, can act as link men. And radio operators as well....'

'What for?' Coustenoble asked.

I told them straight: 'To operate transmitters to flash our information to London.'

Their eyes nearly popped out. A radio set was in itself a weapon of war.

'And how are these sets going to get here?' asked Red, doubt in his voice.

'Perhaps through Spain, perhaps by parachute.'

They broke into smiles. 'In that case,' said Coustenoble, 'we must also find dropping places. Parachutes! Coming down like daisies! Come on, boys!' They stood up and adjusted their leather jackets.

'One word more. If any one of you feels this job is beyond him, let him say so now.'

They gave me a pitying look. I guessed what they were thinking: 'It's odd that *she*·should want to tell us what to do.' For a moment I was afraid they might back out.

'We're ready,' was all that Coustenoble said.

'I wouldn't trust Red, if I were you,' Air Force General Baston confided to me as he watched them go out. 'Before the war he had a very doubtful reputation in Air Force circles.'

'He may have changed; anyway, do you think we must have choir boys for that job?'

'You must have an Air Force General in on it. Then Pétain will take it more seriously,' Navarre had said. Pierre Baston, who had left the inglorious armistice army to deal in Armagnac liquor, agreed to supervise the activities of the 'Reception Centre'.

Observing with considerable anxiety that the Hôtel des Sports became noisier every day, a buzzing hive of conspirators, and learning that Vichy's men were going round with their ears to the ground, Baston began to organize special evenings to camouflage the truth—conducting a choir to sing the Marseillaise at the top of their voices or inventing conversations between Hitler and Pétain, whose speech he could mimic to the life, while the members of the patrols went into the corners to lay their plans.

'Baston will have the chance to do lots more Hitler-Pétain dialogues!' Navarre commented sarcastically. 'Bonhomme tells me that Pétain has gone to Montoire to meet the Führer. The free zone's splendid isolation won't have lasted long! The collaboration agreement has allowed the Nazis to infiltrate everywhere. We shall soon have to take the plunge, Marie-Madeleine! Where's your ambassador to London?'

'He arrived this morning.' My brother, Jacques Bridou, demobilized and newly married to Sylvia Jeavons, a charming English girl, had just told me that he wanted to get to Britain to join the Free French Forces. I called him in and we put him in the picture.

'That alters all my plans,' said Jacques. 'But don't worry, I myself will bring back the answers to your questions. After that I shall return to Britain to join de Gaulle. Your underground intrigues are too involved for me.'

To preserve the absolute secrecy of his mission, my brother was to go to Britain under his own steam. When he reached London he would make contact with a long-standing acquaintance of Loustaunau-Lacau, and he would ask for a meeting with General de Gaulle. Navarre's aim was to inform the British about the creation of our intelligence service and to assure de Gaulle of his complete and warm co-operation in continuing the struggle. Nevertheless, to start with, he would march with him 'in parallel,' for he considered it essential to maintain an underground command in France to take, hour by hour, on the spot, the decisions that changing circumstances dictated. In addition, he was keen to transmit his information directly to the British, who were waging the war on their own, so as to avoid the waste of time that might prevent them from exploiting the situation. He hoped, however, that the means of taking action would reach him via the Free French services, so that their common enterprise should remain purely French in character.

Jacques planned to travel by way of Morocco, where he would leave his wife with one of our uncles who had a farm there; after that he would try his luck. He set off on 7 November.

'Navarre, d'you think he'll succeed?' I asked.

'He was the world bobsleigh champion, that's a help! In any case, I'll use my two other contacts, Fourcaud and Dupuy the Canadian, in case he has any trouble in getting to Britain. Remember this, Marie-Madeleine: one mustn't put all one's eggs into one basket. Bombshell is waiting for you. Now it's your turn.'

'*I'll* also bring you back the goods. Count on me.' Captain Fourcaud was the speaker. Locked with him in a room, I had just written in invisible ink the messages that he was to take to London via Spain: confirmation of Jacques' mission to de Gaulle and the Allies. General de Gaulle's special envoy had quickly become a very close friend. He was a reserve officer of great courage and speed when action was called for. A quick hop to London, a parachute drop into France, then he was off again, his head crammed with the names of contacts and the pockets of his leather jacket stuffed with intelligence information, including ours. Our first report could not fail to be welcome as the Battle of Britain was then approaching its climax.

The Crusade was making headway and the hope of a speedy recovery galvanized its activity. Baston spared no effort to perfect his cover: the sedentary headquarters agents now had a job that was, to all appearances, perfectly legitimate. They were engaged in statistical work for the Marshal's cabinet. 'Who could suspect the old man of being part of our services?' Baston sneered, imitating Pétain's bleat.

A first class recruit had appeared on the scene—Henri Schaerrer, an engineer officer in the Navy who had fled from the Chantiers de Jeunesse. He was in touch with one of his former officers, now in Marseilles, Commandant Jean Boutron, who was willing to serve. I had immediately given the young man the job of forming the Marseilles patrol and he was asking for someone to inspect it.

'You go,' ordered Navarre. 'Marseilles is the gateway to the Mediterranean. And it'll give you a chance to begin with Monte Carlo and see my old friend, Colonel Charles Bernis, one of the Deuxième Bureau's stars. He'll certainly agree to supervise our intelligence. He's a completely dedicated man.'

I was not sorry to get away from the banks of the River Allier, where the weather was horribly cold. Even the hot water bottles froze in the beds. In any event, Marseilles, my native city, had always fascinated me; I adore its vitality, its magnificent position, its delightful, cheerful people.

A few days later I was sitting opposite the 'dedicated man', my heart in my boots. Lunching in the sunshine at the Café de Paris, I felt crushed by the prestige of Colonel Bernis. His deliberately cold tone, his technical way of talking, were utterly different from the vehement outbursts of my patrols.

'I had a feeling that Loustaunau-Lacau was up to something. He's sure about ultimate victory, of course.'

'Quite sure. He thinks that Churchill will hold on, that the Americans will eventually come in. He's pursuing a threefold objective: propaganda, intelligence, action. Since the time's not yet ripe for direct action. . . .'

'That's my view, too. . . .'

'Intelligence is the only weapon we can fight with, Colonel.'

He gave me a quizzical look. 'But do you know what intelligence really is?'

'I know it's a hard job and that I badly need your knowledge and experience, Colonel.'

Bernis got up from the table. 'Not here,' he said. We then wandered along the terraces that looked down upon the sea.

'That knowledge of the enemy should be a factor essential to success in war seems so obvious that no one would seriously dare to deny it. But this knowledge can only be acquired at the cost of a long and difficult search. This means that it must be foreseen, organized and functioning long before its results are actually needed.'

'It's extremely difficult to convince people of the value of intelligence, Colonel. And do you think that what we shall transmit will be useful for the conduct of the war?'

'Since Napoleon's time the British have also believed in intelligence.

Don't worry, they won't let themselves be taken by surprise. That's why they need to know Hitler's plans. They can defy the Nazis, who are a hundred times stronger in men and material, for a certain length of time because of their isolation.'

'But how can we, who are working underground and are fairly incompetent, be as efficient as your well-oiled Deuxième Bureau machine was? Pending definite instructions about what to find out, I've been sending everything that comes to my notice. It's rather incoherent.'

'It's not your job to decide what is important. Use "intelligence maps". As soon as you get a piece of information put it on a map. The questionnaires will undoubtedly arrive one day. Even then we shall probably have to answer only the simplest questions—such as Who? or What? Where? How? Only precise information is of any value. Report only what has been *seen* and *heard*. It's up to the people using the information to draw the proper conclusions.'

'I'm sure we shan't be the only ones to send information to the Allied Staff.'

'No. Results are all the better when cross-checking is spread over a large number of agents. That is how certainty is achieved, the strong evidence the British insist on, which is indispensable when those in authority come to use intelligence. But,' Bernis added with a smile, 'I was under the impression that you had come to recruit *me*. Where must I go? When? How? To whom shall I report?'

Timidly, I made it clear to him that I was the one who was running the service. A worried expression came over his face. Was he going to think better of it? We walked towards the station, down the princely flights of steps that framed the Casino's solid mass. Too bad if I failed to pass the test.

With all the deliberation I could muster I told him that we expected to set up the intelligence centre at the beginning of 1941 at Pau, which had been chosen because it was near enough to the Spanish frontier for couriers to come and go, and also near enough to the demarcation line for agents to slip in and out of the occupied zone. If he agreed to run it he would need an adjutant. I had already chosen one—a woman.

At last he smiled: 'If women are now waging war, a woman it shall be!' He had answered my question indirectly. I had made the grade.

Just as the train was starting the superman handed me a bundle of notes. They contained complete details of army and naval concentrations as far as Genoa. The ace from the Deuxième Bureau had not been caught napping.

'Good God! It's a woman,' roared a voice when, still only half awake, I walked into the buffet at the central station where Schaerrer was waiting to introduce me to his two Marseilles lieutenants. We drank an ersatz coffee and exchanged a few innocuous remarks while surreptitiously studying one another.

Gabriel Rivière was thick set, with fair skin and light blue eyes. One felt him to be solid and optimistic and he smiled the whole time. Emile

Audoly was refined and reserved, but he had a bullfighter's speed of movement. They were perfect foils for one another and bombarded me with searching questions. I could not see anyone pulling wool over their eyes and I cut the conversation short because, at the neighbouring tables, people were pricking up their ears.

'I beg you pardon, madame,' the engineer said as we walked back together to the Rue Thiers, where I was staying. 'I didn't think there was any need to warn them.'

'It wouldn't have worried them if they had known I was a woman, would it? See you tomorrow at ten o'clock.'

Rivière, Audoly and the young naval officer appeared at the appointed time. Schaerrer had prepared the ground very thoroughly and his two companions came straight to the point. Rivière needed a cover; he thought that if we bought a wholesale vegetable business, the warehouse, the various comings and goings, and the money side of the business would provide a splendid front for our activities. He suggested one that was going for 40,000 francs. A partner would do the actual work and Madeleine, his wife, would serve in the shop. Meanwhile his own flat was at our disposal. He knew the underworld as well as the police and ex-army men. He had access to a clinic, an excellent hiding place in an emergency. He also had a radio operator and his adjutant-to-be was itching to get started.

Dumbfounded, I turned to Audoly. 'It's much simpler for me,' he said. His job with a firm of grain dealers gave him access to docks and railway stations. Not only did he have the ships' manifests but he was in a position even to check on the actual cargoes.

'Are the Germans using the port of Marseilles?'

'Not yet, but it's only a matter of time. That's why I must have a transmitting set, because what I shall have to transmit will be valid for only a few hours.'

Now I had only to give the final instructions: Rivière would take on the organization of the Marseilles sector and Audoly would concentrate on the search for intelligence about the Mediterranean. The greengrocer shop would be bought and the second transmitting set to arrive would go to them. The whole thing would be supervised by Commandant Jean Boutron.

'I felt I had to take the plunge,' said Navarre when he greeted me in Vichy. 'Our friends in the "protection group" have arrested Pierre Laval. The Germans are going to demand his release and strengthen their positions in the free zone. The Hôtel des Sports must be liquidated; we must close "the reception centre". I'm replacing it by a floor in the Hotel du Grand-Condé that Baston has just rented for his statistics office. You must disperse your people.'

Our fight in the open died in beauty on a Christmas Day on which the Crusaders and the Patrollers were brought together for the last time. Only three months earlier we had been a mere half dozen. Now there were more than fifty of us, united in the heady joy that is born of unshakeable confidence.

3   THE PATROL

'... Phew ... Phew. ...' mimicked Navarre, shooting his arms out like a swimmer doing the breaststroke. 'The Germans are squeezing the Old Man like a lemon. We must extend the Crusade and establish contacts in the occupied zone.'

'It's a good thing I begged you to keep cover,' I said, deeply moved at the thought of making the journey.

We took the train with Coustenoble. The *Ausweis* for the occupied zone had been obtained for us by a pre-war friend, whom we called Dubidon ('Twister'). He was a collaborator from the start. Navarre—still posted as an escaped prisoner of war—had been assured by him that his high position in the Légion des Combattants was a safeguard against recapture. Nevertheless, although the Germans did not interfere with the Marshal's aides, I felt uneasy in his particular case.

When we reached the demarcation line it was I who was searched by the Nazi women auxiliaries, whom I always referred to as 'the witches' and most French people called 'the grey mice', because of the colour of their uniforms. I had a good personal alibi: I was going to Paris on a business trip to arrange the sale of Indo-Chinese rice to the Spaniards. The strange thing was that this rice deal, in which I never really believed, was in fact eventually clinched.

Meanwhile a witch carefully scrutinized my list of cargoes. Behind her an NCO jotted something down in a notebook. Coustenoble, who was prowling about in the corridor with a scowl on his face, felt his right hand pocket. Navarre, his nose in a German newspaper, watched me curiously out of the corner of his eye.

'Not bad, not bad,' he said when the train started again. 'You were immediately suspected of being a spy. That's a good start.'

Coustenoble, who had now rejoined us in the otherwise empty compartment, exclaimed: 'There must be something fishy somewhere. Why is Madame's name on their list? Are you really sure about this Dubidon fellow?' he asked Navarre.

This incident warned us to split up as soon as we arrived. Both the men had safe hideouts, and since I was 'on the list' I would play the game according to the rules. So I made for the old offices of the *Ordre National*, as I reckoned that a place already known was a good cover for subversive activities.

It was, alas, far better known than I had imagined. The concierge went as white as a sheet when she opened the door. 'Don't you know?' she gasped. 'As soon as they got to Paris the Germans turned the office inside out . . . searched everything. They asked me where *you* were, where the Commandant was . . . and if I knew a Mr Jacob.' Bertold Jacob was the man who had compiled and published the German Army order of battle. 'What are you going to do?' the kindly soul asked anxiously. 'You can rely on me.'

'I'm staying here,' I said, taking the keys. 'The Germans will never guess I've come back.'

I had told Coustenoble to find Pierre Dayne and he arrived with him within the hour. Dayne was a Secret Police agent. I had known him and his family for ten years.

'D'you know what happened when the Fritzes got to the town hall?' he asked, still furious. 'They took the tricolour and flung it into the river. A policeman who was hiding from them pulled it out. I haven't been able to sleep since that day.'

He said he would help. I told him that to begin with he must remove everything from my apartment in the Rue Vaneau and fix me up with a *pied-à-terre* here. Camouflaged in this way, so as to look like a private residence, the old office rooms could shelter our friends passing through Paris and also serve as a meeting place. I counted on him to protect this first hideout by sending in the most innocuous sort of report to the police.

Meanwhile, Coustenoble agreed to go and check up on the safety of another letterbox, my brother's apartment on the Rue Jean-Jacques-Rousseau. A great-hearted woman, Marie-Claire Paupière, whose name was to become famous as a fortune teller, was living there and she had suggested taking messages and storing equipment for us. Afterwards Coustenoble would look for places from which we could transmit. The organization was beginning to take shape.

Defeat had scattered my contacts. Paul Bernard, on whom I was counting most, was away. Fortunately, Henri Champin, who had remained at his job in the Compagnie Française des Petroles, and Nelly de Vogüé, my best friend, were still in Paris. As I expected, they were more than willing to help; likewise an engineer in the Renault factory and an Armenian industrialist, who gave me the key of a maid's room on the sixth floor of his house on the Avenue Foch. That was one more place in which the organization could develop.

Navarre, however, was unlucky. The 'occupation authorities' categorically refused to allow the Legion to be set up and his own relatives looked anything but pleased to see him.

'It'll take a long time to shift that arrogant and stuffy collection. They won't admit we've been defeated and are creating the craziest jobs for themselves. Welcoming the Germans! Undertaking common reconstruction work! "It's like embracing the Devil," I told them.'

'We mustn't recruit the first assault wave from your ranks, Navarre. Let me carry on with my people.'

'You're enjoying it, Marie-Madeleine!' he retorted. 'For once I agree with you. I'll go back to Vichy and see how your new headquarters is getting along and I advise you not to take root here.' And he walked quickly away.

Coustenoble, Dayne and I completed our work and a few days later I departed, leaving behind a fairly solid structure on which to base a patrol. On crossing the demarcation line I realized that the rice business still interested the 'grey mice'. I was again the only one in the carriage to be searched from head to foot.

At the Hôtel du Grand-Condé, instead of the stiff and formal attitude befitting a new HQ, I observed that our visitors were increasing in numbers and importance. Jean Boutron was in Navarre's room. He reported on the progress of the Marseilles patrol. The moment we met I was greatly impressed by his determination. He was a merchant navy officer who had been posted to a warship and had escaped from it at Mers-el-Kébir.

'After that idiotic business there won't be a sailor willing to help us,' said Navarre.

'Make no mistake, Commandant, I've found one who will. Captain Barjot, the Fleet Air Arm and submarine expert.'

According to him Naval Intelligence still functioned with the technical efficiency that sailors bring to everything they do, but the fruit of their labours would simply be pigeon-holed. Barjot, anxious to make practical use of the intelligence that came his way from all over the world, wanted to get it to the British.

'We'll fix it,' Navarre assured him.

'If only we had some radio transmitters,' sighed Navarre after the sailor had gone. 'Things are beginning to hot up in the Mediterranean.'

We did not yet know to what extent this was so. Then the door opened to admit General Baston, back from his daily visit to the Hôtel du Parc, accompanied by an Air Force officer, whom he introduced jovially:

'This is Commandant Léon Faye of the Air Force. He's like quick-silver and completely fearless. I've had the greatest difficulty in stopping him from having a show-down with Pétain. He could only be pacified by assuring him that he would find here the same kind of fools as himself.'

Having been introduced in this fashion, Faye came straight to the point as though we were old accomplices. His whole manner, his drive and the boldness of his plans left me gasping. Until now we had thought of intelligence as the only feasible weapon. Well, we were now being told quite simply that a plot was being hatched across the water, in North Africa:

'Do you want to wait until the Nazis land at Algiers, Tunis and Casablanca before inciting the army in North Africa to revolt?' the airman shouted at us. 'It's our duty to act at once.'

Navarre did not need much encouragement: he was soon galloping along the same course.

'What stage has your plot reached?' he asked.

'The Air Force groups in Tunisia have all agreed. The Algiers Air Force is easy; I've got the telegram ordering hostilities! The Navy's going well. The Army needs to be worked on.'

'I'll go myself,' Navarre exclaimed.

Baston was now looking anything but jovial. 'What have I done?' he stammered, calling me to witness and pointing a trembling finger at the two officers now busy consulting maps and files. 'With those two together all hell will be let loose. A plot! That's all we needed!' he said with a sigh as he went out.

Now that Faye had agreed to head the North African network, I gave him his code. He took the opportunity to ask me endless questions about the way my patrols operated.

'What you're doing is crazy. As soon as I'm back in Algiers I shall act. By the time you're all feeling sorry for yourselves I shall be in a position to save you,' he stressed.

'You and your plots. Nothing could be more dangerous. *I* am absolutely convinced that my job isn't the least bit risky.'

Schaerrer brought along Armand Bonnet, a regular army NCO who had agreed to head the Paris patrol. He was flanked by his adjutant, Jean Toeuf, one of the spahis who had fought against overwhelming odds during the German advance on Lyons. He was tough and inflexible and was, I felt, rather like a sword while Bonnet was like a shield.

I gave them addresses where they would find lodging, an office and a letterbox; three places where the mail could be sent across the demarcation line; the fixed rendezvous where informants would leave their intelligence stuff without being seen; and money. They would have to recruit three fixed agents themselves, one for Paris, another for Brittany and a third for the North. Some day they would have a radio transmitter. The radio operator intended for them was here, but they would not meet him until a transmitter was available.

Bonnet listened like a serious schoolboy.

When I had finished he asked: 'Can I ask a question? If anything happens to me, what shall I do?'

This had been provided for: 'If it's the French police, say that you work for the Vichy Deuxième Bureau. The Chief is a friend of ours, and you can expect to be released. But if it's the German police. . . .'

'OK. But what if I'm tortured? Is it treason to talk under torture?'

I hesitated for a moment. Bonnet had a round, kind face. He was a simple man but no fool. His test reports had been precise. He seemed to possess enough *sangfroid* to manage the Paris patrol.

'I can tell you this, Bonnet. If you have the misfortune to fall into German hands, then everything you know and get to know will depend on your silence.'

Toeuf, who had not uttered a word so far, walked over. Standing to attention, and trembling, he said: 'If I'm arrested I swear on my word of honour as a spahi that I will be shot rather than say a word.'

The conversation shattered me. In the free zone I had, until now, felt no sense of danger. In Paris I had had none at all. I now felt the cruel difference that exists between doing things oneself and ordering others to take risks.

Going to bed after days like those did not mean getting to sleep. I went over my worries. Our personal funds were exhausted. We were living on loans to meet our responsibilities. Would I have to say to my patrols some day, 'It's all over. We're stopping our activities because our money's short?' Yet everything had been going so well for four months. The patrols were snowballing in all parts of France, gathering dozens of recruits.

Philippe Le Couteux ('Valori') and the Salmsons were taking charge of the Lyons-Dijon sector. Newcomers, Dr Arbassier and his mountain guides, kept watch on the Alps, where there were innumerable Italian armistice commissions. 'Lagrotte' had started the Perigueux patrol in the Dordogne with a view to exploiting the Atlantic coast by way of a crossing to Bordeaux. The Vichy patrol was inspired by the young lawyer Jean Labrit and Jean de Malherbe. They skimmed the Ministries. Colonel Bernis, established at Pau, centralized their reports in a pension that also had an appropriate name—the 'Welcome'.

As liaison agents Coustenoble had unearthed two splendid young men, Pierre Berthomier and Lucien Jolly, none other than the pilot and radio operator of the plane that flew regularly to the occupied zone for the Vichy Government. While distributing the Government's despatches they contacted our patrol leaders. In addition, Jolly agreed to be our future chief operator. He had his maintenance men available and their equivalent in the sectors, Pierre Bocher for the Mediterranean, Lucien Vallet for the occupied zone. All we needed now were the radio sets. How could we work efficiently without them? Urgent information—about Barjot's U-boats, Audoly's ships, the decoy airfields that the British were conscientiously bombing instead of the real ones—was going to waste. Furthermore, our headquarters at the Grand-Condé was becoming top-heavy. It was clear that a headquarters must constantly move if it were not to be spotted. I had to press Navarre to go elsewhere.

I switched off my light. Down in the street I could hear people discussing profitable black market deals.

'Bombshell's back. Come on,' whispered Navarre, tapping on my door.

'And Jacques?'

'Your brother's safe and sound in London. He'll be parachuted at the new moon.'

I hurried into the chief's room. On an armchair lay a large leather case. I was intrigued to see streams of plastic-coated wires of every conceivable colour trailing out of it. 'It's Romeo,' Captain Fourcaud told me when he saw what I was looking at. 'My radio transmitter.'

'You're crazy, both of you, to leave this thing lying around. What if anyone comes in?'

Bombshell laughed. 'Nobody knows what it's for yet. The police on duty at the station asked me what I was carrying and I said "You can see quite clearly—a radio set." I suppose they thought no one would be fool enough to flaunt the thing. Anyway, all they said was "Get along."'

'Why is it losing its innards?'

Bombshell's face clouded over: 'That's much more worrying. It was dropped. I hope nothing vital has been damaged.'

'We'll give it to one of our maintenance boys. Meanwhile, if you'll allow me, I'll hide it under my bed, it'll be better for its health and perhaps for yours.'

'Oh, these women,' muttered Bombshell. 'But see what I've brought.' With a grandiloquent gesture, he turned back the lapel of his coat; I saw the badge of General de Gaulle's Free French. 'You can't imagine what an effect it has on people. It's magical. Everybody asks for one.'

'For safety's sake, you'd do better to pin on the Marshal's Frankish axe,' growled Navarre.

He angrily held out to me a handwritten letter. It was signed: 'Charles'. It was General de Gaulle's reply, very brief and ending with the following sentence: 'Whoever is not with me is against me.'

'What about the money and the help we've been expecting?' I asked in despair.

'Captain Fourcaud has been forbidden to help us. He may help only those who agree to wear the Free French label. Let Charles come over here, and see how easy it is to get people to accept it.'

'Keep your shirt on,' said Bombshell. 'There's one thing that's very important for you. The British agree; they admit your complete independence. Of course, they want to see you in person before making a deal.'

'When and where?' roared Navarre. 'Can I afford the time to go to London?'

'They may send someone to meet you in a neutral country,' answered Bombshell. 'Intelligence is the only thing that interests them and your first efforts have been greatly appreciated. You can straighten things out with de Gaulle later. In the meantime, I'm going to share my money with you. Here are half a million francs.'

On 14 March a call from Clermont-Ferrand informed me that my brother Jacques was there. Parachuted with Laroche, Captain Fourcaud's radio operator, he had lost his companion in the dark. Dropped from less than 300 feet, his fall had been heavy. Not knowing how things stood with us after his four months absence, he had preferred not to come directly to Vichy. I left with Navarre to fetch him by car.

I hardly recognized my brother. He was emaciated, and his eyes were feverish; he was visibly suffering from shock and his feet had been badly injured by his fall. I took the wheel when we came to the hectic curves in the Puy de Dome country and Jacques launched into his extraordinary story.

As soon as he had arrived in Morocco, thanks to his English wife he had been able to get transportation to Tangier, and then to Gibraltar, where he had introduced himself to the Admiral commanding the base. Elated by his swift success, he had revealed the purpose of his mission. The Admiral listened politely to this elegantly dressed young man telling him, in the purest English, that an underground organization was sending him to London to see General de Gaulle and the top brass at the War Office. He quickly came to the conclusion that Jacques was a spy and the very same day, with the Admiral's good wishes ringing in his ears, he boarded a troop-ship for England. Scotland Yard men were waiting for him at the gangway; he was arrested and subjected to endless interrogation.

Warned by his first experience, Jacques refused to talk until he was brought face to face with the people he had come to meet—General de Gaulle and a British naval officer, naming as his guarantor in London a Mr Jeavons, his wife Sylvia's father. The crowning misfortune was that this gentleman had not yet received Sylvia's letter of warning. He vehemently denied that a son-in-law he had never met and believed to be living peacefully in the south of France was in England. No one at General de Gaulle's headquarters knew anything about him. Fourcaud had not yet arrived and they were intensely suspicious of everything coming from Vichy.

On the other hand the naval officer remembered perfectly his happy days in Athens where he had done a tour of duty with his great friend Commandant Loustaunau-Lacau. He had alerted one of his cousins, Commander Kenneth Cohen, who held an important position in the Intelligence Service, and who, scenting some really big intelligence opportunity, made praiseworthy efforts to snatch Jacques from the clutches of the inquisition.

To sort things out, Scotland Yard thought up a stratagem. Jeavons was introduced incognito into a room where Jacques was once more put on the spot. Behaving like one of the police inspectors, Jeavons began to ask questions about Sylvia. Jacques, growing increasingly angry at the ill-timed curiosity of these unwelcoming allies, deliberately gave the wrong answers. Why all the fuss about his wife? Very well, they should see the sort of stuff he was made of. What they did conclude was that Jacques was clearly *not* Sylvia's husband; and his father-in-law was about to go, priding himself on having confounded the spy, when Providence prompted him to ask a final question.

'Now, has this Sylvia still got a mole above her left thigh?'

'How do you know that, you old rogue?' roared Jacques, ready to leap at the man who, to his utter amazement, held out his arms and called him 'My son'.

Back in the Hôtel du Grand-Condé, we ran into Fourcaud, who had found the radio operator parachuted with my brother. Our mechanics had lovingly stitched the innards back into Romeo, the transmitter, and Laroche, who had been trained in London, quickly got it working. Jolly and Lucien Vallet were there to be initiated into the mysteries of the clandestine radio contacts. Before our astonished gaze Captain Fourcaud sent his first message to British Intelligence in London.

Then the two men vanished into the darkness with the transmitter.

I now realized that we would have to go on without help for a long time, and went back to the task of building up the sectors. In doing so I met some strange people. A certain 'Rat'—he looked like one—had been recommended to us as being particularly well informed and we had assigned him to General Baston's cover office. In turn, Rat had sent us one of his friends, known as 'Dulack', a deserter from the Deuxième Bureau of whom Navarre thought highly for his professional skills. In this man's eyes we were a bunch of worthless amateurs. Obviously our practices struck him as revolutionary. The improvisation enforced by defeat compelled us to use only volunteers, who sometimes turned out to be more troublesome than efficient, yet we had to trust them. No references, either. And no guarantee that they were any good.

Dulack did not think we were suspicious enough: 'I've jumped out of the frying pan into the fire, madame,' he declared. 'You're surprisingly naïve. You use just anybody.'

'Espionage in enemy territory by professionals is very different from patriots hunting out information in occupied territory.'

Dulack's face went red: 'I'm going to tell you exactly what I think, at the risk of appearing a bastard. I owe my job here to Rat, but it's my duty to tell you that he's a traitor.'

'Dulack, you're crazy! With what he knows, he could have got us locked up a hundred times already.'

The secret agent's face became a mask. 'Perhaps he's playing a deeper game,' he concluded enigmatically. 'Time's on his side.'

He left me deeply disturbed and for the first time face to face with the grim spectre of treason. No doubt about it. Dulack was fanatical. He suffered from an acute attack of spyitis. I rather liked the sentimental Rat and summoned him at once.

'Look, you ought to be careful, you're bringing us some queer recruits!

Dulack. . . .'

Rat never so much as blinked.

'He says you're a traitor.'

'Why does he say that?'

'I don't know. Have you quarrelled?'

'Not as far as I know.'

All the same he became thoughtful. I would have preferred a denial. As though reading my thoughts, he argued that he was doing an excellent job for us and keeping a discreet watch on our patrol members.

'I'll tell you what's worrying me about Red: he's in touch with Geissler,' I went on.

'Geissler? The Gestapo agent in Vichy? Since when?'

This time his question was so much to the point that I did not realize that Rat was dodging the issue concerning himself.

'Oh, I don't think he's betraying us. Red's always shooting a line; he says he sees Geissler just to show off. But at the moment he needs money badly. He's run off with the fiancée of one of the boys!'

'Good heavens! It'll be terrible when he finds out!'

I had really stirred up a hornet's nest. Fortunately Schaerrer was coming back that evening. He would help me get things straight. Then a messenger arrived saying he was from Grenoble. He had no password; but he did have a strong foreign accent.

'I'm Nicholas,' he told me, 'I come from Dr Arbassier.'

'I've never heard of him.'

'Your patrol leader in the Alps, madame!' A pause, then: 'You *are* Marie-Madeleine, aren't you?'

The man persisted and mentioned Red. He handed me some information about the Alpine zone. I jumped up angrily, certain that I was dealing with a *provocateur*. 'Get out, or I'll call the police this instant.'

He rushed away in something like panic. I thought that German agents are no fools and burned any papers that might be compromising.

The phone that rang in Navarre's office early next morning dragged me out of a sleep racked by nightmares. I leaped out of bed. Entering, I had a shock: Schaerrer and a blonde were lying on the divan. After hanging up I heard a double outburst of laughter. The 'blonde' was Coustenoble. He had bleached his hair—normally as black as a raven—and shaved off his moustache. He had certainly gone crazy.

'You must have thought I was overdoing it, bringing a girl here,' said the midshipman, delighted to see me so shocked.

'I must admit I thought you were going a bit far. But why this silly disguise, Coustenoble?'

'D'you really think I do it for pleasure? I've suffered agonies with all this peroxide, to say nothing of the fact that I've had to change my identity. Allow me to introduce myself: Pierre Graimprey.'

'He was betrayed,' Schaerrer blurted out gloomily.

'Was it Red?' I asked, the light suddenly dawning.

The two men looked at me in embarrassment. A traitor can have been a friend. Coustenoble was affectionate by nature; he had been very friendly with Red from the day they met. But he had to tell me about it.

'It happened at Châteauroux. I disagreed about a crossing that Red was using after he'd seen Geissler, and he gave the police my name. I just had time to get away, they're after me now.'

'Geissler! You're mad not to have warned me. No friendship matters, d'you understand? The service comes before anything else. Fortunately for us, if Red's only motive is money, he'll sell his information bit by bit and we'll have time to do something about it.'

'What are your orders?' Schaerrer asked, still upset.

'That was Navarre on the phone. He's in Pau. I'll drive you both there. Vallet will go by train with some of the luggage. We must clear out of this place. Be back here in a couple of hours. But before you go, can you throw any light on a visit I had last night from a certain Nicholas, whose accent gave me a terrible scare?'

'Easy,' said Coustenoble. 'We met him last night in the station buffet. He's of Dutch origin. Poor devil, he was far more scared than you, his legs were still shaking.'

'Then he's genuine?'

'Yes,' the engineer answered, 'and I've got his information.' Dulack was not altogether wrong. I would have to show greater discernment, but how can we judge others when in action oneself, with nothing but instinct to work on? We had nobody to fall back on, nobody to guide and to protect us. We were out on our own and had no alternative but to push on.

I went into the cover office for the last time. Two young heads were poring over a map, a swirling jumble of criss-cross lines and dates.

'We didn't escape from the Stalags just to draw a lot of lines,' muttered Edmond Poulain. 'My buddy, Michel Jumez, and I feel homesick.'

I explained all the difficulties I was having in organizing their mission to the forbidden zone. They might be from the north but even so I could not send them there without a fair amount of money. They said they would keep waiting, though they felt humiliated at being thought to be Pétain's men.

Baston came out of his room looking pink and fresh. 'I'll go and make my usual call at Pétain's Hôtel du Parc,' he began airily.

He stopped short when he heard I was leaving. But he agreed with me that a cover must not be used by so many people at the same time. He would look after the two lads from the north.

It only remained to warn my maid. Jean Toeuf, who had come to contact us just when he was needed, would drive her to Paris that very evening. I had already told her to go and stay in the old *Ordre National* offices and what to do there. She burst into tears. I assured her that they would be using an excellent crossing point and that nothing would happen to her. 'It's not that,' she said, sobbing even more bitterly, 'you know nothing frightens me. It's leaving poor little Marco, the Irish terrier, who had followed us all the way!' I gave him to her. Now the ties were cut.

Nelly de Voguë was passing through the free zone on her way to fulfil a mission in the south-west. So we took the cross-country route to Pau, the picturesque chief town of the Basses-Pyrénées, that I had come to know so well because of the war—the sweep south from river to river, from the secret Creuse and the shady Corrèze to the Lot, with its elegant bends and its lovely castles, houses that one hoped would never change or disappear; then the longer drop towards the Pyrenees, across the dark waters of the Tarn to the Gers with its gay vineyards. Every town that we crossed prompted Schaerrer and Coustenoble to tell a good story about the patrols.

Nelly was aghast: 'You won't get far like that,' she said.

Our arrival at the Pension Welcome in Pau was the crowning moment. The place was a veritable branch of the Hôtel des Sports and the Grand-Condé put together. Should we never go into action?

The Pension Welcome was a quiet family affair, run by two old-fashioned but gracious spinsters. Great admirers of Navarre, the local hero of both wars, they shut their eyes to the peculiar people he brought along. 'No police forms,' he told them firmly. The poor things agreed, feeling that they might nevertheless have a lot of trouble with all the people perpetually coming and going with large suitcases. Could they be black marketeers? They were told in confidence that they were all escaped prisoners.

'Ah! Madame will also look after them. It's so nice to see the French helping one another in misfortune!' they said as they installed me—without filling in a form—in a clean, neatly-kept room with pine furniture.

In spite of the lateness of the hour, Colonel Bernis took me into his room on the next floor. The walls were covered with maps of the Atlantic zone: my eyes were at once struck by cabalistic signs denoting the Atlantic ports.

'We've made a good start,' he said. 'Your patrols are first class. I'm amazed at how well they've grasped the job.'

'Don't tell me they spot submarines everywhere.' I pointed to the intelligence maps.

'No. These also show the coastal trade with Spain. Valuable iron ore for German industry. The U-boats are at Bordeaux. Not yet at Saint-Nazaire —but you must send someone there to watch for them.'

I gave him the information that had come from Paris the night before: airfields bristling with Messerschmitts and a curious report emanating from the White Russians.

'What can they do in this shambles?' Bernis asked in an offhand way, his real attention given to marking in the airfields on the maps.

'Just imagine! The White Russians are convinced that Hitler's going to attack Stalin. Isn't it incredible?'

He spun round as though stung by a wasp. 'I've told you before, it isn't our job to think. All we have to do is to pass things on. The British are the sole judges.'

'Yes, but how are we to send things on?'

'That's the snag. Navarre sent his urgent information through Fourcaud's radio. He's also preparing channels via Spain: the chief customs men at both passes in the Pyrenees are ready to help. On the other hand, the occupied zone is absolute child's play, thanks to Destandau. The grocer in Orthez carries reports and agents in his delivery truck on the pretext that he's picking up food supplies.'

The first of our patrols, operating since 1940, seemed to Bernis to be a model of its kind. In town all the help we needed was available, in particular a car and petrol, thanks to our friends in the Légion des Combattants, even a hiding place for the transmitting set—when it arrived! 'Garvarni', who was being helped by a young garage owner, Jean Broqua, and informants in the Landes, was the head of the patrol in the extreme south-west.

'He's brave,' the Colonel observed, 'but terribly careless. You will have to tell him to stop sending information in clear by interzonal postcards.' I shuddered.

A common friend of long standing, Marc Mesnard de Chal, who travelled a great deal for his insurance company, agreed to be our treasurer and paymaster—when we had the money. Lucien Vallet had arrived a few minutes before us.

Augustine Contrasty came into the room: she was the excellent adjutant-secretary, I had promised Bernis. Quick, cute, always smiling, she had retained all the stubbornness of the religious rebels of the Toulouse region from which she came.

'Here you are at last, Marie-Madeleine! Colonel, you're making far too much racket, you can be heard from the floor underneath and with all this crowd. . . .'

'My maps,' snapped Bernis in annoyance, 'will pass any investigation. The old ladies think I'm a geographer.'

'Colonel, I am, as always, overwhelmed by your knowledge of intelligence work,' I said. 'But there's something else. Can you tell me if there's any way to avoid being taken in when recruiting people?'

'Apart from their ability, I can't see anything to judge by when you're dealing with volunteers. How do you set about it?'

'I'm amazed to see what a hodgepodge this incipient resistance is, Colonel. The loftiest ideals and the most naïve goodwill are all mixed up together. I should like to welcome everyone with open arms. I'm ashamed of suspecting people.'

'And you're the mixer-in-chief. My dear girl, I pity you. Experience, and experience alone, alas, will teach you how much credibility you can place in each person.'

4 HELP

Navarre kept to himself, appearing at the Pension Welcome only at breakfast, which was taken in common at the main table. With his canvas shoes and traditional Pyrenean beret he looked like a genuine local. Like Churchill, he loved the change of uniform.

I was glad to have his broad shoulders on which to unburden my reasons for clearing out of the Hotel du Grand-Condé at Vichy. He took it with his usual calm. I never once saw Navarre look worried. He took the good with the bad. 'Face the facts', was his motto.

Schaerrer came in, interrupting my report.

'You're going back to the occupied zone, old man,' Navarre told him. 'Your mission is vitally important now. I must know as quickly as possible how many German U-boats are at the mouth of the Gironde.'

'I'm ready, Commandant'. Schaerrer clicked his heels nonchalantly and left, sure of himself and of life.

Navarre turned to me: 'Now, here's what comes next. The three emissaries I sent to de Gaulle couldn't persuade him to adopt my point of view. I must save our service and accept the British offer. And so I've agreed to go and see them in Lisbon.'

'And you need Schaerrer's information so as not to go empty-handed?'

'I'm not a beggar. And you will leave for the Dordogne. It's a suitable west-central area and I must have a dropping zone there. Take Coustenoble with you; he can report back with the results. And take the opportunity to have a look at the local patrol. Then go and see your family on the Riviera. I'll repeat what I've told you time and time again: "Don't put all your eggs in one basket". If anything happened to me you would, after reviewing the situation, be able to act.'

'If you're caught, Navarre, then everything will fold up.'

'No, you will simply carry on.'

It's a very pretty run from Pau to Bergerac. As I drove, I chatted to Coustenoble, whom I was now getting to know and to appreciate more every day. His clear-sightedness astonished me, but where did his sound judgement of people and events come from? I also felt that he was still sizing me up. He had been told to obey me and I was not the sort of woman he was used to dealing with.

Darkness fell more quickly than usual as huge black clouds came rolling over the countryside. Then the rain began and grew steadily heavier. I slowed down—which was a real stroke of luck. A rear tyre burst on the left side, then we skidded and finally came to a stop a couple of inches from a ditch just as the full fury of the storm struck us.

'Nice work,' my companion said. 'I'm going to give you a hand with the tyre. It'll take twice as long if you do it on your own.'

We struggled together with the repair, the tools being out of order, and after an hour we set off again covered with mud and frozen stiff. Coustenoble coughed occasionally—a rasping sort of cough that was painful to hear—but he looked pleased.

'And we thought you were a stuck-up sort of dame, a proper wet.'

'I'm wet all right!' I retorted and burst into laughter.

Lagrotte had formed his patrol in Périgueux, the main town of Périgord, the province famous for truffles. Coustenoble and Lagrotte discussed crossing points to Bordeaux and I observed that the principal one was that used by Fourcaud. 'You mustn't confuse the organizations. You must find some other way,' I put in sharply.

'But we get on so well together!' Lagrotte replied. His cold, impersonal expression did not inspire confidence. A certain cynicism edged everything he said. I registered this, but postponed any further analysis of this somewhat shifty character, glad to discover he had a sound knowledge of the district.

'According to your reports, Lagrotte, the Germans are settling down to a hundred years war?'

'It looks like it, madame, but they're sending masses of stuff to Germany . . . vast quantities of supplies, military equipment that they're pinching from us.'

I thought of the White Russians. 'You must find out more,' I said. 'Send your couriers into the occupied zone right away.'

Coustenoble's only worry now was the parachute dropping zone. In his mind's eye he could already see the daisies flowering. . . .

Easter was approaching. On my way back I went and picked up my son, who was a boarder at the near-by Jesuit school. I had decided it was time to let him into the secret of what I was doing. He was not yet twelve and he must not think of my apparent desertion as anything but a necessity dictated by an inescapable duty. I shall always remember the wonderful look that came into his eyes when I described the broad lines of a struggle that I said would end only with the departure of the last German.

'You do understand, don't you, darling? You're the son of an officer, the grandson of an officer, and must be sensible about all the family. If I don't write it's because I haven't the right to get caught: lots of people depend on me.'

'Are you doing something dangerous, mother?' I shall never forget the tone of his voice.

'No more than what all Frenchmen do in time of war.'

'But what if they catch you. . . ?'

'First of all, there are no Nazis—or very few—in the unoccupied zone. And then I take great care. You'll see, it's almost a game.'

We drove back on a zig-zag course as far as Toulouse, visiting various informants or technical experts and not forgetting to note suitable dropping zones as well. Like all towns in the south of France, Toulouse had a population as mixed as it was unfathomable. I decided for the present to set up a temporary relay operation there, a focal point between the Atlantic and the Mediterranean, and thanks to Block, our local agent, I was able to rent a furnished room for Coustenoble in the false name of Pierre Graimprey. My little boy, who was having a tough time as I dragged him everywhere with me, watched us without a word.

'I'm giving you a funny sort of holiday, darling.'

'Don't worry, mother, it's as funny as being at the circus, except that *we* seem to be the clowns!'

Coustenoble left us to report to Pau. Once we were on the coast, amid the roses and the mimosa, the holiday immediately brightened up. The whole family had taken refuge in the farm on our estate, my mother having rented the villa—'to be less conspicuous', she said. My brother Jacques showed me the hiding place he had built under the pigsty and I immediately deposited in it all the files that I had been lugging about with me. But even the shade of the flowering cherries failed to relieve my agony of mind. I had to learn to live with the wound that was beginning to gnaw at my heart, as I thought of Navarre's remark: 'You will simply carry on.'

A clarion voice roused me out of what had become a permanent state of brooding.

'Schaerrer! Why are you here?'

'We've had the Lisbon meeting. The British have come to our help. We've got a transmitter!'

Our six months of frustration were over. I would no longer have to say to people: 'Be patient, help will come.' The real war was now beginning.

'We'll go and take the train at once.'

Crowded cars, corridors jammed with people leaning against the window rail, a chaos of wretched, weary travellers sleeping on the floor amid suitcases and parcels, the smell of dirt, icy draughts or hot blasts of air. Railways were the underground fighter's real home: no forms to fill in, controls easy to evade.

Schaerrer and I at last inherited two corner seats by the window. The sun was almost level with the horizon and I sat fascinated by my companion's steady, unflinching gaze in face of the last dazzling rays.

'How can you stare into the sun like that, Schaerrer?'

'It's a habit I learned as a sailor, Madame. The sea teaches a man a lot of things landsmen don't usually know about.'

'Don't you long to be back at sea?'

'No. Only action counts now. And results,' he added, suddenly looking dejected.

'Our results are going to increase a hundredfold, thanks to British help. And we're not going to muddle along in the old haphazard way. I'm going to set up our own chain of command. As a start I'm thinking of making Coustenoble my adjutant.'

The engineer's smile became even broader. 'That's a splendid idea. Everyone likes him, he never gets tired, and he's shrewd.'

'And I shall suggest you, Schaerrer, as head of our patrols in the occupied zone.'

'Impossible!' He snapped the word out; his face became a mask and his eyes clouded over. 'I cannot accept the honour of being put in command of Frenchmen. I'm not French.' His father was Swiss and lived in the Dutch East Indies where his fiancée also lived. He was fighting for France, to which he owed everything. In return, he would eschew any sort of honour.

'You're an officer, Schaerrer, and far more French at heart than millions of my fellow countrymen at the present moment. A command in the occupied zone is more than an honour: it's a serious responsibility. You cannot refuse just because you think you're not worthy of it.'

We made a bargain: he would carry out my orders, but only after he had made a full list of all the Nazi U-boats in the Gironde estuary.

We were met at the station by Lucien Vallet and one glance at him told us that all was well at the Pau headquarters. 'So you've got your "piano" at last,' I said. 'You can see it isn't just a myth!'

'Four transmissions a day on KVL. The British are very pleased. They receive me QS5. I'm really living at last.'

'KVL? QS5? What does all this jargon mean?'

'KVL is our call sign. QS5 means "receiving you loud and clear",' he replied, in a cocky tone of voice.

The Pension Welcome had organized a fine reception for us. Navarre, smoking dozens of cigarettes that he had brought back from Portugal, was drafting the next day's orders. Marc Mesnard de Chal was counting wads of notes and only looked up to warn the radio operator to be careful. The roving agent, Destandau, arrived from the occupied zone with a gentle-looking, bespectacled young man, Camille Schneider, one of Schaerrer's Paris recruits. Roger Dupuy, Schaerrer, Coustenoble and Gavarni, and the local agents listened open-mouthed to Colonel Bernis dictating their information to Augustine Contrasty, who was tapping away furiously.

It was very late before we were invited to slip away. Then, with a stealth and skill worthy of Indians, we were conducted through the town and taken to the Villa Etchebaster, a solid building, the brain-child of a wealthy citizen, surrounded by a huge walled garden where the plants were running riot.

Navarre explained that this was our new headquarters. People would still think our men were escaped prisoners who were being retrained by the Légion des Combattants. Our attention was drawn to the first floor by the sound of hammering. It was one of our specialists building a secret recess behind the mirror over a wash basin. Vallet was slinging an aerial from this out to a tree by the window, which would allow the transmitter to work at maximum power.

Delighted at last to have a house they could really call their own, the men themselves decided how the rooms should be allotted and organized the chores.

'We ought to have a housekeeper,' insisted the newcomer, Schneider, already infected by the old hands' good humour.

'I think I've got just what you need,' Coustenoble whispered in his most mysterious voice. 'Someone called Josette.'

'Let's leave the rookies to work things out for themselves,' Navarre said to me. 'It's time I told you what happened in Lisbon.' We went into the drawing-room, the walls of which were already covered with maps. 'How did you manage to get to Portugal?' I asked.

'You forget that the Ecole de Guerre has links everywhere, rather like the Masons. In this case the head of Franco's *Seguridad* and the brother of Salazar's secret service chief gave me red carpet treatment.'

'Did they know what you were going to do?'

'They never asked.'

A messenger from the British had suddenly informed him that the meeting would take place in Lisbon as scheduled, and after a non-stop journey, at eleven o'clock in the morning of the appointed day Navarre had found himself once again admiring the tomb of Vasco da Gama in the nave of Santa Maria de Belim, along with Kenneth Cohen, who had shown such understanding when dealing with my brother Jacques in London. After sizing one another up to their satisfaction the two men got into conversation. They talked for three days. Kenneth Cohen, who was known as 'Crane', was adamant: Britain, facing Hitler's Germany alone, would fight to the last man. The land war was lost, the air war was still in the balance, but Britain would hold on at sea. Everything would depend on the Atlantic and Mediterranean lines of communication, which were vital for bringing into play the weapons and supplies that Churchill was extracting from his friend Roosevelt.

Kenneth Cohen had not concealed the fact that the British Intelligence Service in France had been virtually obliterated in the 1940 debacle. Now, in order to win, the British must get out of the fog in which they were waging their desperate fight. They must know everything that was happening in France, which had become Hitler's springboard, since its exceptional position gave him access to three seas. That was why we interested them. Navarre impressed on him that we were not spies but people who were fighting in the only way still feasible—with the only invisible weapon, intelligence. Navarre made it clear that his eventual aim was to go over to direct action when the time was ripe. Until then he would supply the information asked for, provided he was given the help that would enable him to extend and build up every factor of his organization.

'And Crane accepted this?' I asked, astounded to realize that we were now part and parcel of the British Intelligence Service.

'Completely. The British will give us everything we need to get the network really going. I shall remain at the head of it, in France, and absolutely free to act as I think best.'

'And Général de Gaulle?'

'I stand by the proposals I put to him: we will continue to help his special envoys, and Fourcaud will keep him regularly informed of our activities. Crane agreed.'

'But British Intelligence will have prior claim to our information?'

'Naturally; they're fighting the war. You'll have plenty of work on your hands now, Marie-Madeleine!'

He took a novel out of his briefcase. It was Dumas' *La Dame aux Camelias*. 'Here's your new code,' he said. 'I've got other books for your patrols. They've got the same ones in London, in the Nelson edition. Each book has its own sign and the key number for each of our messages will be made up of the page, the paragraph and the word number selected. For example page 20, paragraph 3, word 15—gives the figure 20 315. It can't be broken, thanks to the constant change.

'You will study the questionnaires,' he went on, handing me a bundle of fine, silky sheets of paper. 'You'll see that they are nearly all concerned with ports, airfields, and troop movements, which are bound to reveal the enemy's intentions. Finally, here is a duplicate of the list I have given Crane of eighty of our agents and informants.'

'And these hieroglyphics?'

'Symbols representing my personal assessment that I've given to British Intelligence so that they can judge the value of the source: KSI 42: naval engineer officer, is Schaerrer. COU 72, airforce pilot, is Coustenoble. I, the head of the network, am N 1. You are POZ 55: my chief of staff.'

'You told them who I was?'

'I didn't divulge a single name.'

'It's like a real spy story, N 1. It'll be practical to call one another by our code names, KSI, KIF, TUR, POZ.'

'It's a question of memory. The essential thing is to lose one's personal identity, to become a number.'

'How did you bring the transmitter back?'

'In the diplomatic bag. Imagine, the French Ambassador asked me to go with it! We've also got five million francs to start with.'

'That's far too much!'

'No, it isn't. Think of North Africa. I spoke to Crane about Faye's conspiracy. He'll see Churchill about it. The old lion is haunted night and day by the problem of the Mediterranean. We must help him and speed things up in Algiers. So I'm leaving the direction of the entire intelligence operation in your hands for the moment. Go to Paris with the new questionnaires and use the money where it'll be most valuable.'

At dawn Schaerrer, Coustenoble and I drove to the demarcation line in Gavarni's car.

'You haven't anything compromising on you?' the airman asked me.

'Of course not.'

The boys slipped across the line by road, while I took the train. At Orthez, the frontier station, the horrible search began all over again. I was still trembling with disgust when I greeted my companions, who were waiting in the station buffet. I told them I was the only one who had been treated in this way.

'You'll be searched every time,' Coustenoble said. 'I've discovered why. The little signs typed on the *Ausweis* after the identity details vary—according to how suspect you are. For you it's just short of enough to get you shot on the spot!'

At last we had solved the mystery. To avoid the risk of being tricked by Navarre, Dubidon, who had given Navarre his *Ausweis*, had taken the precaution of getting his German masters to have me watched!

The Paris train steamed in. As soon as we had settled down—luckily we had the compartment to ourselves—I took the questionnaires meant for Schaerrer from the double lining in my hat. Coustenoble put his hands over his face in horror.

'She can't be trusted any more,' he said, furious.

'Calm down,' I said. 'I'd put it all in the next compartment. You must have known, Schaerrer, that the British would ask us to find out what new detection instruments the U-boats are using. How are you going to do it?'

'I shall get a member of a U-boat crew tight, steal his uniform and then go on board.'

'You haven't got a German face! Go aboard a U-boat? What's come over you?'

'My face will be all right. Everyone looks the same in the dark.'

'You're just pulling our legs. Schaerrer, promise me you won't do anything so idiotic.'

'Let's get a bit of sleep,' Coustenoble said. 'This character gives me the willies.'

'*Borrdoxe.*' The station loudspeaker dragged us back to consciousness. My heart was heavy as I watched Schaerrer melt into the crowd of travellers, anxious to escape from the station and its lights.

However, it was spring and Paris was in flower. I went into hiding for a time in the little room on the Avenue Foch. Then, Coustenoble having given me the green light, I hurried off to the old *Ordre National* premises. 'Why aren't you staying here?' asked my maid, Marguerite. 'I completely reassured the Germans who came here yesterday.'

'What Germans?'

'Two very polite men who asked me what I was doing here. I told them that I was expecting you and they made me promise to let them know as soon as you arrived.'

'Now, Marguerite, the day after I've left, tell them that I was simply here on a flying visit to bury an uncle who is leaving me some money.'

'Don't worry! They won't get anything more out of a Norman! I'll soon send them packing.'

A wave of nostalgia swept over me. Piled in the stark rooms where we had once run our magazine were my furniture, and the possessions which had been moved there—all my memories, the precious objects from the Far East where I had spent my childhood, my piano, my music, my books, all my treasures. I looked at them as though I had already departed this world. All that my past now did for me was to attract the enemy: the Germans who appeared to be interested in me must believe that I would come back. although I now had no intention of setting foot there again.

A ring at the door startled me nevertheless. Coustenoble, followed by Armand Bonnet, came in with an armful of information.

'We'll get to work at once,' I said, and added, 'for the last time here.'

The questionnaires I had given him were filled in. There were the plans of the phoney airfields as well as the locations of the German units in the Paris area. Brittany was particularly well covered. 'Your patrols' excellent, Bonnet. Now it must have a name. I'll call it "the Guynemer patrol".'

'What I need is a radio set,' he grumbled.

'We've only got one at the moment. Send more couriers to Pau. Your information will be in London within twenty-four or thirty-six hours. I want you to send someone up to the coast in Brittany, where preparations are afoot to camouflage big units.'

'I've got the very man, Antoine Hugon, and an engineer, Mouren, who's working in the naval shipyards at Saint-Nazaire.'

'Tell him we need to know urgently the changes being made to the bases.'

'He's already told me about nests of U-boats.'

'And your White Russians? They seem a lousy source.'

Bonnet was immediately up in arms. His White Russians were utterly reliable informants. They were sure that Hitler was going to attack the Soviet Union when the weather was good, in the early days of summer. Coustenoble was all enthusiasm. 'So Hitler's going to turn on Russia? That'll make it easier to recruit communist workers.'

The Guynemer patrol was due to get more money. However, I thought Bonnet was demanding far too big a budget, and behind his back I could see Coustenoble making all sorts of mysterious signs, which made me wary about agreeing to Bonnet's requests.

'Didn't you see?' Coustenoble asked me later. 'He's making a good thing out of it. He hadn't a penny when he joined the network but he's gone and bought himself a super watch.' Making a good thing out of it, at a time like this, did not augur well.

I was expecting other visitors. The first to come was Henri Champin. We had known one another since schooldays and had grown up with the same ideals; so he was a very safe contact as well as an exceptional informant in his own line—oil. He brought along a young man of our own age who was working under his orders—Charles Deguy. They pulled out of their pockets precious sheets of paper showing petrol dumps and the amounts the German army had taken from French stocks.

'This is terrific! There's nothing more important at the moment. Do you happen to have any indication of massive shipments of fuel in the direction of Poland?'

'I'll find out,' said Deguy, 'but *I'd* rather have a nice large shipment of hand grenades.'

'Charles, we started with less than nothing and now there's a real gleam of hope. Don't go too fast.' Did he have a premonition that his end was near?

Although it was rather unorthodox, I had promised Fourcaud's radio operator, Laroche, that I would see his parents. They hurried over, escorted by my old acquaintance, Dayné, of the Secret Police. The father was trembling with emotion:

'When you sent word that our son was back in France I was afraid he'd deserted! I would rather have seen him dead. But tell him how delighted I am to know he was parachuted in. And consider me as under your orders. The more you give me to do the better I shall feel.'

They appeared from out of the shadows, and suddenly you felt that you had always known them. The tie formed by a threat to one's country is the strongest tie of all. Everything becomes common property—ideas, feelings, material resources. No mental reservations, no embarrassing questions. People adopt one another, march together; only capture or death can tear them apart. But truth compels me to admit that it has been the modest, less successful people who have given me the greatest sense of kinship.

'You will remain at Dayné's disposal, Monsieur Laroche, here's your secret number: TUR 160.'

His face revealed his joy. Could a resistance pseudonym really inspire such great happiness? It was, in fact, the true *légion d'honneur*.

I gave Marguerite many more instructions and eventually left to fade away into Paris, glad that on my last visit I had set up the hiding places

I would use. My days were spent arranging where the radios were to go, organizing letterboxes and channels of communication, distributing code names, teaching the code and checking information. I saw at first hand what the ideal intelligence cell should consist of: a source, someone who hunts down information; a letterbox for collecting and sending this information; a courier, the local agent who gets the source to search and then brings the report; a radio operator for urgent matters. I could sense the danger in this situation: the source thinking that things were going too slowly. He, too, recruits people and cannot resist the temptation to rally everyone of goodwill; thus he compromises himself. The sector grows in size, but the job becomes unmanageable; small fry begin to cling to the net and this increases the danger that the big fish will himself get caught. And to get this across to the mere handful of men who were bursting with enthusiasm in the spring of 1941 was extremely difficult.

'It won't be carelessness or rashness that will be our undoing. All in all, it's better to have done the best we could. Drive us hard, you'll never ask too much of us.' Coustenoble kept saying.

I went to see Paul Bernard, the manager of the Société Financière et Coloniale, in his office. He was getting impatient at sitting around idly, unable to do a thing. 'Don't put all your eggs in one basket,' I thought, listening to him explain that Paris had now been full again for two months, that the middle classes were no longer scared of the Germans and that collaboration had got really into its stride—had taken 'a terrible hold', to use his own words.

'Paul, we haven't the right to throw a man as valuable as you straight into the front line. I have a feeling, alas, that we shall need to send in wave after wave. Once our patrols have thoroughly tested the ground you'll get your chance.'

There was no point in my hiding anything from this life-long friend. When he heard of the progress that had been made he resigned himself to waiting patiently, certain that one day his call would come.

To get a better idea of 'the terrible hold' the Germans had taken on the capital I begged a friend to take me to lunch at Maxim's. Gathered there were the Nazi intelligentsia and the pretty little 'grey mice' escorted by dashing Luftwaffe officers. These handsome young Germans seemed in no way embarrassed at shamelessly occupying our country for no better reason than that given by Hitler—'in the name of the Greater Reich.' Nevertheless, they must have been aware that they shared the guilt of his torturers. So far I had seen only the ordinary German soldier; now I saw the cream of the German general staff, the aces of the Panzer and the Luftwaffe divisions, the smartest, most decorated and bemedalled tunics, the most distinguished faces and hands, the most arrogant monocles. They were being served with delicate and delicious foods, and I thought of my poor devils travelling the length and breadth of France on empty bellies, down-at-heel, with raincoats for uniform, yet working to get rid of all this arrogant lot and their collaborators with them. Here and there, alas, at equally well-laden tables, I could see Frenchmen who were forming fratricidal syndicates to manufacture German fighter planes, tanks and guns for the Atlantic Wall in our French factories, at a handsome profit to themselves.

I was suddenly overwhelmed by a sense of the futility of our underground activity. We were bound to perish. What could we really achieve against the most powerful military machine in the world and the combined wealth and enslaved economies of a dozen exploited nations? Faced with such odds, had I the right to involve my unfortunate friends in a venture that could end only in our possibly pointless slaughter?

5 NAVARRE

'Things are humming in Marseilles,' said Schaerrer, as he dragged me along to the first train, followed at a distance by Coustenoble, who was going to cross the demarcation line with the courier. We were on our way south again. To evade the witches I got into a third class compartment fully occupied by a family and I nursed the baby on my knees.

But at Moulins the witch on duty led me away, made me undress and carefully searched my clothing and luggage. As soon as the train moved off again I tore the fatal *Ausweis* into a thousand pieces and took my hat with its double lining off the baby's head.

Navarre, wearing the strangest-looking outfit, was travelling as M. Lambin, a wine merchant.

'Why this new disguise?' I asked him, choking with laughter.

'Because I'm making people frightened, as you know very well. So the Gaullists among my Deuxième Bureau colleagues have given me false papers. This way, I can work as I please. I'm sailing for Algiers tomorrow.'

Commandant Faye had sent him a message, urging him to go there, and Navarre thought the time was ripe for a revolt in the African army. If it was successful from Tunis to Agadir, as anticipated, Churchill would seal off the Mediterranean. I told them with considerable vehemence what I had seen in the occupied zone and that there were enough Nazi troops in France to make mincemeat of us and the British as well. To my mind the revolt was premature.

'Nothing's premature in war,' Navarre replied imperturbably. 'The greater the defeat, the greater the effort that must be made.'

'What are you expecting me to do to help these impressive schemes?'

'You will transmit to London the messages that come in our code through the Deuxième Bureau contact.'

Fourcaud arrived in a state of great excitement. 'Everything's going fine,' he enthused. 'I've received confirmation that Churchill is tremendously interested in the whole venture.' I could only resign myself to the situation.

To protect the local patrol from any repercussions I brought the radio operator, Lucien Vallet, and the KVL transmitter to Marseilles. Coustenoble would keep his eyes open. Rivière would maintain contact with the Deuxième Bureau. And while we were awaiting Navarre's messages, Vallet passed on Audoly's information.

The grim news of the sinking of the *Hood* by the *Bismarck* on 24 May, induced me to radio to the War Office expressing my profound sorrow. '*Thanks for your friendship stop we shall avenge them together end*' was their reply.

I was beginning to realize the powerful magic of radio communication. This syncopated dialogue allowed room for human feelings through the harsh vicissitudes of the struggle. I resolved, whatever happened, never to lose contact with the Allies.

When, on the morning of 22 May 1941, Loustaunau-Lacau, alias Navarre, alias Lambin, wine merchant, went to see Faye on the heights overlooking Algiers, he found a happy and determined man and the conspiracy already tied up. Within an hour they were joined by Capitaine André Beaufre, a member of General Weygand's cabinet governing Algeria, and two charming men of sparkling intelligence, Commandant Louis Dartois and Lieutenant de Chassey.

Navarre asked them to call in also a contemporary of his at Saint-Cyr, nicknamed 'Hare Face', who was Deputy Chief of Staff of the 19th Army Corps. Navarre had maintained discreet contact with this man in Vichy throughout the winter. He needed him to pursue his consultations within the army. They seemed to have made a good start. Faye had worked out the African army's needs and drawn up a plan for a surprise air attack on an Italian transport between Bari, Messina and Tripolitania. He had organized the Tunis-Bizerta cell, leaving it to Navarre to set one up in Morocco, where he had his contacts. Captain Beaufre, who was invited to this first meeting, was in touch with the United States Government observers in Algeria.

The question of General Weygand was thoroughly discussed. Weygand undoubtedly loathed the Germans and enjoyed great prestige among the army in Africa. The ideal thing, of course, would be to include him in the conspiracy.

'He won't come in,' said Navarre. 'He's too well disciplined after forty years of blind obedience to the political authorities. Probability is no basis for a conspiracy. Only the British can provide us with the means we need as things stand at present.'

'And de Gaulle?' asked the others.

'I've informed de Gaulle through Fourcaud of what I was going to do in Africa, but it's Churchill who is bearing the burden and the fate of the world on his shoulders. It's up to us to let him know the nature and the amount of help we need.'

In his uncertainty about the United States' entry into the war, the British Prime Minister urgently needed to bottle up the Mediterranean to secure his communications with the Middle East, all of which went round the Cape.

The basis of the conspiracy was thus established when Hare Face came in. Navarre pointed out to him the opportunities that France still had to share in Allied victory. Would the Allies have to land in Africa one day as conquerors, or would the great liberation effort spring spontaneously from French soil? Hare Face soon excused himself. Chatting pleasantly, he shook hands all round and left Navarre, saying: 'Count on me, old man. Come and see me this evening so that I can put your identity papers in order.'

The working session was resumed in the afternoon. It lasted two hours. Some Belgian pilots who had fled to Algeria offered their services. Faye gave details about the Americans, who also seemed to be interested in North Africa. If Hitler occupied the country the establishment of German submarine bases at Tangier and Casablanca would pose a threat to the United States. The plans for action were spread all over the table. Faye recapitulated the decisions taken. He reckoned a thousand aircraft would be needed, two-thirds of them fighters. Navarre began to code a first report for London.

Suddenly men surged into the room through the doors and the windows. A police superintendent, wearing his tricolour sash, strode in. He produced search and arrest warrants. All the officers present were bundled into cars and driven to the main police station.

'The stitch in time' that Churchill wanted had burst. Now North Africa had missed its chance of making a stand on its own.

Three days later, Gabriel Rivière burst like a cyclone into my little studio dining-room where Lucien Vallet was tapping out a message: '*Ships carrying strange cargoes sailing from Marseilles this evening. . . .*'

'You'll have to clear out at once, for two reasons,' he shouted. 'In the first place some nitwit here has told the police he could hear suspicious sounds. . . .'

'It must have been my morse key. It's too noisy,' Vallet explained. 'Even though I turn the tap on while I'm transmitting I can't really drown it.'

'And the second reason?' I asked, rooted to the spot with fear.

'They've all been arrested in Algiers, so the Deuxième Bureau has just informed me. They haven't a hope of being released. What are you going to do?'

My first thought was for Colonel Bernis and our headquarters at Pau. Fourcaud, who had gone white as a sheet, came to the rescue. 'We must warn London.'

'Let me think things out first. In the meantime I must make sure that nothing happens to the organization. I'm off to Pau.'

'You're not going by train. I'll take you by road.'

Wonderful, chivalrous Fourcaud! I had just time to send Coustenoble off to give the alarm everywhere before I was bustled off to the waiting car.

We were shattered by the magnitude of the disaster. Nevertheless Fourcaud continued to make plans involving high political strategy, remote from my ordinary, humdrum worries. Now that all possibility of a spontaneous revolt in North Africa had gone, he still hoped to get the support of Admiral de la Borde, commander of the French navy.

'Don't be ridiculous, Fourcaud! I've spoken in Paris to the Admiral's brother. He advises us not to tackle him on any pretext whatever. The Admiral hates the British with all his guts.'

'I'll try, all the same,' he insisted. 'Even if it's only a thousand-to-one chance, it's worth the risk. You'll see our fleet sailing to help perfidious Albion!'

Our driver, Guy, an old friend, was showing obvious signs of fatigue and we decided to take a few hours rest at Castelnaudary rather than smash ourselves against a tree.

'I'm opening the era of precautions,' Fourcaud announced, describing me on the hotel registration form as his wife. As soon as we met next morning he burst out laughing. 'If you could only have seen the waiter's face when he brought breakfast into the room where I had spent the night in the same bed as Guy!'

As we drove through Toulouse I saw Baston emerging from a large brasserie; we stopped and picked him up. He was shattered to hear the news of Algiers: 'It's just as I feared: Navarre and Faye are an explosive mixture. Bound to go off bang! What have you decided to do?'

'To carry on, General.'

He looked at me sadly. 'Carry on *alone*?'

He did not believe I could, and reproached me for persisting in a mistaken course. But he promised he would keep the whole Vichy patrol together until I could take charge of it again.

Bernis, at the Pension Welcome in Pau, had no choice but to return to Monte-Carlo. He sadly packed up his intelligence maps. Now that Navarre had been captured everything, according to him, would have to stop. If I let him leave feeling there was no hope, a real danger that the network would panic would have arisen.

'It's not the end, Colonel. I'm going to tell the British that you'll take over command of the whole Mediterranean region from Monaco '

He understood that I wanted to ensure that our efforts would go on. Sadness filled his grey eyes; but when, after a pause, he agreed, it was from the bottom of his heart. 'I like your sang-froid, my dear. You only need to give me a sign as soon as you think I can get cracking again.'

He was giving me a chance to prove what I could do.

With everything settled in Pau, I took the train for Marseilles at once, with the idea of setting up my headquarters there. Fourcaud had gone to inform London. What was British Intelligence going to think? Would they abandon us? The stations rolled past, an endless stream of old, familiar names. Well concealed under a broad-brimmed hat I did not look at anybody for fear of being recognized. I had eaten practically nothing for forty-eight hours. It was hot. The book that I began to read did nothing to slake my thirst, and then a traveller who had recently entered the compartment began to annoy me. He had already pressed my feet three times with his own. In a rage I looked up, raising my eyes from his check trousers to the black jacket with its purple rosette, showing that he was an intellectual, then over an enormous tie, such as sported by poets, until they came to rest on a wonderful and grotesque stetson. It was Navarre!

Not a muscle in his face moved. I buried my face in my book again. After some time Navarre got up and went out to smoke in the corridor. Gathering my strength, I followed him.

'Escaped with the help of a police commissioner,' he whispered. 'The boys told me you were using this train and I've come to meet you. Pau's OK for the moment?'

'Yes. You were betrayed?'

'By Hare Face. He rushed off to Weygand the moment he left us.'

'And the others?'

'When I got away they were free on parole, but I'm afraid about the repercussions. It's a pity, it was a good scheme. We'll take it up again.'

It was the first time since the armistice that the Pétain system had cracked in an actual French *département*. Vichy had soon summed up the situation and had given orders for Faye and Beaufre to be transferred to Clermont-Ferrand jail and for proceedings to be instituted against them. Arrest warrants were issued for Navarre and those connected with him. The first to be apprehended was General Baston, who, despite his cover, soon found himself shut up in a hotel-prison in Vals, alone with his beloved Rat.

Although the police never even suspected the existence of our patrols, I assumed my first false identity, Navarre having warned me that my name appeared among the documents that had been seized in Algiers.

'Where do we go now?'

'Back to Pau, of course,' Navarre declared. 'They'll never think I've gone back home.'

The Crusade continued.

Schaerrer found a room in a superb flat overlooking Pau's Promenade des Pyrenees. Only Annick, the daughter of the house, knew that her tenant, a quiet, retired schoolmaster, was none other than the famous local-born Georges Loustaunau-Lacau.

June passed in a flash. At the Pension Welcome I did my best to carry on Bernis' work, keeping closely to his technique.

On 22 June Hitler attacked Russia, as my White Russian agents had predicted. The SS Cathedral Division prepared to move east. So much for learning the local dialect! The officers were disgusted at the idea of exchanging the delights of the Basque country for the less hospitable Russian steppes, and this amused our men, who now redoubled their efforts. They had transformed the Villa Etchebaster into a fortress and

Navarre came and worked there, cycling through the streets of Pau only at dawn or dusk. Josette, the housekeeper, bought our food, which meant that we could confine our own coming and going strictly to the needs of the service. Josette was a phenomenon and did her job with the courage of a lion. To save money, and at the risk of breaking her neck, she would go and fish for trout in the mountain streams; on the other hand she cost us a lot by buying quantities of cigarettes and drink on the black market.

Inspired by the success of his romantic appearance, Navarre thought up one daring scheme after another. His imagination had never been more active, nor reached such dizzy heights. He had got the Tunisian sector going, had established a network to Italy, as well as one within the *Abwehr* itself; he had made contact with the extraordinary 'Dame Blanche' Belgian organization with the help of a priest, and arranged collaboration with the army's Deuxième Bureau through three colonels who could not stomach the armistice. His spare time was spent in setting up a clandestine radio-telephone circuit—'Radio Terror', he called it, bubbling over with enthusiasm and rehearsing his future speeches to our men, who always formed a fascinated audience.

Everything was back to normal. The strength of the patrols now exceeded a hundred and the couriers came and went smoothly. It had been possible to import three new transmitters: BAY for Bernis in Monaco, MED for Audoly in Marseilles. The third, LUX, we held in reserve. We had received them via Spain, thanks to Jean Boutron, whom Vichy proposed to send to the French Embassy at Madrid as deputy naval attaché.

'Just the job, the final link we need,' enthused Navarre, overjoyed at the news. 'It's a real godsend! He'll be able to make sure of direct contact with the military attaché at the British Embassy and thus send our mail in both directions.'

Vichy was really counting on using Jean Boutron to reorganize its Naval Intelligence in Spain. As a 'victim of Mers-el-Kébir', they thought that he at least would not go over to the British.

The British, in fact, received him with open arms. He made immediate contact with British Intelligence and at the same time arranged with the French Embassy to take the diplomatic bag, one or several mail bags, together with a number of Vichy seals. This permitted him, when he stopped at Pau, to open the bags sealed in Vichy or Madrid and insert or remove our secret messages or equipment.

The only drawback to this dazzling operation, as far as I was concerned, was that I had to let Boutron have my beloved little Citroen. Sporting a CD plate, it henceforth maintained a shuttle service between us and the free world.

In view of the growth of our organization, British Intelligence announced at the beginning of July that it was sending us more help. We were going to get a better type of radio and also British specialists to train our operators and teach us a new method of coding.

The RAF had agreed to use the dropping zone that Coustenoble had discovered and the operation was planned for the night of the full moon. We were astounded at our British partners' audacity, for they never hesitated about landing in enemy territory. If only Vichy had not put obstacles in our way. But little did we know. The police were becoming increasingly incensed at not laying their hands on Navarre, who was indispensable for the preliminary hearing at Clermont-Ferrand, where Faye and Beaufre were already. Captain Fourcaud returned from Paris in very low spirits. Charles Deguy was in Fresnes prison. He who was so keen to get things done quickly!

'I walked into a trap,' Fourcaud confessed sheepishly. 'It's a good thing I listened to you, Marie-Madeleine. It was the first time I wasn't wearing my Free French badge and as they observed the regulations and searched me. . . . Things are getting sticky up there!'

'Yes,' Schaerrer chipped in, 'and the controls are being tightened up at Bordeaux as well.'

The engineer was full of gloom and not his normal easy, relaxed self. He had to leave again the next day, 10 July, on a final mission to check on the U-boat situation. I was with him until midnight, passionately urging him to take the greatest possible care and to give up any idea of going aboard the U-boats unless conditions were absolutely right.

'No one's irreplaceable,' he assured me as he nervously collected his bits and pieces. Someone came in and forced us to get our goodbyes over quickly: the escorts at the demarcation line would not wait. Schaerrer, the intrepid, vanished once more into the night.

I was worried about another departure for the occupied zone, that of Poulain and Jumez, the two young statisticians. They were going to set up the Turenne patrol, which was meant to cover the forbidden northern zone. Giving them their numbers, teaching them the code and the questionnaires helped to dull the obsession that was gradually beginning to haunt my mind—that things were going too well on this tightrope. Who would be the first to stumble?

On 17 July, earlier than he was expected, Coustenoble returned from a mission in the Alps. He suddenly appeared before me in his cat-like way, looking abnormally tired and worried. 'Navarre is going to be arrested,' he began.

'How do you know?'

'Never mind. Intuition, if you like.'

'Coustenoble, you have no right to keep your sources secret from me, it's too serious.'

'My sources?' He raised his eyes to heaven. 'I haven't any, it's a certainty. He *must* clear out of Pau today. Tomorrow will be too late. Do something.'

Coustenoble was not an excitable type. No one gave a matter more careful thought than he did before venturing a single step. I had never seen him so tense. Deeply impressed, I got up without a word and went into the map room. Navarre was drafting orders.

'Coustenoble's here.'

'Already? And Schaerrer? Still no news?'

'None.'

'Any need to worry?'

'I'm worried about you.'

'Why this concern about me?'

'The police,' I said, forced to invent a reason. 'When he was coming through Vichy Coustenoble learned that they were convinced you were in Pau. They're going to get you, it's only a matter of hours.'

He put down his pen and began to walk up and down the room. Coustenoble was standing silent in the doorway.

'Listen, both of you. I don't know what your information is worth, but you're right. I've been a bit too smart. I'll get out tomorrow.'

'Why not at once?' asked Coustenoble. 'Everything is prepared for a quick getaway.'

'Impossible. I'm expecting my family tomorrow morning. I must see my wife and daughter one last time. After that I'll put myself in your hands.'

He sat down and started writing again. 'Your family is the only lead the police have. They will certainly be followed,' I said.

'There's a short cut from the nearest church. Annick won't be caught napping.' We knew that he would not go back on his decision.

The afternoon dragged on bleakly, with the usual coming and going. Gavarni signalled that everything was ready for the Turenne patrol to cross into the occupied zone; Vallet brought a message, saying that the first parachute drop would be made in two days time; Josette came in with a bagful of trout. Coding, decoding, arranging missions.

Navarre at last donned his famous stetson. It was the sign for his bike to be got out. Coustenoble and I went and stood in his way. 'We're going with you.'

'Do, if you want to,' agreed the Commandant, in the best of tempers. 'But on one condition. Leave those toys behind, we won't shoot Frenchmen.' He pointed reprovingly at our bulging pockets.

'And what if they attack you?'

'Don't give me that sort of stuff! I know what they're like at night here: they'll be asleep.'

Getting on our bicycles, we glided down into the town, which was indeed sleeping, along the wonderful promenade overlooking the valley. The air was sweet with the scent of blossom. The splendid towers of Henry IV's chateau made an impressive silhouette not far from the house, nto which we stole silently.

Once in the flat, Coustenoble insisted on going through everything. We burned compromising, useless and out-of-date papers and documents that were stacked up in every possible corner. Coustenoble hid the code under the nailed-down carpet. Navarre offered us a glass of Armagnac. The window was wide open. The peaks of the Pyrenees glowed like beacons in the dawn.

'What a fascinating frontier,' Navarre murmured. 'Now try to get a little sleep and tell Josette to cook the trout for twelve o'clock. I shall be here on the dot.'

I decided to wander round the town until lunch time and sent Coustenoble back to the Villa Etchebaster. Apart from the members of the network, nobody in Pau knew me. I did some shopping and spent a long session at the hairdresser's. Then I pedalled slowly towards our headquarters. My head was aching from apprehension and lack of sleep. I stopped at the church. God, I prayed, give me courage! Only the little square to cross. Then I rang the bell discreetly. When Josette came to open the garden gate, I saw at once from her face that the worst had happened.

In the drawing-room with the heavy gold frames and the ugly, shapeless furniture, all the men were standing around in the depths of despair. Coustenoble took me by the arm and dragged me up to the next floor. On the way he told me the whole wretched story. Navarre's family had been followed from Oloron by thirteen policemen that Annick had taken to be people at prayer when she saw them in the cathedral. The major had tried to run for it. He was fired at, but not hit, and was now in Pau prison waiting to be transferred to Clermont-Ferrand. The superintendent in charge of the operation had told the policemen they were after a German spy—in case they should soften, Coustenoble explained.

I was so overcome by a feeling of bitterness and resentment towards Pétain, Vichy and my obtuse, malevolent fellow-countrymen, that I burst into sobs. Coustenoble put his arm round me affectionately and murmured words of encouragement. 'That's enough, little one,' he suddenly said. 'Come and have some lunch. A soldier doesn't cry.'

'I shall never be able to do it, to take the terrible responsibility that is falling on me now. Leave me to think.'

'No, you're coming to eat. If the men don't see you there they *will* feel they've been left without a leader.'

'The trout are ready,' announced Josette. The boys' appetites had not suffered. I managed to slip my portion to Vallet, our Gargantuan radio operator, without my suspicious adjutant noticing.

'What time will you be talking to London again, Vallet?'

'Fifteen hours GMT, madame.' I had barely time to code my message.

6 MY BACK TO THE WALL

'*N1 arrested this morning stop network intact stop everything continuing stop best postpone parachuting next moon stop Turenne patrol leaves for Paris tonight stop confidence unshakable stop regards stop POZ 55 end.*'

'POZ 55 is my chief of staff,' Navarre had explained to Kenneth Cohen. The British might have thought I was a man. I decided to go the whole hog and draft all my radio messages in this way.

The reply came a few hours later, full of expressions of regret and sympathy and ending in the dry little query: '*Who is taking over command?*' to which I replied: '*I am as planned stop surrounded loyal lieutenants. . . .*'

The British were in the picture. Now, with my back to the wall, I must get everything straightened out.

'The Welcome has been raided and the police are looking for you everywhere,' announced Gavarni, who had come to find me. He was a tall, spare, athletic and quick-tempered man, a natural leader. The men liked him and I had the greatest respect for his powers of endurance in action. I looked anxiously at his nervously twitching moustache.

'Do you think it's safe to hide in the Villa Etchebaster?'

'I'll vouch for that personally. My story about prisoners who've escaped from Germany is still believed.'

'Then I'll stay there. What are you afraid of?'

'I'm not afraid of anything,' Gavarni exploded, 'because I have every confidence in you. I've seen you at work for weeks. But there are the others. . . .'

'They think it ridiculous to take orders from a woman?'

'You must admit . . . you're very young, they don't feel sure.'

'In the meantime we must somehow survive and keep things going.'

He soon agreed that it was impossible to dismantle overnight the complicated machinery centred on Pau. Knowing his ability to act quickly, I made him my chief of staff. Top priority was to raise the alarm everywhere and to get the men of the Turenne patrol on their way.

'We're still going?' exclaimed Poulain. He and Jumez were overjoyed at the news. I was expecting great things of these cold, determined young men who were resolved to drive out the invader they had hated since childhood. Our chief escort, Jean Broqua, tall, well-built, a little embarrassed by his physical strength, looked after them with an almost motherly care.

We embraced. Then, fearful of the answer, I asked: 'Broqua, there's still no news of Schaerrer?'

'No, madame, not a word.'

Whatever the danger, I had to go back to the Pension Welcome. When night fell I stole there, hugging the walls, and went into the small drawing-room where one of the old ladies—the one I liked best—was sewing by the light of a dim lamp.

'You know what has happened?' I asked. 'The Commandant has been arrested.'

'Sweet Jesus,' she said, putting her hands together. 'Such a gentleman. Is it possible?' I talked to her for a long time about France, and the British who, I said, were going to win the war. 'Yes,' she replied, 'yes'. She was becoming dimly aware of the strange world opening up before her.

'So, you understand, if the police come here you'll tell them I left for the Riviera on the early morning train. I'll fill in a form to cover you.'

'Do you want the horse carriage to take you to the station?'

'There's no need, a friend is coming for me.'

The sweet, gentle old lady brought me a cup of hot tea while I was collecting my things. She told me that I had nothing to fear from her.

Lucien Vallet knocked on the door at the agreed time, dashed in and grabbed my cases. We pretended to set off towards the station. My kind hostess waved goodbye with her handkerchief until we were out of sight. Then, after a good ten minutes we crossed the street, keeping close to the wall, and walked in the opposite direction. Creeping along like Red Indians, we eventually slipped into the Villa Etchebaster through the iron gate that Josette had left undone. I made for the first bed I could find. Sixty hours without sleep was rather long.

To sleep . . . and to forget. . . . But it was still early when Gavarni came in and shook me awake. 'You've given me a fine fright!' he said. 'I've run here like a madman. The police have been at the Welcome since dawn.'

'Well, I'm on the Riviera. You say *I've* given *you* a fright and then *you* come along and wake me up and give *me* a start! Let me sleep.'

My story did nothing to calm him. I agreed to follow him to a temporary hide-out in the house of an industrialist whose wife was English. Though their home was an oasis of happiness, I had to move on.

The ideal headquarters was quickly discovered in the very centre of Pau, at the Hôtel du Lycée. Its owners agreed to put me up without filling in any forms and to serve all my meals in the spacious but bare room where I resigned myself to living, to all intents and purposes, the life of a prisoner, never going out by day and very rarely by night. It was the only way to save the organization.

The fact that everything went on as usual gave the men confidence. Shocked by their chief's arrest, they put twice as much into their efforts.

A veritable flood of mail converged on my hotel. I coded the urgent information, which was sent by radio. The rest was despatched to London via Madrid in Jean Boutron's diplomatic bags.

News about the Clermont-Ferrand prison began to arrive. The hearing would take place in October.

Writing messages in invisible ink, coding and decoding; my studious incarceration was a credit to the *lycée* after which my hotel was named. Josette and Vallet came once a day, acting as couriers and bringing and taking my messages. Every morning and evening Gavarni would come to plan the hunt for the information requested in the questionnaires we received by radio—'please send more information about the mass production of landing barges . . . please send more information about the "Cathedral" division about to leave for the Russian front . . . more about the installation on the Atlantic Coast of the 47s taken from the Maginot Line . . . please send more about . . . please send more about. . . .'

It was Coustenoble who brought the dreadful news: Henri Schaerrer, the first of us to fall into Nazi clutches, had been captured on 11 July in the U-boat nest that he had attempted to infiltrate in the guise of a German sailor. From the little that we knew, Schaerrer was imprisoned at Fresnes under his assumed name. Since his arrest he had not divulged a thing about what he knew. His behaviour in adversity matched his courage in action.

The August moon renewed our preoccupation with the parachute drop that I had cancelled after Navarre's arrest. The British had almost stopped parachuting their agents blind, in the way they had done with my brother. They insisted on a 'reception committee' to lay out proper ground lights to mark the dropping zone and to give the prearranged light signal. The thought of receiving an Englishman made us wildly excited. Coustenoble suggested playing 'God Save the King' on the gramophone while the parachutist floated gently down to earth: 'After all, we can't receive him like a sack of peanuts!'

Everything was laid on for the special envoy. His false civilian papers had been sent to me. On the basis of this document we had also concocted a false identity card for Josette, who would assume the role of his lawful wedded wife.

The agents who were to learn the new ciphering methods were called to Pau and shown how to operate the new type of radio. Once the Englishman's job with us was finished, he was to be taken to Normandy, where he was to set up an independent sector. Later on I would have to send him money and receive his messages. He had his own personal code and radio. A second parachute would drop us spare parts, transmitting sets and a few weapons.

The drop on 5 August went well. In less than twenty-four hours Gavarni and Coustenoble were back. It was a fateful night when I was brought out of my lair to inspect the rare bird in the brilliantly lighted drawing-room of the Villa Etchebaster. Coustenoble, never at a loss for ideas, had me make my entrance to the first bars of 'God Save the King' followed by a resounding rendering of the Marseillaise. I stopped and gaped. Before me stood the most ridiculous, most grotesque parody of a 'typical' Frenchman. He was attired as if for a village wedding—short jacket and waistcoat, striped trousers, a spotted cravat, a stiff shirt with cutaway collar beneath a little goatee beard, a pair of pince-nez, and as a crowning glory, a bowler hat. Was this British Intelligence? The boys burst into roars of laughter.

The unhappy parachutist blinked his big, round, milky blue eyes at us. I decided to console him by saying a few welcoming words in English.

'Don't bother, Madame,' he answered in excellent French, but with a strong cockney accent. 'I've spent more of my life in France than in England.'

The new radios that had been dropped by parachute were much smaller than the first ones. Vallet was already fiddling about with his (OCK), intended for the Paris area, which Coustenoble was to smuggle into the occupied zone as quickly as possible in a cartload of vegetables. I admired the new office material: extra fine, silky paper for messages, more invisible ink, lots of little gadgets to make our job easier and to fox the enemy. I fingered the first envelope to come stamped with the royal coat of arms and containing a letter of encouragement addressed to 'POZ 55' and, couched in the politest possible vein, suggestions regarding the organization and its future work.

The sight of 'Bla'—our name for His Majesty's ambassador—and the sight of his lifeless face and defeated expression led me to end the session pretty quickly. I told him to take forty-eight hours rest, get a complete change of clothes and shave off his beard.

The next day Lucien Vallet came to see me. I sensed that something was wrong. He came straight to the point: 'He's going to kick the bucket.'

'Who?'

'The Englishman.'

He explained. After I had left, Bla had started to complain of pains in the head and the stomach. Josette had taken his temperature. It had been 104. They at once diagnosed acute appendicitis.

'We can't let him die just like that. He must be looked after at once.'

Vallet's blue eyes went purple; he clearly felt no liking for Bla. 'He's a queer fish, Madame. You ought to let him go. He's already shown me the code. I can explain it to the others, there's nothing very difficult about it.'

I was very angry and gave orders that Bla should be taken to a hospital. We managed to save him. Josette stayed at his bedside and played the role of wife to perfection. When the patient came round and began talking in English she threw herself on him to stifle his Shakespearean moans and groans, covered him with resounding kisses and added her own cries to his, to the nurses' astonishment. A few days later everything was going well except that Bla, developing a taste for the game, pestered Josette with his demands and devoured everybody's rations on the quiet. Consequently Vallet's animosity towards him increased tenfold.

However, my radio operator was due to leave for Paris. He departed all smiles to take up his job in the occupied zone. The OCK set had arrived safely and was already installed where 'Tadpole', one of his friends, was living, and before leaving Pau Vallet carried what he called the 'flirtation' to the point of fixing a date in Paris with the British in London. I received an enthusiastic message of congratulations from British Intelligence when everything went off as planned and without a hitch. OCK was certainly one of the very first transmitters to operate in Paris and Vallet was a champion operator. The departure of this gay and inspiring fellow left a great void at our headquarters. We had been such a closely knit entity that I had the sad feeling we were cutting ourselves into pieces. Vallet's successor, who had been trained by him, took over the KVL transmitter at the Etchebaster. We called him 'Tringa'.

The appendicitis episode meant that I had to keep the parachutist in Pau longer than had been anticipated and his behaviour continued to worry me. Having presumably been properly trained, he should have known better than to give his coding lessons in a loud voice, sitting in the public park; nor should he have introduced himself to every visitor who came to the Etchebaster or exchanged names and addresses with all and sundry. Who would distrust an agent parachuted by the British? Although I had warned people to be careful, they were around him constantly.

The last straw was when my brother, whom I had called to the rescue, came and told me that, on learning he was a journalist, Bla had suggested buying from him, at a very good price, information for the British press. He said he would radio this information to London on a wavelength that British Intelligence knew nothing about. I was frightened. Was Bla here to test us, I wondered. The best thing was to get him to Normandy as quickly as possible, but he gave endless reasons why he should delay going. In the meantime he continued to offer his services to anyone and everyone and discovered more and more of the secrets of my organization.

One morning Antoine Hugon appeared from Paris. He was a garage owner and had the unusual distinction of having been awarded the Iron Cross for having saved the life of a drowning German soldier in the First World War. He made a point of wearing it openly, which presumably made his missions into the less accessible zones that much easier. He proudly unfolded a huge plan that he had wrapped round his body and smuggled across the demarcation line. It showed all the U-boat pens recently built at Saint-Nazaire, reproduced to scale, down to the last inch, by the engineer Henri Mouren.

Since the arrival of the Turenne patrol and Lucien Vallet, the Paris organization was expanding in a remarkable way. The only doubtful element was Armand Bonnet, the leader of the Guynemer patrol, who was cheerfully engaging in the black market. It was imperative that we should get rid of him and we agreed to remodel the organization. With the help of a post office official, Amedée Pautard, we would henceforth be able to address the mail to a fictitious name, care of the Post Office in Paris, without going through Bonnet, who would thus be automatically eliminated. Hugon, knowing all our sources, would take over the leadership of the Guynemer patrol.

This conversation with a sensible and intrepid man greatly cheered me. In spite of Schaerrer's disappearance and Bonnet's deficiency I would be able to equip the terrible occupied zone. I did not know that before leaving Antoine Hugon had, against my orders, arranged to meet Bla in the capital.

Everything comes to him who waits and Bla, looking very different from the day he first appeared, announced that he was ready to set off for Normandy. To get him there safely I detailed Jean Lefèvre, whose skill in crossing the demarcation line with the most compromising messages guaranteed the success of the operation, which was planned to the last detail.

Lefevre returned forty-eight hours late. Throughout the whole trip his protégé, who was supposed to pretend he had a bad attack of toothache and was not to utter a word, had never stopped talking, asking stupid questions at the top of his voice and fooling with his transmitter, SHE. It was a miracle that they had got through safe and sound. Once there, Bla had vanished into thin air. And so Lefèvre, greatly concerned, had thought it wiser to come back and report. I congratulated him. Bla was in contact with London on SHE and with the network through the lawyer Bouvet at Dax. I would eventually find out what had happened to him. In actual fact, a short time later the British informed me that Bla had made contact with them by radio and they were delighted at this success. So Bla, for all his disconcerting antics, was perhaps fundamentally a sound man.

The day before Bla was parachuted into France, Jolly had been killed. The plane of the internal French airline in which he was flying had crashed between Vichy and Pau.

'Robert Philippe has agreed to take over as head of the radio service,' Coustenoble commented sadly.

My adjutant's account of his recent inspection of the occupied zone was hardly encouraging. Pétain was collaborating more and more actively; Admiral Darlan, his present heir apparent, was instructing the police to take the toughest possible action against the Resistance. We must create such a psychological shock that waverers would understand that the nation was not taking things lying down. 'We must liquidate Darlan,' the fiery airman concluded. 'I've discussed it with our comrades. They hold Darlan responsible for Navarre's trial at Clermont-Ferrand.'

The implacable reality that I had been refusing to face for so many months now became crystal clear to me. So far, apart from Schaerrer, all our friends had been hunted and struck down by Frenchmen. Our splendid Fourcaud had joined Navarre, Faye and Beaufre in the dungeons at Clermont-Ferrand, along with Claude de Boislambert, a rebel from Dakar, and many other victims. Their attempts, the very first, at liberating our native land had failed, and Vichy was to blame.

Some gleams of hope, however, were beginning to appear. Hitler, plunging headlong into Russia, seemed to have abandoned the idea of invading Britain. Several African countries had rallied to de Gaulle's cause, but Pétain and Darlan, putting aside all thought of revenge against the Germans, governed under the Nazi aegis.

'Yes, it would be a marvellous diversion,' Coustenoble insisted. 'That would really put the cat among the pigeons!'

I gave him permission to go into the matter and he set off hot foot, although the possibility of assassinating a Frenchman, one of our own people, shocked me immensely. Would we now be forced to such extremes in order to carry through our mission and liberate France?

Clermont-Ferrand, October 15, 1941

'*The Marshal of France, Head of the French State, Decrees and Orders . . . the carrying out of the majority sentence condemning:*

'*1. The accused Loustaunau-Lacau, Georges, to two years imprisonment and to confiscation of his present and future property.*

'*2. The accused Faye, Léon, to five months imprisonment. . . .*

'*3. The accused Beaufre, André, to two months imprisonment . . . for an attempt against the external security of the State and by inciting North Africa to revolt, for having made themselves guilty of having endeavoured to remove from the authority of France a part of the territories over which this authority is exercised.*

'*A president, General Chaudessole, six colonels and lieutenant-colonels, three of whom were from the Army and three from the Air Force, have pronounced this sentence by four votes to three.*'

These ridiculous sentences—too severe not to tarnish the Army's honour, but insufficient to relate to a real crime—had a shattering effect on my organization. The myth of Général de Gaulle conducting shady intrigues with Pétain behind Britain's back was an idea quite seriously discussed at the time and many of our people had been looking to the Clermont-Ferrand trial as a test. The sentencing of Navarre meant that the Marshal was once and for all slamming the door on hope.

Some of Navarre's loyal supporters felt it as a personal condemnation. They were not slow to let me know that, at least for the moment, I must not count on their co-operation. I myself had nursed no illusions about a justice that had already condemned Général de Gaulle to death and I had prepared myself for the fact that the full responsibility for continuing the struggle would fall on me. I knew exactly where I stood.

In the autumn of 1941 six transmitters were in operation—KVL at Pau, MED at Marseilles, BAY at Nice, VAL at Lyons, OCK in Paris, SHE in Normandy. Other reports were sent every week via Madrid and were in London a few days later. The patrols were beginning to increase greatly in the occupied zone and in North Africa. The British, to whom we had given proof of our efficiency, had promised me a second parachute drop for the November full moon. I was expecting six more transmitters, a radio engineer, Julien Bondois, and a large sum of money.

On the other hand, I could consult no one but myself. Navarre, unless he escaped or was reprieved—an unlikely contingency—would not be available until the end of hostilities. And when Faye was released from Vichy's jails he would have to lie low for some time.

There was no alternative. I must hold to the course that the network had irrevocably mapped out.

On 17 October I sent emissaries to tell the patrols that we should soon be getting more help and to ask them to widen the scope of their activities. I brushed the defeatists aside.

Confidence was reborn. More and more reports piled up on my desk. I spent whole days copying them out by hand, removing all compromising traces, correcting the geographical details, touching up the sketch maps. With the agents who had come to deliver their reports personally I discussed the information they were to seek along the lines of the British questionnaires. This search for information was agonising, like an aching tooth.

'About the Darlan business,' Coustenoble began as he got out of the Vichy train in a state of great excitement. 'Everything's ready. We're all agreed. I've come to get the green light.'

'Kill Darlan? I don't feel I can give you the order to do that.' This time I *did* rebel. He looked at me askance: he thought I really had gone to pieces.

'The fact is,' he said very firmly, 'the men want to avenge the Clermont-Ferrand sentences. They insist on making an example. If you don't do it, they'll think you lack guts, that you're not a real leader.'

Giving me no chance to interrupt, he went into detail about all the possible ways they had discussed to kill Darlan for certain; but of these all but one had been rejected. The exception was to shoot Darlan with a revolver, and Coustenoble was to be the assassin.

'You're quite mad, Coustenoble! If you're caught the network may as well shut down. After me you're the only one who knows just what we're doing. Why should it be you?'

He took his head in his hands. The minutes dragged by. I did not move, for I was even more stubborn than he.

'I have more confidence in you than in anyone,' he began. 'That's the very reason why I'm afraid of losing your respect. You won't believe what I'm going to say. It is quite out of this world. Since this damned business began I've gradually become aware that I'm different from the rest, that I am, in fact, a sort of medium. My first shock was the death of a comrade named Graimprey, whose name I adopted a little while ago as a pseudonym, you remember. He had been to me like a brother. When he died I thought I should go mad. However, I gradually became convinced that he was still with me, and I then tried in every possible way to catch his thoughts, and I prayed fervently. I was living in complete spiritual communion with the man who I was sure had found eternal rest and one day, when I was writing, my hand, moving as though it were guided by an unseen hand, began to draw a propeller. Automatically, and against my will I covered whole pages. Then a name came and added itself to the drawing; Graimprey, and the signature was *his own*. I realized that he had chosen this way to communicate and he has been speaking to me ever since. Whenever I have an important problem to solve I put it to him. He never fails me. . . .'

'So that was why you suddenly came back on the very eve of Navarre's arrest to tell me you were certain he was about to be caught?'

'Yes,' he said, 'and also the day you were hesitating about assuming command.'

Petrified, I watched his pencil beginning to draw propellers on the paper on my desk, then a signature and finally a sentence: 'Darlan will die by the revolver. . . . Darlan will die by the revolver. . . . The man who kills him will be executed.' The words streamed on in endless repetition. 'Darlan will die by the revolver. . . . Darlan will die by the revolver. . . .'

I took the paper and studied it for a long time. What I saw was definitely not Coustenoble's own writing.

'You do understand, don't you?' he asked. 'Knowing that I cannot in all decency entrust this mission to anyone else. You'll give it the green light, won't you?'

'No green light from me, Coustenoble!' I replied. 'Your life is worth a hundred thousand Darlans.'

He did not argue. 'But,' he pointed out, 'our colleagues will think us. . . .'

'They can think what they like. Go along to bed and tomorrow you can catch trout with Josette. I'll see to the rest.'

I wrote to the various men, who, I knew, were pushing the whole business. Darlan's execution did not come within our province. We had given our word of honour to our allies to confine our struggle to the invaders. I thought that was the end of the Darlan affair.

I was rather absentmindedly sorting some papers when the engineer Mouren burst into the room. One look at his agonized face and I knew there was no point in asking him if the news from Paris was good. Two radio inspectors had discovered documents and weapons in a disused cloakroom while they were searching our box at Post Office No. 118. The handwriting of the post office worker was immediately recognized. The men could not deny the evidence. During the day the patrol's agents who were on their way to see him were arrested. The affair was in the hands of the Paris Criminal Investigation Department. Superintendent David was in charge of the case. I shuddered at the thought, for David was reputed to be a merciless torturer.

'Who was caught?' I asked in a whisper.

'Pautard, Daigremont, Hugon, Vallet. . . .'

'Did they get the OCK set?' I shouted.

'. . . Armand Bonnet, then Vallet's assistant and probably Poulain,' the engineer continued remorselessly, ignoring my question. 'But worst of all was number eight, my friend Sgier, the engineer, my best friend. . . .'

'Where is OCK?'

'Annie, Hugon's girl friend, managed to get it away in time.'

'Thank God; then they may be able to clear themselves.'

'Maybe, maybe,' Mouren went on, echoing my words. 'I understand the police thought they were dealing with communists.'

This gave me renewed hope. It meant that we must immediately inform our accomplices in the Deuxième Bureau, who would be able to intervene if the Germans were not involved. I alerted Gavarni, who got cheering messages of assurance from Vichy.

I was, however, quite unable to calm Mouren's agony of mind. He could, he said, continue to help only if all of his future letterboxes were kept by beautiful women. 'Like a sailor,' he explained. 'A girl in every port. I shall arrive and knock. If a Boche opens the door I shall say: "Is my girl friend in?" And that'll be that. . . .'

He began to worry me and since he was in the free zone I went to the greatest trouble to convince him that he should get in touch with the Navy Ministry in Vichy to glean information about the Japanese, who I had heard were building and using blockade runners.

'That'll change my ideas,' he admitted at last, 'I can find out all you want to know about Japan. But on one condition, remember, a girl in every port. . . .'

The families of our unfortunate agents who were under arrest were in urgent need of help and we had to do something about it. Jean Lefevre left for Paris to make a preliminary reconnaissance. Would I ever be able to get used to these sudden and irremediable disappearances which brought the permanent threat of the guillotine?

My presence in Pau was becoming a liability and the arrival of Rat, who had been released from confinement at Vals, where he had spent a miserable time with Baston, gave me an unwholesome feeling, like finding hairs in one's soup. He did, however, bring me a report on the world economic situation entitled 'The Synarchy', which he enjoyed retailing in whispers. I asked Rat for news of Dulack, who had left the service, sending me an inflammatory letter. In point of fact he was right. He had warned me about what he thought was treason on the part of Rat. I had naïvely divulged this to Rat who, understandably, had reproached Dulack. The two of them had become reconciled behind my back. This was to teach me that silence is golden and our interview proved to be the last.

Everything was ready, however, for our second parachute drop at a little hamlet called Saint-Capraise-d'Eymet, near the farm belonging to the Lauzeilles, who were part of Lagrotte's patrol.

The wait began. British Intelligence had suggested a number of sentences that they had agreed with the BBC, but our listening system was not yet good enough and so the reception committee had to go out every night and await the possible arrival of the plane. They spent hours on end watching the stars, listening for sounds in the sky and quaking with fear at the dark shadows cast by the moon! Poor Coustenoble! I thought of his hacking, rather suspect cough and I vowed I would make him take a long rest after this operation was over and decided that it was my turn to go out and scour the countryside.

Marc Mesnard came to Pau to be on the spot as soon as the money arrived, so that he could distribute it among his various branches. His smiling punctuality, his naturally benign gestures had earned him the nickname of 'The Bishop'. I had ordered him never to put all his eggs in one basket, and this time we had a giant omelette on our plate. It had been agreed to send me ten million francs, three of which were to come by parachute and three by Commandant Boutron, whom we were expecting daily from Madrid with his famous diplomatic bag. The remainder was to be deposited in a British Intelligence box in Barcelona.

The days and nights around the time of the full moon passed in an atmosphere of feverish, nightmarish anxiety. At last, on 8 November, Coustenoble arrived looking pale, unshaven, and dirty, wearing very muddy shoes. He proudly plonked down a lovely case, complete with gleaming locks, a thing so beautiful that it might well have come from one of London's most elegant shops. Everything had gone off admirably. The parachutists? Marvellous. For there was a second one, whom we were to help join his organization. The radio operator, Julien Bondois, intended for us had sprained his foot slightly on landing. He was being looked after at the Lauzeilles' farm. The six new radios had been stored safely in Coustenoble's house in Toulouse.

To spare me needless worry my adjutant had immediately set off for the station with the case full of money. How he watched that case! While waiting in the buffet for the train he kept it gripped between his legs and had the greatest difficulty in not sinking into the sleep he had been denied for thirteen days. Fortunately, a poor girl had come over to his table to cadge a cup of ersatz coffee and this had kept him awake. She had talked to him about her sad life, her aspirations, her dreams. 'You can't possibly understand,' she had told him. 'What I want is a millionaire!'

'A millionaire!' Coustenoble repeated, laughing loudly. 'If she had only known what I had in the case!'

He clicked it open to reveal the three bundles of notes. They lay on a base of Craven A cigarettes; their red packets had the same effect on me as a matador's cape has on a bull. Then came two large envelopes with diagrams of the radios, new codes, questionnaires, microphotographs of innumerable vehicles, unit signs, letters in code admirably typed on elegant paper. And then all sorts of gadgets, boxes of soap with false bottoms, fake pencils. Also coffee, sugar and tea. I suddenly remembered that it was my birthday. What a great birthday these kind allies were giving me!

The Bishop, beaming, began to divide his money into little packets which he would hide in six different places, when Jean Boutron burst in with a large linen bag slung over his back. He gave a great gasp at the sight of the treasure spread out on my bed.

'Well, we're getting things from all quarters,' he murmured, undoing the Pétain seal on his bag. 'Here's my contribution.'

Three more bundles disappeared into the Bishop's satchels. There was a pair of shoes for me, and presents of chocolate for the Etchebaster's agents. Gavarni, who had come running over when he heard the news, blinked like an owl in the sunlight, but the Bishop was worried. Taking me aside, he said: 'Aren't you afraid that it's counterfeit? The notes make an odd sort of crackle.'

I stood rooted to the spot. To be arrested as spies, fine, but as a bunch of forgers! I began to look at the bundles, all of brand new notes, with great suspicion.

For three days every minute of my time went in seeing that all these things were distributed. Jean Boutron had left again for Vichy with what remained of the genuine diplomatic bag and to pick up the one to go back. Gavarni was making arrangements for the departure of several agents who were going into the occupied zone to reorganize the Paris patrols, as well as for my mother, who insisted on crossing the demarcation line with the members of the underground. I was expecting the liaison agents who were coming to get their orders and the material that had been parachuted.

Coustenoble came in. 'I'd like to ask you to do one last thing,' I said to him. 'Help me to put the final touches to everything. I should have been in Marseilles before now. There's too much coming and going here. The feeling of safety has gone.'

He poured himself some coffee. 'I'm expecting the worst,' he began.

'You're not telling me that the propeller-man. . . .'

He pulled a wry face. With a sign of resignation I lit a cigarette. 'Look,

Coustenoble, everything's going well. The parachute operation went off without a hitch, all the things have been distributed. The Etchebaster is as quiet as a monastery. . . .'

'Exactly, the Etchebaster!'

'Well, if you have a hunch that some dreadful blow is about to fall we must move the transmitter and hide it somewhere in the town.'

It hurt me to see him go; I could still hear his dry cough as I looked through my shutters and watched him turn the corner. I began coding.

In the early morning Tringa, the radio operator who had replaced Vallet, came to take my messages. 'Coustenoble's mad,' he said by way of greeting. 'He wants me to move the set as soon as I've sent your messages; what's more, he's been rummaging around all night and burning masses of stuff. He told me to bring you the records that he's left.'

'Did he get any sleep at all?'

'No, he left to go and meet Gavarni.'

'One can never be too careful. Go and get these off quickly and then do what he said, Tringa. As soon as you reach the Etchebaster, send Schneider and the new man, Gerard Novel, over here. I want to see them before they cross the frontier.'

I waited for hours and hours. Nobody came. The brutal truth dawned on me and I realized how utterly dependent I was on these men who for so many weeks had been my legs, my ears, my eyes: like periscopes above the jungle they allowed me to act and to live. What if they should vanish?

Camille Schneider appeared at last with his travelling companion, Novel. 'Tringa told me to tell you that everything was OK! Messages sent, set gone.'

'And where has *he* gone?'

'He went to look for Coustenoble, who didn't come back to lunch.'

Beads of perspiration broke out on my forehead. Searching painfully for words, I explained what was expected of them in Paris, where it was necessary to rebuild the decimated patrols. Time went by and for the first time since I had known him Gavarni, who was to take them to the frontier, was late, terribly late. Understanding my feelings, Schneider suggested that he and his companion, Novel, should go out and reconnoitre. Stupidly, I agreed. Ah! How much I had still to learn!

Darkness had already fallen when suddenly the light was switched on. A young couple whom I had not seen for a long time, Jean-Philippe Salmson and his newly married wife, Jacqueline, rushed in, brushing our kind host out of their way. I then remembered that they, too, were to reinforce the patrol in the occupied zone.

'They've all been arrested,' they said. 'Your mother as well. A trap at Gavarni's. A raid at the Etchebaster. There are police everywhere. They're hunting high and low for you. We've come to get you away.'

7 THE MAIL BAG

Because of the difference in the running times of passenger and freight trains, I had been doubled up in the mail bag for nine hours. Jean Boutron kept saying: 'Stick it out, we're coming to the customs. Our friend will clear us very quickly. Courage. Stick it out.'

But I had had enough, more than enough; tears rolled down my face and the pain in my hips was unbearable. The train carrying my old car, lent to Boutron for his journeys to and fro, wheezed and jolted along. One of the four new tyres piled up on the seat to camouflage the appearance of the diplomatic bag had just slipped and was cutting into the back of my neck, already pressed down by the seal on the bag. In the boot at the back I could hear the heavy breathing of the British Intelligence agent, Jean Schoofs, whom Boutron had also promised to take back to Spain for Christmas. After we had put the car on the train Boutron had not been allowed to remain in the vehicle.

'Imagine how dangerous it would be for you if the car broke loose!' the station master had said. 'Go to your compartment.' Poor Boutron. It made no difference when he pointed out that there were state secrets in the three bags on the back seat.

During the journey, however, Schoofs had been able to get out of the boot and stretch his legs, and he had freed my head from the bag so that I could gulp in great draughts of the icy air blowing down from the Pyrenean peaks. We were frozen stiff. To get into the regulation mail bag—four feet by two feet—I had had to wear a minimum of clothing. And Schoof, in his tiny cage, was in the same state.

'But for us,' he declared sententiously, 'there are no frontiers.'

'I don't feel like laughing,' I replied. 'Look out, the train's slowing down, get back in.'

Before each station Schoofs tied me up again, so that my chin dug into my chest, and the little engine once more began to puff and pant, monotonously, slowly, terribly slowly, through the tunnels and up the iced gradients towards the frontier. In my numbed hands I clasped the enormous pair of scissors that I could use, if need be, to slit the bag open and escape.

At the customs post at the top of the pass Jean Boutron, who had joined us by leaping from car to car in the Somport tunnel, jumped down before the train stopped to avoid being reprimanded by the station master.

A seemingly interminable quarter of an hour dragged by. I heard him return with several railwaymen. The car was unloaded roughly and this time the whole pile of tyres landed on my shoulders. I dared not make the slightest move. There were people everywhere, all armed with electric torches and I could see the beams gliding over the unusual-looking bag.

'It's the diplomatic bag,' the naval officer explained in a choking voice. 'Three bags. The tyres are for the Ambassador. They're part of it. Hurry up. I must get to Madrid as soon as possible. . . . Important diplomatic mission. . . . The Marshal . . . the bag . . . the mail bags. . . .'

The voices drifted away and we waited again. Suddenly I became aware that someone was feeling the door. An arm appeared and groped inside the car. A hand lifted the tyres, slid along the seat, felt the bags, soon reached the top of my head, stopped, felt its shape. Fingers closed on my face. Frightened to death, I held my breath.

The hand, at first hesitant as though suspicious, became bolder. The feeling changed to tapping, then the tapping changed to real blows. At last I heard a low voice speaking.

'OK, old chap? It's me, Lelay. Answer, Schoofs old chap! Imagine burying you in that! Boutron told me you were in the boot. . . . Have you fainted? Don't be afraid. It's me, Lelay.'

Boutron had obviously told his friend, the customs officer, who knew Schoofs from having smuggled him across the frontier several times, that there was only one passenger. I did not answer. The tapping increased.

'Speak for, God's sake,' begged Lelay anxiously. 'Otherwise I'll pull you out. Nothing can justify dying like that.'

'Shut up!' The effect on Lelay of these words from Schoof in the rear trunk was so startling that they might have been a command from the Holy Sepulchre. The hand was snatched away from the car door as though it had been stung by a wasp.

'I'll speed up the customs,' Lelay said in a whisper.

'He must have thought we were Ali Baba and the forty thieves,' muttered Schoofs. Through the bell-like ringing of the blood in my ears I could vaguely hear Lelay growling: 'How many have you got in that car?'

'I haven't time to go into that,' replied Boutron, settling himself at the wheel, lighting his first cigarette and starting the engine. With a ringing '*Adios, amigos*' to the customs men at the frontier post, where the Abwehr official was nosing into things, he accelerated down the slope. Bend after bend after bend. Suddenly he stopped, turned round and drove back the way we had come. In the inky darkness of the now deserted station Boutron, under the impression that he was making a clatter like a cat with a battery of tin cans tied to its tail, found his way to Lelay's room by striking matches.

'What's happened?' asked his friend, frightened out of his wits.

'My extra petrol. I forgot to take it out of your office.'

After much groping they discovered the ten gallon drum and the car once more took the road into the uncertainty of Franco's Spain.

'Jean, I can't go on, I'm thirsty.'

'Yes, of course. You've been over ten hours in that thing!'

I could no longer hear him. My numbed, cramp-racked body was sinking into a vast whirlpool. . . . When I recovered consciousness I found myself at the edge of a mountain stream. The moonlight revealed the anxiety engraved on my companions' faces.

'What she needs now,' said Boutron, in his relief, 'is a decent cigarette. Then off we go.'

In the Spanish capital Jean Boutron put me up at his house and handed me over to the British Intelligence group in the city during office hours. The group consisted of William and Zette Sleator (Schoof's sister and her husband) and the dynamic Georges Charaudeau. They did everything possible to make me feel myself again. I was given a charming black silk dress, wonderful shoes with cork soles—my French ones with their wooden soles were unbearable—and a whole range of skirts, sweaters and lingerie. All the cigarettes, whisky, coffee and tea I could possibly want. After the threadbare clothes, the corncobs, the infusions and boiled turnips, it was a very strange experience to be treated like a princess and yet be cut off from everything I loved most in the world. I was haunted by the thought of my deserted children, my friends and my mother, who had been imprisoned instead of me.

As soon as we arrived, Georges Charaudeau had alerted the British Ambassador and the military attaché had let him know that I was expected in Lisbon. This meant setting off again in the Ambassador's car to the frontier, and as I had no identity papers, even false ones, I would have to cross the Tagus by ferry and risk having to dive overboard at the slightest alarm. Once in Lisbon it was planned to take me to London.

I rebelled: 'I don't mind swimming across the Tagus in mid-December if it's absolutely necessary. But England's out of the question. I must be back in France on 1 January at the latest.'

Not many hours later my messenger returned from the Embassy all smiles: 'They've changed their minds. The people in London now know you're a woman. The meeting will take place here.'

The tall, fair, youthful major with the open, smiling, but serious face was known as Richards. I thanked him for having spared me more travel adventures.

'It's perfectly natural,' he replied. 'When we finally realized that POZ 55 was not the mustachioed officer we imagined, I was ordered to come to Madrid. You fairly took us in!' he added, pressing his nose to his clasped hands.

'You're disappointed,' I said, suddenly embarrassed about myself and my role. I began to feel terribly small and useless in this conflict that was now assuming gigantic proportions. I continued: 'If I have concealed the fact that I am a woman it was because of those who are working and risking their lives every minute of the day. I didn't want them to be abandoned— I thought you might not take me seriously. I had to prove myself before revealing myself.'

He looked up at me with his kind blue eyes and brushed my words aside with a wave of his hand. 'We appreciate courage,' he replied firmly. And then with a touch of anxiety: 'You're still a volunteer, aren't you?'

I recovered my confidence. Volunteers were needed, whatever their sex. 'Richards, the day after the November parachute drop there was a dreadful tragedy in Pau.'

He let me talk almost without interruption, merely punctuating my sentences with little grunts of encouragement. It was a difficult conversation, as Richards knew us only by code numbers. I now had to translate them into real names.

'All my staff at Pau, agents in transit, my own mother, N 1's wife and son, were arrested in our various headquarters. From what I heard they were ill-treated, especially COU 73, my adjutant, Maurice Coustenoble. From the start he took full responsibility on himself, declaring he was the leader. The police forced him to kneel on a ruler for hours on end, they ran lighted newspapers over his whole body. Above all they wanted to make him confess that we were in contact with the British.'

'Too bad,' said Richards.

'Fortunately, the KVL radio had been removed from the Etchebaster in time, but the man who had it took fright and broke it up into hundreds of little bits that were thrown into the river. The arrival of the young Salmsons, NEG 83 you know, saved me. The owner of the hotel moved into the room I had been living in for four months. When the police appeared at dawn to pluck me from the nest—someone had given them the number of my room—he was able to prove that the bird had flown.'

'Well done!'

'The respite allowed me to leave Pau the following night. I reached Tarbes with the Salmsons, who got me a room with a couple of awkward friends. Jean Boutron was alerted and rushed over. He tried to find me a safer hiding place. Not even the convents wanted to have anything to do with me. . . . Meanwhile, things were going from bad to worse. Through Coustenoble's false identity card the police discovered his home in Toulouse. All the radio equipment you'd parachuted on the 7th was seized.'

'Bad luck!'

'As I no longer had any transmitter in Pau and as I didn't want to compromise the sectors that were still intact, I accepted Boutron's generous offer to come here inside one of Vichy's sealed mail bags. Fortunately the money you sent is in a safe place, even the millions stored at Gavarni's were not found.'

'Yes,' Richards said, 'that's right. The millions are safe so far.'

I looked at him dumbfounded, as at a conjurer producing baby rabbits from his sleeve. 'How do you know?'

'From a message he has sent.'

'Gavarni? How could he telegraph you from Pau prison?'

'He never was in prison. He's free in Vichy. His telegram came through MED.'

'My God! Then Marseilles is compromised?' Our conversation, carried on in both languages so far, was continued in English only. Richards seemed to think that by using his own language it would be simpler to find the words best suited to soften his cruel news.

'I don't think Marseilles is compromised. But there have been other arrests: the whole Lagrotte patrol, the reception committee, the radio operators who were parachuted. We realized that was where the disaster began. Apparently it was the patrol leader who was caught first. . . .'

'Lagrotte. . . . I really could have. . . .' But I thrust aside my dreadful suspicion to concentrate on the damage that had been done.

'Another thing,' Richards continued methodically. 'Valori was picked up at Lyons. It was his Dijon agent, MOU 100, who betrayed him. He, too, has been arrested.'

'Anything else?'

Richards looked down again for a moment at the newly decoded notes scattered about on the table. 'Paris,' he said, and my heart missed a beat. 'In Paris the French police have turned your friends over to the Abwehr: the Guynemer and Turenne patrols are in Fresnes prison.'

To learn of this damage without being able to do anything about it plunged me into the depths of despair. 'Who has given you all this information?' I asked.

'MED at Marseilles and BAY at Nice are your only transmitters still functioning, but your operators are going beyond the limits of security.' He squeezed my hand sympathetically.

'Your chief of staff, Gavarni, is in Marseilles at the moment. Rivière told him you were in England and he wants you to make a decision.'

Gavarni had made a pact with the Vichy police, negotiating with Commander Rollin, head of the Surveillance du Territoire, responsible for state security. He had convinced Rollin that the network had collapsed and in exchange for the release of all the agents in the free zone he had offered to surrender the transmitter and the millions still in his house. The Vichy police knew that we still possessed at least two transmitters. Gavarni had been able to show a few bits remaining of the KVL set that had been thrown into the river Gave at Pau but he now wanted to hand over MED, the one at Marseilles. Naturally Rivière and Audoly refused.

'Give MED to the police! It's out of the question! Better to hand over LUX, which hasn't yet been used.'

'Very well, then. But what about the money, Poz?'

'Why does the fool want to give Vichy the money?'

'He maintains this will prove that all these sectors are really knocked out.'

How could Richards keep calm and collected in the midst of this shambles? Gavarni driving around in a police car, playing with the radio sets and the millions of francs smuggled into France with so much effort and at the cost of lives and then selling them to Vichy. I had to make a decision.

Jean Boutron arrived from the Embassy. I put him in the picture. 'The dirty bastard!' he roared. 'Gavarni the traitor! I never liked the skunk.'

Greatly surprised by this reaction, Richards remarked: 'But doesn't *he* also run great risks?'

'To hell with his risks,' Boutron snapped. 'He has gambled and lost. Let him keep quiet. You Intelligence people calculate everything in terms of risks. We run one long risk. There aren't two, there's only one and it's permanent. D'you understand, Richards? *Permanent.*'

'Calm down, Jean,' I broke in. 'What Richards says is true. At this distance we can only give Gavarni the benefit of the doubt. If he were a traitor he wouldn't ask permission to act in this way and we would all have been picked up ages ago.'

I told Richards I agreed to surrender the LUX set and the two million francs to Commandant Rollin in exchange for the release of all the prisoners. After all, that Vichy official—a naval officer, I emphasized, to pacify Boutron—might be the sort of man who simply deserves everything that comes to him. Richards went off to radio my orders to Rivière via London.

But there was no point in deceiving ourselves. Fourteen months of hard work were coming to nothing. The number and the quality of the captures made by the Vichy police and the Abwehr were annihilating the whole of the first wave. We had now to rebuild the network.

I had taken the precaution of leaving my book of coded records under the coal stored in the cellar of our Tarbes friends and in my mind I feverishly ran through what remained intact: Marseilles, Nice, Grenoble, Vichy, a few sub-sectors—a lot of sources certainly, scattered all over France, liaison agents, reserve radio operators, centres in the process of formation. . . . But the shortage of people to get everything going again was becoming desperate. Should we ever again see Schaerrer, Coustenoble, Hugon, Poulain or Vallet?

'Richards, you've bombarded us with questions about Hitler's invasion of Britain. Do you still believe in it?'

'We shan't stop considering the possibility before the beginning of 1942,' he answered frankly. 'The deeper the Nazis become involved in the Soviet Union, the greater are our chances of not having their jackboots on our soil. It is of the greatest importance to us now to keep the seas free. Supply us with as much authoritative information as you can about port installations and the movement of ships and U-boats. U-boat hunting is problem number one today. Our troop transports, our convoys must be preserved at all costs. Shipping . . . shipping. . . .' he repeated over and over again. 'Your new network *must* last! The priority at present being given to U-boats may shift to mastery of the air tomorrow. You will undoubtedly come across some secret weapons as you go on. Quality and safety first.'

Quality first! I was overwhelmed by the vague and dizzy prospects of U-boat interception and the discovery of secret weapons. . . . I came back to the question of security. 'You've sent us a strange character in Bla. Was it to test us?'

Richards face froze. 'Shame on you, Poz, to suspect us of such a trick.'

'Rubbish! People in France have fantastic ideas about British Intelligence, you know. At the moment you're generally taken for a sort of cunning and bloodthirsty Lady Macbeth. And so the business about the newspapers hardly surprised me.'

'What newspaper business?'

'The crystals, the wave-lengths that Bla has for communicating with London newspapers. Is it a trap?'

He looked genuinely surprised. I told him about his radio operator's abnormally careless attitude. 'Look, Richards, what has been worrying me since you told me that our Paris patrols had been handed over to the Nazis is the thought that Bla is involved in this whole business.'

Richards became very thoughtful. 'I don't think your fears are justified, Poz. We're very pleased with Bla's work. SHE is operating admirably in Normandy, sending us first-class information.'

'Are you sure that SHE *is* transmitting from Normandy?'

'Didn't you have it sent there yourself in September? It's still there.'

'It certainly is not. Bla told us his own set had gone wrong and asked for the loan of OCK, Lucien Vallet's set that hadn't fallen into the hands of the police.'

Richards face went livid. 'How do you know that?'

'I had inquiries made of the arrested agents' families. Bla terrorizes them. He keeps pestering them with questions. He's in Paris the whole time.'

'There must be some misunderstanding. Bla may have done some careless things but he's not a bad lot. You shall have your fears set at rest before you leave.'

The report I received from British Intelligence a few hours later confirmed Richards' opinion of Bla. The only thing that London was willing to do to appease me was gradually to ease Bla out of the network.

In London, Richards bore the sole responsibility for our organization and the portraits of various people that I was able to sketch out for him meant that from now on he would understand our reactions and know how much credence could be given to our sources. He constantly reviewed our intelligence service.

'And the report on synarchy?' I asked.

'The syn . . . what? I don't remember anything,' he said.

'What a nuisance. That report contained a paragraph that gave me a great shock, tracing back the channels of business deals that certain American firms—and by no means only small ones—and certain British firms were making with the Nazis in the middle of war through Switzerland and Vichy's French synarchs. One is never very pleased to learn that one is being shot in the back. . . .'

Richards left me earlier than usual, saying that he had an appointment with his military attaché. When Boutron returned I asked him whether he had in fact sent the report.

'Of course,' he replied. 'Sent the synarchy stuff like the rest. I remember the tube it was in. Any idea who does the sorting?'

Next day Richards began our conference by saying: 'I've found the synarchy report. It was the Ambassador: not thinking the document was serious he'd stopped it en route.'

I exploded: 'Look, Richards, I'm not working with your ambassadors. What right. . . .'

'Take it easy, Poz. It won't happen again.'

The conversation switched to the pick-up operations and we immediately launched into the organization of what was to be a clandestine airmail service, selection and lighting of the landing places, and the authority of the reception committees.

When the whole gamut of military intelligence, all the subjects ranging from sources to headquarters staff, from types of radio transmission to air operations and various forms of help and their distribution, had been dealt with in the minute detail and with the planning precision that is generally recognized to be a major obsession with the British, Richards informed me that his mission to me was ending. He had taught me a lot of things, given me a new, very practical ciphering code—a key phrase easy to remember—and two transmitters for use in the Paris area, reduced to a quarter the number of suitcases we were in the habit of carting about. Also an excellent invisible ink and a set of KVL2 crystals for my own head-quarter transmissions. We shook hands with a warmth that went far beyond the solemn framework of our mutual promises. A real friendship, springing from respect and a sense of fair play, had been born between us.

I continued to work at our own internal problems with Boutron. The Pau business made it imperative to establish a direct radio link among ourselves to avoid the delay of waiting for transmissions from London. Boutron, never a believer in half measures, had installed a British trans-mitter in the roof of the French Embassy and the official radio operator thought this secret traffic with London went on with Vichy's knowledge. Imagine the Embassy man's surprise, therefore, when one day the operator he was in touch with answered him with an ear-splitting 'OK'. It was of little use for Boutron to tell him that 'OK' was used all over the world; the good fellow still remained suspicious. The most difficult thing of all was to bring him into a new radio link between Madrid and Marseilles. The night or day frequencies most favourable to this supersecret link were calibrated on the crystals that we possessed—four or six per set. A key phrase was agreed on as well as a code of call signs.

'I'll tell the operator it's still Vichy,' Boutron concluded optimistically, after I had voiced my doubts about the wisdom of this. 'Above all, tell your operator never to say "OK"!'

At last it was time to go back. Marshal Pétain's diplomatic mail must have its usual escort. We went. This time the freight car attached to the train was waiting for us at the customs post on the pass and I did not have to endure hours of further agony doubled up inside the bag; but as I lay on top of my new transmitters, my jute prison seemed to me more cramped than ever. The pain racking my twisted limbs was made worse by the biting cold. Although I was jolted about on my tiny platform, I was nevertheless conscious of the luck that allowed me to bring my mission to a successful conclusion.

Boutron extricated me from the bag in a deserted spot in the country. It meant the end of the dreaming, the thinking and the planning; now we must act, quickly and with the utmost vigour.

Jean Broqua's kindly face appeared as we approached the garage where we had arranged from Madrid to meet him. He had never missed a rendezvous, never failed to cross the demarcation line and I felt the greatest affection for him. He told me at once that my mother was free. With a great load taken off my mind, I immediately asked Broqua to fetch Gavarni. His tall body gave a start and his broad shoulders shook.

'I should love to, chief, but he's in Vichy.'

'What's he doing back there?'

Broqua thought for a moment then blurted out: 'Spending our money on himself.' It cost him a lot to say that about the leader in whom he had believed so blindly. 'He had sworn that if we handed the stuff over our pals would be let out. Well, they're still behind bars. Chief, Coustenoble *must* be got out! He has not breathed a word about us. At one time he was made to kneel for hours on the edge of a ruler, stark naked and with all his skin burned. He muttered something and those brutes thought he wanted to talk; so they beat him up to make him repeat what he was saying. He told them: "I'm praying."'

'He's a saint. I know that.'

'And what was the use?' Broqua went on. 'When he was caught in the trap at Gavarni's, the poor boy tried to swallow the identity card that gave his Toulouse address. They already knew it. All so that Gavarni can strut around like a peacock.'

'What . . . who makes you think that?'

'You'll learn by experience, chief.' He spontaneously used the same expression as Bernis. At this juncture he would say no more. I gave him money to get a huge Christmas dinner for the men.

'Holy Mother! You *are* thin,' exclaimed Rivière when he saw me.

In the back part of the Marseilles vegetable shop—last year's acquisition was proving a very profitable business as well as an ideal cover—we clinked glasses and exchanged ideas. There were Gabriel Rivière and his wife Madeleine who, like me, suffered from a congenital dislocation of the hip, a common burden that inevitably drew us close together; Alfred Jassaud, a strongly-built, open-faced lad who looked curiously angelic despite his muscular frame; Emile Audoly with his delicate, mobile face and his nasal laugh; Marc Mesnard with his puns and his witticisms; and Jean Boutron was the king of the feast. Over in one corner the chief radio operator, Pierre Bocher—who had fifteen years' experience of listening through the roar of typhoons during long voyages to the Far East—was examining the new radios with great admiration and scrutinizing the transmission schedules. Get Madrid as well? That would be child's play.

After we had said all that could be said without breaking the sweet peace that springs from the satisfaction of knowing that duty had been done with mutual affection and respect, I ventured to ask: 'And Gavarni?'

The interval was over; the curtain was rising again on the tragedy. 'He'll doubtless be here tomorrow,' Audoly began, after a heavy silence. 'He's going to suggest a plan. His line is that the network's absolutely finished and will never be able to function again. He, of course, would be the only one who could remedy the situation by getting us all work with the Deuxième Bureau, which would mean severing our links with Britain. He's scared of your reaction.'

'Do you think he has betrayed us?'

'Certainly not in the sense of informing against us. Vichy knows only what has actually fallen into their hands, and what's more, that's not Gavarni's fault.'

'That's just what I'd sensed from Madrid. So have confidence in me. The Gavarni episode will soon fade away, like a bad dream at dawn.'

'Heavens! Talking about dawn, here we are at the first day of 1942,' sighed Rivière. 'It's time we drifted. Here come the Provençal peasants in their old crocks to deliver their stuff. Better not let them see the happy family!'

Going out into the vegetable store, I admired the piles of carrots, turnips and spinach that Madeleine was beginning to sprinkle with water from a watering can.

'Why are you doing that?' I asked naïvely.

'To give full weight!' laughed Rivière. At least the vegetable business would not be a flop.

SECOND PERIOD

1942

THE ATTACK

If one army knew what the other army was doing,
that army would beat the other army.

Old French proverb

8 THE SQUADRON

The weather in the early part of 1942 was severe. Huddled under bedclothes that felt like blocks of ice, fully dressed and with fingers frozen, I drafted messages that my radio operators sent off at once. Although the place where I was living, a cottage rented by Audoly for transmitting, was very good for its purpose—'direct producer to consumer service' as he said—it was not suitable as a headquarters.

'I've found what you need,' the Bishop (Marc Mesnard) told me. 'The Jeanne d'Arc hospital, where Alfred Jassaud's mother is matron. His grandmother's living there too, and will look after you. It'll be easy for all of us to come and you'll get more than just carrots to eat.'

So that he should not find out where I was living, my meeting with Gavarni took place at the vegetable store and I received him in the back part. Jassaud, leaning against the frame of the glass door, acted as bodyguard. Gavarni appeared, still angular and morose; only his expression seemed to have changed, for there was now something very hard about his eyes and something very unsympathetic in his manner. However, seeing him again after the dreadful ordeal in Pau brought great lumps into my throat. I could not forget his devotion at the Hôtel du Lycée and the disciplined example he had set when Navarre was arrested. We embraced without saying a word, like brother and sister.

He did not tell me very much. He had carried out the orders I had sent from Madrid. Yes, Lagrotte had indeed been behind the arrests in the free zone. 'He had become the lover of a policeman's daughter. This man had had him pulled in and the leader of the Perigueux patrol had talked.' Instead of doing as ordered and saying that he was working for the Deuxième Bureau, he had informed the police about the parachute drop at the Lauzeilles' farm and handed over the parachutists—poor boys who had dropped in France only to go to prison. Lagrotte had also revealed the names of agents, the hideouts of the Pau staff and the whereabouts of Captain Fourcaud's transmission centre!

'I suddenly realized,' continued Gavarni pompously, 'that in the face of such a disaster it was necessary to knock loudly in high places, and when I was arrested I asked to be heard by Commandant Rollin, head of the Surveillance du Territoire. This man was against my being imprisoned and allowed me to act in the way that has received your agreement. When our boys are let out they'll be able to work with papers from the Deuxième Bureau.'

I felt my eyes growing bigger and bigger. 'And what's happening to the network inside?'

Gavarni's face became a mask. He chewed a cigarette nervously, but did not smoke it. Then came the revelation.

'I'm fed up with your British friends. Anyway they must fork out, you understand, fork out! Vast sums. I need money, a lot of money. . . .' And suddenly rushing at me, he began spluttering and babbling sentences that were almost unintelligible: 'We shall be in a unique situation. Protected by Vichy, fooling the British, accumulating masses of stuff whose existence nobody will suspect. . . .'

Through the glass panel I could see Jassaud standing quietly on guard with his back to the door. How could I attract his attention without shouting. Had I done so, he would have come in and shot Gavarni.

Pushing Gavarni away with a desperate effort, I knocked the desk over. The door opened. 'Do you need me, madame?'

'Yes, Jassaud, I'm very much afraid our friend will miss his train. Will you please drive him back to Saint-Charles station immediately?'

'But,' Gavarni began in astonishment, 'you haven't given me an answer.' Jassaud started flexing his shoulders.

'Your plan's so novel, Gavarni. Go back quickly to Commandant Rollin. Tell him that I agree to the disappearance of my network. When he has released everybody, I promise you we'll have another meeting.'

'Not before?' he asked, with a surly look.

'No not before. If you want us to embark on your second stage,' I said dishonestly, 'I mustn't compromise myself!'

A fresh gleam of hope appeared in his eyes. 'Quite right. Thank you, thank you, I was sure you'd agree.'

'By the way,' I inquired, 'why did you give up your two millions? I should have thought you would have got the same result with a few notes. . . .' My words seemed to go home, for he did not answer. He was docile as Jassaud took him outside.

Towards evening Jassaud came to the hospital with a message from Audoly. Our agents from the port area had met two Paris policemen who said they were being followed. They claimed they belonged to the network of a certain Micheline, known as 'The Cat'. She had betrayed everybody and they had been forced to flee the capital, leaving their families behind. They wanted to continue the fight and begged to be taken on. But their story smacked of provocation. I drafted a radio message to Richards. We would see whether this 'Cat' really existed.

While I was coding the message Jassaud paced up and down the room, obviously wanting to say something. 'This talk about money is horrible,' he eventually said. 'I must confess that I heard everything and was afraid you were going to give him an answer.'

'Then you believed I was going to agree to this disgusting offer?'

'I didn't know. I'm suspicious of everything. I'm a sergeant air-gunner, you know. All these sordid stories about Vichy, all this money business, is beyond me. . . .'

As bees return to the hive, the agents found their way to Marseilles. The hospital was full at all times. As everyone admitted, my presence there, even though it was under Joan of Arc's banner, was becoming a liability. One fine day the Bishop informed me that he had now discovered the ideal hideout. Quite by chance he had met a charming woman from his own town whom we at once called 'The Cousin'. She was very much a Gaullist, he assured me, and ready to hide me in return for a tidy rent that would entitle me to a room overlooking the sea. The sea! I could not resist the offer. I had to see the place at once. In the Old Port we took a rickety old trolley that twisted and ground its way for a long time along the Corniche coast road, got out at a remote stopping place, went up a flight of steps between bulging walls down which hung branches of fig and eucalyptus trees, and arrived, panting, in a square. There, standing wide open, was the door of a house in the style of the twenties, built into the rock. We went down two floors, past mouldy walls, and, after striking fifteen matches, discovered the door bearing the Cousin's visiting card.

A troglodyte's nest, but what a view! A hundred feet below me I could see beached boats, faded sails and a swarm of children shouting and playing in the light reflected from the Mediterranean, that stretched away, vast and voluptuous, to the horizon. The Cousin, young and plump, said she would get my food for me and I immediately clinched the deal. At least I should sleep peacefully there. How wonderful not to be haunted by the fear of being awakened by the police. Nobody but Mesnard was to know where I was. It meant that I had to go down into the town once or twice a day, using the Marseilles trolleys, that were to play a big part in my life.

One morning I found Léon Faye waiting at the vegetable shop. His prison ordeal seemed to have left no mark on him. Absolute determination could be read in his rather pronounced but balanced features and in those large eyes so accustomed to studying the infinite spaces of the sky. His smile was gay and kind. Perhaps he was not as erect as he had been a year ago. There were touches of white in his wavy hair, now thinning, as it does with almost all men who have worn a flying helmet for a long time. His slightly muffled, sometimes rather lisping voice added to the charm that emanated from his tall, athletic figure. He was elegantly dressed and I suddenly felt very ashamed of my own third-rate tailor.

'At last! Is this the soonest you could get here?' I said, trying to sound ironic to hide my emotion.

'It's very bad of me,' he began. 'I delayed amidst the pleasures of Capua.

Then a triumphal jaunt to North Africa, where my friends lent me a crate. A tour of the messes. Back to France, a tour of the chateaux. I even went as far as Paris! It does you good, you know, Marie-Madeleine, after five months in the jug. I definitely cannot stand prison. . . .'

'Who can?'

'You're right to pull me up,' he said, blushing. 'I was lucky to get out so soon, while poor Navarre. . . . In the courtroom, after the sentencing, I promised him I'd fly to the aid of the organization. It's inexcusable to have taken so long to come here, but you're not easy to find!'

'No, fortunately! Anyway, here we are, face to face. What are your plans?'

'First, to take you to somewhere safe. Some very good friends, the Dartois, are expecting you in Algiers, where they will hide you. The liberation of North Africa is under way. Last year's plot has borne fruit and started a fashion. Nothing has stopped.'

'And you'll take the network too?'

He gave me a long, steady look. 'The network? But it doesn't exist any more.'

'Who told you so?'

'Navarre himself thinks so.'

'And if I told you it's not true, that it's carrying on?'

'I *would* be delighted!' he exclaimed. 'Tell me, quickly.'

'In a minute. I've some people to see. You can join us, you'll find it an eye-opener.'

At that moment Jassaud brought in two strapping men—one, Ernest Siegrist, very tall, burly and with slightly protruding ears, the other, Georges Guillot, just as hefty but more thick-set and darker skinned. Two open, frank and determined faces—they were the policemen from the Cat's lair.

'I'm pleased to meet you,' I told them. 'London has confirmed your story. I just need two security men and it appears that you're both professionals.' They grinned broadly.

'One of you will be put on to forging identity papers, the other will keep an eye on the headquarters and the agents. I imagine you don't mind hard work and moving around? You'll be directly attached to my headquarters.'

'And our wives?' asked Guillot.

'Perhaps I'm in a bad position to advise you about your wives,' I replied, 'but they're an excellent way of getting caught. In a normal war you'd never think of taking your wives into the front line. We'll help them, of course. Have you any children?'

'I've got two small daughters,' the huge Siegrist replied, anxiously.

'Think of them. Don't forget that your safety will be their best reward.'

He looked down, his great ears shaking. 'We're very pleased,' he said at last, 'to have found your organization. If we hadn't, we'd have worked as dockers in the Old Port until the end of hostilities.'

A small, tubby, intelligent-looking woman came in: Denise Centore, the headquarters secretary sent to me by my mother. Denise was the niece of the great musician Germaine Tailleferre; a trained historian, she embarked on underground work as one approaches history. Lucid and methodical, one would have said she acted with a certain detachment from the times.

'Is the ciphering going well, Denise?'

She looked questioningly at Faye.

'You can speak quite frankly, it's Commandant Faye.'

'Commandant Faye! You *must* tell us about the Algiers affair.'

'Wait,' I interrupted. 'What about the codes?'

'I'm trying to work them out in record time. I understand them basically but need practice. I prefer invisible ink, though the stuff we're using at the moment worries me.'

I almost dropped dead when she showed me a piece of light brown wrapping paper covered with great screeds of dark brown writing describing anti-aircraft sites in the Boulogne sector.

'It's the heat,' Denise explained. 'It brings the writing out.'

'But this is dreadful! Quick—draft a message warning London about the horrible brew they're sending us. It's a miracle that the postman hasn't noticed anything.'

Interested, Faye fingered the offending paper. Denise explained to him how we used innocent-looking parcels from the occupied zone to smuggle in information written in invisible ink.

'There's a better way,' he exclaimed. 'Interzonal cards in code. I'm going to arrange that for you right away.'

I calmed his enthusiasm. He smiled at me, still disbelieving but captivated by the brand new venture unfolding before his eyes.

Henri-Léopold Dor, a friend of my brother and the son of a great Marseilles-born maritime lawyer, was brought in. 'Great news, Madame,' he said. 'My father's agreed to get me an *Ausweis*. I shall be able, as you asked me . . .' When he saw Faye he suddenly became embarrassed.

'This is Commandant Faye, Dor, you can continue.'

'It's like this. I shall be described as my father's secretary. People won't suspect me and I shall forward all your parcels, all your mail, anything you want. . . .'

'That's marvellous, Dor. Thanks for acting so quickly.'

He dropped his eyes a little. 'The thing that worries me is deceiving my father. He belongs to another age, you know, and he doesn't understand what's going on. He think's the Marshal's a great man. Dad's torn between my mother's English family and Vichy France.'

'And you are torn between your Marseilles blood and your Oxford tastes.'

'I'd much rather write fairy tales ,' he confessed with a laugh.

'I won't stop you from sending the British radiograms in verse, as long as they're in code. To start, you will be our liaison agent with the occupied zone. See the Bishop about your expenses.'

He blushed. 'I don't want money. At least let the family dough look after that side of things.'

One person after another came in until after one o'clock. Cobra, the courier, brought a copy of the daily radio messages sent by Audoly, whose agent, Michel the Sailor, opened the Nazi Armistice Commissions cases at night; in the guise of innocent merchandise they contained war material for Rommel's Africa Korps. The ships carrying them were intercepted.

Pierre Giovaccini arrived out of breath from Melegnano, near Milan, to let us know about the movement of Fascist flotillas bound for Italy. Robert Philippe came to suggest a new radio operator, 'Canary', whom I took on as an extra. Emile Hédin suggested that we should buy a bar to duplicate the vegetable store cover. I agreed.

'Don't you think it's time to eat?', sighed Faye during a pause. 'How long will you go on like this?'

'Oh, we haven't any set hours! It's such a joy not to have any periods of idleness, any long, agonizing gaps any more. If things could go on like this. . . .'

He then took me off to the Hotel Terminus, where he had taken up residence. 'We can talk more quietly there and I've got a few goodies in my cupboard. They're also clandestine.'

Sitting opposite one another, between us an exquisite *foie gras* which we spread on some 'white' bread, and pouring out generous draughts of Montbazillac, I dared not broach the vital issue. I told him about everything I had done since Navarre's arrest and the programme we had mapped out with Richards in Madrid, the parachute drops and the pick-up operations to be organized, the plans that had to be put into effect to unearth information that would be helpful in closing the Mediterranean sea routes, the battle of the Atlantic, and the interception of ships and aircraft.

'What's your main worry?' he asked at last.

'I need specialists to reinforce the sectors and to create new ones.'

'Since I've begun to feel that the thing is possible again, my head has been seething with ideas. Specialists? Would you take me?' And throwing his napkin nervously down on the table he exclaimed: 'There's no point in beating about the bush. It would be utterly mean to leave you to sort out this mess on your own. I'm at your disposal, along with all my friends.'

'It would be wonderful to be sure that, thanks to you, everything could still go on if I disappeared. The greatest difficulty is to ensure the survival of what one creates and my life is one long fear that the service may go under when we come up against the next obstacle.'

Faye's face lit up. 'I've got it, Marie-Madeleine! I've got everything you need for attacking the enemy: Colonel Kauffmann, a very experienced officer from Morocco who's bored with stagnating in his artichoke fields at Sarlat; Colonel Morraglia, the bravest of men, who fought in the 1914 war; and Colonel René de Vitrolles, both are nauseated with the armistice commissions they've been pushed into; and Commandant Verteré, one of the leading Air Force experts; and Maurice de MacMahon, the Duke of Magenta. He wasn't an instructor in aerobatics for nothing. Is he restless! What a man! And in lesser ranks, some young lieutenants and NCOs. A whole squadron.'

I had a dazzling vision of France as one vast aerodrome covered with airmen racing into battle and myself flying with them. Reluctantly I came back to earth. 'All these friends of yours, Faye, are regular officers in armistice jobs who want to get out, but do you realize the sort of life I can offer them? They will be terribly lost; everything will be completely different from what they're used to and, what's more, can you see senior officers taking orders from a woman?'

'*I'm* prepared to,' he said, laughing.

'I'm very grateful to you, but isn't your job really in North Africa?'

'Nothing's easier than to do both at the same time! André Beaufre has kept in touch with the Americans; I'd be kept informed, especially if you could install a transmitter in Algiers. At least, let me help you to get things moving again here. I'll go to Africa afterwards.'

'I'll give you my answer tomorrow.'

'I'll go back with you,' said Faye.

'All right, just to the tram, but first we'll make the evening visit to the shop.'

Night had fallen and it was snowing. The dreadful chilblains on my feet started itching when we left the hotel, causing me to stumble on the dark dirty pavement where silent, shadowy figures were scurrying along. A great hush was settling on Marseilles, embarrassed by shameful presences: *bersaglieri* flaunting their arrogant cocks' feathers and mysterious German figures in heavy, padded raincoats, their felt hats pulled down to conceal their faces.

Gabriel Rivière was sitting alone behind his ledgers, his fair, bushy eyebrows knit in a frown. 'A fine thing to go and do,' he began with enforced cheerfulness. 'Salmson had just broken his leg at winter sports.'

'Jean Philippe's at winter sports?'

'Yes, the fellow at Tarbes with whom you parked your records before your sack race was going. He refused to turn the records over to Jean Philippe. "She gave them to us to look after, she must come and get them herself," the guy said. So Jean Philippe decided to ski with him to try to wheedle them out of him.'

'He'd have done better to bash the fellow's face in than break his own leg,' Faye shouted. 'Are the papers compromising?'

'Only for me,' I said. 'Everything's in my handwriting. The real names of the agents and the towns are in code. But I've got to have the records of the information we've sent, the unit signs, which I can't remember very well, and the questionnaires for the occupied zone. I've got no copies.'

'We must go immediately and show this slob in Tarbes what's what,' Faye declared.

Rivière looked at him astonished, as if to say, why is he butting in? But I felt he had something important to tell me. He stood up, pressed both my shoulders very hard and looked me straight in the eye:

'Now be brave, chief. I've got bad news. Henri Schaerrer was shot on 13 November.'

It seemed to me that I had always known; and then, suddenly, I had the feeling that he had returned, that he, the first member of the network to be killed, was there with us and that he was saying, 'I have passed through their bullets. I'm with you again. Carry on, always carry on! Deliverance will also come to you.'

'How did you hear?'

'Through his uncle, Henri Blandin. The German chaplain sent him a letter,' he said, taking it out of his pocket. 'Look. After the sentence he had dated this letter every day, always with a question mark; the date of his execution is marked with a cross.'

I bent over the simple, upright handwriting that covered two sheets of the squared paper from Fresnes prison that I knew so well from the engineer's reports. I forced myself to read:

'Dearest Uncle and Godfather. . . . I shall soon have been four months in the prison . . . I have been condemned to death . . . I am deeply in your debt for the two things that you inculcated into me—loyalty and courage, and it is thanks to those two qualities that my judges could say after they had passed sentence on me: "Everywhere you have been since your arrest you have, thanks to your dignity and your sense of honour, made the best possible impression, but we are obliged to comply with international law on espionage." My only words were: "I am glad I have preserved my honour . . ." I have wept only once since my arrest, after I had made my confession and taken holy communion . . . I do not fear death, it is only a trial.'

'I am glad that I have preserved my honour. . . .' That meant: 'You have nothing to fear from me, I said absolutely nothing, I have carried out my mission to the full. . . .'

He had been arrested on 11 July and his first interzonal card from Fresnes to his family had not been sent until 3 September, when his true identity, which he had tried to conceal throughout the whole period of his ill treatment, had been discovered. But who was responsible for that? None of our men, who had been handed over to the Abwehr well after that date, had any reason to identify themselves with a spy who had been caught red-handed. Who was the traitor?

I turned to Faye despairingly. Pale and speechless, he gazed at the heart-rending message.

'Since 1917 I've seen many comrades disappear,' he said at last, 'but I know only too well that men like that are few and far between.'

'We will avenge him,' said Rivière.

'I don't think he would like that word. We shall carry on. That was his great wish.'

It was nearly time for the last trolley. The two men escorted me to the port terminus, where a crowd of people was waiting. I managed to cling to the iron handrails of the rear platform. At each stop I found a little more room. When we reached the Corniche I was the only passenger. Alone in the wind, the freezing cold and the darkness, I was afraid. I stumbled up the dark steps, a prayer on my lips. 'Notre-Dame de la Garde, give me strength. Help me to carry on. Notre-Dame de la Garde, pray for them, for all of them, those who are with you and those who will come to you. I did not think it would be so terrible. Notre-Dame de la Garde, give me the strength to carry on.'

Back in the darkness of my room I opened the windows. Black waves were rolling in from the sea. Beyond lay Algiers and its promises of deliverance. Perhaps it would be a good thing to go there? Perhaps I should let all of them leave? I sank into a nightmare-haunted sleep.

I was awakened by a scratching at my door. It was Mesnard. A winter sun poured in, pale as mimosa. The sea was once again blue and bewitching.

'Lord! We really had the wind up. It's the first time you've failed to turn up at the shop. As I didn't want to let on where you were, they've sent me in the role of ambassador.'

We sat down on the divan. 'Bishop, you know about Schaerrer? I don't want to go out today.'

'It's ghastly, but there are the others to consider. In war one must never talk about the dead. Like him, we know that our turn may come. We have accepted that in advance. Come on, hurry up and get dressed.'

When I got to the shop they were all there. I saw the smiles on their faces, and I realized that I could never retreat.

'I have something of great importance to tell you,' I began. 'Faye has suggested he should stay in France. I have offered him the post of chief of staff, which he will hold until events in North Africa have reached the point when he must resume the armed conflict. If you all agree I will inform London immediately.'

At that moment I knew what they were all thinking: if she has taken this decision it means that she has given up hope of Navarre's return. The shadow of the leader who fascinated them weighed heavily on the group. They longed again for his tremendous, fiery drive, his electrifying outbursts, and to feel the spark that he was so adept at kindling in their ranks. I read the silent question on their lips.

I continued: 'It was Navarre who, on the day the Clermont-Ferrand verdict was pronounced, asked Faye to come to our rescue.'

'Wonderful!' exclaimed Rivière. 'They're both in the same rank. Long live the commandants!'

A great hubbub broke out and congratulations were exchanged all round. Said Faye: 'My first act will be to try to organize Navarre's escape. Now to work.'

That evening letters went off, fixing a number of different rendezvous with the volunteers for the 'Squadron'. The second wave would soon take the offensive.

There remained the task of fusing the Patrol and the Squadron. Faye and I left for Tarbes, where we called without warning on the shifty couple, who were obviously taken aback and claimed that my records were hidden away in a strong box. For extra safety the key had been entrusted to a Jewish friend who was away at the moment. But we need not lose any sleep: they would let us know as soon as they knew the man was coming back, which was absolutely certain.

'It sounds fishy,' was Faye's verdict as we hurried to catch a train for Pau. 'It's just a yarn.'

I felt there was something odd about Gavarni's negotiations with Rollin. The whole Pau team had been released and allowed to return to the villa Etchebaster, but the victims who had been parachuted were still in prison. We must get to the bottom of the mystery.

Pau! its station by the River Gave, the nineteenth-century elevator up to the Promenade des Pyrénées, the parks and trees. We hurried along the streets close to the walls. Broqua escorted us, watchful and alert, which made him look even more awkward than usual.

'Since the police raid everything has changed a lot, including the people; they need taking in hand again,' he whispered.

Coustenoble came to the iron gate. 'You shouldn't have come,' he growled. 'It's been difficult enough trying to protect you in the interrogations. Now you've put yourself in the lion's jaws. You should have called a meeting where you were.' I was shocked to find my first lieutenant so curt, distant, almost vicious.

Gérard Novel, Camille Schneider and Tringa came running up. The poor fellows were unshaven and in rags. Accustomed to walking in the restricted space of a cell, they dragged their feet along in the tattered old slippers they were wearing.

Faye's presence had a tremendous effect on them. I told them immediately: 'Faye is replacing Gavarni.'

An excited buzz broke out. What did they think of Gavarni? Now that they were out they no longer bore him any grudge, provided they never heard of him again. However, they were still dependent on him, having promised the police to work under his orders for the Deuxième Bureau, which had given them false cover papers.

'Have they given you any money or any orders?'

'No, nothing like that.'

'Then accept the false papers. But I release you from your promises. Everyone must go into hiding.'

Schneider would go to the Dordogne, Novel to the occupied zone, and Tringa would come to Marseilles as the headquarters radio operator. Coustenoble would naturally resume his former duties with me.

'You've still got confidence in me?' he barked.

'More than ever. I've missed you very much indeed.'

'To go and get caught like a fool, and when I was expecting it. It shall never, never happen again, I swear.'

While Faye was discussing technical details with the others, Coustenoble and I went into Navarre's old office, still a shambles from the search.

'And how's your cough? I'm told you spat blood in prison. You ought to rest before you start.'

'Rest! I've had plenty of that. You know perfectly well, little one, that I shall never voluntarily take any rest. There's the Paris crowd to save and if that proves impossible, then it will mean working like hell to be worthy of them. That's my fate since Schaerrer's death.'

He knew! Yes, news gets around in prison as everywhere else. He began to call me 'little one' again, the intimacy of the early days of our venture was reborn and a rediscovered sense of confidence shone through the confused stories we had to tell each other. . . . I and my Madrid adventure. . . . He and his ordeal at the hands of the torturers and his difficulties in preventing the boys from talking and giving away secrets.

'Tringa especially,' he said. 'It might be better to drop him. He's as soft as butter. Use him with an iron hand. That ruffian Lagrotte has taken us for a ride! And what a damned fool I was to carry that Toulouse address around. I'll never be taken alive again! If you'd seen those dirty cops' malicious glee when they found the four radios in Toulouse.'

'Four radios? There were six, Coustenoble!'

Now completely relaxed, he laughed his head off. 'I disobeyed you! I'd left two hidden in the Lauzeilles' farm. The police haven't discovered them, they're still there.'

'Well done, Coustenoble! At last I'm going to be able to start transmissions. The two sets I've brought back from Madrid will be for Paris, yours for the provinces.'

Faye was becoming impatient. He did not want me to hang about the villa a long time. Coustenoble frowned slightly. While I was giving him a warm goodbye embrace he said under his breath: 'I hope it's still *you* at the helm!'

So that was what was irritating him! I arranged a rendezvous with him in Marseilles as soon as he had straightened out his position with the Deuxième Bureau. Gavarni, of course, would not be told about my visit to the Etchebaster. They dispersed that very evening.

We could now fly off to meet the Squadron.

At the far end of the lounge in the Hotel de Paris in Toulouse I caught sight of the picturesque figure of Colonel Kauffmann in heavy boots, ancient army trousers and a big grey cape. He was the first of the airmen to arrive. From out of this strange garb there appeared a sensitive and distinguished face. He spoke loudly, too loudly, I remarked to Faye later.

'He's slightly deaf, even more than I am,' he replied, 'like everyone who's had to put up with the drone of aeroplane engines in his ears for hundreds of hours.'

Colonel Kauffmann, 'old Kuf' to close friends, like many officers demobilized from the 'armistice army', was farming his property in Sarlat in the Dordogne and for him it was a godsend to find a way of serving his country in his own place. He'd fix things for us in no time. Crossing places to Bordeaux? Easy. Getting information from the south-west? Child's play. A woman running the network? He didn't mind in the least. He already had a radio operator in mind, a letterbox and couriers. Faye told him that Camille Schneider would be coming with the TAP set, saved from the raid. There could not have been a better start and I sighed with relief to see the Dordogne patrol on its feet again so soon.

When we got back to Marseilles we found the old members already deeply engaged in an exchange of ideas with two airmen who had rushed over on receiving a message from their old CO. One of them, Pierre Dallas, was twenty-six, slim, and with a swarthy face that denoted gipsy blood; the other was Lucien Poulard, not yet twenty-five, plump, fair-skinned, whom Faye called 'Jack Tar'.

It was simple to make Pierre Dallas understand what was expected of him: to organize the Avia crew, the clandestine airmail service for which London, delighted with our progress, was clamouring. By common consent the Lyons area was chosen for the dropping zone, because of the open country along that river and the Saone that favoured such operations. Guillot, the policeman, would ensure its security. Dallas was to suggest as soon as possible a choice of sites for which I gave him the topographical requirements laid down by the RAF. He would soon receive a personal operator and radio. Lucien Poulard would remain for the moment at headquarters as Faye's adjutant. After a period of instruction he would be sent to his native Brittany.

Now looking twenty years younger, Faye was always on the move. Each time he returned from these trips he brought the names of new recruits who were present or former air force men. Colonel Morraglia and Colonel René de Vitrolles, who were stagnating in the armistice commissions, Commandant Félix Cros of the Air Force General Staff, and Georges Lamarque, a young undergraduate, agreed to join the squadron.

'It's going like a bomb, spreading like wildfire!' exclaimed Faye delightedly.

There remained Paris. I had warned Faye to be on his guard there: 'You won't find Vichy's bungling or indifference in Paris; it's the Abwehr there and its highly skilled professionals. Since our principal agents are in their hands we must go carefully. For the time being I've ordered Jean Jackson, a friend of Edmond Poulain, to tie up the broken threads until I find someone of real stature, someone who can build things up again from scratch, working on his own.'

'My comrade Verteré is just the man you need,' Faye had exclaimed. Faye may have overplayed the 'expertise' on which he had kept harping. Verteré did not have a very martial look about him, and his appreciation of the situation seemed to me both half-hearted and complicated. I gathered, however, that Paris suited him and I gave him the list of our major sources in the occupied zone. Dor would be his liaison agent and Coustenoble would be on hand to put him in touch with our contacts in the forbidden zones.

Verteré himself said he had lots of friends he could rope in. A woman named Gertrude would be his alter ego. His cover would be as sensational as it was unexpected: Marcel Déat, the man who had 'refused to die for Danzig', now a Nazi party chief, would be able to provide him with a press card for his *rassemblement*.

We finally agreed and Verteré, who had at the outset insisted that I should obtain London's agreement to his employment and his cover, left, assuring us that he would be on the other side of the demarcation line on 1 April at latest, when he would ask Marcel Déat for an *Ausweis*. Getting the leader of the *rassemblement* to work for British Intelligence! Could anything be better?

To welcome the squadron and its services our Marseilles 'aircraft carrier' had to undergo a thorough overhaul. In order to free the local sector from the constant turmoil among the national staff, I had set up the headquarters in Pierre Berthomier's flat at No. 355 on the Corniche. A nearby villa, 'La Brise', housed our information centre. The Saint Charles bar, bought in Emile Hédin's name, at the foot of the big flight of steps at the station, was used as a place where agents and couriers on the move could come and leave their envelopes and receive their instructions. Siegrist, the policeman, saw to the safety of the entire complex, which now embraced a dozen letterboxes, transmitter sites and hideouts.

I assigned special names to the towns, the regions and the commonest objects. A system of numbers was worked out for our sources, the places where messages could be left or people could meet. We finished up by speaking a jargon that was absolutely incomprehensible to anyone but an initiate, especially to people who did not come from the same region.

Another innovation was the 'Corniche' code, invented by Faye for corresponding with the occupied zone. Each agent received a key word that enabled him to insert a secret message into the innocent text of an inoffensive-looking inter-zonal card. This gradually became the normal way of corresponding throughout the network and it saved us a tremendous amount of travelling.

At last our links with Spain had been perfected. An additional channel of communication had been established for our mail, thanks to the SS *Coëtlogon* and SS *Saint Brieuc* plying between Sète and Barcelona, where we had two contacts. The Marseilles-Madrid radio link was still working marvellously. Every day Jean Boutron let me know the information he had managed to obtain. One day he had a real scoop: '*Old cruiser Gueydon camouflaged battle cruiser left Brest stop departure of two German cruisers therefore apparently imminent stop Scharnhorst ready stop Gneisenau not yet stop they are going to sail stop do not miss them end*'. Why was this not believed? History will say that other sources geographically nearer had been poisoned by the enemy.

Precisely a week later the two German cruisers sailed calmly out of Brest and, after running the gauntlet of British air and sea action, steamed home to North Sea ports.

9 *A ROPE ROUND MY NECK*

It was just when things were going well that the blow fell. It came in the deceptive form of Commandant G. Georges-Picot, my elder sister's husband, an officer in the colonial army. We had had a warm and affectionate feeling for one another since my youth. And so I was greatly surprised to see him come charging down on me with his lower lip thrust out menacingly and anger in his voice: 'Who is ASO 43? Who is PLU 122?'

In a flash I realized that my Tarbes files had fallen into enemy hands and that I was going to have no easy job to extricate myself from what was obviously a very tight corner. 'Have they got my papers?' I asked.

'Yes, they have got your papers. They're hunting for you more actively than ever now. You're known to have gone to Madrid in a way that makes the Marshal look ridiculous. You're accused—and there's documentary proof—of wanting to kill Darlan! You've gone completely mad! Meanwhile this ASO 43 and this PLU 122 of yours are going to be lured to Paris, where they are expected any minute. You're in a fine old mess. Fortunately, I'm on the spot,' he said, suddenly much more gentle. 'For once, you pig-headed creature, you're going to do immediately what I tell you. You're going to catch the train for Vichy with me this very evening.'

'To be handed over to the police?'

'You'll look fine if the police find you in Marseilles.'

'But what they've got hold of doesn't mean a thing. Names, radio messages. . . .'

'All in your own handwriting! As for the names, they have their suspicions. The police have woken up to the fact that your Gavarni was a minor figure. They hoped to trace you through the agents who were freed in Pau, but you seem to have spirited them away already.'

'Your solution makes their job very much easier, my poor dear. If I go to Vichy they'll lock me up.'

'Not a bit of it. Not with me there. You're lucky that Commandant Rollin is a good Frenchman and a friend. I've convinced him that you were incapable of such baseness and he's offering you a forty-eight-hour truce so that you can go and explain yourself.'

'And what will happen afterwards?'

'You'll have proved your good faith and you may have saved your ASO 43 and PLU 122 and shaken off the police. Haven't you got your hands full enough with the Germans?'

'Of course, but who can promise. . . .'

'*I* do. I give you my word of honour. If you don't succeed I'll help you to get away.'

'It's very sweet of you to compromise yourself so completely but I beg you to wait a bit. Tell your people anything you like so that I can gain time, and come back for me in two days. Then you can put the rope round my neck. I swear.'

ASO 43! That was Jean Boutron, who was due to arrive from Madrid at any moment with a very important message. PLU 122 was our 'Pluto', Commandant Barjot, serving in Dakar, whence he continued to send us messages. How could they be saved? I could see no other way than by submitting to the ordeal Picot had proposed. We held an immediate council of war, comprising the Bishop, Audoly, Rivière and, of course, Faye, and we agreed on a plan of action: to inform the British, who were thrown into a panic and radioed back at once, begging me not to walk into such a crude trap; to warn Boutron by the Marseilles-Madrid radio link; and to alert our main agents. The Bishop would retire to bed, saying he had 'influenza' and would stand by night and day for a telephone call from me. Faye would follow me, ready to give the alarm, depending on the outcome of this strange rendezvous.

Georges-Picot reappeared two days later, fairly dancing with impatience. 'They're waiting for you!' he shouted in his stentorian voice the moment he spotted me. 'The hunt for you has been called off while the truce is on; we're going to have a marvellous trip.'

A marvellous trip indeed! The train wheels clicked and clacked implacably and my head seemed to be filling with inky-black clouds. We had been destroyed once already; the whole of the first wave, headed by Navarre, had been smashed. I had believed I could rebuild the organization on the same foundations and, through sheer carelessness, the second wave was about to suffer the same fate!

I now remembered. The British had, rather foolishly, radioed me that they had identified PLU 122 as Commandant Barjot. British Intelligence is good, I had thought. And full of admiration I had stupidly recopied the message, leaving the rank and initials of the proper name.

On the other hand, in the case of ASO 143, Vichy could only proceed by deduction or on the strength of gossip. Apart from the infuriating mistake about Barjot, I was absolutely certain that my records contained only pseudonyms and symbols. I went over them again and again, racking my memory, when a sort of dream crystallized, alongside my feverish thoughts. I closed my eyes to catch it: amid hostile people who were throwing stones at them, my friends the symbols underwent a metamorphosis, changing from symbols into hunted animals. All kinds of animals, from the humble ant to the proud king of the beasts, the lion. At one moment the animals were speeding across the plains; at another they were pacing restlessly behind the bars of endless cages. They were shut off from the side where the human beings were. What was I among all these? A hedgehog, curled up with all quills bristling.

I came back to normal consciousness. Dozing in the seat opposite me was Georges-Picot. His great height—he was well over six feet—inspired an obvious parallel: he would be Giraffe. And Coustenoble, with his feline prowl, would be Tiger. Siegrist, the huge policeman with the flapping ears, could only be Elephant, and Dor, the poet, was like a Fawn, Denise Centore like a Sable, Augustine Contrasty like a Gazelle. And Bernis suggested that marvellous, faithful gun dog, a Spaniel. Rivière was a Wolf, and Audoly a Fox.

I elaborated the picture. Why not give all the airmen the names of birds? All the radio operators the names of fledglings? No more patrols: from now on there would be just a jungle. Regions divided into sectors in which dogs and wild animals and game of every variety would breed and multiply; in the ports, fishes. The whole of creation was rising up to face the enemy, except that most of the human species rejected us. Even the Flood had not been able to destroy us, the animals.

The barrier at the Vichy station struck me as a veritable trap, but it did not frighten me. A second sense, a sort of animal flair, had been born in me during the journey. I saw Faye get out at the tail end of the train. He followed us, arching his arms over his head, as though he were drawing breath deep into his lungs. He would be the Eagle that soars above the mountain tops.

I was literally bristling when, early next morning, I went to Commandant Rollin's office, where I was immediately shown in, pushed along by my brother-in-law.

The Commandant, responsible for security in the occupied zone, stood up and pointed an accusing finger at the photostat copies of the notebooks that I had entrusted to the 'Tarbes friends' and of which an incredible number of copies were now spread out over his desk: 'So you want to kill the admiral?' was his opening gambit.

In a flash I saw, enlarged out of all proportion as if seen through a telescope, the phrases written down by Coustenoble: 'Darlan will die by revolver. . . . Darlan will die by revolver. . . .'

I burst out laughing. So these were the 'documentary proofs'? Taken completely aback, Rollin's only reaction was to push a chair at me so that I could sit down.

'You want to kill the Admiral,' he went on, 'and all you do is to laugh your head off. The Admiral can't sleep any more. Will you please explain?'

I asked him to let me look closely at the incriminating sheet. 'Take a good look, Monsieur le Directeur, at these downstrokes, at these identical and never-varying phrases that are repeated *ad infinitum*; do you consider that normal?'

'That's true,' he said. 'Since I've been looking at these papers I've been trying to fathom what it's all about.'

'Now look at the photostat copies of my notes and messages; is the writing the same?'

'No,' he admitted, 'it's not the same at all. The experts also agree. Then whose writing is it?'

The whole business was beginning to take a nasty turn. Coustenoble must certainly be kept out of trouble; I must think of something else at once. 'It's a clairvoyant's prophecy.'

Rollin sat down again, screwing up his face and goggling at me in astonishment. He was short, thick-set and greying. One could picture him, binoculars in hand, on the bridge of a warship ploughing its way through mountainous seas. At the same time he also had a fatherly side, which he was emphasizing, no doubt to draw me out. I quickly repressed an instinctive liking that began to well up.

'And where is this clairvoyant of yours?' he asked.

'In the occupied zone, in Paris,' I thought of Marie-Claude Paupière. If he asked for her name it would be easy to give it since she was a member of the network.

'She would be in the occupied zone! You know perfectly well we don't like having to deal with two police forces. . . .' This was news to me. 'You're lucky. Before the war I carried out a big investigation of necromancy and clairvoyance for *Le Temps*. What method does she use?'

'Mediumistic handwriting. Her "spirits" dictate to her. As you can see this is always the same one. He announces himself by drawing a propeller. He's an airman who was killed in 1940, one of her old clients.'

He scrutinized the paper, scrutinized my face and asked more questions. 'Why did she send this to you?'

'Oh, she keeps sending me her prophecies. I usually throw them straight into the wastepaper basket. I kept this one. One never knows,' I said craftily.

'And just as I was going to say that the Admiral would feel much relieved to hear it was nothing more than that. . . .'

'You see, you see,' cried my brother-in-law, delighted. 'I knew it. Kids' stuff. Nothing to make a fuss about!'

Rollin picked up his inter-office telephone, called the Admiralty and I heard him say: 'The person is sitting opposite me now. Tell the Admiral that he has no need to worry, there's nothing to make a fuss about. I will explain it all, no need to worry . . . for the moment,' he added, after he had hung up.

My clairvoyant story had obviously interested him tremendously. 'When there's time, you'll tell me everything you know about this woman.'

He had forgotten to ask me her name.

Rollin offered me a cigarette which I gratefully accepted, aglow with a sense of satisfaction at having got over the first hurdle so well; he gave me a light and, adjusting his sights, so to speak, fired point blank: 'We're going to arrest ASO 43 tomorrow morning. Admiral Delay, the naval attaché in Madrid, will put him on the plane to Istres. It's Jean Boutron, isn't it?'

Boutron had been warned. If he arrived at least he would have nothing compromising on him. I decided to avert their suspicions again. 'ASO 43 is not the man you think.' I said. 'He's a Frenchman living in Spain, all right, but Jean Boutron has nothing to do with this business.'

'But you do know Boutron?'

'Of course! He sailed for the Compagnie des Messageries Maritimes, to which my father belonged.'

I felt Rollin's conviction weakening. He picked his phone up again and called the police at the Istres naval base: 'Go easy with tomorrow morning's arrest. ASO may not be ASO.'

'Then who is ASO?' he continued, hanging up and looking at me this time in a most unpleasant way.

'Listen, Monsieur le Directeur, don't expect me to give you one single name to tie up with the symbols you've discovered in my wretched files! I came here to see if we can ever hope to find patriots in Vichy and to establish an acceptable *modus vivendi* with them.'

'What do you think?' Rollin shouted, thoroughly riled. 'Do you really think we aren't patriots? We're far greater patriots than you. You people are a confounded nuisance with your fatuous networks. I long to get rid of the Germans as much as you do, but believe me, Britain won't help us.'

I threw my arms up in despair. 'But you know perfectly well that we no longer have any contact with Britain. Your police have seized everything.'

'Then what did you go to Madrid for? The bull fights?'

No one could have put on a more bewildered look than I did at that moment. I launched into a flood of denials.

'We'll go into all that again tomorrow,' he said, dodging the issue, 'I must hurry off to interrogate your friend Barjot. He at least is helpful. He never denied a thing when he was picked up in Dakar.'

I didn't flinch, but I had to swallow so hard that Rollin became much gentler again. 'You need have no fears about Barjot. He's too big a fish. Because the Admiralty is afraid his example might start a fashion they will be content merely to silence him. By the way,' he added maliciously, 'your friend the vegetable dealer's going to have a funny sort of awakening tomorrow morning!'

I went away feeling more dead than alive. The Barjot affair could be settled on a sailor-to-sailor basis, but *I* was not a sailor! Nor was poor Rivière, who was going to be picked up with the vegetables, and possibly the entire organization would be drawn into a new trap.

Faye was waiting for us at the hotel. I explained the situation and he dashed to the phone to call Mesnard at the Hotel Terminus. He gave the alarm, using the formula agreed upon before we left: 'Clear the vegetable shop, dismiss everybody and store the pianos.'

Late in the evening Faye called the Bishop again. The job seemed to have been done. Another agonizing night began.

Our appointment was not until ten o'clock and Rollin greeted us in the majestic manner that set me thinking hard. After making a few cracks about 'the vegetable dealer who will soon be in the soup,' he plunged a dagger into my heart. 'When your friend Boutron was questioned by my men at Istres he went with them like a lamb. So who is lying? He or you?'

'Bring us face to face, then you'll see for yourself.'

'Not before inviting you to come and have lunch with us out in the country. My wife's dying to meet you,' he said cheerfully. 'I like stubborn people,' and turning to my brother-in-law, 'I thought you were talking through your hat, but she's worse than a mule.'

Away from his office and the danger that any indiscretion might be overheard, Rollin was a different man. His wife told me at once how completely she understood my point of view, that her brothers had crossed swords with the Gestapo and that her husband would do well to leave me in peace, otherwise. . . . She looked at him hard with her dark, velvety eyes and he dropped his formidable manner. He began to tell me that his wish was not to defeat us but to canalize us, to put us in a position genuinely to serve the cause of France.

'In point of fact,' I told him, 'you're arresting us in order to help us.'

He said he was sincerely sorry to have to do it but others were involved and we were so careless and illogical. What a curious mixture he was, torn between his wish to go over to the Allied camp and a Vichyist subservience that made the slightest confidences risky. Undeniably, he had a heart and I decided to appeal to his generous side. I spoke to him at length of my ideal of fighting to the bitter end, of what some of his police at Pau were doing, of the tragedy that was being played out in the occupied zone.

'You've done enough,' he said to me at the end. 'Your duty now is towards your children. I'm going to spread my protective wing over you. Take advantage of it, it may not last long. I also feel threatened. My police are not the only police in Vichy. Darlan has a force of his own. Watch out for him!'

Watch out for Darlan! What would happen to my friends if Rollin fell?

'I won't accept a thing from you,' I snapped, 'if all my comrades who are still in prison aren't out within the hour.'

'But they are going to be freed! If they want to carry on the fight you'll tell them to join the Deuxième Bureau, which is in dire need of men of their calibre.'

'I'll willingly let it have Gavarni, if he volunteers. He has fleeced us completely.'

'Rubbish. The miserable eighty notes he brought back with him couldn't have run you short. You're reckoned to have received fantastic sums.'

'People have been quick to turn everything into fairy stories,' I put in to hide my astonishment. Eighty thousand francs! The rogue had surrendered only eighty thousand francs out of two million!

When we returned to the Security office, Boutron and Rivière were there already. Rollin allowed me to see them. Boutron was in despair, the tears streaming down his cheeks upset me terribly.

'Why didn't you protest when you landed?' I asked him.

'The police probably saved my life,' he whispered. 'On leaving Madrid I noticed that two men on the plane were keeping me under observation the whole time. Abwehr agents. They were only waiting for a chance to bump me off. It was far less dangerous to come here. Don't worry, everything is OK in Madrid. I haven't said a word either about the bag or the other things. They're completely at sea.'

I told him that as Rollin had his doubts he was going to detain him in the Alps, from where our Grenoble agents would arrange his escape, and that Barjot would be silenced in Algeria. I urged him to be patient. I assured him that everything we were doing would continue.

The shouting that began to come from Rivière in the next room soon put an end to our emotional conversation. Yes, he knew dear old Barjot very well. He was an old friend and therefore he knew Marie-Madeleine. She was an acquaintance who had lent him money for his vegetable business. Resistance? Heaven forbid, that was too dangerous. Transmitting sets? Good heavens, that would be real suicide. It was true that there was a certain Gavarni, an odd fish who had turned up at his house with a suitcase that he called LUX. . . . It was a transmitting set? Impossible. He thought it was black market stuff and luxury articles. . . . Well, Gavarni had come to collect LUX and said 'It's for Vichy.' Well then! If it was for Vichy what did they want with him?

There was nothing further they wanted with him. He travelled back to Marseilles the same evening.

When I got back to Rollin's office he asked me what identity I wanted to adopt.

'None,' I replied, 'since you're very kindly going to protect me. I'll be delighted to resume my own.'

'I prefer to make you out a genuine false identity card. I've been bombarded with phone calls about you all day. You've been seen walking about in Vichy. People are asking why I don't pull you in.'

'That's the end! If it's no longer possible to be safe with the head of Security, make me out a phoney card.'

He called in a colleague whom he felt he could trust and I dictated to him: 'Claire de Bacqueville, born in Shanghai, China. . . .'

'Let me know how you're getting along from time to time,' Rollin concluded. 'From this minute all the searches will stop and I'll send the order for the release of the people still in prison. Philippe le Couteux in Lyons and your parachute friends will be freed tonight. In Boutron's case it will take a little longer. As for you, go back to your family and your children. . . .'

On leaving Rollin I bumped into Gavarni, whose face turned a sickly green. 'I've been looking everywhere,' he began. 'Things are going from bad to worse. Rivière, Boutron and Barjot have been arrested.'

'Take it easy! I've followed your trail. I've seen the top police officers.'

His face fell. 'You've seen Rollin?'

'Yes, at great length. You're out. Goodbye.' He turned wearily away and I felt profoundly sorry for him.

My brother-in-law dragged me towards the train for the Riviera, where he wanted me to get my second wind and also to make sure that I was no longer being trailed. It was very wise advice. What's more, I was dying to take my children in my arms.

10 *THE WORM IN THE FRUIT*

There is a fundamental fault in the construction of Fresnes prison. It stands in the bottom of a valley; the damp creeps up into the masonry and the cells at ground level are partly rotten. The food was indescribably bad. About once a month, each prisoner was given a very small piece of paper and pencil and allowed to write a letter. Ferocious threats, minute searching gave rise to a form of sport engaged in by the prisoners. Its object was to acquire a stock of tiny bits of paper a few centimetres long, easy to conceal.

Neighbouring prisoners corresponded with one another by tapping. Direct conversation was more cheering: it was possible in the case of common law prisoners occupying the parts guarded by a French staff. The windows of their cells were often left open until night fell. From these, warnings to members of the Resistance, as well as news about what was happening inside, were passed on. Sometimes, when the Nazis had been on the rampage, everything was silent.

People sang a lot and that was also a distraction. Often, towards dawn, the knell would toll for the hostages. Cries of revolt bordering on madness rose from groups of the condemned who were being led away to their deaths, mingled with the grumbling of the warders and the barking of the dogs. Soldiers charged along the galleries, flung open the doors and ordered the inmates to dress. As the steps neared one's cell, one wondered, 'Will it be me this time?' and as the Germans passed one went to sleep again with a feeling of shame, relieved that this time death had passed one by.

With rage in his heart, Coustenoble prowled around the huge, ramshackle building, studying its massive, grey walls. He had to abandon the idea of organizing an escape. 'You'd need an armoured division to attack this fortress!' he decided.

At least he was able to breach it from inside. He knew for certain who was behind those blind walls, and he gradually discovered what his comrades, who had been handed over to the enemy in the very heart of their native land, were thinking. Dispersed all over the prison, they were unable to communicate with one another and had no way of learning what was happening. Superintendent David began to agree that he had made a mistake in taking them for Communists, but one day, despite the intervention of the Deuxième Bureau, he had handed them over to a platoon of German soldiers. Yet Coustenoble heard that the investigation had yielded nothing.

'It's enough to drive you mad,' the imprisoned network people said in messages that they managed to pass out. The women—their wives, mothers and sisters—constantly pleading with the enemy, succeeded in getting through to them clean underwear, food parcels and scraps of information which relieved their gloom. Often the dirty linen picked up by the families in exchange bore the marks of torture. They examined that linen carefully, running their fingers through it, and soon discovered, in the hem of a skirt or a handkerchief, tiny, almost invisible rolls of paper engraved with a pin-point, or covered with capitals pencilled with scraps of lead that had been missed when the men were searched.

Coustenoble knew those messages by heart, but he had carefully kept those from Lucien Vallet that were in code. The radio operator had not revealed his code and Coustenoble knew that, apart from London and his chief, nobody would be able to understand them. 'There's a worm in the fruit,' he thought. 'Perhaps Vallet will give us the key to the riddle.'

Mechanically pulling his sodden old hat further down over his face, the airman walked reluctantly away from the impregnable and hated bastion.

Nice was fragrant with the scent of carnations and violets, but my brother-in-law Georges-Picot watched my slightest movement like a hawk, which meant that I was able to check very quickly that I was no longer shadowed by Rollin's police. I could safety re-establish contact with the network construction without endangering Rollin.

Coustenoble appeared in response to my call. Without a word, he handed me Lucien Vallet's messages. I decoded them eagerly. They all ended with the word 'hungry'. It was clear that there was something of a devil's hand guiding the interrogations and that in the end the beating, the brutality and ill-treatment, worse still the traps that were laid for them, forced involuntary admissions. 'The Fritzes know more than we know ourselves', Coustenoble admitted.

'How is that possible? Who's giving them the low-down?'

'Bla!'

'But, that's not possible. I've told British Intelligence all about his curious ways, but they think he's OK.'

Coustenoble refused to be convinced. In spite of my explicit orders, Bla kept coming back to see the families of those in prison, but he knew nothing about the new organization.

I told Coustenoble what I had decided as a result of my latest reflections. To avoid the disasters of the past year we must decentralize the network to an even greater extent, create independent services for radio, air operations and sending mail, and increase the autonomy of the sectors whose job was to gather information. I then came to my decision to replace the English symbols by animal names.

'So we're going to turn into a menagerie!' was Coustenoble's comment, 'and for me you've chosen the tiger, a splendid beast with a mighty bite. If I understand your scheme correctly, it'll mean a fair amount of moving about?'

'The British tell me they're sending a massive amount of material and two operators, one an expert in landing aeroplanes, the other an expert in the appreciation of intelligence. As soon as Mahout is ready. . . .'

He pulled out his moustache to give himself a tigerish look and began to growl: 'However much you bristle, Hedgehog, you'll always be "little one" to me. So now to business! I go through Marseilles to report to Fa . . . Eagle, I return to Paris to wait for your Colonel Ve . . . Hyena. He can come and he will be helped.' Coustenoble (now Tiger) broke off, then said: 'Don't worry about the occupied zone, little one! We shall soon know what Bla's game is. I'm on his trail. . . .'

How was I to leave my family without revealing that the organization was continuing? It was becoming urgent that I should take up the fight again and it was not long before a sad opportunity to do so came my way. It became clear, alas, that one of my daughters must have an operation. We heard of a Dr Charry, who lived in Toulouse and who was said to perform wonders, even in those days when there was an acute shortage of medicines. I took my child to see him and he agreed to take us into his hospital. After the operation there would have to be a fairly long period of convalescence. And so I set up my new headquarters in Toulouse.

We installed ourselves in the Clinique des Allées, where we had a large room containing enough furniture to hide the things I needed for my underground activity and to work in comfort.

Dr Charry soon tumbled to what I was doing. 'Are you writing a book?' he inquired one evening.

'Not exactly. At the moment I'm busy collecting my material.'

'I thought so. Can I be of any help?'

'A great help—if only by allowing me to receive a certain number of callers here.'

'Anyone can have a large family! They may come to the hospital whenever they like. You have only to let me know what you want.'

In this way I acquired an established and solid headquarters. The bridgehead was formed at once by a Polish engineer, Mouchou Damm, and his wife, Nelly, whom I had already seen on Faye's recommendation. Everything I had asked them to do had been done: they had found an adjutant, in the person of their adopted son, Arnold Gartner; an intelligence chief, Superintendent Philippe; and a hideout in the Hotel de Paris. They would put the radio operator up in their own home. I completed this excellent team by the addition of Guy Mesnard, the son of our treasurer, who was studying at the university and giving them a sub-sector of informants in the surrounding towns. I had them come to the hospital.

'From now on we shall cut out real names,' I explained. 'Your name, Mouchou, is Griffin, your wife is Vicuna, your son is Zebra. As soon as I have fixed things up with Superintendent Philippe he will become Basset.'

'I didn't think I'd be going into a zoo!' commented Mouchou Damm with a laugh. 'If you'd like to see Basset right now, he's downstairs.'

I asked Basset (Supt. Philippe) if he could organize the search for information in the Toulouse region and the neighbouring *departments*. 'You're quite right to be concerned about this area,' he replied. 'I'm wondering whether Hitler means to occupy it.'

'Would Pétain invade his *own* free zone? Would he violate the armistice terms so blatantly?'

'It's being violated the whole time. What difference does a little more or a little less make?'

Basset had people everywhere. Now he could employ them. His whole manner was open and forthright and he looked at one directly, his eyes bright with intelligence. I knew I could have complete confidence in him.

My daughter's operation was a complete success. I spent many hours sitting with her, especially as she found her plaster cast very trying. But Marseilles insisted on my presence and I had to go, though it broke my heart to leave my little girl weeping her eyes out.

The moment I arrived I could see the tremendous progress that had been made since the reorganization. At the Saint-Charles bar, run by Emile Hédin, the hard-working Beaver, incoming agents were directed to the addresses in the city where their particular lines were handled. Faye, more like an Eagle than ever, met me at the bar and I followed him, at a discreet distance, to his house on the Corniche, at the highest point on the rocky road, overlooking the whole of Marseilles bay. I had hardly sat down in front of the dream-like prospect than a servant appeared wearing a white jacket and carrying coffee and liqueurs. 'This is Albert, alias Mastiff,' Faye (Eagle) explained. 'He runs our mess.'

I drank my coffee in silence and refused the liqueurs. The Mastiff took the glasses away. 'It's very nice indeed to have one's creature comforts,' I said, 'but what about Intelligence?'

'Come and see your mail.' He pointed to the desk with its orderly piles of messages from London and information from the sectors. Eagle had wanted to save me worry during the difficult weeks in Toulouse, and the day-to-day routine was under control.

This was when the Desert War was raging and British Intelligence inundated us with questions concerning the movements of Axis land, sea and air forces. To answer these Audoly (Fox) went to ground in a deep, out-of-the-way earth, for London attached increasing importance to his Mediterranean intelligence. Bernis (Spaniel) had reinforced his effective strength by contacting a small network of Italian anti-fascists who said they were connected with Pietro Nenni, the leader of the underground socialists, with whom we had a contact at Nice.

'They're asking for a transmitter for northern Italy,' Eagle told me. 'Is it OK with you?'

'Richards will be delighted. I'll draft the message right away.'

'You can add that we're keeping an eye on the Italian air force in Turin, thanks to Pierre Giovaccini. Our friends have been able to get him assigned there from Melegnano as mechanic to the Vichy commission's airplane.'

'How did you come to think that up?'

'British Intelligence is afraid that Fascist squadrons will soon be sent to reinforce Rommel's army. Giovaccini will have a ringside seat for assessing the situation. What alias have you given him?' I asked as I finished my radio message.

'Pelican; but that's not all. Tell them also that supplies are on their way to Rommel. From Grenoble, Dr Arbassier (Snail) reports massive shipments of material: torpedo boats are going by river from the Rhine down the Rhone to the Mediterranean.'

'Fox must nab them when they arrive in the Gulf of Lyons.'

'That's fixed. Commandant Mahé is going to set up an observation post en route. His photographs will be sent to Fox within an hour. Mahé's alias will be Pike.'

'By the way, what's the reaction to the animal names?'

'They're a fantastic success. The habit caught on instantly. People are using nothing else now.'

Mastiff knocked at the door.

'Can Tiger come in?' he bayed.

Tiger, of course, was Coustenoble who entered out of breath, his voice hoarse and almost inaudible with emotion. He brandished a coded message from Vallet:

'Decipher it, decipher it quickly. I'm sure it confirms what I told you. Bla's the traitor. I became certain when I checked his contacts. He's had his entire network in Normandy arrested. And thanks to him the Boches were already shadowing Hugon and Pautard when Superintendent David arrested them. Furious to find their lead gone, the Germans demanded that the French police should hand the patrol over.'

'Can you imagine the haul there would have been if the Nazis had gone on watching us?' Eagle asked as he prepared the deciphering grid with his usual dexterity.

Vallet's brief message appeared: '*Last interrogation made me certain treachery Bla stop I've been handed set OCK which was delivered to him after my arrest by Annie Hugon ostensibly to repair stop don't forget we owe all our misfortunes to him stop pray for us stop regards hunger.*'

'The investigation's been speeded up,' commented Tiger. 'The British commando raid on Saint-Nazaire on 28 March landed at the spot described in the Mouren-Sgier plan of the U-boat pens. Since then the Boche have been making a tremendous effort and now they're forced to reveal their informer. To confuse Vallet, the interrogators haven't hesitated to show him the OCK set that was sent to Bla.'

'Obviously,' I commented, 'They don't suspect that we correspond with their prisoners. What a marvel Vallet is!'

I immediately sent an urgent message to London, summing up the situation. Their answer was that Bla's SHE set was continuing to operate and sending excellent information.

'A dialogue of the deaf,' said Eagle. 'I propose that Tiger should go back to Paris to fix this bastard.'

'No, let's cut the melodrama. Let's give the British all the proof we can. I haven't given up hope of convincing them.'

I despatched another message. We waited another day. Tiger was about to leave, completely disgusted, when Jassaud rushed into the office with a message. 'The radio operator said *top* priority, to be decoded at once,' he said.

We got straight down to it. '*No. 218 for POZ 55: You were right stop Bla a traitor stop working for the Gestapo stop secure everything he knows about that is still intact stop we are issuing execution order stop Richards.*'

Orders to execute Bla? British Intelligence never gave orders! It was true that a British subject was involved, but did the British have to vent their fury in such a violent way?

'It's incredible!' said Eagle.

'And what's the use of British Intelligence?' asked Tiger, dumbfounded. 'Can't they do it themselves? It's like looking for a needle in a haystack now that Bla is exposed.'

'Make secure everything he knows about? But he knows Tiger, he knows me . . . he knows the Bishop, he knows my brother . . . he knows. . . .'

'. . . Bouvet!' I yelled.

Bouvet was the Dax solicitor whom Bla had been using as a letter box in the occupied zone and who had been sending money on to Bla every month—which was undoubtedly the reason why the traitor had spared him so far.

Tiger picked up his bag: 'I'm off to warn the solicitor.'

I caught him by the arm. 'Tiger, before you left Paris, did you receive a visit from Jean de Malherbe and Joseph Ornstein, little "Gigot", who left here a week ago?'

He shook his head.

'Then there's no point in going,' Eagle cut in. 'They were to cross the line to see Bouvet in Dax and join you in Paris when they got off the train. They've undoubtedly all been caught.'

Two days later we knew that altogether sixteen of our patrol members were in Fresnes. How many would survive?

I could only reply to Richards: 'The damage is done.' He immediately suggested that since Bla was still playing a double game by using his SHE set and yet complaining that he was cut off from the network, I should arrange a rendezvous with him in Lyons where we could renew contact with him with a view to bumping him off.

It was the Bishop who volunteered to do the job. He waited at the appointed place for three hours. Bla, of course, never turned up; but the Abwehr thugs were there. As they could not accost the Bishop openly, they attempted to grab him and it was he who was nearly kidnapped. A real song and dance!

After that all we could do was to send all our agents a description and particulars of Bla. I was certain that he would now try to get in touch with me again on his masters' orders.

'It's incredible, incredible!' muttered Eagle. We had good grounds for astonishment. The first man sent to us by British Intelligence was working for the Nazis. We began a race against the Abwehr.

11 *THE INTELLIGENCE SERVICE ARMY*

The convent atmosphere which I returned to in the Clinique des Allées allowed me to come to grips with the host of complex problems requiring urgent attention. In the room where my daughter could lie and regain her strength as she looked out at the spring through wide-open windows, I could safely spread out the plans for the organization of the network, diagrams that I burned as soon as they had been drawn.

Since returning from Madrid I had followed Richards' advice: 'Take your time over your network. It must last!' Its reconstruction seemed to be going very well. The original patrols that had come through unscathed, amalgamated with the squadrons that had come to swell our numbers, were being brought up to strength and supporting each other in a brotherly sort of way throughout the whole territory. I now had to reinforce their positions and plug the gaps.

I marked the firmly-based, strong districts in green ink—Grenoble, the Alps and Savoy; Marseilles and the Riviera with its extensions into Italy and North Africa; Lyons and the Rhone Valley; Toulouse, of course, Pau, the Pyrenees with their connections with Bordeaux and the Atlantic coast.

Lieutenant Dallas' (Mahout's) Avia crew was consolidating its position in the Lyons area; the policeman Siegrist (Elephant) was setting up the security centre at Marseilles, forging every kind of false document and keeping a watch on the headquarters: Pierre Berthomier, called Goeland (Seagull) after his Goeland plane, continued to use the official Air-Bleu circuit to pick up information from the various towns; Robert Philippe (Parrot) maintained the equipment in Vichy's radio stations.

Vichy? Since October 1941, thanks to British Intelligence, who had put us in touch with one another I had been corresponding with General Camille Raynal, whom I considered to be one of our most remarkable Intelligence experts. His age, however, precluded him from bringing into play the dynamic elements that he had ready to hand and I had not yet succeeded in getting him placed. Lieutenant Lenoir of the Blue-White-Red patrol had been recalled to Saint-Cyr as an instructor. Nevertheless, Vichy retained its importance as the cross-roads of defeat. In red pencil I underlined the words: *to be reinforced*.

The occupied zone presented very definite worries. Commandant Verteré had returned to his post in Paris and said in every report that he would keep his promises. To make things easier for him, Eagle (Faye) had released his own adjutant, Lieutenant Poulard (Jack Tar), who had left for Brittany, and I had sacrificed the services of Tiger (Coustenoble) who, together with Jumez, went to pick up the severed connections with the forbidden northern zone. Gérard Novel was tackling the Alsace-Lorraine region, where we had not yet managed to penetrate. The first feather in the Squadron's cap there was Capitaine Maurice de MacMahon, Duke of Magenta, who had answered Eagle's appeal and brought us invaluable elements in Normandy, Burgundy and the capital. We had detailed him as Verteré's adjutant. Verteré was now known to us as Hyena.

The obvious choice for the Contentin district was Jean Sainteny (Dragon), who had been recruited by Navarre as early as October 1940. Since then he had settled a team of sailors and mechanics in the coastal sectors and these were now ready to go into action.

Robert Philippe (Parrot) had smuggled out the two radio sets I had brought back from Madrid and these were now in the hands of the two fledglings discovered by Tiger, Robin and Wren. I was anxious for this new Paris radio centre to contact London and I was furious that Verteré had done nothing about it.

Fortunately, the liaison agents were indefatigable: Jean Lefevre, who went by the name of Gorilla because of his powerful physique, and the romantic Henri-Léopold Dor, now Fawn, and especially two young women, Odette Fabius, called Doe because of her alert, nervous look, and Else Erzberger, who was of Swiss origin and called Adela because of her loyalty. Our couriers were continually on the move, slipping from zone to zone and provided with lots of double-bottomed Gibbs dentifrice tins containing secret messages.

Organizing these journeys from a distance, and the co-ordination of old and new agents, getting hold again of the best sources in the sectors that had been decimated and putting them in touch with reliable go-betweens, resuscitating the sectors from their own ashes and creating new ones from them, were extremely tricky operations. I went on plastering red circles all over my diagram. A transmitter must be earmarked for this place; more money must be sent to that place; bases must be set up in Bordeaux, Brest and Strasbourg, and so on.

The problem of actual numbers did not worry me, for Eagle, dodging about and going to the four corners of the so-called free zone, made it a point of honour to bring back first-class recruits from every journey he made, and all I had to do was to allocate them. His fertile imagination also drove him to extend the network in far less orthodox directions—to create a network of agents in Germany itself by exploiting Vichy's agreement to send Frenchmen to work in Nazi factories and plants; to make preparations to mobilize the organizations created by Pétain so as to have fighting troops; to set up cells and infiltrate staffs, headquarters and industries; to secure suitable cover.

I had wanted him to remain based in Marseilles, where our radios were, with an agreement that we should visit one another in turn and that he would send to Toulouse the people I simply ought to see, but his final words had alarmed me: 'I've finished with retail business,' he said grandiloquently. 'I'm now in the wholesale business. An agent must work in dozens. We're better than the Army's Intelligence Service, we're the Intelligence Service's Army.'

I saw that I should also have to damp his ardour.

A scratching at the door made me whisk my papers hastily out of sight. The stranger who came in was by no means unknown. He was a real flesh and blood Gulliver, and that is what we called him. At once tall and powerfully built, with copper-coloured hair and an open face, his Herculean appearance inspired confidence. 'I come from Tiger-Cat,' he said, trying hard to muffle his natural boom.

Former minister, Louis Jacquinot, Navarre's lawyer, now working in the network under the name of Tiger-Cat, had successfully defended him in an arms shipment case. On leaving prison, Gulliver had found his organization disbanded and he asked me to help him revive it. His forces were concentrated in central France. He lived in Vichy.

'You couldn't have come at a better moment. My network is facing something of a crisis; I need to strengthen it by setting up withdrawal areas to be used in case of emergency.'

'The *département* of Corrèze is the obvious place. My partner in the arms job, Jean Vinzant, lives there, at Ussel. He already has a whole circuit of hiding places in the Auvergne mountains that you could at once use for your men and equipment. Have you any escaped prisoners that you want to hide? If you have an airplane we've got a perfect landing place.'

I thought of Navarre, Boutron, my brother and of Claude Hettier de Boislambert, General de Gaulle's first collaborator in London, who had been captured and sentenced to transportation with forced labour as a result of the abortive Dakar landing. I had promised our mutual friend, Jean Sainteny (Dragon), that I would snatch him out of prison, but all these plans had been postponed because we lacked any means of evacuation.

I grabbed a Michelin map. Gulliver marked the Thalamy landing ground near Ussel and painted a rosy picture of the withdrawal area he could create in the vicinity.

'I have a first class leader on the spot in Vichy,' I told him. 'As you live there would you agree to be his adjutant?'

Gulliver looked as though I were some Lilliputian that he would gladly devour.

'It all depends,' he scowled.

'He's a general, and he's old, but you'd more than hold your own.'

'I bet it's Raynal!' he exclaimed, suddenly excited. 'If you mean him, then OK.'

He was able to provide Raynal with some fifty volunteers, both men and women, who were ready for any kind of mission, and he went back to set about organizing the Ussel and Vichy sectors, which were assigned canine and bovine names. General Raynal would be called Sheepdog, and Gulliver himself had taken the name of Ram.

The second part of Richards' programme ('and hold on') seemed to have got off to a far better start. With a feeling of relief I turned my attention to practical jobs.

Working by the dim light of my little girl's bedside lamp, I was deciphering the last batch of messages that had come through on the headquarters radio. Questionnaires, more questionnaires, pieces of information for the Avia crew. Suddenly I received a shock, for the message that emerged under my pencil was unusual:

'*Richards to POZ strictly confidential stop have learned heroic escape of General Giraud stop repeat Giraud stop believed to have fled to Lyons stop would be most happy if you would agree to contact him to discover his intentions stop would he serve again stop if so where stop end.*'

Since 1940 I had had complete confidence in those who had shouldered the task of fighting the war; political events had scarcely affected me. All of us in the network were like that. Only the final objective mattered. How could I become involved in this Giraud business? It was certainly not a question of suggesting to him that he should do intelligence work for the British. What then? What kind of service did the British expect of him? Political, undoubtedly.

It crossed my mind that Churchill wanted to set up a rival to de Gaulle. I put the suspicion aside. It was not my job to think; my job was to help General Giraud if he intended taking up the fight again. I remembered that Hitler had been mad with rage at Giraud's escape from the fortress of Koenigstein and had suspended the repatriation of our war prisoners. As the price of resuming it, he demanded that Giraud should surrender again. It was better to suggest that he should go to Britain.

The following day I told Eagle, who had come to Toulouse on a liaison visit, the conclusions I had come to about Giraud. He considered me very naïve. 'You're right off beam. If the Allies need Giraud it's for the North African landing. I learned to my cost that the African Army is not Gaullist —nor pro-British. A general from France would oil the wheels. Especially Giraud, who is so well known there. Can you imagine? The whole world would sit up.'

'Who would be the best man to contact him?'

'I have it! Saluki! He's coming to see me in Marseilles tomorrow.'

Saluki, the Duke of Magenta. His dash, his martial bearing, the secrecy with which he surrounded his activities, guaranteed success, at least of the part I was asked to play. I informed London.

Saluki found it fairly easy to meet Giraud, but the General was not so easy to persuade. He could not understand why Britain was interested in him. Since he was being asked what his intentions were, he declared that he had not the slightest wish to go to London, but that he was ready to become chief of the European Resistance if the British agreed to provide him with money and assistance and to put him in touch with the various Resistance chiefs in Europe.

I explored every conceivable way of handling this unusual matter. To become chief of the European Resistance! How could that be possible, somewhere in France? It was not all that easy then to be even a minor network chief in one's native land, and at this critical stage in the war I understood my British friends' mentality well enough not to send them a reply of this sort without generously sugaring the pill. But one thing seemed clear and all-important: even if the General's knowledge of underground work were as original as his ambitions, there was ample evidence of his eagerness to take a leading part in the fight against the Nazis.

I therefore sent Richards the following message: '*Giraud alias Degui repeat Degui thanks you for your interest in him stop Eagle repeat Eagle will be detailed to put authorities in picture about what can be done to help him stop Degui wishes for the moment to remain in France and play a leading role in Resistance stop please avoid all publicity on BBC stop end.*'

We had agreed with Richards that Eagle would pay a liaison visit to Britain as soon as the rebuilding of the networks would allow. In any case to do that we had to await the arrival of the expert who was to teach Mahout how to land and take off in a Lysander. This would mean a saving of several weeks in the Giraud affair, which might become clearer with time.

It was once more my turn to go to Marseilles where we were fortunately able to make useful contributions to the desert battle. A report from Giovaccini (Pelican) in Italy gave details of the flight timetables of important Italian squadrons being flown to reinforce the Afrika Korps–and this within the very same hour that Pelican had been able to observe the operation on the Turin airfield. My radio operator was at that moment transmitting to London, so he got the British to wait while I coded a message and the information went out at once. British Intelligence sent us warm congratulations and told us that the Italian planes had been intercepted, depriving Rommel of the air support he needed for his advance on Tobruk.

We were also thanked for Fox (Emile Audoly), who never missed a thing to do with the shipping that went in and out of Marseilles: German raiders sailing under neutral flags; consignments of arms and material loaded under French commercial labels and intended for the Afrika Korps; French tankers with which the Nazis tried to obtain oil from Roumania; torpedo-boats attempting to get to sea and spotted by Commandant Mahé watching the Rhone. (Fox's information was so 'hard' that the Royal Navy was redeployed on receipt of every message from him.)

I was able to return to Toulouse, and Tiger was waiting for me at the Clinique des Allées with Gorilla (Jean Lefevre). This time the defending counsel held out no hope for the members of our network in Fresnes prison. The two men handed me a message from Edmond Poulain, one that had been tucked away in the hem of some dirty linen. The microscopic block letters, jumbled together in groups of five, yielded their meaning: '*I shall certainly be condemned to death and I have only one request, save the girl I should have loved to be able to marry stop don't let anything happen to her stop I entrust her to you stop farewell.*'

Unable to utter a sound, I looked questioningly at Gorilla. 'She's here,' he said, 'I thought it better to bring her right away, she's so reckless, isn't she, Tiger?'

'Yes,' he agreed. 'Just imagine, she climbed up the trees to catch a glimpse of our friends at their cell windows and shouted to them to cheer them up. One day she managed to get right into the corridors of Fresnes to try to see them through the peep-holes.'

She came in, shy but determined, an exquisite picture with her long fair hair, her little cotton skirt and cork-soled shoes. She smiled at me. 'Look, madame, I agreed to come with your Gorilla so that I can serve under your orders. Whatever you do, don't send me into hiding,' she begged. 'Give me something to do, I must be on the same footing as the rest!'

'I don't doubt that, and you're going immediately to the Marseilles headquarters, where you're badly needed,' I said, impressed by such directness and integrity. 'We shall meet again soon. Your name will be Ermine.'

The time eventually came when Dr Charry considered that I could take my little girl away. She was now making very good progress. I rented a chalet in the Pyrenees where the entire family could come and spend the summer and I left her there in the care of my own relatives, never suspecting that I would not see her again for years. Perhaps her child's instinct sensed this, for I had literally to tear myself away from her tiny arms.

After making a minute inspection of all my sectors I finally got back to Marseilles. Faye was hard at work on the links with North Africa. At his request Pierre Bocher ('Nightingale' in our first phase) was working again on the liners. His trips between Marseilles and Algiers enabled us to maintain relations with our friends who had taken part in the abortive conspiracy of May 1941.

'Aren't you afraid we might be dispersing our forces rather too much, Eagle?' I asked.

'Everything's going like a house afire,' Eagle replied and he radiated such confidence that I caught his optimism.

The arrival of Henri-Léopold Dor (Fawn) made us change our minds. I had been expecting him for some days, feeling vaguely uneasy, and I was not altogether surprised when he turned up at the Corniche headquarters with his suit badly crumpled, his shirt anything but clean and his hair full of dirt and dust.

'You don't look as though you've just come from a sleeper, Fawn,' remarked Eagle.

'I haven't,' he snapped, looking rather shame-faced.

'And what about your magnificent *Ausweis*, which was going to make everything nice and easy?'

'How right you are. I had a lot of documents and I thought it wouldn't be very nice for Dad if I was caught with them on me. So I asked Tiger to smuggle me across the frontier in a market gardener's cart; but I had the *Ausweis* in my pocket,' he said triumphantly, 'and if I'd been caught in the cart, even with the *Ausweis*, it wouldn't have been the same thing. I could have kept Dad out of it!'

Eagle laughed. 'Let's have a look at the documents you've brought.'

Fawn swallowed hard again: 'They're mainly verbal.'

'What? You waste three days in a vegetable cart to bring what you call verbal documents, when all the time you've got a perfectly good *Ausweis* in your pocket. Never mind, now tell us!'

'The fact is,' he said, extremely embarrassed, 'I can only speak to Hedgehog on her own.'

Eagle leapt up in a fury. 'You mean I'm in the way?'

'Yes,' the unfortunate fellow spluttered. 'I'm very sorry, Commandant, but you placed me under the orders of Commandant Verteré, who told me to speak to Hedgehog and to Hedgehog only. It's a question of hierarchy.' He dropped into an armchair.

'Come, Fawn,' I said, taking him into the dining room. 'You need a drink. I think we've a little whisky left from the last lot parachuted.'

At last he brightened up and spoke. Fawn's story proved to be an odd one. Verteré (Hyena) no longer wanted to serve under Eagle's orders; being senior to Eagle, such a situation could not possibly last. He had information from Déat (Fawn handed it to me) but he begged me not to send it on to London, thinking it was shameful to betray the man who was acting as his cover. Had not the moment come, he finally suggested, to put himself under General de Gaulle's orders and leave the Intelligence service?

Through this melodrama, described with picturesque and colourful details by Fawn, I could see what I thought to be an intrigue taking shape. If Hyena was flattering me, was it not in order to get rid of Eagle more easily and then take over leadership of the organization? I recalled conversations I'd had with other agents serving under him. He was in no hurry to establish any radio link with London; he was half-hearted about military intelligence; he constantly talked politics, saying that he wanted to make contact with the Communists and other organizations, all in complete disregard of orders.

Worse was yet to come: the messenger (and a letter from Verteré confirmed this in veiled terms) then told me of the arrest of a certain Jean

1 Marie-Madeleine Fourcade at the time of these events

Georges Loustaunau-Lacau (*Navarre*)

Paul Bernard (*Swift*)

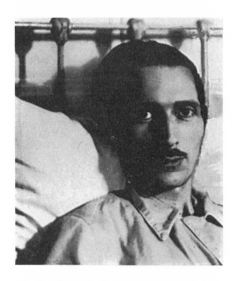

Maurice Coustenoble (*Tiger*)

Colonel Charles Bernis (*Spaniel*)

3

Jean Boutron (*Bull*)

Henry Schaerrer

Pierre Berthomier (*Seagull*)

Lucien Vallet

Gabriel Rivière (*Wolf*)

Jacques Stosskopf

Colonel Jean Carayon

Colonel Morraglia

Henri Freméndity (*Osprey*)

Jacques Bridou

Ernest Siegrist (*Elephant*)

Robert Philippe (*Parrot*)

Jeannie Rousseau (*Amniarix*)

Madeleine Crozet (*Mouse*)

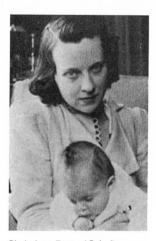

Christiane Battu (*Cricri*)

Michèle Goldschmidt
(*Hummingbird*)

Marguerite Brouillet (*Bee*)

Henriette Amable (*Tomboy*)

6

Colonel Edouard Kauffmann (*Cricket*)

Lieutenant Lucien Poulard (*Jack Tar*)

Maurice de MacMahon,
Duke of Magenta (*Saluki*)

Capitaine Helen des Isnards (*Grand Duke*)

General Camille Raynal (*Sheepdog*)

Admiral Pierre Barjot (*Pluto*)

The disguise created in England: Housewife 'Mme. Pezet'

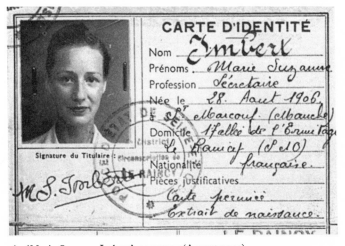

As 'Marie Suzanne Imbert', secretary (August 1944)

After her escape at Aix through
the 'bar of freedom'

From the Gestapo records

Joël Lemoigne (*Triton*)   Félix Cros (*Aurochs*)

Georges Lamarque (*Petrel*)   Dr Marcel Gilbert (*Toubib*)

Rousseau, who had recently been promoted head of the Lille sector.

'Who is this Jean Rousseau?'

'The cousin of one of Verteré's adjutants, an industrialist, but he knows Verteré personally, his address and his post boxes in Paris.'

'And Verteré has made no changes since learning of Rousseau's arrest?'

'None at all. He says the man's tough and won't talk.'

'Fawn, it's a strict rule. Even the walls can talk if they get into the hands of the Gestapo. You will go back tonight.'

When Eagle was told he flew into a rage. Hyena had turned into a 'treacherous viper', he averred, and I had the greatest difficulty in getting him to view the affair more calmly. Eventually, we handed Fawn a long reply in which we reminded Hyena of the promises he had deliberately made concerning the network and the British.

I still felt hopeful. One could not blame a man without any real experience in underground work for having had a moment of doubt in the terrible conditions of the occupied zone. I found Jean Rousseau's arrest in the forbidden zone much more disturbing. Hyena must clearly leave Paris as soon as possible and we invited him to come to Lyons to take over command of the eastern region. I had already chosen his successor—Saluki (the Duke of Magenta).

But Eagle was not to be placated; he thought these measures inadequate and wanted to take the train to Paris himself 'to raise Cain there'. It is undoubtedly what he ought to have done and I was quite wrong not to let him have his head.

The July moon brought us Crawley, alias Heron, who was dropped by parachute. He was the air liaison expert who was to teach us how to bring in and send off a Lysander at an emergency landing place. His arrival was marked by a sensational mishap. One of the three parachutes released that night failed to open and I thanked God that Heron was safe when I saw the mess of what had been the containers. The lucky young fellow was welcomed with open arms and put straight into the Avia crew, and I came and confirmed that his job would be to support Mahout (Lieutenant Dallas) in all operations.

What a leader of men our Mahout was! Besides housing the Avia headquarters, his little villa on the banks of the Saône was a veritable underground community. His very pretty wife, his two small sons—who took after their father—his sister, Marten, as brave as she was intelligent, lived there with the policeman Guillot's family. Called Dromedary because of his powers of endurance, Guillot had finally incorporated his wife into the network as a courier. As she was seen here, there and everywhere she was called Grasshopper. Arnold Gartner, the indomitable Zebra, had joined the crew, saying he preferred action to teaching.

Our pseudo-refugees were favourably viewed in the town where their sporting nature took the form of a real enthusiasm for cycling, camping and even canoeing, whatever the season.

'Why all these canoeing expenses, Mahout?' I asked, intrigued.

'It's a real brainwave. As most of our parachuting and landing sites are near rivers I ship our cargoes by canoe. If the operation causes an alarm *they* will always be able to close the roads, but *we* shall be well away.'

It was now a matter of distributing what was left of Heron's parachuted stuff. Robert Philippe, the ever-punctual Parrot, urged me to send as many transmitters as possible to the occupied zone. I had a volunteer for the job, a very young man who had already proved himself in a number of small jobs and was always eager to do any mission.

Robert Lynen, our French Jackie Cooper, had played the lead in the film *Poil de Carotte* and his face invariably expressed the spirit of the little boy that the author, Jules Renard, had imagined. I had given him the name Eaglet.

'It'll be my finest role,' he had said. 'Unlike the others, I'm lucky in being well known. I can go anywhere and everywhere. "Carrots", secret agent! People would hoot with laughter at the very idea. Let me take the radios. You'll see the value of an actor!'

Parrot let him have four transmitters and these were wrapped up in his stage wardrobe and smuggled out. What I did now know until later was that Eaglet, preferring to remain incognito, had borrowed the *Ausweis* of someone he had impersonated.

Nightingale, on the other hand, had got radios into Algiers and Tunis, but he had failed to link up with London and was urgently demanding additional wavelengths. Hence the appearance of Louis Jacquinot, who had come to the Corniche headquarters to see whether we could give him a mission in North Africa, where he was going for professional reasons.

'Our missions are a bit risky, Minister, but I can lend you my suitcase with a false bottom if you agree to take two sets of crystals, operational plans and a fairly large sum of money as well.'

Louis Jacquinot (Tiger-Cat) had acted as counsel in all the Resistance cases in the free zone, but he replied that he was perfectly willing to appear in the dock instead. While I sewed back, saddler fashion, the skilfully filled lining of the best suitcase of its type I had ever seen, Eagle gave the minister-turned-smuggler his instructions. Thanks to the contacts he made, Colonel Bouscat, 'Maxime', who was later to become the head of the Air Force in the Provisional Government, agreed to command our Algiers network.

In Tunisia, however, the situation was anything but certain. German secret agents were going there in large numbers, which made our people's work much more hazardous. Why were they going there? Something was undoubtedly brewing.

I resumed my inspection of the sectors, and when I returned from one of these larks early in the morning of 22 July, and got off the train at Marseilles, I found our agents unusually active. There were some at every barrier. Eagle, who was directing the exercise, was the first to spot me and seized my luggage. A car was waiting for us, its engine running.

'Quickly! To the headquarters!' he shouted to Jassaud, who drove off at great speed.

Eagle screwed up his eyes. In his case it was a sign of great tension: 'They're after you again,' he told me. 'And this time the Boches are handling the job. In Paris they're going round to all your relatives. The Gestapo have been to see your old friend, Henri Champin. They raised merry hell, said you were another Mata Hari and that they were putting a price on your head.'

'What's the danger from the Boches in Marseilles?'

'Greater than you think. The Germans have complained to Laval about the number of secret transmitters operating in the free zone, draining information from the occupied zone and smashing up their convoys. In flagrant violation of the armistice, they've obtained permission for their agents to drive about disguised as French policemen in cars with direction-finding equipment. They use this cover primarily to carry out personal investigations and to kidnap people.'

'Good. The main thing is to see that our sets are not located. Have you sent out any orders?'

'Sure! Maximum sixty groups. Maximum transmission time twenty minutes. And to change frequency during transmission. And *you* must just disappear.'

'Not on your life! I certainly don't regard myself as Mata Hari!'

'I'm leaving for London in a few days. If you're caught in the meantime I can't possibly go.'

It was a convincing argument, but where was I to go? 'I've got it all fixed up,' he said. 'They won't get you.'

Odette Fabius, the smiling Doe, came to pick me up in a car two days later. I looked forward to the drive; it would allow us to get to know one another much better.

We were approaching Saint-Clair de Lavandou, a small seaside place among the wooded, rocky headlands of the Riviera. Here a woman friend whom I could trust completely was waiting for us. Maritou Brouillet (Bee), a slim, dark, laughing young woman with huge green eyes and regular features, took us into her tiny, cool, clean house, where her two teenage sons, Jean-Claude and Michel, were companions, aides and runners rolled into one.

'You can never ask enough of me,' she said suddenly, 'nor of my sons either.'

The two boys hustled us down to the sea where we were able to wallow at leisure, trying to forget everything else. Neither the brilliant sunset and scented pinewoods, nor the smell of fish soup drifting down to us from the big pot wedged in its bed of shells and glowing vine shoots could, however, ease the sadness in my heart. I was spending these first 'holidays' since the war without my children—thanks to the Gestapo's kind attentions.

Saint-Clair de Lavandou rapidly became a good withdrawal centre. We made a number of devoted friends whose help proved inexhaustible: Dr Lacapère, known as Dolphin, an outstanding doctor as well as a scholar; Ulysse Richard (Lobster) the schoolmaster who had been badly disabled in the 1914–18 war, and his wife and daughter; Lieutenant-Colonel Lucien Pinault (Dorado) and his shock troops, workmen and local winegrowers. I sent for my brother to come and take over the secretarial side of things. Couriers guaranteed daily links with Marseilles. Bee was living in a seventh heaven, and her sons strained every nerve to be like the grown-ups. Who would have dreamed that a very different sort of play would shortly be enacted in this peaceful spot!

There were many things to be arranged with Eagle before his departure for London and he came to fetch me. He had a surprise. In the compartment in the Blue Train into which he helped me at Toulon I found myself face to face with Saluki and his wife. I had known him since the thirties, when, an elegant and dashing bachelor haloed with citations and titles, he was famous for his aerobatics and his original behaviour.

And his wife! A miracle of grace—tall, willowy and radiant: she was born a princess and she looked a princess in her every movement, in her smile, in everything she did. I immediately called her Firefly.

This exceptional couple could have lived on the fringe of the storm. Instead of which I heard them laugh about the tricks they were always playing on the Gestapo, and Saluki longed to do even more. Of course, the proposal to replace Verteré as head of the network in the occupied zone suited him down to the ground.

The two airmen then plunged into a veritable orgy of planning. The Duchess, Saluki's wife, blessed with that sense of humour that naturally criticizes the most brilliant ideas, quickly joined with me in censuring their zeal.

The hour it took to get to Marseilles passed in a flash, but I arrived feeling easy in my mind because the Intelligence Army was clearly fighting fit.

12 SQUALLS

Now that she was our accomplice, the moon's only significance lay in marking our air operations. We could never imagine her as the moon that looked down on lovers gliding in gondolas along Venetian canals. The August moon brought a parachute drop and our first Lysander landing.

Armadillo (Michel Gaveau), the military intelligence expert, came down without mishap in the fields beside the Saône. He was to relieve me of the burden I had borne single-handed for such a long time—sorting out the reports coming in from all over France and selecting urgent information for transmission by radio. This landing operation involved our first use of the Thalamy field near Ussel, and it whisked Eagle away as though by magic. The following morning the BBC broadcast a prearranged sentence that told us that Eagle was at that moment walking in the streets of London.

It was no longer possible for me to go back to Le Lavandou as planned, because a serious hazard had just arisen to upset the course on which I was set. It occurred in connection with one of our channels of communication with Spain. As the growing needs of the organization had exhausted the Bishop's (Mesnard's) monetary reserves, I had three of the four million francs deposited in Barcelona sent to France. Fox thought that no risk was involved in shipping this money. The vessel chosen, the SS *Saint-Brieuc*, and her skipper had been employed several times already by Jules Gony, who brought our mail. No check had ever been carried out at the customs in the port of Sète, but for greater safety Gony was to leave the *Saint-Brieuc* with only one million on him, leaving the other two millions on board. We were thus in a position to salvage something in the very improbable event of a disaster.

But nothing is improbable. Gony found the police waiting on the quayside and he was immediately put under lock and key and the million francs impounded.

'He has been betrayed,' I said, white with anger, to poor Fox.

'His son believes he was followed in Barcelona and a tip-off sent by telegram. The only thing I can do now is to go on board and look for the rest,' he concluded woefully.

It was dangerous, but he came back looking even more crestfallen than the night before. 'The swine,' he muttered, 'that swine of a skipper has done us. When I asked for the parcel Gony had given him to look after before coming ashore, he growled threateningly: "The unfortunate thing is that I threw it into the furnace, as I was afraid of being searched, *d'you understand?*"'

'And what if it had been dynamite?' was all that Fox could reply as he came back down the gangway. Since he had robbed us and as we could not take him to court, rather than hand us over to the police this rogue would prefer to digest his little haul, we thought.

The Bishop, whom I had alerted, exploded: 'How are the sectors going to manage? How are our people going to live?'

Together with our paymaster I had worked out a scheme which laid down a scale to cover the pay and other requirements of the various sectors. Rates of pay were equivalent to those of the army in the field. In addition, expenses, travelling, rent, unforeseen purchases, were reimbursed if justified. The only general worry was having enough money to carry on.

'That's not all,' the Bishop went on, 'it's the consequences! I've been wanting to talk to you about it for a long time. They're cashing in on it. They're trying to pinch our specialists and are offering them as much as 10,000 francs a month!'

'They' were the escape routes, networks, movements of every conceivable shade, and the embryonic secret armies that were springing up.

'It can't be helped, Bishop. I shan't change our system in any way. Those whose idea is to get rich are welcome to go elsewhere and act the gangster; there's no place for them in a military network. Let them go.'

'It's our radio operators I'm afraid of. They're the ones most in demand.'

'Come now, Bishop. They love their job, it's a vocation. They don't give a damn for money.'

'You're wrong there. Canary has taken those 10,000 francs and chucked us up. If he were to be captured in his new organization. . . .'

Jeanne Berthomier was as beautiful and graceful as a seamew and that was the name I gave her. She arrived one evening at the Corniche headquarters where, since Eagle's departure, I barricaded myself in at night with Denise Centore, the brilliant Sable, my secretary, and Ermine, the young girl coming from the Paris patrol, who now acted as my personal courier. Taking her cloak off with evident relief, Seamew immediately began to undo the stitching in order to extract some closely typewritten sheets of paper.

'Terrific!' she said enthusiastically, rumpling the gossamer-like tissue in her hands. 'The grey mice ran their hands over me at the demarcation line. You can't feel a thing, it's like silk. I wish them luck!'

'And then there's this,' said Sable, 'a scrap of paper with an azymous paste base that melts in the mouth like an eclair.'

'And you don't yet know the latest model,' interrupted Ermine, applying her cigarette lightly to a rectangle that went up in a flash.

'As for me,' I said, still sore about the Tarbes archives affair, 'I roll them all into tiny balls. You can search anywhere you like, they're impossible to find.'

Seamew was the sister of Seagull (Pierre Berthomier), head of the Air-Bleu air link. As a civil servant in the Ministry of Public Works in Paris she had access to top secret information. That evening she brought me excellent news of the capital, where Saluki had taken command as planned. Hyena (Verteré) hung on in Paris and even tried to entice our agents away from us, but the radio circuit was no longer at his disposal and our men indignantly refused to follow him. Hyena had a perfect right to seek to create a network of his own. What was more serious was the fact that he had in no way modified his habits since Jean Rousseau's arrest in Lille in the forbidden zone and that he continued to see some of our people.

Nor had all hope disappeared in the north, Seamew confirmed. Due to his admirable recruits, Tiger, with his usual energy, was busy making his region one of the best in the whole network.

While passing through her native Cusset, Seamew had seen Sheepdog (General Raynal), whose sector was fully operational, thanks to Gulliver. He wanted to send me as direct attachments two men whom he considered would be best able to organize a real naval intelligence service: a certain Joël Lemoigne, who could do something I had always dreamed of—reeling off, with their numbers, all the enemy vessels stationed in our ports—and a certain Maurice Gillet, an ideal sector leader, particularly for Brest. We must put him in urgent contact with Jack Tar (Lucien Poulard) at that moment in Brittany.

We spent the night making sure that everything was properly tied up. Not one of us seemed to notice how much the women's role in life had changed.

Determined not to be outdone by her friends who were detained in Fresnes, Ermine was, without my knowledge, getting herself sent on missions she should never have undertaken. Afterwards she would say to me, in her innocent way: 'Hedgehog, I must! Those poor boys are so tired! And so from time to time I stand in for them.' Her escapades meant that she saw many more people than I did.

For some time now she had been mentioning a young man who was hiding with our friend Dr Claude Zimmern, a Jewish refugee living in Marseilles with his family. We often used the doctor's villa for transmitting messages and he also supplied me with first-class information about the bombing raids on Normandy. One day he decided to introduce his own secret agent to me. This agent was a very young boy who had made for London in a sail boat as soon as war broke out. After having gone through all the preparatory courses in training for secret warfare, he had been parachuted over the Dordogne, but not at the right place. As all villages and farms look more or less alike, he had confidently made his jump over what looked to him most like the description he had learned by heart.

The reception he met with from growling dogs and hostile faces made him beat a retreat. Forced to abandon the case containing his transmitter, he owed his escape solely to an agility acquired in a youth devoted to every kind of sport. He was a strange creature. The ease with which he moved and carried on an intelligent, well-informed conversation proved he was a cut above the usual run of recruits. He always affected a nonchalance and a simplicity of manner that were too simple to be true, and he obviously wanted to be taken for something that he was not. I did not ask what he was, convinced that I was dealing with an exceptional person. This discretion on my part seemed to please him. He suggested that, under my orders, he should carry out the mission he had undertaken on behalf of the BCRA, the Central Office for Intelligence and Sabotage, de Gaulle's intelligence services.

This was the first time I had heard the department mentioned by someone who had come from it. Since the days of the nebulous organization that Captain Fourcaud had known after the fall of France, great progress had been made across the Channel; but my interlocutor had not been able, after his arrival in France, to contact anyone in the service who might enable him to resume his mission.

'Employ me,' he urged. 'I'm a radio operator. I've been trained to gather naval intelligence. Send me where I ought to have been for months; to the Atlantic coast.'

I was dubious about taking on an agent who was not intended for me. Nevertheless, British Intelligence confirmed his story and declared they were delighted that I had found him when he had been given up as lost. And so, all my doubts dispelled, I sent him with a delightful lad, known as Poodle, as his escort, to Sarlat, so that Colonel Kauffmann (Cricket) could install him as leader of the Bordeaux-La Rochelle sector.

Though I thought he looked like a Little Lord Fauntleroy, we called him Mandrill because, he said grimacing, he loved that sort of monkey 'with its blue, white and red face.' Mandrill's arrival at his post produced real trouble for U-boats.

Before Eagle's return, which I suspected would cause quite a stir, I wanted to create a withdrawal centre near Marseilles. Why not Avignon? That aristocratic city is the key to the south of France. That key was missing from my interlocking organization. So I had arranged to meet Hubert Fourcade there. He travelled from Paris and I found him waiting for me under the ramparts.

We had heard about one another through a friend, and I had been told he wanted to serve. I knew that he was reliable, but how was I to ask him point-blank to take command of a headquarters? He spoke first:

'I've always felt the greatest admiration for you, especially when I heard you were not just standing passively by in the present situation. I find it disconcerting to think that it's *you* who are going to help me. . . . Let me come straight to the point. I can't stand this Hitlerite France any more. Get this clear, Marie-Madeleine, I feel a physical and moral need to seek revenge by fighting.'

My castle in Avignon was crumbling. 'You . . . you want to leave?' I asked.

'I thought you were in the picture,' he exclaimed in alarm. 'I was told you had escape routes.'

'It's not exactly my line,' I said, mastering my disappointment. 'Escape routes are only a sideline. I'm the head of an intelligence network.'

His dark eyes lit up: 'How I wish I could help you! I envy you, but I'm not made for that sort of thing. I feel a real call to a different sort of struggle and if I didn't follow it I shouldn't feel I deserved a future.'

'You really want to get to Britain?'

'I want to join de Gaulle. He alone is right. All Frenchmen of my age should be with him. I'm still sick with disappointment that I couldn't fight before 1940. I was finishing my military service in Marrakesh when war broke out. My comrades and I had to stand by and watch the fall of France. I had the luck to be directly under Colonel Monclar's and Captain Koenig's orders and those two are now fighting in Africa with de Gaulle. I can't possibly wait another minute.'

'I'll help you,' I said.

'I'm not going alone,' he quickly pointed out. 'I've promised to fix it for several friends.'

'That's going to complicate things. The Lysanders can take only one passenger at a time . . . but I do have a number of assembly points for getting to Spain.'

He looked at me as though I were a fairy who could change pumpkins into airplanes. 'I'm a swine,' he said suddenly. 'Compared with what you're doing my personal worries are simply nothing. Thank you for the offer but I'd die rather than compromise your work. Instead, is there anything *I* can do for *you* before I leave France?'

'Nothing,' I replied sadly. 'I must go back again immediately.'

'You can't do that. I've been lent a car and we're going to lunch at the Prieure.'

He took me firmly by the hand and led me away. There was no longer any need to talk to him about my agonizing mission. For once I forgot my obsession with the underground struggle. We talked about ourselves, our hopes, the desperate plight of France that we both loved with the same deep love, and the uncertain future that lay ahead for both of us.

When he was taking me back to catch the night train he finally said: 'If you were thinking that I could join the network. . . .'

'Goodbye, Hubert,' I said hurriedly. 'Follow your conscience. Join de Gaulle.'

He pressed my hand in his. 'Wherever I am, Marie-Madeleine, you can always call on me. I'm sure we shall meet again.'

I ran off into the night to catch my train, which was already on the move. I did not know then that this was the man I would marry after the war.

Superintendent Théus of the Surveillance du Territoire, muffled up in the big scarf that he abandoned only during the summer, put his hand to his mouth and gave a little cough. The young man who had been brought to him, caught red-handed making a clandestine broadcast, stood before him signing a confession concerning the Pat O'Leary escape network, whose existence Théus had never suspected. Having divulged everything when he was asked nothing, he merely inspired Théus' disgust.

'Guards, you can remove the prisoner,' Théus said wearily.

No doubt mistaking the significance of the superintendent's contemptuous tone of voice, the handcuffed young man turned round slowly and said: 'That isn't all. I should like to add something.'

'Enough, enough,' coughed Théus, 'I'll hear you some other time.'

'No, no; now, at once.'

The superintendent looked up. He was not sure of all his staff and he dared not compromise the underground activities he was engaged in at the very heart of the police force by too overt an attitude. He had been given orders by his network to stay as long as possible in his job, where he was in a position to give the greatest service, so if this idiot insisted. . . .

'What I have omitted to tell you,' the traitor went on, 'is that I previously worked as a radio operator in a military intelligence network. My alias was Canary. . . .'

The radiant summer was fading; early mists heralded the approach of autumn and plunged us into a state of anxiety: Eagle's return was planned for the full moon. Preferring not to use the Thalamy landing ground for two successive operations, the RAF had chosen the one used by the Avia crew on the banks of the Rhone. With the nights getting longer, it could still be used despite its remoteness from base. Our second Lysander landing—Operation Vesta—was fixed for 11 September.

Jean Boutron, nicknamed Bull in memory of Madrid, was due to go back with the plane. He had finally been rescued from his fortress when our agents had inoculated him with a disease he did not have, necessitating his transfer to hospital, from which escape was easier. As I was keen to repay him with interest for my journey in the mailbag, I had had him driven to a place not far from the landing ground, where he was to lie low in an inn, waiting until it was time to go.

I had gone over the details of Operation Vesta with Mahout (Dallas) a hundred times. Now began the depressing nights spent in waiting, nights in which hope alternated with frantic anxiety. Would the Lysander come? Even when its departure had been announced, it might still turn back. It might also disappear with all hands, blown to pieces by anti-aircraft fire. The Avia team might be captured. They had gone to earth in the surrounding countryside, on the alert for a police raid, hampered by their passenger and the bags of mail they had to lug about on the landing ground for several days and forced to maintain a permanent radio watch.

On the evening of the 11th Mahout phoned to say that the plane was leaving in spite of the foul weather conditions—rain and cloud. On 12 September there was no news. And on 13 September Mahout informed me that the team had waited in vain. I myself had radio contact only in the late afternoon and I spent a grim day, imagining the worst, looking out for the liaison agent who would bring me the message that would confirm Eagle's fate.

Rivière (Wolf) appeared. His bleak look was like a blow: 'I must tell you at once,' he began, weighing his words, 'that we shan't have any radio contact tonight. Wolf thought it wiser to send out a general alert. Fox has been arrested.'

'Wolf, do you think they'll stop at that?' I asked.

'Chief! Of all of us Fox is the one who is most worried at the prospect of imprisonment. Trust him, he'll see that he covers up all traces.'

'Have you any suspicions, Wolf?'

'Hell! Not suspicions, proof! It was Canary who betrayed him. . . .'

'Canary!' I nearly fainted. Canary had not been recruited locally. He was the son of the best agent in Boulogne and it was Robert Philippe (Parrot), our chief radio operator, who had brought him to Marseilles.

The Bishop was right: a boy leaves you to earn more, then he sells you. And it meant that the entire central organization of the radio network was threatened—not to mention the collapse of Audoly's sector. I pulled myself together. The gaps must be filled. 'Can you take over from Fox?' I asked Wolf.

He waved his big hands. 'Fox left everything in perfect order for taking over. Cobra, his secretary, is fully in the picture. Michel the Sailor knows all the dockers and I know the other sources in the port of Marseilles. All we have to do is to continue along the same lines.'

We concentrated our attention on the problem of regaining control of the sector and the threat to Parrot and his radio headquarters, which must be moved.

Suddenly Wolf exclaimed: 'What with all this shemozzle, I was forgetting. . . . The Avia crew have had news of Eagle.'

Eagle's plane, which had left Chichester on the night of 11 September, had been forced to turn back because of bad weather. On the return flight to England they had suddenly found themselves being tailed by a German fighter! The German pilot could have shot them down with a touch of his finger, but he did not open fire. Apparently he mistook the queer-looking British plane, unarmed except for what looked like a torpedo slung under the fuselage, though it was really the extra petrol tank, for a German plane of some strange new type.

Immediately on landing, Eagle asked to be flown to France again that very night. It was impossible—the weather forecast was foul. By the time it had improved sufficiently the September moon was lost. They would have to await the next moon.

From the headquarters observation post I followed the squalls spattering the sea with broad iridescent stains. The mistral whipped the Corniche into an ocean of dust. I caught sight of Sable, who was finding it difficult to get off the trolley-car. I slipped on a coat and went out to meet her.

'Parrot's here. He's just escaped, I've got him hidden in my house,' she said, panic in her voice.

'Good, I'll follow you. Go on back.'

Slumped in an armchair and washing a mouthful of sandwich down with a swig of beer, Parrot was methodically polishing off the food that Sable had put at the disposal of his legendary appetite. We looked at one another in silence, he chewing and swallowing hard, I thinking of this man's tremendous achievement since 1940. They weren't going to take him from me, and I told him so.

'Chief, you're a real tonic. And so's this,' he added, turning to Sable with a look of infinite gratitude.

'What happened?' I asked him.

'Well, it was like this. I was doing a spot of work at the Vichy state radio—must put in an appearance there from time to time. Some inspectors from the Surveillance du Territoire came for me. Nothing I could do but go along. I was told I was a dangerous terrorist, that my wife was under arrest, as well as a certain Fox. If I wanted to be free again I had only to give them the low-down on the network I belonged to.'

'Did they find anything on you?'

'Not a thing, but they thought they were on to a real scoop. Then I put paid to their chances of learning any more. For one moment I was left on my own in the room where I was being interrogated. I didn't stop to think twice. I jumped out of the window and ran like mad back home. I was shaking with anxiety—I always kept a transmitter and a case full of crystals and spare parts there. If you could only have seen me. I didn't waste any time. I got everything packed up in five minutes and left again, still running, carrying the cases.'

'It's marvellous to have saved the equipment, but what if you'd been recaptured in your own house?'

'Even in a car they wouldn't be able to go faster than me. My legs are still shaking like a jelly. Anyhow the equipment was the really important thing. It takes too much trouble getting it. Who spilled the beans?'

'Canary. Since they have nothing to go on except that rat's word, the whole business might easily just peter out. They might simply be released.'

'I only hope you're right. I feel I'm going to be able to sleep at last.'

I had no such feelings. This business worried me deeply. Since Laval's return as Pétain's heir-apparent, Rollin no longer possessed any real influence and I felt Vichy's claws once more menacing the network.

Thanks to my brother-in-law George-Picot's insistence that all the police dossiers on the Gavarni affair be burned, there was, to my intense relief, no longer any trace in Vichy of our past, but I remembered Rollin's remarks about the parallel police. I knew that we should not be let off the hook that quickly and that the slightest thing would spark off their viciousness again with even greater violence. I felt I was sitting on a gunpowder barrel. And with Eagle's return delayed until the next moon, I was also going to find myself without a penny.

With an improvement in the weather on 20 September, Eagle's plane took off when night fell, and as they approached the coast of Normandy the moon appeared from behind the veil of cloud. The coast crossing went off without incident, and the plane continued on its south-westerly course. Suddenly, a number of searchlights caught it in their beams. The pilot veered away, reduced speed and dived towards the ground. The searchlights swept the sky in an attempt to pick him up, then went out one by one.

Above the bends along the broad river Loire the sky clouded over again and the machine flew low in almost pitch darkness. Only a few gleams here and there revealed the ground, and villages, trees and streams appeared only to disappear again in a flash. They now soared above the Morvan mountains, then over the mountains of the Lyonnais—a dramatic way to see things, for the plane flew lower than the mountain ridges that were no more than vague outlines in the clouds. What a pilot! He cut down towards the Saône, flying close to the ground in lashing rain. Thick mist covered everything and he was compelled to bank.

At last a feature on the river told them they were very near the rendezvous and without a moment's hesitation the pilot circled at ground level. As Eagle feared, there was no light signal to indicate the men's presence. Trees, roads, fields spun in a terrifying merry-go-round under the plane's wing. The pilot never faltered; he continued to circle.

Suddenly, from across the Rhone, jerking flashlight beams betrayed the panic felt by the men who held them. But it was the recognition letter that had been agreed on for operation Vesta: 'A' for the ground. 'W' replied the plane, blinking its landing lights. The Lysander dropped into the blackness and Eagle, now unable to see a thing, felt they were taking a horribly long time to reach target. At last they were there; the engine was just ticking over when they could see the flashlights forming an isosceles triangle. The plane touched down on the sodden ground that the rain made heavier every minute.

The pilot turned to get into position to take off, when suddenly a wheel sank axle-deep and the Lysander tipped over on its right wing. Revving hard, the pilot tried in vain to free the plane. The din was tremendous. Leaping to the ground, Eagle signed to the pilot to cut out. He pulled his cases and his bags out and handed them to the Avia team who had gathered round the stricken plane.

Mahout had gone to the rendezvous only because he was conscientious. How could anyone imagine that the operation would be carried out in such appalling weather? He had left Bull—due to go to England in the plane—at the inn, but the mail was there and it was loaded on board. The rain pelted down. The pilot insisted on starting back at once. He climbed into his seat, restarted the engine and gave it full throttle. Using their hands, Eagle and his men dug a furrow in front of the wheel, but as there were only four of them they had little hope of success. Then, in a desperate effort, they clung to the fuselage; this did the trick and the Lysander heaved itself out of the rut. Letting the engine race so as not to lose impetus, the pilot raised his plane into the storm.

One, two, five seconds. The throbbing that continued above their heads gave the poor fellows new hope as they stood there exhausted, drenched and covered with mud from head to foot. They dragged themselves towards Mahout's famous canoes, stooping under the weight of the baggage and thinking less about their own plight than about the pilot flying back to base, his sole companion the inconstant moon.

Mahout laid two large and muddy suitcases at my feet with the gentleness of a nurse.

'Operation Vesta was fifty per cent successful,' was his sober comment. Bull was still out on the job. Eagle arrived by the next trolley-car.

'Well! I've got what you wanted,' Eagle announced gleefully, hurling himself on the suitcases, flicking open the locks and tearing at the envelopes that spilled out onto the floor. 'Here are two large bundles. The network will get the same amount every month and, on request, as much equipment as we need will be parachuted. As for specialist reinforcements, I saw the radio operator who's coming at the next moon. He's fine: simple and direct and speaks French without a trace of accent. I've called him Magpie. The British reckon he's the best man they've got.'

I stood speechless. Like Navarre in Lisbon, like myself in Madrid, Eagle had completely succeeded in London. There was nothing like direct contact.

'So Madame's not pleased?' he asked, worried by my silence.

'Eagle, look at these questionnaires, they're done as microphotos! What a tremendous advance!' I replied stupidly.

He looked at me out of the corner of his eye. We both burst out laughing.

'I see your imagination has run away with you again. When will you stop worrying for no reason?'

'Wait till you understand the reason!' I retorted. 'Did you see Richards?'

'Yes, and lots of other people,' he replied importantly. 'I could see how highly British Intelligence regards our network.'

Mastiff brought in Saluki (the Duke of Magenta) and his wife. On hearing the news, they had hurried over with armfuls of their superb white burgundy.

'I hope you've got something for General Giraud,' Saluki said at once.

'It wasn't as easy as he imagines! Giraud's ambition to become the head of Resistance in Europe knocked the British flat.'

'I thought it would,' I said. 'What did they expect?'

'That he would go to London. When I got there neither Churchill nor de Gaulle was in London. . . .'

Firefly, the Duchess of Magenta, and I looked anxiously at one another. 'You had the nerve to ask for them directly?'

'Of course. Anyway, de Gaulle was somewhere between Cairo and Beirut, Churchill was in Moscow, and I immediately got a very definite impression that the Giraud problem would not be solved in their absence, especially without some quid pro quo.'

'That's dreadful. Our Army comrades will be shattered.'

'Don't forget, I pleaded their cause, Saluki. I told the British that it was quite wrong to drop all the people who wanted to fight. I went on about it so much that our allies did something. Fortunately for General Giraud my early setback didn't last. While I was champing at the bit, Churchill, who had returned to London, sent to say that the Giraud affair interested him. One of the British Intelligence chiefs, whose home I went to a lot, sent his expert down to the airfield with a message to say that Giraud can count on the Allies' full support. Saluki, you'll inform him, but in return you'll ask him to send us a memorandum.'

'Then they mean to help him in France? And so your theory that the Allies needed him to back a landing in North Africa was wrong,' I said, disappointed.

'Not as wrong as all that,' Eagle murmured under his breath. 'I'm terribly thirsty,' he added hastily. I did not pursue the matter.

'We must drink to your health, old chap,' said Saluki, opening one of his delicious bottles. 'You've done a damned good job. What's it like in London?'

After a pleasant hour or two spent listening to his account of wartime London, which gave us a comforting picture of a country that had remained resolute and relatively normal, Saluki and Firefly, carrying a large sum of money for the occupied zone, hurried off to solve their problems and left us to ours.

'Eagle, why were you so cagey when I spoke to you about the landing in North Africa?'

'Because I was asked to say absolutely nothing about it, except to you. Churchill is using all his powers of persuasion to get the Americans to make a landing. I have a very definite impression that the thing has been agreed. All the evidence goes to suggest that the liberation of Europe can be launched only from two platforms. The British Isles is too vulnerable on its own. And so a second platform must be created to get the enemy on the run on two fronts.'

'In a word, the obsession you've had for so long is becoming a reality. Well, it's about time! The day after you left for London, on 19 August, a second commando came to test the cliffs at Dieppe.'

'It was wiped out.'

'Alas! But what a splendid opportunity for the Vichyists to push collaboration to the limit. Sheepdog's latest reports are revealing: bogged down by his Russian and African campaigns, Hitler is thinking more and more of using Pétain's armistice army to cover the Atlantic front.'

'Defend France side by side with the Nazis! That would be abominable!'

'It's almost come to that, Eagle! Sheepdog (General Raynal) has just informed me that after the Dieppe affair Pétain sent Hitler a telegram proposing that "France should contribute towards the safeguarding of Europe." In other words, if the Allies land the French will receive orders to fire on them.'

'You've radioed to let London know?'

'No, Eagle, I was too ashamed.'

The Corniche headquarters had served its turn and I was lucky enough to discover a huge villa, called La Pinède, that was situated in the hilly part of Marseilles and surrounded by gardens. It was not a long tram journey to the centre of the city and we would at least be spared the risk of indiscreet neighbours. The owner's name was M. Giraud, a coincidence that augured well.

I got Bee to come and she completed the tenancy formalities on our behalf and then moved in with her elder son, Jean-Claude. Then she brought in her 'family', that is to say Eagle, myself and Ermine. 'Cousins' who had fled as refugees to the free zone constantly visited her under M. Giraud's compassionate eye. If he had only known what they were doing!

On the ground floor a drawing room had been turned into a general office for the secretaries. My brother and a new operator, André Liess (Stork), for radio messages, and Elephant (Siegrist), dealing with identity cards, spent their whole time writing. A chest of drawers filled with revolvers and sten guns inspired a confidence that I personally considered very relative.

On the first floor was Eagle's office, where there was an impressive array of transmitters, of which one, perhaps the only one of its kind in France, could transmit in duplicate on two different wavelengths at the same time. It had been built by our experts from all sorts of odd bits and pieces. My old KVL 2 was used for our staff traffic and the third was used for internal listening.

Internal listening was an idea of Eagle's, with which I disagreed. He thought that the sector leaders often moved liaison agents for no particular reason when a single radio message would avoid the dangers involved in their comings and goings.

My brother, who had a small fine, neat, monkish handwriting, had been asked to write out on a single sheet of paper all the details of the sets in the network: names, call signs, answering signs for the central station, wave-length details and operating schedules. He had covered a whole sheet, which remained permanently on the listening table where Stork and Tringa worked shift and shift about to pick up the transmissions put out by the sectors that might also contain a message intended for us. There were two other transmitters in the town.

A house a few hundred yards away from ours was rented for Alligator, Capitaine Crémieu of the French Air Force, the new head of the HQ intelligence unit, who had Armadillo and Sable under his orders. He had gone to live there with his entire family, a genuine one, which he reckoned was the best kind of cover—and the most original. In the rooms, where the walls were covered with maps that made a brilliant sight with their many-coloured flags and where the tables were strewn with photographs and typewritten reports, you would come across toddlers perching on their pots or eating some sort of mush from a spoon that Alligator now and again pushed at them while dictating the most terrifying operational orders.

Nevertheless, we had kept the Corniche headquarters open, leaving Mastiff there as watch-dog.

13 *THE FASCIST*

One morning, when I had thought Eagle was out on a tour of inspection, I saw him running breathless into the villa La Pinède.

'Bla's in Marseilles!' he gasped.

'Who told you?'

'Heron. They bumped into one another at the station. They were together at the radio operator school in London and Bla recognized him at once. Delighted to see him again, he explained that the organization to which British Intelligence had attached him and which was run by a woman had been smashed, that he himself had just escaped being arrested by the Gestapo, that he had lost his transmitter and was wandering about without a penny in his pocket looking for another organization. Heron kept his head and arranged to meet him this afternoon in a bar in the Rue de Paradise.

'I shall go.'

'No, you must not. He knows you. This is what I plan to do.'

When Heron (the Englishman, Crawley) walked into the little bar he saw at once that Bla was waiting for him. They had a drink together and exchanged a few commonplaces. After making sure the man was really alone, Heron invited him to go outside and there began to explain that the head of his network would like to meet him.

Two policemen in khaki-coloured raincoats, their hats pulled down over their faces, came up to check their identity. Heron objected violently but Bla agreed. He handed them his real identity card giving his true name, his address in Paris, and nationality as a British subject.

'That's odd, sir,' one of the policemen said. 'Will you be good enough to come with us. A British subject living in Paris; that needs checking.'

Heron raised further objections. 'Shut up,' whispered Bla, 'you'll see, it'll be cleared up in no time.'

In the car into which they were bundled he gave the police a small piece of paper on which an address was scribbled. 'You've only to phone there and you'll soon find that everything's all right.' It was the address of a shady German office.

The driver skirted the Old Port, climbed up on to the Corniche, skidded round the corners and came to No. 355. The car stopped. One of the policemen got out, then came back in rather a bad temper.

'These office types are all the same. They've gone out to lunch and locked the door,' he said to his colleague, jerking his head in the direction of the nearest cafe.

The other policeman set off at a gallop while Bla chatted to Heron. He was not surprised by the appearance of the building; he knew that the Surveillance du Territoire used middle class flats, but rushing back with the key the inspector pushed him into a dark entrance hall on the right of the ground floor. The door closed.

'We've got you at last, Bla,' roared Eagle, giving him a tremendous blow.

'You've made a mistake. I don't know you,' the other whimpered, peering hard because his glasses had been smashed.

It had been agreed that I should not appear, that it should be settled man to man, but that first it was vital to extract from the traitor the maximum amount of information about the arrest of the Paris patrols. I did not expect to see Eagle return until late that night, but I was worried to death. This act of violence in the heart of Marseilles would undoubtedly turn out badly.

'Oh no, it won't,' Ermine said in a calm voice. 'With Beaver sitting beside him and Bison at the wheel we can be easy in our minds. If he moves,' she added fiercely, 'they'll shoot him and scram.'

The front door shut with a bang and made us jump. 'It's done,' said Eagle. 'Quickly, give me a drink. Don't look at me like that.'

His face lost its strained look. 'What has happened is that he's in our hands but he won't say a word. He keeps trying to make us believe we're mistaken and that he's never been called Bla in his life. I'm very sorry, Marie-Madeleine, you're the only one left who may be able to get something out of him. I shall have to take you along.'

'How did it happen?'

'Nothing went wrong with our plan, except that Mastiff was in the café instead of waiting behind the door! I could see the moment coming when everything would be messed up because of him. Bla was sitting in an armchair, Bison was guarding him with a revolver in his hand. Beaver and Wolf were keeping a general look-out. I gave Jack Tar, who arrived back from Brittany yesterday, the job of controlling the operation.'

'Didn't he try to shout out and attract attention?'

'Not at all. He laughed and joked. I don't think he has grasped the situation yet. He keeps insisting that we phone a Gestapo address.'

Although it went terribly against the grain, I put on my trench coat and took my bag.

'I want to come too,' Ermine pleaded. 'It was he who betrayed us in Paris!' She began to weep convulsively.

We boarded the trolley-car. It was a long journey, with a change at the Old Port in the gathering darkness. When he saw me appear in the glare of the naked office light I saw an unmistakable look of terror come into that soft, smooth, flabby, clean-shaven face, which sagged as he realized that I was there.

'You have a funny way of observing the laws of hospitality, Bla,' I said.

'You've won and I've lost, madame. You were the person I was looking for in Marseilles,' he retorted like a flash.

His interrogation then began. I had given orders that the prisoner should not be touched, but he had to answer standing up. Yes, he told us, he had betrayed everyone. He had come for that purpose. He had infiltrated British Intelligence on behalf of Mosley's British Fascists. What then? He and I had very different ideas about things. I was a republican and he was a fascist. As I could see for myself, *my* English friends were not *his*.

He told us everything—how he had gone about betraying our comrades, how he had wormed his way into their confidence. He told us how angry the Germans were when Superintendent David had accidentally tumbled on the network! He had quickly been told to lay off, the fool, with his story about Communists!

'Within two months we had everybody. Even you, whom we lured into a trap in Paris. That's what you mean by infiltration,' he explained, chortling. 'And the transmissions we sent to mislead British Intelligence! We gave a lot of genuine information, that we knew they already possessed, and then one day we slipped in a false piece, something that sent them running round in circles.'

Had he been in Normandy? Hardly ever. In Paris all the time. The SHE set was at Abwehr headquarters, but he did the transmitting himself because London recognized the operators by their touch; each used the Morse key differently.

'That's called a *Funkspiel*. . . . If you hadn't unmasked me, we'd have continued to infiltrate the free zone and you'd all have been caught. . . .'

We had radioed London the moment Bla was in our hands and by dawn London's reply was lying on my table. '*Well played confirm execution order*.' But the man went on talking in a never-ending flow; a psychiatrist might have said that he was insane, for his eagerness to admit his crime was a sort of madness.

'What are your contacts in London?' I asked. He immediately stopped talking. I insisted: 'Who are you secretly in touch with in London? You told my brother you had a secret wave-length for contacting a paper.'

I felt him make a tremendous effort to remember; his thickset body began to sway to and fro. 'Did I tell him that? And did he believe it?' he added giving a forced laugh. 'You know I'm such a liar. Don't wear yourself out, madame. I won't tell you anything about that. Never. That's *my* affair.'

I asked him the same question again and again. But he continued standing at attention, rather unsteadily, as he had been for hours, never complaining. He would tell us hardly anything that we did not know already.

'You may sit down, Bla.'

'Thank you, madame.'

I went out of the smoky room where the boys had taken turns to stand by me on guard. Eagle was working in the dining room. Mastiff brought us a cup of hot coffee.

'You've got nothing out of him?'

'He's confirmed what we knew. He also told me he was scouring the free zone to find me. The only new fact is that if he failed to find me, he had orders to go to North Africa by the end of October—with the second identity we found on him, a teacher's identity card. He wouldn't explain that, either. He was going to Algiers, that day, for the Nazis.'

'Go back to La Pinède, Marie-Madeleine. What happens now doesn't concern you.'

'What are you going to do?'

He took a tube of white lozenges from his pocket. 'I was given these in London. All the men who are afraid of talking under torture have them. I understand they work very quickly.'

'Above all I don't want him to have the slightest inkling.'

I went back into the office. 'Bla?'

'Yes, madame.'

He jumped to his feet, looking infinitely less tired than we did; he saw the boys dropping off to sleep where they were sitting. No, it must go on no longer.

'Bla, you have refused to tell me your personal secrets, so I'm going to send you back to England.'

He gave a start. 'I'd rather not go,' he said emphatically.

'Then think again. Either you tell us everything or we send you back tonight.'

'Very well, madame.'

I took the tramcar as the milkmen were beginning their rounds and the October sea rose and fell in a dark green swell.

At La Pinède, where Ermine was the only one who knew what was happening, I found the usual chaos of messages and visitors. Superintendent Cottoni (Alpaca) of the Surveillance du Territoire insisted that Parrot should give himself up to the police, for his flight in itself gave a suspicious appearance to the whole affair. In return Alpaca guaranteed to secure everyone's release. I went to see Parrot.

'Do you trust Alpaca, madame?'

'Absolutely. You know perfectly well he's one of us. Put yourself in his shoes: they arrest three innocent people, one of them flees, automatically becomes the guilty one and the others remain suspect. How can the thing be fixed up without you?'

'Chief, if you order me to surrender, I'll go.' He turned his kind eyes on me with an imploring, trusting look. To go and give oneself up to save one's friends, even with all the assurance possible, is not easy. I knew that.

'I'll never again give you an order like that, Parrot, but it's the end of your work in France. I'm going to send you to London. We'll spread the rumour that you've joined the Free French. . . .'

'Thanks,' he said beaming, 'I didn't really like the idea of giving myself up.'

I left, pondering over all the tricky problems involved in getting people out of France. There were so many men to be evacuated as a matter of urgency on one single aircraft: Operation Achilles, planned for the next moon. How many more would yet have to be saved?

When I saw Poulard (Jack Tar) turn into the avenue leading to La Pinède just as I did, the drama that was being played out on the Corniche stuck in my throat. Poulard's kind, round, simple face, dirty from his all-night session, showed extreme tension.

'You ought to go back there, we'll get it over!'

I felt a chill run down my spine. 'Jack Tar, you don't want me to. . . .'

'Oh no, chief! But you can't imagine what it's like . . . After you'd gone the Eagle interrogated him again, for a long time. He repeated your threat about sending him back to England. Bla wouldn't talk. With you he restrained himself a bit, but . . . when there were only men there! Then Eagle said to me: "Jack Tar, we won't waste any more time with this bastard. Give him his soup." I poured out two plates of soup. I was trembling so hard I was afraid of mixing them up. We began eating. I looked at him. . . . Nothing happened. Then I thought it was I who. . . . Imagination, you understand. I began to have one of those stomach aches. . . . We went on eating. Still nothing happened. I was almost passing out. Eagle had said it would be all over in a flash!'

I stared at him in horror as he continued his story. 'Suddenly he stood up, then doubled up, gave me a funny look and said: "I get this sometimes, a legacy from rugger days. I should like to lie down." So I said stupidly: "Lie down, old man."'

'You did right.'

'He lay down and then he began to talk and talk and talk. . . .'

'Did he ramble?'

'Far from it. He talked about all sorts of things, told dirty stories. . . .'

'Had he finished his soup?'

'Sure! More than I had! I called Bison to come and take my place. We waited one hour, two hours, three hours. He talked constantly. He even got up to show us some dance steps. Then Eagle said: "We must get it over, Jack Tar, go and make him a cup of tea." We waited until it was dark and went back into the office. He was lying down again with his back to us. I called out to him: "Bla, here's a cup of tea!" He took it, swallowed a mouthful, pulled a face and said to me: "Is it an order from London?" I said, "Take it as you like."'

'Was it hot tea?'

'Yes. Then he drank it up in one gulp and said to me again: "Thanks, it can't be much fun for an officer to do this sort of thing." I shook my head. I waited. Nothing happened. It went on like that for two hours and still nothing happened.'

'We must go back.' We took the trolley.

Bla was lying on the couch in the corner of the office. He was talking almost non-stop. The two boys on guard were staring anxiously at him. In the dining room Eagle was in conference with Wolf.

'You made a mistake mixing that drug with hot water,' I said as I went in.

'No doubt, but they assured me that it would work any time. It's a good thing to know in case we have to use it ourselves. . . .'

'Stop joking and please go and throw everything down the lavatory. It's a horrible business. How are you going to act now?'

'I have the answer,' said Wolf. 'The little network of gangsters I've often spoken to you about got me three men who will go out with the fishermen tonight from the Old Port. We'll climb down the cliff and wait on the little beach at the bottom. When the boats are level with us theirs will break off and come into where we are. I'll go aboard with the brute and . . . out at sea. . . .'

'And what if he starts screaming and fighting?'

'That's the risk,' said Wolf.

'I won't take risks over a traitor.'

I went back into the office. 'Bla?'

'Yes, madame.' He struggled up painfully, trying to get on his feet.

'You can lie down. Are you in pain?'

He looked at me for a long time. 'No, madame, but I should like a cold drink.'

'I'll get you a whisky.'

I had the bottle and two glasses brought in, poured out my own drink at the same time as his. He watched me, a smug smile on his face.

'This is what we've decided to do,' I told him. 'A Royal Navy submarine is cruising off the coast. Tonight we'll put you on board from a fishing boat. I know what your promises are worth, but all the same I want you to tell me that you'll behave properly during the trip.'

'You've treated me with humanity and dignity,' he said pompously. 'Whatever you've decided, I accept my fate.'

Once again I took my trolley-car back to La Pinède. I spent the night standing with my nose to the window and my ears straining to catch the slightest sound. At last I heard the first tramcar of the day grinding its way up the hill, then Eagle's swift step on the gravel, and saw his tall, slightly bent figure gliding towards the door. He walked in and flopped down full length on the couch in his usual attitude, as though this could relieve him of a crushing burden.

A long silence followed. 'Something went wrong?' I asked.
'Yes.'
'I thought it would, with the gangsters in an unfamiliar set-up. . . .'
'The whole thing was ghastly. We set off with Wolf in the lead, Jack Tar, Beaver and Bison in a circle round the man, and me bringing up the rear. The climb down to the cove was hell. I made everyone hug the rock so we shouldn't be seen from the road. We waited. What a wait! It was a marvellous night. The sea was faintly phosphorescent. The boats left one by one. You could hear the fishermen's voices clearly across the water. It was so beautiful, so peaceful. Then they all sailed out to sea.'
'How did he behave?'
'He never flinched. I'd placed myself beside him, ready for any eventuality and then gradually, as the minutes went by, I told myself that we couldn't do it, that it was horrible. I prayed to God for inspiration. Suddenly a huge shooting star flashed across the sky. At that moment Wolf said to me: "It's long past the time, what shall we do?" I replied: "Go back." We climbed up the cliff and back onto the Corniche.'
'Listen, Eagle, we're all going mad. We're waging a dreadful war, attacking U-boats, armoured divisions and air squadrons and all the time we're completely defenceless, at the mercy of a Canary, of a Bla, of any traitor who talks or betrays us. We're putting our own lives into this fight, and also those of the people helping us. This business is despicable and ghastly, but we haven't the right to let it drop. You're exhausted, your men are worn out. To their simple souls, this villain will soon seem like a nice person. They'll pity him, whereas he is in fact an enemy. A German spy. Already you are in two minds yourself, so imagine their reaction. . . .'
Eagle turned and looked at me, his face dark and attentive. 'What prison are you going to put him in until the end of the war?' I continued. 'Are you going to give him a seat in a Lysander and let Bull, Parrot, my brother and all the others die? Pull yourself together. I'm sorry I gave way to a feminine impulse, to a feeling that I wanted him not to suffer, not to notice anything. It's entirely my fault. We're going into reverse. We're going to put him on trial, then it will no longer look like a liquidation. We are in the field. We have the right to do so, and it's our duty.'

Once again we found ourselves around the big table in the office on the Corniche. Eagle presided, seated between Jack Tar and Wolf, who were flanked by Jassaud and Beaver (Hédin). I sat a little to one side. Facing us, on a chair, was the accused, looking pale and blinking. Eagle rose and read a lengthy indictment. I then rose and asked him if he wanted to write to his bosses in England.
'No,' he shouted defiantly. 'Everything is true. I worked for the Germans. I've betrayed you. I've gambled and lost.'
'Then,' said Eagle, 'we condemn you to death by virtue of the fact that we are on the battlefield and have the right to execute you. We at this table

are five French army officers who have rejected the armistice and by our verdict we ratify that of your London bosses.'

He produced the message from British Intelligence: '*We confirm execution order.*'

I walked over to Bla. 'A year ago, in Pau, when you were dying, I sent a surgeon to you. Today, I ask you: do you want a priest?'

'No, thank you, madame, we don't agree about that either.'

Then I returned to La Pinède and took a strong sleeping draught before I went to bed.

'Hurry up, Hedgehog, you're going to miss your train.' Ermine was pounding me in the back. 'Jack Tar's waiting for you.'

I was to go to Toulouse to get everything ready for Magpie, the sensational radio operator British Intelligence had promised to send.

'Jack Tar. Oh yes, Jack Tar! What happened?'

'It's all over,' said Ermine serenely.

'Where's Eagle?'

'He went out early. He had an appointment in Beaver's bar.' She handed me a slip of paper. I read: 'I'm going to fetch the Giraud memorandum. Don't stay away too long.'

A cold shower, a comb through my hair. Then the trolley.

'Ermine, I'll be back tomorrow evening.' I rushed to the trolley, followed by Jack Tar carrying my luggage. He had become his stolid Breton self again. Happy age when fatigue fades at the touch of sleep. 'Let's stay out here,' I told him, and we remained on the rear platform.

The conductor moved up and down, handing out tickets, while I stared down at the cobblestones as they flashed past.

'Thank you for your help, Jack Tar. It wasn't too difficult?'

'No. It was necessary. But you needn't worry any more, he. . . .'

'No details here.'

'I must tell you all the same. He gave me a message for you. He said: "You will tell your chief that it must be terrible for a lady to do all the things she's obliged to do; and I want my last act to be of help to her. . . ." '

The conductor came back, called out the name of the stop, and a bunch of chattering women surged onto the platform. Jack Tar leaned forward and whispered into my ear: 'He said: "She must leave Marseilles. The Germans will invade the free zone on 11 November." '

14 *OPERATION MINERVA*

Back at La Pinéde the following evening, I found Eagle puffing away at one of his innumerable pipes and studying a document intently.

'Look at this!' he said abruptly.

I looked. It was Giraud's memorandum, running to some fifty type-written lines—a sort of strategic delirium. Giraud thought that with the large quantities of equipment he was asking the Allies to give him he would be able to win the armistice army over by assigning it the leading role—that is to say, by opening the battle to liberate France with it alone.

I looked up. 'It's incredible,' I gasped. 'Even if one were to admit that the plan were sound, it would collapse if it's true that the Germans plan to invade the free zone, as Bla revealed at the end.'

'Do you think it's certain, Marie-Madeleine?'

'A man about to die hears the hour of truth strike, whatever kind of man he is.'

'But how could that third-rate spy know the secrets of the Third Reich?'

'The bigger the operation the greater the chance of a leak. Don't forget that he'd been told to go to Algiers before the end of the month.'

Eagle began to pace up and down the room, gesticulating. 'You're right. If they send radio operators like Bla to North Africa it's because they're afraid they'll be cut off. The Germans will be here on 11 November. We must do something, but this memorandum is so fundamentally different from what I and the British envisaged last month that all my efforts are wasted.'

'I'm going to transmit it all the same. To me the strangest thing about it is that he completely ignores the possibility of a landing in Algiers.' I prepared to code the document.

'Look,' said Eagle, thinking aloud, 'if the free zone really is invaded we won't need to get stuff sent in, we shall have to get it out. Our last planes, our last pilots, our fleet. . . . It's mad . . . it's enough to send you mad.'

'Go and tell Pétain that and no doubt he'll follow you! And try to make less noise or I'll make a mess of the coding.'

He went off, grumbling, to look for Beaufre, who was bound to know more than Giraud about the Americans' intentions in North Africa.

We were informed that the Lysander operation, code-named Mercury, would take place in two days, on 22 October. I had finally surrendered to my mother's entreaties and given my brother, whose state of health was very worrying, priority to leave. Heron, the radio operator for the Avia team, was already in Ussel, and Mahout, normally very punctual, was late. At last he came in, looking harassed. I handed him the bag of mail and with a very heavy heart said goodbye to my brother.

Forty-eight hours later they were back, laden with suitcases. Mahout had fallen asleep on the train and my brother, travelling separately for greater safety, had waited in vain for him in the Ussel station buffet. Seeing that time was getting short, Heron sensibly decided to go to the Thalamy landing ground. He did not even have the flashlights, which were all in Mahout's luggage. But the radio operator had a little solid meta fuel, and he organized his triangle with these improvised lights and used a pocket flashlight to give the recognition letter.

The aircraft landed. Magpie, the brilliant British operator whose true name was Ferdinand Rodriguez and for whom we had been waiting impatiently and a young woman who was unknown to the network and was to go to another organization, climbed out. The Lysander took off just as Mahout and Jacques came tearing into sight like a couple of Olympic sprinters.

'I'm very sorry, madame,' apologized the Avia leader, who was on the verge of a nervous collapse.

I was utterly dismayed. A second Lysander going back without a passenger! But I could not really blame these men who for months on end had been sleeping with one eye open and had been perpetually on the move, in trains and waiting rooms, always carrying equipment and documents that were sheer dynamite. At least I had the suitcases from London. I started to list them and to hand out the cigarettes and the provisions.

'One good thing has come of this,' I said to comfort Mahout. 'The Lysander can carry two passengers at a time, since Magpie and a girl were obviously on board when it took off.'

'Why not three?' he suggested with alacrity.

'Work out how it can be done, Mahout. It means we can make up for everything come the next moon. What's Magpie like?'

'He seemed splendid, and he was speaking French without an accent.'

I had arranged everything for Magpie in Toulouse. The Damms would put him up and he would be able to spend all his time familiarizing himself with life under the occupation. His first job was to put up an emergency aerial powerful enough to allow Marseilles to function independently if need be.

My brother, dejected, exhausted, terribly thin and weary, was still consoling his escort. I sent them off to bed with a promise that they would have another splendid chance, although I had not the least idea what it would be. But within the hour it emerged.

Eagle stormed into the office. 'I've just seen Beaufre. He's certain that the North African landing is imminent, but as communications with the Americans are very tenuous he's asking us to organize the operation.'

'I don't quite understand. What operation?'

'General Giraud's departure to take command in Algiers. . . .'

'How long have we known that? And what about the General's memorandum?'

'A dead duck. It's all going to be settled by a personal meeting, as I always expected.'

'How are we going to get Giraud away? The moon's on the wane. . . .'

'You don't need a moon for submarines. It won't be just Giraud going; there'll be a whole retinue of high ranking officers.' I was stunned. Was the old dream of putting the armistice army back into the war going to become a reality?

'Marie-Madeleine, while you're making preparations for Giraud's departure . . . via the Mediterranean, of course. . . .'

'Thanks, that goes without saying. What are we going to call this operation?'

'Minerva,' he said with a laugh. 'It'll all be up to you, because I'm going to have to leave you. I must go and alert my Air Force comrades.'

'Who do you think you are—Moses at the Red Sea? The idea of going to warn your friends is too dangerous. Supposing Vichy learns about the landing!'

'Don't worry, I'll talk only to people who are absolutely reliable and are fed up. Given due warning, they'll start the great exodus moving one by one.'

'You're very cheerful, Moses. I hope nothing happens to you, because we're staying with the network.'

'Exactly,' he replied, suddenly preoccupied. 'When the time comes we'll take all necessary precautions. I was forgetting: General Giraud wants the submarine, which will have to be British, to be operated by an American crew.

'It's a mania with him.'

'Yes, it *is* an obsession. Giraud wants to collect as many officers as possible. He considers them mostly to be anti-British.'

Once Eagle had gone I sent for Colonel Bernis (Spaniel), who was all agog to do the job I was giving him. He came back in record time with two suggestions about places that would be ideal for the embarkation. In Le Lavandou there was a boat we could use that would take five or six passengers. The owner, a fisherman named Crest, was well known by our local leader, Ulysse Richard (Lobster), and his disinterestedness and discretion could be relied upon. He would need only to be provided with enough petrol to make the open sea if need be. Bee's villa would serve as a hiding place.

The other possibility, the small resort of Cros-de-Cagnes, also offered excellent prospects. There, again, we could use a fishing boat that belonged to one De Stefano, but it had no engine and could only take three or four passengers. Not far from the sea there was a comfortable hotel, the Auberge du Moulin, run by the Bensa couple, that could shelter the General for a day or two.

Delighted and encouraged by the way the Giraud affair was turning out, Saluki had hurriedly come down in answer to my call and helped us thrash out the security aspects of the respective places suggested. We decided to inform the British about both of them, stressing our preference for Le Lavandou, where the enemy units seemed to be less on the alert than they were in the Nice area.

Finally I coded all the aspects of the problem in the simplest and most concise terms possible. Nevertheless this ran to five messages, each comprising at least sixty five-letter groups. It looked difficult to send such a large batch in a single transmission. Since we knew the Gestapo's detector vans were prowling in and around Marseilles, the operators had instructions to send the messages in short bursts.

I heard the men on duty tap out our call sign: D — . . D — . . N — . . D — . . D — . . N — . Suddenly, instead of the normal *ti ti ta* we heard a string of oaths. Tringa appeared: 'I've burned out my frequency,' he reported.

'Use another.'

'It's the 6897 that's gone, the one I always use. The others are blanketed out right now because it's autumn.'

Apparently zones of silence occurred in the mysterious realm of radio waves. Sometimes the night frequencies were inaudible, sometimes in daytime certain wavelengths, however carefully tuned, would not work. Autumn plunged us into one of these mysterious complexes.

'Try the others all the same.' He tried in vain.

'What about the emergency sets in town?'

'You know very well, chief, that in order to spread the risk this set's contacts with London are fixed for night time. At this moment London won't be listening to the night frequencies.'

'So we're cut off! Look through your spares and quickly give the numbers of three new frequencies nearest to 6897.'

'I know them off by heart—7004, 6952 and 3334 kilocycles.'

I repeated one of the five messages, explained our difficulties and asked that we should be listened to on the three new frequencies as soon as we were being received. Bernis suggested I should transmit the messages on his BAY transmitter in Nice. I agreed and sent Jassaud off to contact the radio operator, Pigeon.

Jassaud came back in high spirits; Cockroach, the head of the unit, said the messages would all go out when he was in radio contact during the day. I checked the time on the general schedule and allowing a normal time for decoding and transmission by London, I gave Tringa orders to send out the call sign.

He generally picked up his contacts in a few seconds, but now nothing came through. Beginning to have doubts about the whole business, I sent Marten, Mahout's sister, to Nice. She came back to tell me that Cockroach sent his apologies, that he had had technical trouble, but that BAY would function that evening. Tringa repeated his call sign, changing his frequencies every five minutes amid a silence that seemed like eternity. Now convinced that Cockroach was just not bothering, I sent Marten back to Nice once more. She was to insist that Pigeon should transmit the messages in her presence. If he refused she would bring them back. Marten returned with the messages in her bag without having been able to tell whether the radio operator or his chief was responsible for the set's failure.

General Giraud's departure was going to be compromised by lack of foresight on my part. I should have had eight crystals lined up.

It was the British who through Kauffmann (Cricket) came to the rescue. Worried by the fact that they were no longer picking up Marseilles, British Intelligence had asked Cricket to clear up the mystery as a matter of the utmost urgency and he had sent Camille Schneider (Jaguar).

'Providence has sent you, Jaguar! Take these messages straight to old Cricket and phone me as soon as you've been told you've been received.'

How long would it take him to get back to the Dordogne with those impossible train connections? By catching the Geneva-Bordeaux train at Lyons it would be at least twenty-four hours!

It was 28 October when Eagle, whom I was not expecting before 1 November, suddenly reappeared. 'The landing's going ahead,' he announced, beaming with delight.

'You're imagining things!'

'No. Vichy knows that large Allied convoys are moving from west to east and thinks they're making for Malta, but I'm sure it's on.'

'Impossible, Tripe is in Marseilles.'

'Tripe' was the alias—it tickled him no end—that I had given to Jacques Lemaigre-Dubreuil, an African oil magnate. He had figured in the May 1941 plot and had pursued it subsequently with what he had called the 'Algiers Group'; General Mast, Lieutenant-Colonel Jousse, Henri d'Astier de la Vigerie, Van Heeck and Rigault, who had been joined by our friend Pluto, Commander Barjot. Lemaigre-Dubreuil was in France at the time to report to General Giraud on his negotiations with the American observer, Robert Murphy, which had taken place on 15, 18 and 19 October.

'Marvellous!' Eagle exclaimed. 'I'm off to see Tripe. He must have fantastic sources of information.'

They were indeed. But hardly encouraging. General Giraud had finally accepted the terms laid down by the United States General Staff for the landings in Algeria and Morocco, but true to his ideas he wanted the North African operation to be combined with a landing, on the French Mediterranean coast, of personnel from Ireland and supplies and equipment from Gibraltar when he requested it by radio.

Another piece of news was that the Americans were opposed to any sort of Gaullist intervention. Convinced that the African Army was ready to come in on their side, they considered that the effect of any participation by Gaullist or even British troops (shades of Mers el-Kébir!) would destroy any hope of a peaceful landing. On the other hand, Lemaigre-Dubreuil assured us that Washington planned to employ a force of 500,000 combatant troops, 2,000 aircraft and about a hundred supporting warships, including cruisers and aircraft carriers.

On hearing the details of this sensational armada, Eagle no longer had any doubts that those were the big convoys that were worrying Vichy. Lemaigre-Dubreuil, however, convinced that he was the only one who could deal with the White House, in Giraud's name, now that the North African landings were unlikely to take place for at least another month, departed again for Algiers to check on this.

'With their pretensions to lay down the law about everything,' I said, 'these gentlemen are very keen to put on a show. I wonder what they'll do if we can't get them a submarine?'

'No submarine?' said Eagle, going all the colours of the rainbow. 'Haven't you got the operation tied up?'

I told him about the frequency trouble and the wretched business with Cockroach. He collapsed on the sofa like a bird with broken wings.

A breathless old gentleman ran along the convoy of cars that was waiting to take General Eisenhower to the aircraft in which he would fly to Gibraltar, via Scotland and Northern Ireland. That was the curious route taken by Allied aircraft flying to the south. He waved a batch of five messages that had been taken to him the moment they had been decoded. The convoy was about to move off when, not without surprise, Eisenhower saw the elegant but breathless figure appear.

'Giraud, of whom we had had no news,' the old gentleman said, 'General Giraud has just been in touch again through the oldest of the networks working with us. He wants to leave France and is asking for a submarine commanded by an American officer,' he added with a smile.

Eisenhower also smiled: 'Winston has agreed to send the submarine. Tell General Giraud that one of my officers will be on board and that I shall expect him in Gibraltar.'

The phone call from Jaguar to tell me that the five messages had at last gone out on Cricket's set put new heart into Eagle. I took him into the room where Tringa was looking in a dazed sort of way at his transmitter, which had been silent for some days now.

'My dear man, if my calculations are correct,' I said, 'there's no point in wearing yourself out. Put the earphones on, they're the ones who are going to call us now.'

We sat down round the radio. The regular contact time came and went, as well as the regulation fifteen minutes grace. The little hand on the clock had not reached the next hour before the operator turned towards us with an ecstatic light in his eyes.

'W.C.S. . . . W.C.S. . . . they're calling!'

'Then answer, for God's sake, answer,' Eagle shouted.

The operator worked his key, sent his call sign, told them he was ready and switched over to receive. His pencil moved and the groups took shape; I copied them as they appeared in order to prepare the grid and finally decoded the message from London that would enable us to sort out this mysterious venture.

The submarine would come. An American officer would be on board. It would cruise in the vicinity of Le Lavandou from 4 November onwards. Giraud would be transferred out at sea to a seaplane that would fly him to Gibraltar. Then came details of the instructions to be observed for the operation, and the recognition letters for us and for the submarine. It was to be the *Seraph*—commanded by Lieutenant-Commander N. L. A. Jewell.

'That's real proof that the landing is imminent and that our Allies are as thick as thieves,' I said, relieved. 'But if they're speeding things up it's because they're afraid the Germans will invade the free zone on 11 November.'

'Once Hitler's got to Marseilles and Toulon he's not likely to let them sail so easily in the Mediterranean,' commented Eagle. He rushed into town to tell Captain Beaufre the good news.

I had hardly finished the message informing London that we were ready before Eagle reappeared with a worried frown on his face: 'The General's delighted about going to Gibraltar, where he's now certain to meet Eisenhower, but he wants a second submarine. . . .' I threw my arms up in despair.

'He maintains that four places are not enough. He's taking with him his son; Beaufre, who is now his military principal private secretary; Viret, who is his aide-de-camp, as well as his personal bodyguard. But he also wants several generals to accompany him.'

'Where are *they* coming from?'

'They'll be streaming into Marseilles and I've arranged for them to use Beaver's bar as a rendezvous.'

I exploded: 'It's unthinkable, Eagle. I'm not a public transport firm. I'll make every possible sacrifice for Giraud, but the rest must do like us and fend for themselves. First of all, what will you bet me that your generals won't come?'

'They've received orders to come. I implore you, Minerva; it would be wonderful to grab half a dozen from Pétain!'

'Listen, Eagle, I want to please you and ask for a second submarine; but to make sure that the British are not going to all this trouble for nothing, get our three friends who've definitely had it—my brother, Bull and Parrot—and Beaufre's wife, who's going to be in great danger, ready in reserve for the embarkation. . . .'

He looked at me in utter amazement. 'Why do you think the generals won't come?'

'They'll be falling over one another—when they're sure that Giraud has won, not before.'

'I didn't dare admit it to myself, but that's exactly the impression I got during my trip. I'm afraid, too, that not a single air crew will take off, nor one more ship. . . . We're alone, terribly alone.'

The following day, 3 November, Lemaigre-Dubreuil returned from Algiers looking very crestfallen. General Mast had informed him on 31 October that the American landing would take place during the night of 7 to 8 November.

Poor old Tripe was still in high dudgeon over what he called ill-advised haste and distressing lack of confidence on the part of the Americans. Giraud had been swayed by Tripe's virulent protestations and had reverted to the original position set out in his memorandum: he no longer wanted to leave France.

'And the submarine's turning up off our coast tomorrow!' I said, thrown into a state of panic when Eagle told me of this new turn of events. 'That lot are going to drive us crackers with their politics.'

'That's what I told them, and added that when they were in prison they'd have all the time in the world to discuss the best way of taking command of operations.'

'But it might be *us* behind the bars. Wolf and Elephant ran into a different lot of patrols in town. They're hunting for Giraud in these parts. With his figure'—Giraud was extremely tall—'he won't get away with it for long.'

'I believe he's finally going to make up his mind. I know him of old. He has a nose for battle.'

All was calmness and determination again by the evening. Lemaigre-Dubreuil left once more for Africa, armed with a proclamation to the Army drawn up in Giraud's own hand, but he bitterly criticized the diversion that the General had to take via Gibraltar. As if the British submarine—even if it were called the *Seraph*—could pop up with Giraud, like Venus rising from the sea, bang in the middle of Algiers harbour under the Vichyists' very noses!

D-Day dawned. I left for Toulouse with Armadillo—an essential withdrawal action in case things went wrong. The network must not suffer because of the venture.

Neither the warmth of the Damms' reception, my introduction to the handsome British officer, Magpie (Ferdinand Rodriguez or Rodney), who was bored to death and restless for action, nor the settlement of the final details of the organization of Basset's sector succeeded in dispelling my qualms about the outrageousness of Operation Minerva. . . .

The phone call received by Gazelle—once more an innocent post office official in the principality of Monaco—was immediately passed on to Spaniel, who arrived at Le Lavandou about six o'clock in the evening on 4 November. Mahout, already ensconced, told him that General Giraud was expected from Marseilles that evening.

There was an air of gloom about Maritou Brouillet's villa. Waiting set everyone's nerves on edge. Bee and her young son, Michael, tried in vain to dispel the general anxiety by preparing a veritable banquet. The hours went by. The food went cold. Colonel Lucien Pinault (Dorado) repeated his original wish to go to Africa with Giraud. Spaniel tried to dissuade him, telling him that a submarine was not a pleasure steamer. Then at last, about ten o'clock, two cars drew up. The General, his youngest son, Captain Beaufre, Sub-Lieutenant Louis Viret, another aide-de-camp whom Spaniel did not know, and finally Eagle got out. Bee anxiously reheated the food. While the others were dining, Eagle took out of his pocket a bundle of messages that he decoded on the corner of a table.

The feeling among the members of the network was quite different from that among their guests. Giraud's appearance in their midst disconcerted them. Actual experience is always more terrifying than one expects. And now, standing there smiling, leading the same underground life that they knew, was the great leader they were being asked to help escape from France. He talked about everything save the gravity of the hour. At Dorado's request he described how he had escaped from the fortress of Koenigstein and in a burst of smiling cordiality reminisced with Spaniel about the battle on 28 August 1914, in which Giraud, at the head of a crack infantry company, almost fought their way through the German lines to General von Bülow's headquarters.

'I can't say the same about the submarine,' sighed Eagle, who had just finished his deciphering. 'It will probably not arrive in time for them to embark tonight. Three o'clock in the morning is the absolute limit laid down by London.'

Accustomed to leading a disciplined life, the General and his officers went to the rooms that had been prepared for them, while Spaniel and Mahout, the one a 68-year-old Colonel of the General Staff, and the other a 26-year-old Lieutenant-Pilot, scanned the horizon for signals in answer to the ones they themselves were flashing in vain. They kept watch until the latest deadline fixed by British Intelligence. Then they returned to the villa.

The operation was postponed until the night of 5 to 6 November.

The Spaniel-Mahout combination, which was to remain unbroken through thick and thin, ran down to the shore as soon as the first rays of the sun appeared. The state of the sea worried them: it was surging and booming but not bad enough, they thought, to prevent the embarkation. In order to avoid attracting attention to the house, where everything seemed to be asleep, they went and breakfasted with Dorado, who, having failed for a second time to persuade Giraud to let him go to North Africa, made no bones about his profound disappointment. Mahout created a diversion by switching on the radio and the Allies' successes at El Alamein raised their drooping spirits. The three men took the news to the General. Optimism revived again when Lobster arrived, flanked by Crest, his fisherman friend. But their news was disturbing. A terrible wind had risen—as long as it lasted the boat could not possibly leave harbour.

In the evening Eagle, who had gone to Marseilles, returned all bounce and enthusiasm. The submarine was prowling off shore ready to begin the operation. Eagle insisted that an attempt should be made. Beaufre, calm and methodical, argued that the decision must be left to the fisherman's judgement. Giraud, determined and self-assured, declared that he was willing to take any risk. Spaniel, who was worried by the weather conditions, but really terrified by all the coming and going, tried to reconcile the two points of view. 'We'll go if the boat is able to get through the harbour entrance.'

Towards eleven-thirty that night the howling of the wind died down. A car dashed to Le Lavandou with the General's son, Sub-Lieutenant Viret and the escort officer to help the fisherman Crest get the boat into the water. A procession formed by Giraud, Spaniel, Eagle, Beaufre, Dorado and Mahout approached a rocky headland. Mahout slipped away and hurried to the extreme tip of the headland from whence he flashed the signal 'wait' to the submarine.

The sea subsided. The boat, with Viret and the General's son already aboard, soon drew alongside a rock. A few rough steps that had been hacked out by the local inhabitants made it easier for Giraud and Beaufre to embark. Mahout leaped into the bow and swept the inky-black void with the light signals showing the agreed letter. Soon there came an answering letter from the dark mass of the *Seraph*, which had surfaced only a few hundred yards away.

Crest and Mahout were back in less than a quarter of an hour. Eagle hugged them. The five officers, Eagle, Spaniel, Dorado, Lobster and Mahout, had the same thought in mind—a gnawing regret that they could not leave to follow their tradition, their profession as fighting officers and to go to the real war.

The animals' humble task was not yet done. Another submarine was coming the following night.

15 *THE ANIMALS ILL WITH THE PLAGUE*

In a fever of impatience and curiosity I had left Toulouse by the night train, earlier than planned. At the bar Beaver gave me the green light and I arrived at the villa La Pinède, with a great feeling of relief, at the same time as Eagle.

'Everything's going well. Now we've only got to get them to send the second submarine,' he said cheerfully.

'And the new passengers? There wasn't a sign of your famous generals in the bar.'

'Don't let's get into a state, the day's young yet.'

Next morning the only people waiting unobtrusively in the bar were my brother Jacques, Bull, Parrot and Leila Beaufre, all praying that the army would not roll up.

In any case, we could not possibly change our timetable. The operation—which the Royal Navy had christened Neptune—had been scheduled, still at Le Lavandou, for the night of 7 to 8 November, and British Intelligence had warned me that no more submarines would be available after that date. This was obvious, if the landing in North Africa was to take place on the 8th!

Late that evening the telephone rang and Bee's hoarse voice informed me that she had 'flu and couldn't take the holiday party. This was a sentence we had agreed on and meant that Le Lavandou was out as an embarkation point. We must divert the submarine to Cros-de-Cagnes with the utmost urgency.

'Don't you worry, madame, I'll send that out in tonight's transmission,' said Tringa pocketing my message. 'The sub will be alerted in time.'

In the morning Eagle returned from Beaver's bar very angry indeed: the top brass were still conspicuous by their absence, but he had given Mahout the bag with the network's mail to be put on board the submarine, and said that my brother would be coming in the morning to say goodbye to me.

La Pinède awoke to its usual bustle. Elephant and Stork sat down at their desks. Ermine came in from the shops with Jean-Claude, who was carrying the basket. They seemed uneasy.

'There are some strange men walking up and down the avenue,' insisted Jean-Claude, to whom we were paying little attention.

'A pal of mine in the police knows that the detector van is on the point of locating a set in Marseilles,' added Elephant.

I pricked up my ears. 'Go back into town and find out more. We've exceeded the safety limit,' I said, addressing Eagle. 'We must move our headquarters.'

Tringa suddenly appeared, unwashed, unshaven, his hair unbrushed and his voice sepulchral: 'I called and called and called all night through, long enough to sprain my wrist. But I never got them. I could hear a distinct whistling, but it was impossible to establish contact.'

'Then the submarine's had it! Have you got a transmission scheduled now?'

'No, chief! But they've been listening every minute for the last four days. As soon as I go out on my best frequency they'll come in, I'm certain.'

Tringa took my message, crumpled and dirty, from his pocket. He sat down, carefully put his cap straight, laid his watch, his schedule, the Morse key and the telegram on the table, plugged in his favourite frequency and while warming up the set looked up at me inquiringly.

The submarine off Le Lavandou was in mortal danger. Unless we sent a counter-order it would steal in to the coast where it might be misled by false signals and run the risk of getting caught in the nets laid by the Italian patrols alerted by Operation Minerva. Whatever the truth about the detection stories, I had to warn the British; one can't let an ally fall into a trap.

Eagle had retired to the bathroom. Ermine, Stork and Jean-Claude were busy on the ground floor. Elephant had disappeared. I looked out of the window to contemplate the park which was stirred by a light wind playing through the trees and providing the music for the dance of the dead leaves. Everything was so peaceful! I signed to the operator to start transmitting. 'Got them!' he said immediately and began to tap out my message.

Back in my room I heard the Morse signals winging through the air like regular, pathetic music scales.

'Make him work quickly, God, make him work quickly, more quickly!' I prayed.

At last the key stopped tapping and a click told me that the operator had switched over to receive. At the same moment an avalanche crashed on to the calm and peaceful house, making everywhere echo with the cries of 'Police'. A quick glance outside showed me that we were surrounded.

I rushed into the office. Tringa was holding a cigarette lighter unsteadily in his hands and trying to set fire to his schedules and the last message. A man with a revolver in his hand was tackling him. Another was already searching the drawers: I attacked him at the same time, screaming insults inspired by twenty-four months of underground activity. He stared at me in astonishment from behind his spectacles and thought it wiser to entrench himself behind a chair, which he held out in front of him like a shield.

He looked perfectly ridiculous. He must be the leader, I thought, and then, in a flash, I remembered that I had something better to do. I rushed back into my room, hurled myself on my bag, which was crammed full of little paper balls. In a trice the whole of my small travelling library of secret notes was firmly clenched between my teeth.

The 'leader' pushed his bespectacled face cautiously around the door and gave a start: 'Spit that out! The lady is swallowing *papers*!' he yelled to one of his squad.

In bounded a thin, brown-haired, little man, who grabbed me by the throat.

'Boche! Dirty Boche!' I choked, crunching up the papers that were now swelling up with my saliva.

The grip on my throat tightened. Apparently satisfied with what he saw, the 'leader' turned around. Was it an illusion? The grip around my neck slackened slightly. I seized the opportunity to shout again: 'Boche! Dirty Boche! Revolting Boche!' and swallowed a great mouthful of papers.

The little man looked at me intently. Suddenly, I saw tears come into his blue eyes. 'I'm not German,' he whispered. 'Go on shouting, but chew everything up quickly. Go on shouting and pretend.'

It was a sensible precaution. The 'leader' showed his face from time to time, as if he were part of a Punch and Judy show. Still chewing, I muttered between two insults: 'Then who are you? Prove it.'

'A friend, a French policeman forced by Vichy to escort these bastards. They're only allowed to do the actual detection work, they can't touch anything.' The face popped through the half-open door again.

'You swine of a Boche,' I spluttered, shaking my fist at him. 'You've no right to lay a finger on us, you're in the unoccupied zone.'

The face vanished. 'What can I do to help? What must be done?'

Help me! I analysed the clouded eyes, the honest, yes certainly honest, face. But the accent? The accent had teutonic overtones. It was obviously a trick. 'I don't believe you.' I said.

Giving me a despairing look the little man whispered again: 'Hurry up, I'm risking my life, don't wait any longer. . . .'

'Your accent?'

'I'm a Breton. My name's Goubil. I and my pal Pierre who's somewhere near are with you. I swear it's the truth!'

'Has she spat it up?' asked the 'leader' anxiously.

'Yes, it's coming,' replied the man called Goubil as I spat out into his handkerchief the remains of a shapeless mess that he quickly tore into shreds.

Heartened by this proof of co-operation I put all my cards on the table: 'There's a parcel of documents under my bed. . . . They're military documents. . . . And we're also expecting some people, they mustn't come in. . . .'

With the agility of a cat the little man grabbed the parcel and held it gingerly in his embarrassed hands. Where could it go? He flung it on top of the cupboard. His friend Pierre arrived, young, dark, very simple. His obvious confusion was written all over his face.

'Go to the garden gate,' the Breton whispered to him. 'Don't let anyone in, don't let anyone be caught.'

Pierre disappeared looking greatly relieved. 'We must go on struggling,' said Goubil, dragging me into the next room where I saw I would have to launch another formal attack on the 'leader'.

Tringa had been driven into a corner and was shaking in every limb. The 'leader' had a revolver in one hand and, in the other, he was holding an all too familiar piece of paper, at which he was looking in triumph.

'*Ach so . . . ! Ach so . . . !*' he cried.

'You mean, dirty Boche, you've no right to keep that paper,' I said snatching it away.

He leaped after it. For a moment I thought the revolver was going to go off, but it didn't. The Breton intervened: 'Steady,' he said to the 'leader', twisting my wrists and recovering the paper, which he stuffed into his pocket. 'I'll put it in a sealed envelope.'

'Make sure you do,' barked the Gestapo man. 'I'll see to that! It's the plan of their whole radio circuit.'

So much for Eagle's brain wave! The number of times I'd told him that his internal listening was stupid. Because of his damned radio plan all our sets were going to be captured in one fell swoop! As though understanding my dismay, Tringa began shouting loudly: 'QS 5! QS 5! QS 5!'

'That man's mad,' remarked the 'leader', lashing out at Tringa and making the terrified operator tremble even more violently.

QS 5 meant: 'They've received me! The submarine is saved! They received me, loud and clear, at maximum strength.' And grief-stricken he looked at the love of his life, the duplex set which the German detector chief, himself a radio enthusiast, was smashing up.

'It was bound to finish like this, with Vichy shooting us in the back with the enemy's help!' I fulminated, beside myself with rage, as I walked into my room, where the sight of my brother standing there, smiling cheerfully and dressed from head to foot ready for the great departure, made me recoil in horror. If he had been able to get in, my two policemen were no better than a couple of phoneys. I had allowed myself to be taken in like an idiot.

'Jacques, why did you come in?'

'To say goodbye to you, darling, and it wasn't easy. Some clown of a chap shouted: "Don't go in, the Gestapo's there." A likely story. The Gestapo in Marseilles, I ask you! A joke's a joke, but it's a bit much when you overdo the cowboy and Indian stuff like this.'

'It's true, Jacques,' I said, feeling completely beaten. 'We've been arrested. The Boches are here. How did you manage to get in?'

'Other people were arriving. The clown at the gate rushed out to them, so I barged right in. See what I've brought you.' In a corner of the room was an old, roped-up, mud-stained, mouldy, bashed and stinking suitcase. I frowned. 'Oh I agree, it's not a thing of beauty,' Jacques stammered, 'but, you know, it's been lying under the pig in our farm at Mougins for a year now and I thought the papers would be ruined. I thought it wiser....'

My archives. The original documents setting up the network. General de Gaulle's letter to Navarre!

The Breton appeared, his eyes followed mine. 'D'you take me for a furniture remover?' was his crack as he threw an eiderdown over the salvaged case. 'I'll go along to the gate and take my pal Pierre's place,' he added, giving my brother a reproving look.

The sounds in the villa grew louder. I opened the bathroom door. Eagle, looking magnificent, was carefully shaving in front of the mirror that reflected the faces of an astounded audience behind him.

'I'm glad I'm in my shoes rather than yours today, gentlemen,' he declared in a calm voice. 'In a very short time you will see that your wicked conduct has been completely wasted.' He gave his kindly laugh. 'And you'll also see that we shall all meet again in the same cell, because the Germans are going to invade the free zone.'

His audience shook their heads. Who was this imperturbable and prophetic person? Obviously a visionary! Within a few hours he would be locked up and he stood there massaging his face and giving advice. Pierre, now back from the gate, opened a cupboard on the German's orders. He wept: on the Commandant's uniform hung the Croix de Guerre with ten bars.

A very young, fair, distinguished-looking man, who seemed to be the superintendent, appeared on the scene. Addressing the Nazis he ordered them, politely but firmly, to leave—which they did, but not before they had made it clear, through the 'leader's' voice, that they were going to put in a report about the importance of their capture.

The young superintendent then asked us to pack our cases and tactfully withdrew to the ground floor with his men.

Eagle bounded over to me: 'The dirty dogs. We can't get away for the moment, but you can be quite sure that I shall fix everything.'

'I've made a start already,' I said, describing the episode with the Breton. 'The others didn't seem tough. I feel quite hopeful.'

Reassured, Eagle's one thought now was for my brother: 'Poor old Jacques! You've missed the boat again!'

'I'd do better to cross the Pyrenees,' said Jacques. 'With all your cloak and dagger stuff, the Lysanders and submarines, there's nothing to equal good old-fashioned shank's mare.'

Four lots of belongings were crammed into a bag and we all assembled on the steps of the villa. Ermine, smart as usual; Jean-Claude, joking and whispering to me, 'I've hidden the plank' (our secret papers were hidden in that fake plank, which had therefore escaped the search), Jacques, worried; Tringa still shaking from head to foot; Stork resigned; Eagle majestic, and I bringing up the rear and feeling I was in a really tight corner. We got into the police cars under the horrified gaze of the owner of the villa, M. Giraud, who watched in bewilderment his very peaceful-looking tenants being treated like common criminals. How was he to know that there, in his villa, the curtain had just come down on the last act in the escape of his illustrious fellow countrymen who bore the same name as himself?

As we passed through the gate I noticed Elephant, completely poker-faced, standing with his nose to the wall. It warmed my heart to see him. He was free and would give the alarm.

The French police were shattered. They were conscious of the odious role assigned to them by Vichy, and when we were taken to the building used by the Surveillance du Territoire we were given a good meal. Then the interrogations began. We were split up among the various rooms of the comfortably furnished suite that they had requisitioned.

I asked my interrogator if I might lie down on a divan. 'What is your name?' I was asked.

'Bacqueville.'

'I'm not asking you *my* name, but yours.'

'Bacqueville, Claire de Bacqueville.'

'*My* name is Bacqueville,' he said icily. 'But what is yours?'

I was astounded as he was and showed him my identity card, which had been made out in this assumed name by Rollin's office in Vichy. I had decided to stick to this, my grandmother's maiden name.

'But *I* am also a Bacqueville!' he exclaimed.

'Then we're cousins!'

And so I launched into the whole history of the Bacquevilles, from my ancestor the marquis who flew across the Seine in 1742 with his extraordinary winged machine to the great aunts exiled in Russia. What a stroke of luck!

'Yes,' my cousin broke in. 'I've heard that . . . and that. . . .' He seemed delighted to get out of his unpleasant duty, thanks to a family history that was so fascinating and would give him real pleasure to type out.

We were put that same evening into the cells of l'Evêché, a sordid, vermin-infested prison. It was cold and I had put on my American goatskin coat, which I had lugged around every winter since the beginning of hostilities. I was also wearing my jewels, a pearl necklace, a diamond ring, a signet ring and a gold bracelet that I never took off, reckoning on being able to sell them in case of need. The clerk of the court's wife made me deposit them immediately in a large envelope which she sealed up. She advised me to leave my goatskin coat as well.

'Oh no, I should feel too cold.'

'As you like,' she said. 'But you mustn't come and complain afterwards if it walks out by itself.'

'But it hasn't any feet,' I said, trying to be equally funny.

'Feet! There'll be thousands of feet! As soon as you're in the cell. Every hair will have feet. Keep it, my beauty, and hang on to it,' she insisted.

From a distance I saw the line of men disappearing into a corridor. Ermine and I were marched off in the opposite direction and I had, alas! the honour of a separate cell. A swinging bail, a WC into which the water gushed regularly and noisily, rapidly affecting me like the Chinese water torture, an electric light bulb up near the ceiling, window-bars completely out of reach, and a door with a bolt that made a noise like thunder. Wrapped in my goatskin I perched myself on the swinging bail and took a cigarette from my coat lining. The feet soon appeared on the scene.

I found it impossible not to think of the operations that were now going on. I only hoped that Giraud had arrived safely at Gibraltar and that the second submarine had managed to get away. That alone would justify our present plight. I had to get some sleep so that I should have the strength to cope next day.

It was an hour before midnight. The train from Marseilles drew into Cros-de-Cagnes station. Dallas got out, followed by his passengers: Leila Beaufre, Bull (Jean Boutron), Parrot (Robert Philippe), General Koenig's son-in-law, General Giraud's chauffeur, a sergeant who had helped him escape from Koenigstein fortress, and a friend of Lemaigre-Dubreuil who had taken my brother's place at the last minute. Spaniel choked when he saw none of the expected generals. 'That was a waste of effort,' he thought when Dallas told him what had happened.

Mahout was very worried, for he did not know the recognition letters or the password for Operation Neptune. He presumed that the telegram announcing the change of embarkation place had in fact been transmitted but he had still received no answer—and for a very good reason. Nevertheless, he must carry on, and he decided to do precisely as he had done for Operation Minerva. At exactly the same time he piled his people and the bag of mail into Di Stefano's boat. Standing in the bow, he flashed his torch.

The unbelievable skill of the British sailors, navigating close in at the risk of running aground, soon brought the impressive bulk of P 217, a 750-tonner, out of the darkness. Turner, the submarine commander, appeared on deck surrounded by his crew, armed to the teeth. He was obviously expecting to take on a whole crowd of VIPs and was taken aback to see that his passengers were just a bunch of ordinary people in tattered old clothes and shivering with cold. Now suspicious, he began to parley. In order to convince him Leila Beaufre, who was English, sang one of the latest London hits. Jean Boutron gave his alias, Bull, as a password and mentioned Richards' name.

Although he was still suspicious, Lieutenant-Commander Turner nevertheless hauled everybody on board and the P 127 headed out to sea again, while Mahout and Di Stefano returned to the shore, managing to make it just in time between two Italian patrols. Bernis guided them on to the beach and went sadly back to his next tasks.

The first thing he did was to give the alert and the machinery was set in motion. As soon as British Intelligence had been informed, they would send a sentence to the BBC to warn all sectors: 'Be careful! In the south of France the animals are ill with the plague.'

In the yellow dawn that gradually vied with the light shed by the bulb, I saw a police inspector appear. He was brisk, close shaven and very chatty. 'I shouldn't really tell you,' he said, 'but it's absolutely marvellous. They seem to be landing in North Africa in all their glory.'

In my joy I gave the policeman a mighty hug. 'Yes, it's too wonderful for words! What a splendid 8 November, and my birthday too! What a fantastic birthday present!'

At noon we were all back at police headquarters. The officer in command, Chief Superintendent Léonard, allowed us to get together over lunch and we ate with far greater relish than the night before. Around the table the inspectors of the section looked at us with growing benevolence. More details of the great news had come in and there was a family feeling in the air.

Eagle told me of his plans. He knew through Léonard that the Vichy Government was in a state of complete panic and insisting that he should go there. Laval personally wanted to see him. Eagle had replied that he would agree, on condition that his friends in prison were released. That assumed that we would remain there until Eagle had arrived in Vichy.

Eagle's plan did not appeal to me at all. The interest that we inspired, once it was known, through a blunder by Tringa—Tiger had warned me that he could not hold his tongue—that we had got Giraud away in a submarine, and the enthusiasm that the unhoped-for news of the landing inspired in the breasts of the police, led Eagle to believe that in Vichy he would find an audience receptive to the suggestion of armed opposition to the invasion of the free zone that we knew to be imminent. I felt nothing but pessimism on this score and I begged him to escape during the journey.

Intoxicated by his grandiose plans, he smiled gently. 'No, eternal Minerva, I won't play safe. I'll go to Vichy. It is my duty to convince them. You'll see, everything will go according to plan.'

'And what if you're betrayed? What if the Germans arrive?'

'I've taken care of that,' said Eagle. 'You see that small, fair-haired superintendent? If the Germans come he has promised me to see that you escape.'

The afternoon dragged on in routine interrogations. From time to time a strange person, whom everyone saluted respectfully, came through the offices. I immediately got the impression that he was conducting the whole affair. That evening, while we were dining, the door was suddenly flung open by the policeman Goubil, who announced:

'Someone called Mahout wants you to know that the embarkation was successful. I don't know what it's all about, but it's not fair, they don't trust me,' he added in a peevish voice that made us laugh. '"Mind your own business," the barman said, "pass it on to the chief, she'll be pleased." Another thing, they're preparing to rescue you. Now I'm off to see the Boche. Yesterday they left my friend Pierre and me on our own at your villa and we put masses of things aside.'

'You see?' cried Eagle beaming. 'Everything's going very well.'

Like some supernatural confirmation, the door opened again to admit Superintendent Cottoni (Alpaca)! Vichy had picked on him as a reliable person to fetch Eagle. We all laughed and congratulated one another on this happy omen, while the excellent Alpaca shook my hands warmly: 'I'm sorry to make the acquaintance of the leaders of my network under such sad circumstances, but it's a stroke of luck to be in on this party. Be very careful about everything. Since your capture, the Boche have been on the rampage.'

Turning to Eagle, Alpaca suggested he should take him not to Vichy but to Geneva.

'Eagle,' I said firmly, 'you're leaving in a few moments and we may never see one another again. This time I order you to follow the superintendent. You've been unmasked. You must grow a new skin. Your Vichy plan won't work. They're all rotten to the core, corrupt and trapped. I'll give you fair warning, I'm going to do everything I can to get away.'

Attentive and torn as he was, Eagle stuck to his guns: 'You know me, Minerva. I must do this. I must try to keep my word. If you don't hear from me in forty-eight hours, go your own way. We shall meet again. Rendezvous at the Danois' house in Ussel.'

As he took him away Alpaca whispered to me: 'I'll try and see what I can do on the trip.'

The two figures, wearing bulky overcoats and hats pulled well down over their faces, vanished into the night. Eagle would certainly go to extremes to preserve his honour. We were taken back to the Evêché prison, where I went to sleep feeling heartbroken.

The very next day things worsened. As soon as we arrived at police headquarters, I saw from Superintendent Léonard's face that Eagle had not been received in Vichy like the prodigal son. What was more, the Nazis were agitating and insisting they should get the sealed envelopes, particularly the radio plan that had been on the operator's table.

I exploded: 'You know what that means, Superintendent? You're going to hand all our sets over to the enemy! It's sheer murder!'

'I have no option,' said Léonard, badly shaken all the same.

I got him to see at last that the Boche would be completely hoodwinked if we substituted a false plan for the original. He agreed, provided that the copy looked exactly the same.

It was not an easy job. Accompanied by two policemen, I went to La Pinède to get the necessary material, squared paper, fine pens, Chinese and various coloured inks. It was the same material that my brother had used to write out in his own hand the internal listening table on a sheet of paper measuring ten inches by eight that contained no less than twelve little station schedules, each with hundreds of call signs.

We buckled down to the job. All night, under the eyes of three benevolent inspectors, together with Stork, we dictated to Jacques the apocryphal plan that he managed to copy with such accuracy that towards dawn Léonard was in raptures: 'I can't tell which is the genuine one!' he confessed admiringly, and so as not to risk making a mistake, I pointed out the good one and he burned it before our eyes. My radios were saved.

Nor had the mysterious superintendent with the bad throat wasted his time. He had hardly moved out of the office all night. On my way to have a wash and brush up in the tiny, all-purpose kitchen, I discovered a heap of ashes in one corner and the suitcase in bits. Had he burned everything? I stirred the heap; it must have weighed pounds. My mind was now at rest, so were my files.

During the subsequent interrogation I was shown only unimportant papers and I agreed that they should be sent to the Gestapo. The plan was simple: to make the Germans believe that the captured group was an isolated commando whose only job was to organize General Giraud's departure.

Feeling light at heart, at midday I rejoined Ermine, Tringa and Jean-Claude, who had slept at the Evêché prison, and we sat down to a meal. Suddenly there was a phone call from La Pinède to say that Tiger-Cat, Louis Jacquinot, had just been caught in the trap laid on at the Germans' request. Tiger-Cat had been a former Minister of the Interior and Léonard's old boss, so that the Superintendent was more than annoyed.

I was even more annoyed as I suddenly remembered that he had an appointment with us that same day to introduce us to one of the main leaders of the underground Communist Party. The latter wanted to discuss with the network the question of transmitting to London the huge volume of information that had been gathered by the Communists, but which remained dead because they had no radio links. I only hoped that the Communist leader had not been with Tiger-Cat.

We must think up an immediate alibi. Tiger-Cat was a lawyer. What, then, could be more natural than that my family, hearing of my arrest, should send such a man to defend me. And so he soon appeared, under strong escort.

'How kind of you to come so quickly, sir, to take up my case.'

'Not at all,' he replied in a lordly manner. 'These gentlemen have arrested me as well.'

While sharing our sausage, Tiger-Cat whispered to me that the answers he had received by phone before coming to keep his appointment with us were off the record. He had destroyed everything compromising in his pockets and got rid of the Communist leader, but he did not think he would have to give up helping us eventually.

'It is obvious,' I said to Léonard, 'that the Minister cannot be considered an agent. You're surely not going to arrest our lawyers to please the Boches! Wait for them to do that themselves!'

'Of course not, of course not,' Léonard retorted. 'That's the line I shall take.' And so he secured the release of the Minister, who left as calm and serene as he had arrived.

Towards evening the Breton, Goubil, reappeared looking very worried and drew me into a corner: 'Look out! The Germans have persuaded Vichy to transfer you all to Castres prison. Be careful; it's a veritable Bastille. Above all, don't go or you'll be extradited immediately and taken to Fresnes. . . .'

'Don't go!' That was a good one! But it was an excellent tip. The first thing to do was stay in the police premises at all costs. Superintendent Léonard followed immediately on Goubil's heels. Then, with a casualness that seemed to me completely false, he told me that it was impossible to keep me for the night, but he solemnly swore that he would come to collect us from the Evêché at dawn.

'Superintendent Léonard, I refuse!' I said. 'We made a tacit agreement. Eagle agreed to go to Vichy only on condition that we were released.'

'But, madame, I have not received an answer from my superiors!'

'So long as you have no answer, negative or positive, I refuse to allow us to be taken off to prison. I give you my word of honour that we will make no attempt to escape unless Hitler's army marches in.'

'Come, come, madame, I have no indication that the Germans are in Marseilles. It's sheer fantasy! We shall see where we are tomorrow. Allow us to take you to the Evêché.'

'I'd rather die, Superintendent! Tomorrow is 11 November and the Boche will invade the free zone. They'll capture us at the Evêché, because you'll not even have had time to come for us. So you *will*, in fact, have handed us over.'

Léonard gave way again and we barricaded ourselves in with three volunteer inspectors, who immediately turned the place into a sort of barracks. I asked them to check up on the news and one of them rang through every quarter of an hour to the police stations in what they called the 'Great North'. While Lyons and Vichy kept on replying 'nothing to report', towards midnight Moulins told them that the troop concentrations along the demaraction line that had so far been considered inoffensive were giving cause for alarm. Then threat became fact: the Nazis were about to march in. They marched in, fanned out and occupied the whole countryside. We were all lost.

In the little kitchen I forced myself to make my toilet minutely, and to freshen up carefully the old clothes I had been wearing for the past four days. The goatskin, now deprived of its feet—no easy task—and my blue tailor-made suit, now reasonably spruce after a good brush-up, gave me courage and it was with a stout heart that I saw Léonard come in, head bowed, and shut himself in the big directorial office. Mobile police soon appeared and a truck parked at the door.

I went into the superintendent's office. The whole police section was there, dismay written on their faces. I was conscious of their tragic role under the German jackboot. They had arrested German spies in the free zone, they had even shot some, but Vichy also compelled them to track down Allied agents. I knew, however, for I had just been living in their company, that not one of them wanted to hand us over to the enemy and that they had done their best to save us. Léonard told me that Eagle's negotiations had failed and that he had received orders to transfer us to Castres. 'You will be safer there than in Marseilles, where we expect the German troops any minute,' he added to encourage me.

Could this man who, only the evening before, regarded this prospect as sheer fantasy, really not know that Castres was simply a springboard for extradition? I turned to the small, fair-haired superintendent, whose name I now knew to be Piani, as my last hope. I said to him: 'You promised Faye that if the Germans marched in we should be freed. I absolve you from your solemn promise. It shall not be said that a Corsican pledged his word of honour in vain.'

I left the room. My friends were standing together in a group, waiting to see my reactions, and in their eyes I read such hope in me that I had not the heart to tell them there and then what was in store for us. Something stronger than reasoning told me that the die was not yet cast.

The husky-voiced superintendent, buried in his scarf, walked up the stairs. He dismissed the guards standing round the entrance with an angry wave of his hand and drew me aside: 'Madame,' he said, 'I have just warned your friends in town. They're going to attack the police van. Don't worry, we're with you.'

'Whom did you see?'

'Rivière, Hédin, the whole lot.'

This marvellous person was Léonard's adjutant, Superintendent Théus. He commanded a network inside the police force itself. I had no time to tell him what I felt before Piani joined us: 'I have only one word, I'll keep it. Léonard has agreed to send the mobile police back. I'm going to take you to

Castres with two Corsican inspectors. Our van driver is also a Corsican. On the way all you have to do is to direct the operation.'

Then something quite extraordinary happened. The whole police section helped us to pack our things up. Taking advantage of the general confusion, my friends seized a few revolvers and Sten guns that were lying about in the rooms. One of them, on the pretext of shaking hands with Léonard, quickly picked up the sealed envelope containing the 80,000 francs that had been seized in the villa. Superintendent Théus leaped on the pile of interrogation reports and burned them. 'They shan't even have the cans,' he muttered.

Goubil had carried kindness to the length of bringing us our suitcases from M. Giraud's villa. When we all shook hands and wished one another good luck, two inspectors, Le Tullier and Gautier whispered to me: 'We know what's happening. We're joining your network in Nice tonight.'

At last we piled into the van, guarded by the three Corsicans. Sitting in front, by Piani, I promised him that he and his two inspectors would be in London in a week. Hearing this, the two inspectors, Rutali and Reverbel, who were sitting inside near the door, exclaimed loudly: 'But that changes everything. In that case we must say goodbye to our families.'

'That's right,' replied Piani and ordered the driver, who was beginning to think we were an odd lot, to drive to the policemen's homes.

It was a strange van, full of arrested escapees, sauntering through Marseilles on 11 November 1942, the day that was to see the arrival of the Nazis. The families exchanged kisses and they were all in the best of humour, but I personally was nearly dead with fright, scared that the enemy would suddenly appear and that our beautiful dream would vanish. 'We must push on, we must push on,' I kept saying.

'Not yet,' the three policemen protested. 'And what about your jewels, madame?'

'What do they matter? You've gone mad. Freedom's worth all the jewels in the world.'

But they insisted. In spite of my protests, we stopped in front of the Evêché prison. Piani got out. For what seemed an eternity I was racked by doubt. What if the whole thing was play-acting, a put-up job to avoid the attack on the van planned by the man with the sore throat? My friends had also fallen silent. The superintendent came out again and brandished the clerk of the court's large yellow envelope. 'Your jewellery, madame,' he said, delighted with himself.

We sped along the road to Avignon. The plane trees flashed past under the smiling winter sun. The familiar countryside spread out before my eyes that were now shining with happiness.

A car appeared in the distance. We stiffened. It was going along slowly with its hood down. It was a German car, a Nazi vanguard. The officer seated by the driver was reading a large map spread across his knees. They were completely unprotected. They were quite at home, like masters. The same thought struck us all; we could kill them. The boys seized the Sten guns and loaded the revolvers.

It all happened in a flash. I reacted violently. No! It would be too idiotic after our providential luck. Our duty was elsewhere. I shouted: 'Don't move.'

The German car disappeared. 'A shame,' I said, thinking aloud. 'We would probably have been the only ones to open fire.'

16 TO PASTURES NEW

'Come on! We can't hang about!' exclaimed Wolf (Rivière) clambering down from the huge, wheezing, steam lorry that had brought him to the rendezvous arranged by Théus.

'Where are you taking us?'

'To Chateaurenard, where the early vegetables come from. But I know a black market café. . . .'

'Is it wise, Wolf?'

'Blimey, nothing's wise, but everything's worth trying.'

The joy of having a meal that was washed down with an old Chateauneuf-du-Pape soon banished our pessimistic thoughts. The first thing Rivière told me about was Navarre's escape. On the pretext of going for a medical examination, he had been able to arrange to be taken to the Jeanne d'Arc clinic, where the Jassaud tribe immediately took charge of him. But the arrival of the Germans naturally created a new and dangerous situation. In principle Navarre could be safe again with the Damms, who had already been warned. And Elephant would come the following day to make false identity papers out for us. Everything else was going like clockwork. As I had anticipated in the event of our headquarters being neutralized, Spaniel had taken over command of the southern zone and Saluki had taken command of the northern zone.

Rather heavy and unsteady, we went back to the truck, which soon landed us at Chateaurenard. Like shadows, and moving in extended order, we slipped along to the lodgings that we had been offered by the patriots in the little town. My troop dispersed. Ermine and I were taken to an old couple who gave us a big Provençal bed to share, with sheets smelling of mountain lavender.

That same day the P 127 entered the Algiers roads, where Lieutenant-Commander Turner received orders to surface. That meant that Operation Torch—the Allied landing in North Africa—had been successfully completed.

During the voyage, which lasted over thirty-six hours, Bull (Boutron) and his friends were unhappy. They had gone aboard dying of hunger and had devoured all the crew's ration of white bread; and in the daytime, when the submarine was submerged, the air became dangerously rarefied. At least, Bull had been able to use the submarine's radio and, with his own code, had given London all the details of the captures made in Marseilles.

A launch drew up alongside the P 127 in a mighty shower of spray. Two British Intelligence officers leaped aboard the submarine and demanded to speak to Bull.

'Where's General Giraud?' they asked.

'Not here,' Bull replied dumbfounded. 'He left well before me.'

'The General hasn't arrived in Algiers,' said one of the officers. 'We were hoping you'd taken him to Gibraltar.'

'Then who's in command here?'

'Admiral Darlan, put in by the Americans.'

All that effort and the net result was to find Vichy again, across the Mediterranean! History, thought Bull, moves faster than men.

'Then allow me to introduce myself,' he said, selecting a false identity card from his briefcase. 'I am M. Robin.'

'Oh yes, poor cock robin,' said the British Intelligence officers, taking him along with a lot of friendly back-slapping.

'Don't forget the bag with the network's mail,' said Bull in consternation. 'This drama must at least serve some purpose.'

In Castres prison Eagle was in despair. His failure in Vichy burned into his soul. He suffered intensely from France's acceptance of defeat. No one would listen to his plea to throw the 'armistice army' back into the war. No one would pay the slightest heed when he promised that General Giraud, in agreement with the Americans, would send immediate help.

A warder came in and warned him: 'Silence is the rule in this prison. All noise is forbidden. The slightest sound and it'll mean solitary confinement. Come along and wash.'

Eagle followed him into a sort of inner courtyard and, left alone, concentrated on enjoying the icy stream of water from the tap.

'Who are you?' a voice whispered.

'A French Air Force officer, a Commandant,' Eagle whispered back, looking up to the bars of a cell.

'We, Yugoslav officers, volunteers in the French army.'

'What are you doing here?'

'Waiting to be handed over to the Germans. They take a few of us at a time. You'll also be extradited.'

'Be brave,' said Eagle in a louder voice, 'the Americans have landed in North Africa.'

The gaoler came back shouting, 'I heard something!'

'It's your tap spitting,' Eagle replied contemptuously, shaking his dirty water over the man.

The news from Algiers was curious. Apparently Giraud had not reached North Africa, but that no longer worried me. I had altered course to save a ship in distress and had nearly gone down with it. A new era was opening before me: the Marseilles page had been turned over, Beaver's bar closed, the agents dispersed, the connections severed. I was eager to pick up the broken threads of the network again but the day after we arrived my landlady, Mme Stingue, had begged me not to put my nose out of doors, as the police were roaming the town.

With the Gestapo taking a hand the situation could change radically, and I decided to stay indoors until Elephant arrived. It was a wait of forty-eight hours, and I spent the whole of the time wondering if everything was lost.

'With all those trouble-makers around,' Elephant explained by way of apology, 'I had a hard time making up a new set of blank papers. My new tin seals are impeccable, chief; you'll soon be able to get away.'

Our identity photographs had been taken locally, each of us trying to look his best. Going from one hideout to another, Elephant inserted our names and latest descriptions and finger-prints, and expertly stuck our portraits on the cards and impressed them with his own perfectly forged seals. He also provided us with cards for food and clothing—a total of twenty-four in all—plus various driving licences and other personal papers appropriate to our respective personalities. I had become a citrus fruit dealer, cut off from Africa by the landings.

My brother and the two radio operators were expected at Nice, where it was hoped that they would have further chances of getting away by boat. The three Corsican policemen would go direct to Ussel, where I had asked for a Lysander to be sent, and Operation Apollo had been approved. As everything was in order, I did not wait a minute longer but went straight to the Toulouse headquarters with Ermine and Jean-Claude.

In the Damms' cosy flat in the Rue Clauzel in Toulouse the exquisite Griffin-Vicuna couple, surrounded by the whole Toulouse headquarters staff, received me with open arms and affectionate smiles, which were a great comfort. Magpie, the radio operator, re-established my direct contact with the British with a flick of his wrist. There was a never-ending stream of news for me to hear.

'You know,' Basset told me, 'I'm snowed under with search warrants. You've caused untold havoc. Six people escaping at once, three policemen subverted, two who've deserted to join your network. And Superintendent Théus has also had to flee. Vichy is raging. The Germans, who still haven't a clue, are insisting that every possible effort be made to recapture the mysterious spies who have vanished into thin air. By the way,' he concluded with a laugh, 'a price has been put on the head of a certain Claire de Bacqueville. I could become a millionaire!'

From Castres, where we were to join him, Eagle had been transferred to Vals-les-Bains in the Ardèche. Our escape had clearly saved him from being extradited; in the Giraud affair, which was so difficult to swallow, it was not possible for Pétain to hand over just one regular officer. Instead of hiding with the Damms, Navarre, who always did the unexpected, had reported spontaneously to the Toulouse police with a view to 'strengthening his legal position'. Ordered to reside in Albi, he went to an excellent inn in the little town on the Tarn and spent his time letting the days flow peacefully by. The police chief had promised not to surrender him to the enemy. I therefore decided to check up for myself and left for Albi with the Bishop.

We found Navarre looking thin and sallow as a result of prison life, but his eyes still burned with their indomitable orange fire. He behaved as though nothing had happened for the last sixteen months and talked at length about his philosophical discoveries while in prison but never once mentioned the network. Did he even think of it?

'Poor Marie-Madeleine,' he suddenly said in his old caustic way, 'are you angry with me for letting myself be caught so stupidly?'

'I'm angrier still that you've done it a second time.'

'What? I've got complete freedom by a trick! If you only knew how pleasant this inn is after sixteen months in prison!'

'But, Navarre, you must flee immediately. Leave for Ussel without a moment's delay and I'll get you out of the country by Lysander in three days time.'

'The police chief promised to warn me if I was in any danger. Give me forty-eight hours.'

'If Eagle makes his escape tonight they'll grab you again.'

'I'm expecting my son. He's getting to the age when he needs some guidance.' It was the Pau story all over again. The Bishop added his entreaties to mine but they had no effect and dawn was breaking.

'If you won't think of yourself, think of the network.'

He looked at me, quite taken aback, and his eyes softened. 'The network! I think it would be more honest if I tell you at once, Marie-Madeleine, to remain head of it. I'm a has-been. It's a job where one mustn't miss the bus.'

'Very well, Navarre. You're handing over command of the network to me? Good, I'll take advantage of it. I order you to follow us.'

He roared with laughter. 'Order? That's funny! You know perfectly well, both of you, that I've never obeyed an order in my life. I'm a rebel. Look, I'll make one concession to you; send someone to fetch me tomorrow.'

'We're making a mistake in leaving him,' sighed the Bishop as he got into the train in the pale morning light.

'One confidence deserves another. I'm afraid the die is cast, Bishop, but we couldn't stay. A terrifying thing has just happened to me; even when he's free Navarre leaves responsibility for the network to me. I'm definitely no longer my own master.'

Fawn (Dor), whom I had sent to fetch Navarre, did not return to Toulouse for another two days, and then he was alone. I had waited up all night and knew in advance what had happened.

'Where is he?'

'In the station waiting room, between two gendarmes.'

'Why didn't you take last night's train?'

'He insisted on spending one last cosy evening by the fire,' he said disconsolately. 'I went to bed and when I came out of my room at five o'clock this morning I saw the two gendarmes standing in front of his door. I walked past them without stopping. . . .'

'You did quite right.'

'I went straight to the station. Ten minutes before the train left the Major arrived handcuffed to the gendarmes and I heard him say to them: "I'm a badly wounded man, take my handcuffs off, I give you my word of honour not to escape." He was joking with them.'

'Why were they in the waiting room?'

'They seemed to be waiting for another train. What shall I do now?'

'Warn Basset at once. He can lay on a rescue party.'

Basset was accordingly informed at once.

It was possible to get near Navarre but the only way to rescue him successfully at Toulouse station was by shooting down the gendarmes. So Navarre refused. He could not bear the thought of having French blood on his hands.

Arriving from Monaco immaculately dressed, calm and realistic as usual, Spaniel had heard this report. This new blow against his lifelong friend disgusted him.

'Why didn't you rescue Navarre?' he asked me reproachfully. 'After Eagle's escape that was fatal.'

'Eagle's escaped?'

'It's odds on. By now Eagle is well on his way, if my calculations are right.'

'Your calculations are always right, my dear Colonel.'

'It's easy to calculate for others,' he said modestly.

'And what about us, Colonel? I'm ashamed to say I haven't sent a single piece of information since 7 November. It's not our job to play hide and seek with the Nazis, but to destroy them.'

Spaniel's half-suppressed laugh cheered me. 'The others are doing that for you. The alert system you arranged has paid off. Everything is intact. Galvanized by the Giraud affair, our friends are working twice as fast and twice as hard. I've split up the Marseilles sector, Panda is reforming it and the money is still undiscovered. Wolf is in Lyons. Armadillo and Bison are in Paris. Alligator and Beaver are in Nice. That's where things are worst. Not much credit to me.' he added, looking contrite.

'Elephant told me that you've got a bottleneck.'

'Yes. Now that the Algiers business has come off hordes of people are turning up from all over the place. Some of our agents want to be evacuated so that they can take up arms again and then lots of colonels and generals are convinced that we have only to ring up to get a submarine. I don't known how I'm going to feed and house them all.'

'You'll get two million francs via operation Apollo, Colonel. Deposit them very carefully in Monaco, but take what you need to save our people. How will you be able to evacuate those who are compromised most?'

'The Royal Navy will risk no more submarines now that the Germans are on the shores of the Mediterranean too, but the British inform me that some large, inoffensive-looking fishing boats, feluccas—you know the sort of thing—are on their way from Barcelona. The operation's code name is Nomad. I shall be able to put the whole caboodle into them.'

'I'm not at all happy about this business of sea caravans. I'd much rather organize the same sort of thing across the Pyrenees.'

'That's just what Jacques said to me. He's gone to try his luck that way.'

My brother! The only one for whom I had not been able to do anything had lost confidence in me. He was truly one of those people condemned by fate to travel alone through life.

Seeing how affected I was, Spaniel went on quickly: 'The British are definitely expecting you to go and see them this moon. They keep reminding me in all their telegrams. That's the main reason why I'm here.'

'I'm very sorry to have to disappoint you, Colonel. I didn't escape to go dashing off to London.'

'I had a feeling you wouldn't,' said Spaniel and got up. 'Look after yourself, my dear.' He kissed me on the forehead with such sadness that I felt guilty about letting him go back.

Thanks to the Damms' extraordinary sense of hospitality, I was able, in their house in the Rue Clauzel, to pick up the threads of the network again and to enjoy at last a rare happiness—to see my young son. In October I had sent him to the Jesuit college in Toulouse, where Josette, whom I had made his local contact, was going to fetch him and employ all kinds of subterfuge to bring him to me. I had been told that somewhere in the school there was a priest who had been one of the leaders of the famous Belgian network of the First World War, known as 'La Dame Blanche'. I was sure he would protect my son should he be in danger.

Vals-les-Bains is a splendid little fortified town in Ardèche. Policemen, sentries, guard post, a gendarmerie section—nothing was missing in the way of armed welcome in this one-time spa.

General Cochet, one of the very first members of the Resistance in France, had through his sister been able to obtain the things needed for the escape that the two airmen determined to make together—a long rope and a hacksaw. Also through his sister, Eagle organized outside help, for they could get away only by throwing the rope weighted with a bundle of clothes over the surrounding wall. As both of them were being kept on the fourth floor this would be difficult.

Eagle had already dealt with his lock by replacing the screws in his door with hair. On the evening of D-Day, when his guards were having their meal, he went and sawed through the bar across the lavatory window while Cochet kept watch. Eagle was locked in at nine-thirty as usual. In bed, he got the rope and his own things ready. A gendarme had been posted six feet away as a special precaution, and a policeman had arrived the same day and was in the next room, so Eagle had to make all his preparations quickly and silently.

At the appointed time he pushed the lock. It yielded and he went along to Cochet's door, past the snoring gendarme, and opened it. The two men stole behind one another along the corridor, brushed by the gendarme and went into the lavatory, where the bar had been sawn through. Leaning well out of the window Eagle hurled forth the bundle of clothes and the weight took the rope with it. Boys from the network, waiting outside the wall, seized it and he only had to tie his own end firmly. Hanging on by one leg, Cochet slid quickly down the sloping eighty feet of rope and reached the bottom head first. It was then Eagle's turn. He took a deep breath and savoured the icy air that filled his lungs. He launched himself out of the window. He was heavier than Cochet and thought his aerial acrobatics were much superior. But now taut with the greater weight, the rope offered no proper hold. Eagle got down safely, but although he was wearing gloves his hands were raw.

A car was waiting nearby with the engine running. At the wheel was Paul Joyon of the Vichy sector, who drove off westwards. At his side was Jean Grappin, who had organized the affair and explained that they were going to Sheepdog's.

'Vichy again!' exclaimed Eagle, startled. 'That's the end!'

'But Faye,' said Grappin (Panda), 'it's the last place they'll look for you.'

I learned of Eagle's successful escape on 23 November and then, almost at once, on the 25th, of the success of the Lysander Operation Apollo that had taken place on the Ussel landing ground. It was a triumph for Mahout, for it was found possible to fit my Corsican rescuers into the one cockpit. Their aerial baptism—it was their first flight—could not have been happy. 'One of them had to be hauled in upside down,' Zebra reported. 'I felt sorry for him.'

It was an interesting innovation, but for the moment my whole attention was taken up with another problem. British Intelligence had approved my caravan project *tra los montes*; I received a telegram giving a long list of names of Canadian airmen, followed by their ranks, who were believed to have baled out during air raids over France and Belgium. I was to allot these identities—false, of course—to the people I wanted to evacuate. This piece of deception would allow them to by-pass the Spanish internment camps, because the same list had been sent to Franco's *Seguridad* and they would be accepted as combatants at the frontier posts. True to his alias,

Dromedary, together with genuine smugglers, would organize the passage of the 'Canadian' caravans along the mule tracks through the towering, snow-capped peaks.

Since Eagle was free again, we needed a more central headquarters than the charming but vulnerable one in Toulouse. So it was decided that I should set off with Ermine and Magpie, who refused to be separated from his transmitter, for the retreat at Ussel in Corrèze, 150 miles north, in a car belonging to Gulliver's team, with an escort of good solid 'animals' armed to the teeth.

'Welcome, madame! Quickly, Marie, the dinner, they're frozen.' Jean Vinzant (Great Dane) fussed around us and ushered us into his large family house in Ussel.

'Great Dane, I thank you from the bottom of my heart. Already three successful landings on the Thalamy landing ground! And now we come and invade you!'

'I shan't be able to keep you,' he said sadly. 'This house isn't safe enough. It must stay intact, like a glass house, so that we can continue our work. But we're going to take you, by stages, to an inaccessible headquarters.'

'You're right, we're going to cause far too great an upheaval here.'

'You'll find we'll try to cope,' smiled Great Dane. 'Let me introduce you.' He took me into an office where I found a whole crowd of people gathered: Dr Syriex (Fox Terrier) and Dr Bellecour. They worked for us, but they were also setting up bases in the region for the secret army. And then there were the leaders responsible for the network in the town of Tulle: Louis Lemaire (Setter), and his adjutant Fernand Allibert (Barbet). Mme Dumont (Cicada) kept a mountain hut. And there was Marty (Hound) and Hummel (Cocker), and his niece and Roland Creel (Labrador). They had already tramped hundreds of miles to help the cause.

I was dazzled by the sight of this squad of men so inured to the harsh mountain climate, so deeply imbued with the silence of the forests and so familiar with the twisting paths of the Limousin region that they constituted, in fact, a natural pack of hounds ready to attack the enemy. This was the astonishing hidden face of France, the inexhaustible spring of spiritual values and courage.

The cold seemed less sharp at midnight when Ermine and I were taken the first stage, to stay in a real farm smelling of good cow's milk and where the bed, with its red eiderdown and stiff sheets, seemed to me like a little corner of paradise. Eagle joined us there on 17 December. We hardly had time to tell one another about our various adventures before we were off again, along the twisting mountain roads, heading for the inaccessible headquarters promised by Great Dane: the Lemaire farm.

Lemaire, the farmer, was an enthusiastic listener to the BBC, to which he solemnly tuned in at every meal. 'Since you claim to be in touch with

London,' he said to me, doubt in his voice, 'give me proof! I shall expect to hear a sentence you send to London radio.'

'Child's play,' I replied, adding to my daily message a sentence specially agreed with my host.

'We're going to be in a fix if he doesn't give us anything to eat until it comes,' said Eagle anxiously, while Magpie was setting up his transmitter and Ermine helped the old servant to take the buckwheat pancakes back to the hearth.

Our good farmer, however, knew the requirements of hospitality. He invited us to go in for our meal, but slyly switched on the radio. Boum, boum, boum, BOUM. 'Frenchmen speak to Frenchmen. Here are the personal messages: The eel has been caught, I repeat: The eel has been caught. . . .' Suddenly: 'We thank the Mayor and we are counting on him. I repeat: We thank the Mayor and are counting on him.'

We looked at one another in amazement. Our M. Lemaire (the Mayor) was staggered and got up stammering: 'Well, I'm damned, I never thought it would be so quick.' Nor did we.

After that our trek to new pastures began again. It took us to a hotel in Terrasson in the Dordogne. A whole floor to ourselves. The owners were utterly devoted to our cause. Nothing could be more practical. At last we could take up the reins of command again in reasonable ease and with a sense of security.

The Duke of Magenta (Saluki) was the first to appear, his hands full of good, solid provisions and no less substantial reports. He beamed to find us safe and sound. We hugged one another like children. He thanked us for having managed to send warning messages over the BBC after our arrest. The whole of the northern region was peaceful and fully operational. Animated by a spirit of rivalry, he was even evacuating people to England by sea, using fishing boats that he chartered at Carantec.

The Bishop had arrived on Saluki's heels but we could see from his face that the news in the southern zone was far less good.

'Things are bad,' were his first words. 'We're afraid of a revolt. Spaniel gave Cockroach the bag with the two millions francs and the mail so that he could put it in his safe. He won't give any of it back. Worse still, he's taking our agents. Tringa is joining him and urging all our radio operators to desert us.

'This wretch and his lies nearly made us miss Operation Minerva,' I said in my exasperation. 'I've never been able to find out why he didn't transmit my messages to London. In any case, I'd given orders that he was never to be used again.'

'I know,' said the Bishop, 'people begin by lying, go on to stealing, and end up by betraying you.'

'He's a real traitor,' said Eagle, cutting in. 'Bishop, go off at once with Saluki and smash this dirty plot. Get hold of the men who volunteered to go to Paris and the northern sectors. That's where everything is going to happen from now on. Since the American landing and Rommel's retreat, the south of France is becoming less and less important. If that crook of yours makes one false move he'd better look out! Meanwhile we're more broke than ever. Our people are going to starve.'

We were expecting General Cochet, Eagle's escape partner, to arrive in Ussel at any moment with Claude de Boislambert, who had been rescued from Gannat prison. They had to be evacuated. Eagle, too, must be got away. Another Lysander Operation had to take place at all costs. The gales began and the December moon was born under unfavourable auspices; the wind howled and rattled the shutters, the rain beat down and lashed the windows.

While we were settling the details of the Lysander mission, called Operation Ajax, with Magpie, we heard a furious banging on the office door.

'Who's that?'

'Pony. Open the door quickly.'

To our surprise, the man who entered was Cricket (Colonel Kauffmann), his shoes and greatcoat soaked, the rain streaming from his hat. He coughed, sat down heavily and looked at us in bewilderment. 'Well, aren't you going to ask me anything?' he asked. He had come from Paris, where he had gone to glean what news he could about the fate of our patrols now in enemy hands.

'I'll tell you the news,' he said heavily. '*They have been shot.* Sentenced on 13 November. Shot on the 30th. Vallet, Hugon, Pautard, Poulain, Bouvet, Toeuf, the two Bonnets and Ornstein have been shot. Jackson and Jean de Malherbe have been deported. The two engineers, Sgier and Blanchard, have been released for lack of evidence.'

Bla's ghost walked between Eagle and me. Cricket mechanically wiped his wet face and continued to stare at us as though he could not see us, as though a horrible premonitory vision of further killings and further slaughter had risen before his eyes. Blindly, he handed us a sodden piece of paper—Lucien Vallet's last letter:

'. . . *My hour has come, I am leaving you, Mother darling. . . . I have had courage and hope to the end. . . . Poor Mother! I thank you, for the last time, for everything you have done for me and ask forgiveness for all the worry that I may have caused you. . . . I have just received the last sacraments and I await the decisive hour with courage and peace in my heart. . . . I think of you . . . of our dear family. Of all the very dear friends who have helped me in this final episode of my life. I think I have done my duty to my country and my comrades, you will never need to blush on my account. That is a great comfort to me. . . . Be courageous. . . . Be courageous, all of you. Farewell, everybody. Farewell, Mother.*'

Operation Ajax was announced. Silent and bruised in spirit, we left Terrasson for Ussel.

Our fugitives had arrived and once again Great Dane's house was full. Boislambert had only one thought in mind—to rejoin de Gaulle, whom he had been serving since 16 June 1940. Cochet, a rebel against Pétain's regime since Vichy's early days—which was the reason for his imprisonment at Vals-les-Bains—now wanted to leave to take up a command in Algiers commensurate with his abilities. He transferred his organization to my care and introduced me to its leader, René Nougués, a tall, fair-haired lawyer whom I immediately called 'Auvergne Bleu'.

I was very fond of Boislambert and Cochet, but they posed a tricky problem. British Intelligence made it quite clear that they were not Thomas Cook and Son and that the RAF would not take unwarranted risks. Henceforth the Lysanders should be used only for the needs of the service and only our agents, equipment and reports would be given top priority.

I suspected that this decision had been taken as a result of the evacuation of my Corsican rescuers. In fact the British had been disappointed to see them arrive instead of me. They had been waiting on the airfield to receive me with pomp and ceremony only to see three complete strangers. They obviously had good reason for astonishment, but they had forgiven me for this deceit when they discovered that a debt of honour was involved.

I had therefore drawn up my own priority list and the first to be approved was Fawn (Henri-Léopold Dor). Eagle's departure, too, was now obviously vital, so that the British and French commands could better appreciate the situation created by the total occupation of France and the scuttling of the French fleet at Toulon. That left only one place free. I took the risk of telegraphing to suggest that this should go either to Cochet or to Boislambert. I was staggered by the reply that came back: 'Let them go through Spain like everybody else.' Boislambert demanded that General de Gaulle should be approached personally. I radioed back. The next time we were in contact with London we were told that General de Gaulle was most anxious to see Boislambert and Cochet very nobly stood down.

A six weeks' backlog of reports from all over France flowed in. Eagle and I went through them with a feeling of pride: many of these described airfields with their anti-aircraft defences and the numbers and types of machines based on them; the identification signs and location of the divisions massed in the north and in Brittany; troop movements towards the Russian front; samples of synthetic fuels and strange metals; a new type of gas mask; the 'troop movements in course of preparation'; the cargo lists of Japanese ships, and also the intelligence maps depicting the gigantic works of the Todt organization that ran the whole length of the French coastline, encircling and encasing the 'Fortress of Europe' in a concrete suit of armour.

'Has Hitler got the wind up!' said Eagle, with a whoop of delight.

A year earlier there had been about a hundred of us, now there were nearly a thousand preparing the monster's end. Each one of our friends founded a family, so to speak, even those who had disappeared and whose legacy we inherited to the full.

Feeling an intense glow of pride at this stupendous effort, I closed the cases, wedging the documents between pretty bottles of nectar, for if we liked English whisky and cigarettes, our British Intelligence friends thoroughly appreciated Paris perfumes and cognac.

All that was missing was the plane. It would not come. The weather was absolutely thick and the full moon was on the wane. There was nothing to do but change the plans.

For the animals the trek was not yet over. I could not remain in the Ussel sector, which had to be reserved for operational purposes. Cricket had unearthed 'something extra-special, a chateau', for us about a hundred miles away, near the old town of Sarlat. Eagle, forced to wait for the next moon, had already switched the regional leaders we were expecting to this new style headquarters. Elephant was presented with a car which he handled on the ice-covered roads in masterly fashion and which, a most unusual luxury, was always purring at the door.

Gathered all together for the last time around Great Dane's hospitable table in the beneficent truce that Christmas brought, we were merry in spite of everything. We relished the fact that we were free and able to serve our cause and our country again, and the kiss of peace that we exchanged when we parted and went our several ways was that of men of good will.

We knew that at Stalingrad the arrogant Wehrmacht was beginning to feel the bite of the Russian frosts and that one day the Nazi wave would break up on the colossal Soviet iceberg. It would then flow back over us in a furious flood unleashed by its Führer's frenzied, impotent wrath.

Gone was the illusory unoccupied zone and its relative oases. Farewell, Vichy policemen, with your easy-going instincts! Now operating over the whole territory, the Abwehr and the Gestapo had suspended their rivalry to advance like a steamroller of deadly efficiency. The Abwehr with its subtle infiltration methods was the demoniacal intelligence. The Gestapo with its arrests, tortures and killings, was the blind, bestial force. We should have to brave them with our poor weapons and on our forefathers' soil for a very long time yet.

The terrible year was about to begin.

THE TERRIBLE YEAR

*The true Resistance lost
two-thirds of its members.*

André Malraux

17 MALFONDS

The Château of Malfonds at Sarlat well deserved its name. No doubt it had been opulent in the days when a happy family lived there to enliven its huge rooms, its vast corridors and its English-style gardens. But on the evening of our arrival it struck us as a sombre, melancholy, dusty place, dead except for its draughts. We were frozen as soon as we entered the fake baronial hall.

'You'll soon thaw out,' Cricket (Colonel Kauffmann) said as he welcomed us. 'Come into the kitchen all of you. Tomboy!' he called out. 'Tomboy!' A charming young country girl appeared, curiously dressed in a severely tailored suit. Her hair had been permed and her hands were nicely manicured. 'This is Henriette Amable, "Tomboy". She's a formidable young woman and acts as my special courier. She'll look after you. You won't lack for anything.'

In the huge kitchen the enormous, ancient stove was roaring cheerfully. 'If the boys arrive in time we shall even be able to see the New Year in,' Eagle remarked, peering at the Sarlat hams, the truffles and the splendid assortment of bottles that the far-sighted Tomboy had laid in.

A hoarse cough told me that Tiger had already arrived. I could not suppress my shock at the sight of his haggard appearance. His eyes were like carbuncles set in a wax face. In spite of the total Nazi occupation, the demarcation line had not been abolished. He had just crossed it and had nearly been caught. He had been fired at and had to dodge from side to side as he fled, the bullets whistling about his ears and going through his coat. As he ran he swallowed the secret papers he was carrying. He embraced me convulsively.

'Little one, little one,' he finally managed to say, 'to think we nearly finished you off with that submarine business! But I'm sure you'll survive. You'll always survive.'

His cough racked him the whole time he was speaking. Then he spat up blood. 'Tiger,' I exclaimed, 'you're in a dreadful state.'

'It doesn't matter," he replied. Suddenly his face lit up at the sight of Jack Tar (Poulard), who had arrived dragging his large blue fibre suitcase with him.

'And how did you get across the line, Jack Tar?' He pointed to his jacket, which Tomboy was mending neatly.

'Well,' said Jack Tar, pausing at the sight of the bullet holes. 'It was much less trouble for me. I was arrested.' We started in surprise. 'Getting out of the train, on the wrong side as usual, I fell bang on top of an officer doing his rounds and was grabbed by the seat of my trousers.'

'You should have left your suitcase on the track, Jack Tar!'

'And what if I'd abandoned all our friends' reports, eh? I sat down hard on it when I got to the Kommandatur at the station. The Nazi officer was the sententious rather than the loud-mouthed type. He asked me why I was slipping across the line illegally. I told him I was a student and coming to visit the prehistoric Eyzies caves. "That's good, my lad, that's good, les Eyzies. Usually it's terrorists who slip across the frontier. They transport weapons, documents that lead to the death of thousands of Germans."

'"Oh dear," I said, "the dirty dogs," thinking if you only knew what's under my backside. . . . In the end he let me go and even gave me an *Ausweis* for both ways. The things one has to do to win the war!'

'How's Brittany, Jack Tar?'

'Splendid, chief. Thanks to my boys,' he hastened to add, ever modest, 'especially Maurice Gillet (Unicorn). We're doing fine. Octopus sets up police roadblocks so as to get better confirmation of the Nazi regimental signs. Urus is doing his stuff at the Saint-Nazaire base and keeping an eye on the Atlantic coast.'

'What about Unicorn? He's madly pro-British.'

'If you could only see him, making out he's even more short-sighted than he is and bumping deliberately into the sentries to get better photographs of the submarine pens with his tiny Japanese camera! But our real triumphs have come since I took him his radio. A word to London and down go the U-boats.'

'Who tips Unicorn off about when they're sailing?' I asked fascinated.

'A little dressmaker, a girl called Shrimp, working at the submarine base. She repairs the lifebelts, sort of Mae Wests. She repairs them by pricking little holes in them. "Like that," she says, "they'll float longer." What's more, she knows that when the pressure's on it means a unit is going to sail within thirty-six hours. The sailors turn up, demand their lifebelts and chat to one another. By keeping her ears cocked she picks up the numbers of the U-boats that are leaving. Then she runs quickly to Unicorn and says: "The U 92 is leaving Brest." The British do the rest. It's not difficult.'

At that moment Mandrill walked into the welcoming kitchen, which had now become an operational headquarters. I looked with absolute amazement at my little Lord Fauntleroy, whose aristocratic face had matured into something manly and determined, a real tough guy. He was as thin as a lath and black as a coalman.

'Bordeaux feeding doesn't suit you, Mandrill.'

'Buddha preserve me from it, madame. If I liked it I wouldn't be able to get into Marco's tender. Marco's an engine driver. I don't like walking, so I cross the line with him. When the train from Bordeaux has steam up, Marco gives a special whistle. I slip into the station and he shoves me into his tender. Same thing going back.'

With Mandrill things were both simple and complicated at the same time, for his region had shrunk considerably. The Royal Navy was extremely appreciative of his skill in hunting down U-boats and blockade runners and I passed on the compliments I received about him.

'It's purely a matter of cunning,' he explained in his off-hand way. 'You can't imagine the number of marvellous people I bump into wherever I go. Nearly all my agents are volunteers and unpaid. And they come from every class of society—regular and reserve officers, workmen, priests, even a canon, Monsignor Bordes, and even a Protestant pastor, Yann Roullet, the son-in-law of Colonel Delmas-Vieljeux, the mayor of La Rochelle, who also does his bit. I've got them everywhere, as far as Poitiers, where a boy we call Asp performs miracles. And Saint-Mixent, where General Faucher has just agreed to take on the sector. I've called him Pekinese.'

'Isn't it too much for one man?'

'I love travelling around and seeing the country. I find it refreshing,' he replied, delicately rubbing his long, tapering, bony hands together.

'So the British have damaged your notorious blockade runners in the Gironde estuary?'

'Yes, on 18 December,' he said, brightening up. 'I'd been signalling the presence of the *Dresden* and the *Tannenfels* for days on end, giving their position almost to the inch. The *Abbama*, the *Portland* and the *Sperr Kecher* were anchored by them. When they blew up on 18 December I went absolutely crazy with joy.'

'How did the English manage it?'

'No doubt some men were put into a dinghy from a submarine off the mouth of the river and laid magnetic mines. It was a fantastic explosion. I'm ashamed I didn't do it myself.'

'Mandrill, you know perfectly well that I won't let people do lots of different jobs.'

Tiger and I were now alone.

'Did you see how the Darlan affair ended?' he began. 'He's dead, assassinated by a young man, Bonnier de la Chapelle, who was sentenced to death at once.' Like a lightning flash, the propellor-man's prophecy shot through my mind.

He got up to take a little of the milk that Tomboy had warmed up on the corner of the stove. 'What did you think of Verteré's arrest?' he continued

Verteré (Hyena) had been arrested in Paris on 10 November. Rumours had reached me in Toulouse and Ussel, but as we had broken with him completely I had not given it much thought, for it occurred at the time of our own trials and tribulations in Marseilles.

'He was transferred with his girl friend Gertrude to Loos-les-Lille prison, like several of his Paris agents. Since then there's been a complete round-up in the north. Everything must be started again from scratch,' he said bitterly.

'And so, as I feared, the north was fatal for him.'

'He didn't talk, but he fell for the classic trick—the stool pigeon put in the same cell, in whom you confide when you're at the end of your tether.'

'What effect will it have on the network?'

'Hyena knew a tremendous amount. Saluki and I have changed and duplicated everything we could.'

'Eagle claims that he will behave like an officer and say nothing.'

'In the Nazis' hands, little one, some people turn into monsters.'

Tiger returned repeatedly to the subject of the action he was undertaking in the huge region where Saluki was sparing no effort or expense to keep things going, as though the stream of words in itself had the power to exorcize the lacerating memory of his comrades who had disappeared in Fresnes. Once again I was moved to tears to see the way old and new came to merge.

The regions of Paris, Normandy and Brittany were now all covered by our agents and transmitters. Tiger had reserved the forbidden zones for himself. I would have been astounded if he had not done so! The east, alas, had been in a bad way since the arrest of the local leader, Gérard Novel.

'It's a miracle, Tiger, that apart from the hard blow of Novel's arrest, that region has not been the centre of any catastrophe for thirteen months, since the Bla business.'

'People are still transmitting, getting over difficulties and obstacles. I tell you, little one, it isn't lack of work that will be our undoing.'

Eagle, Cricket, Jack Tar, Magpie and Mandrill had come in in a body and raided the kitchen. The ham was piled thick on the plates, the truffles gave a wonderful aroma to the eggs that Tomboy deftly scrambled, the good wine from Cricket's cellar gurgled as it was poured into the glasses. The chateau lost its Sleeping Beauty air.

Tiger did not join in the feast but went on sipping his hot milk. He wanted to fulfil his mission as long as he had the strength left and the serene and loving look that he bestowed on each one of us was the heart-felt farewell of a prince to his trusty lieges.

Lying in my icy room on the first floor I found it impossible to sleep. Downstairs in the drawing room that had been converted into a dormitory, Tiger's cough rent the silence of the night. I had told him before we parted that he would not be going back to Paris before I'd got to the bottom of his lung trouble, but the sidelong glances that he exchanged with Jack Tar worried me. I crept down and made sure that my little troop was asleep. I then went back and followed their example while the dawn and the frost turned the ancient trees in the park white.

'Breakfast! Breakfast!' cried Magpie, hammering on my door until it rang. 'Or rather lunch,' he announced when I appeared in the dining room where Eagle and he were facing the leftovers from the night before. 'It's noon, madame.'

'Where are the others?'

'Gone, flown,' said Eagle gloomily. 'I've only this minute come back in and they especially said they didn't want to wake you.'

'I couldn't stop them from taking French leave, madame,' said Magpie, 'but I understand them. Duty first.'

A sharp pain that pierced the very depth of my being told me that I would never see Tiger again.

One of Sheepdog's (General Raynal's) couriers came to inform me that they needed me in Vichy to give them advice about organizing Navarre's escape. I went, made up so effectively that my own mother would not have recognized me.

'I nearly missed you at the exit from the platform,' Gulliver said as he took me off to his lodging near the station. 'Women are dreadful frauds,' he added reproachfully. Behind us I could hear the sure, springy step of his right-hand man, Paul Guillebaud, a fierce Moufflon who was there to protect us.

Sheepdog was waiting for me, sipping an ersatz coffee. 'My dear child—excuse me calling you that, you could be my daughter—we have so many things to do!' said the old soldier in a voice that might have been General Joffre's at the battle of the Marne. 'First, our great leader's escape. His prison at Evaux-les-Bains in the Massif Central is only a fortified hotel used for prisoners in transit. We can hide him beneath a pile of poultry cages in the prison van when the driver goes out on odd jobs. It's all been fixed with him.'

'What do you know about him?'

'Name, Chambon. Bachelor, jovial, short and fat.'

'Fat these days? That sounds fishy.'

'Moufflon met him several times and thinks he's reasonably safe. He must get his food on the black market, hence his exorbitant charge, 100,000 francs.'

'That's an enormous sum, General. I don't like people who put that sort of price on the risks they take. Does he know any other agents of ours?'

'I'm afraid the driver also knows the General,' said Gulliver in a reproving voice. Sheepdog flushed like a boy found out.

'I suppose you told this money-grubber who you were, General?'

'I had to. What does an old man like me count compared with Navarre?'

'Promise me then, not to keep anything compromising in your house, so that you're not at the mercy of a search. The Gestapo rules in Vichy now.'

'I'm not afraid of teutonic policemen,' he answered. 'My transmitter is in the care of my gardener, who'd rather be hacked to pieces than betray me. All my records are made out in a sort of punning style and written in a language that only I can translate—one word in Breton, one in Polish.' From his pocket he took a notebook filled with the most extraordinary scrawl. 'I speak Polish fluently. I learned it when I was doing a tour of duty in Poland in 1920, and I'm a Breton by birth.'

'You've been deceiving me, General. Since you keep your archives handy, allow me to ask you for the full details about your naval specialist. It's more necessary than ever to create a naval sub-network with the sole job of keeping tabs on activity in the ports and bases occupied by the Germans. The fleet was scuttled at Toulon, but British Intelligence is afraid that the enemy will raise part of it. In the Atlantic the U-boats are multiplying like shoals of sardines. It's absolutely vital to keep up a continuous watch. Send your sea god to me quickly, we'll call him Triton.'

'He was only awaiting the summons. Now it's time I went home; my wife doesn't like me to be out too long.'

The dear old man squared his shoulders and drew himself up. He gave me a magnificent military salute. 'Bless you,' he said, 'for what you are doing. You make it possible for an old soldier like me to serve his country again.'

For some time Gulliver had been stamping around in the room restlessly. He muttered: 'She hasn't come home, the bitch, she hasn't come home.'

I sent Moufflon to watch the station approaches and now that I was alone with the leader of the flock I questioned him gently: 'Something wrong, Gulliver?'

'Why should I keep it from you, chief? I'm going mad.'

'This underground existence doesn't help one's nerves.'

'It isn't that. But I'm going mad with jealousy. I think I shall kill her.'

'Who?'

'My wife.'

'That's all we need to put us really in the soup, a crime of passion. Look here, Gulliver, one doesn't go mad with jealousy on mere suspicion. I know your wife and she seems perfectly all right to me.'

'It's no longer just suspicion. I'm sure she's being unfaithful to me with the Boches.'

'Heavens, that's more serious. You're afraid that she tells them secrets in bed?'

'I don't give a damn about the secrets! I love her, you understand. It's sheer torture. I can't sleep and I can't eat because of it. *I* don't give her those pretty dresses and those jewels, I just couldn't. So, chief,' he said shaking with anger, 'one day I'm sure I shan't be able to stop myself. I'm asking you to get me out. Over in England I shall suffer just as much but I won't be able to do anything dreadful.'

'It's an excellent idea, Gulliver. I've a caravan leaving for Spain. I'll squeeze you in. I imagine Moufflon's the best person to take your place?'

'Yes. Like me, he knows all the details about the sector I've built up, man by man, and to which I'm devoted.'

'Then don't leave, Gulliver.'

He looked down. 'I'd rather go.'

Putting on my Salvation Army-like clothes I followed him to the station when the first street lamps were lighting up. Vichy had not changed: there was still no sign of war.

Before we went into the station, Gulliver said: 'One more thing, chief. If I get to England the sentence on the BBC will be: "The ram has got its horns."'

I took the night train once again, haunted by the tragic picture of the man and his obsession. Was the wife passing information to her German lovers? Was the fat little driver an *agent provocateur*?

The new January moon appeared and with feverish impatience we began to watch its slim crescent swell. After the December gales the success of the Lysander operation Ajax II was a matter of life or death for us. Saluki and the Bishop had been able to recover a few bits and pieces from Operation Apollo at Cockroach's, but that would not last very long. The felucca operation had been cancelled; one little boat had sunk off Barcelona and very wisely Spaniel had switched the passengers waiting for it in Nice to Toulouse, the assembly point for the crossing of the Pyrenees. Tringa, our greatest worry since he had started urging our operators to desert, had obstinately refused to follow them. And so we had carefully parked him in the mountains of the Massif Central under Beaver's watchful eye. Boislambert and Fawn were back in Ussel. Eagle, escorted by Magpie, joined them there on 13 January.

Now left on my own at Malfonds, I barricaded myself in the chateau in the evening. In order to be ready for any eventuality I did not go to bed. I whiled away the time by preparing the tobacco leaves that Cricket (Colonel Kauffmann) had kindly brought me. 'They're Manosque,' he told me. 'Put them in salt water, dry them, cut them into thin sheets and tell me what you think of them.'

But these manual feats failed to allay my anxiety; I wrote to the Damms and asked them to find me a less isolated headquarters as a matter of urgency, and I was overjoyed to see my old friend Camille Schneider appear on a liaison visit from Marseilles.

My joy was short-lived. After describing at length the progress being made in the Marseilles sector recently revived by Grappin, and handing me a charming letter from Tiger-Cat, who apologized for leaving the organization without permission because his position in Vichy had become impossible, Jaguar (Camille Schneider) produced his shock.

'We've brought off a real scoop,' he said in his calm voice. 'We've got a German sailor to desert from the Kriegsmarine.'

'I don't really see why that's interesting,' I replied, pulling a face. 'How did it happen?'

'Eagle's brother-in-law spends all his evenings in a bar where a lot of Nazi soldiers go for a drink. He says he picks up a lot of valuable information there. One of the Fritzes he talks to had been going on about deserting for some time. He wanted his help. The fellow begged to be evacuated through Spain, so Panda had him brought to his headquarters and gave orders that he should go through our Béziers escape route.'

'The one Tiger-Cat used?'

'Yes, Pony, the courier, was to drive him there.'

I could not believe my ears. I looked hard at Jaguar. His kind, healthy, pink, bespectacled intellectual's face, with its halo of light brown hair, was the very essence of good faith. Since March 1941 he had been performing the most thankless tasks for the network, without which no action would have been possible—travelling thousands of miles by train, endlessly waiting around at rendezvous points, and making hundreds of bicycle trips carrying compromising messages and material.

'My dear Jaguar, you're to return immediately—hell for leather, as you're fond of saying—and you'll chuck this deserter into the Old Port. He's a phoney, don't you understand? A *provocateur*. This sort of thing doesn't happen, at least not like that. Straight into the Old Port, you understand.'

'I hope there's still time,' he said, putting his coat on again. 'I came to see you for enlightenment. I'm scared of this fellow, too.'

He left, his old bike squeaking as he rode down the avenue. Enlighten him? My God! What more could I do? Whom could I appeal to for help? Eagle had just flown to England and I was once more alone in a dark and sinister world.

I started to tremble when I heard the sound of tyres crunch on the road. Magpie could not possibly be back so soon. I turned out the light and, squeezing myself behind the door, I waited for the enemy with the safety catch of my revolver off. It was Magpie.

'Relax,' he exclaimed delightedly, seeing my pile of tobacco. 'The moon was as round and clear as in a film. Ajax II went off like clockwork. I've got my pockets full of Craven A's. I knew you were half dead with anxiety, so I took a car to get here more quickly than by those old puffing billies.'

I unpacked British Intelligence's suitcase, full, as usual, of charming gifts, encouraging letters and coded missives to do with the top secret problems on which information was urgently needed.

Magpie opened a tin of powdered coffee so that we could warm ourselves up. He took out the brick-like bundles of 5,000-franc notes, compressed so tightly that they looked like tinned ham. I smoked, sipped my coffee to savour it to the full and devoured the messages from my English friends. The first light of dawn found us talking about our happiness at knowing that Eagle and Boislambert were safe and picturing Fawn already strolling along the Strand and calling 'Taxi' in his inimitable accent.

The parachute drops directed by Seagull (Pierre Berthomier) with Magpie's help went off successfully. We were able to let people have their own individual weapons as well as shoes and warm clothes. Cricket got his new accumulators, for transmitting in the open air, from the middle of his artichoke fields—a remarkable innovation that gave the TAP set almost total immunity—and a whole shipment of transmitters was unpacked.

It was Georges Lamarque, the student recruited by Eagle, who now took over direction of the radio service. We called him Petrel. Travelling continually between Paris, Lyons, Marseilles and Vichy, he steadily built up his stocks and methodically delivered radio sets and recruited operators.

He had been unable to come on that particular day and had sent his liaison agent, Michele Goldschmidt (Hummingbird) and his chief operator, Armand Siffert (Oriole), an Alsatian and a fervent patriot as well as an outstanding engineer. With her broad smile, her superb complexion and colouring, her discreet and refined elegance, Hummingbird well deserved her name. She also seemed the obvious choice for distributing equipment in her own inoffensive-looking suitcases.

'How's Lyons, Hummingbird?'

'Absolutely fine. Wolf turned up at the end of November with a charming little Marseilles girl, Madeleine Crozet (Mouse). He's taken the Rhone region well in hand with Lazard, who spits fire.

'Lazard from the bank?'

'Yes, he's asked to do all the lousy jobs.'

I gave Hummingbird orders for Petrel and Wolf. She left again with her assured and dancing step and her beautiful face shone like the face of a saint in an Italian primitive. Behind her trotted Oriole, happily carrying his brand new equipment. I watched him go away, thrilled by the dynamism of this new recruit, but I suddenly had a vision of a martyr's halo behind his head. I almost called him back.

I was working on a research plan based on the latest British questionnaires when Magpie, who was drumming away on the window, roused me brutally from my cogitations. 'Look what's here,' he said.

I looked out and shook with terror at what I saw. A police car had drawn up in front of the steps. From it there got out a superintendent in full uniform, flanked by two burly policemen. While I was thinking I could already hear the words 'In the name of the law . . .' the superintendent shouted out: 'Open the door! It's Basset.'

It's a trap, we thought, as the visit was out of the blue. 'I recognize him,' said Magpie. And he ran to open the door.

'I'm sorry, madame,' said Superintendent Philippe (Basset) who could see from my white face that I had nearly passed out. 'I wanted my last job to be to present my respects to you dressed in my full official uniform.'

Recovering my composure with great difficulty, I had him sit down on the corner of the stove, the most comfortable place in the house. 'You'll all end up by giving me a heart attack,' I said, still badly shaken. 'What's happened to you, Basset?'

'Nothing's happened to me, but a circular arrived from Vichy this morning ordering us to round up Jews and hand them over to the enemy. From 1940 until now I've managed to perform the rare feat of not arresting a single Frenchman. Now, I'm going to be under pressure every minute and I've come to request the honour of being allowed to join the underground. I have too great a respect for my uniform to soil it.'

'I can only applaud your decision, Basset; but have you got everything tied up properly?'

'The two men who're with me are policemen with long and trusty records. They've fixed me up with an extraordinary hideout. From there I shall be able to command my sector. Six breaks in the chain and six checks. As safe as houses!'

He then described in detail the progress made in his district but he asked me to assign Zebra to him for his exclusive use. He had never seen anything so quick or so courageous as the young Pole, the Damms' adopted son.

'Do you think he'll agree to leave Griffin?'

Basset smiled: 'I've promised him lots of excitement.'

I gave him a considerable amount of equipment and money and the police car disappeared like a great wind sweeping over young wheat. As though it had been his cue, Zebra appeared, on foot as usual; walking was as easy for him as breathing.

'Griffin's found a house in Cahors belonging to a Spanish dentist,' he told us. 'It meets all your requirements: seven trains in both directions, a mirador and a double exit. You can move as soon as you like. Here's the map reference. Dad's expecting you there with Ermine.'

'Thanks, Zebra, you can tell your father that I'll join him tomorrow morning; but I've a personal question to ask you. Would you be willing to leave him and go and work for Basset?'

He nodded his proud, young, blonde head. 'Griffin is my father, but Basset's my master,' he said as he turned away.

'I'm leaving', I said to Cricket, who had been summoned urgently.

'You don't like my chateau?'

'Frankly, no. Since the Marseilles business I've been suffering from claustrophobia.'

'You're safe here!'

'Maybe, but I prefer my form of autonomous headquarters, which I've always found successful, and I shan't compromise your people. I am referring to the radio operator Blackbird, the liaison agents Bichon and Lacroix, your adjutant Poodle and his exquisite wife, and the Delpechs, who spared no effort or expense to see that everybody got to the right place.'

'That's what we're here for,' Cricket commented.

'No. Your role is intelligence pure and simple,' I answered.

He promised to get me a removal van for the following day, driven by Horvilleur, his operational chief. Elephant, who had been at Malfonds for several days, would take Magpie and me in his car. We arranged to meet at eight o'clock and I began feverishly to get my things packed.

Early next morning, the two vehicles purring in front of the steps, I was waiting for Magpie to finish the first contact of the day with London. I had not slept all night and I knew from experience that that sort of insomnia presaged grave developments. The exceptional life that we were leading compelled our overworked organs to perform new functions; a sort of radar was grafted on to a supercharged, hypertensed nervous system.

'Will you be long, Magpie?'

'QS 5, madame, I want to send all your messages.'

'No. Stop. I don't want you to.'

'It's going so well,' he complained and continued to transmit, tapping faster than ever.

A kind of frenzy possessed me. We must leave. Leave at once. 'Elephant, switch off the power.' Elephant switched off.

'A pity,' said Magpie, carefully folding his aerials. 'I've never had such a good time.' He looked at me in a way that implied: she's losing her nerve. Tomboy removed all trace of our presence and disappeared into the mist. We got into the car.

The next day Elephant went back to Malfonds to fetch a reserve transmitter that Magpie, to spread the risks, had hidden at the bottom of the garden. Some peasants stopped his car just before the chateau.

'Watch out,' they said. 'The Germans arrived hard on your heels yesterday, before the dust settled. They drew their revolvers and surrounded the place. We told them that the house was empty. They said they were after a "Mrs Harrison", a dangerous spy. They seemed absolutely furious at not finding her.'

After slipping into the copse to dig up the set, Elephant had driven back at top speed.

'It's certainly weird,' said Magpie. 'If you'd let me go on transmitting for another ten minutes longer, we'd have had it.'

I burst out laughing: '"Mrs Harrison"! *Herisson* (Hedgehog) my alias! They thought it was Harrison! They don't know who I am. They think I'm an Englishwoman!'

Well situated in the hilly part of the city, on a kind of spur, the house at Cahors, sixty miles north of Toulouse, overlooked every road. Ermine, who had already arrived with Mouchou Damm, had soon made sure that our rooms were as comfortable as possible. The whole house radiated a gentle warmth. It was the ideal headquarters, too good to be true.

I imposed draconian regulations. Magpie had discovered a hiding place for his radios in the moulding of the dining room ceiling and we took turns keeping watch. Every visitor arriving by one of the seven trains in both directions was observed while still a long way off and should we receive a visit by car we could, if necessary, escape into the country through a secret door. Damm watched all our doings with a certain scepticism. He was a very good fellow and warm-hearted, and gave little heed to the rules of ordinary common sense.

'Griffin, everyone in Toulouse knows you and we've been using your house in the Rue Clauzel too long. The time has come for you to go underground.'

'Brrr, in this cold,' said Damm jovially. 'What are your orders?'

'You say your wife is hiding somewhere on the Riviera. Go and get her at once, and rejoin me here, the two of you. You'll take charge of the headquarters secretariat. Magpie's leaving soon for Toulouse, where he has to check on the frequencies of the local set. Go with him but be careful. Don't leave the station. Don't get in touch with anybody.'

'Not even my son?'

'No, my dear Griffin, Zebra's Basset's agent now.'

'That's a nice thing! You forbid me to go home and you take away my son!'

'The Gestapo couldn't have known I was at Malfonds just by guesswork. They must have traced back some of our communication channels.'

'Our boys can't be suspected.'

'Of course not, but don't you think one of them may have been followed?' I then noticed his heavy fawn-coloured leather brief case. 'What have you got in there?'

Tucked away among all the business papers was the lease he had signed with the Spanish dentist who owned the house, which Magpie consequently called Castel Lolita.

'Well,' I said, 'it'd be disastrous if that paper was found on you. Now show me your wallet.'

'This is a regular search!'

'What's this?'

'Basset's address,' he said with some embarrassment. 'I'd promised Zebra to destroy it after learning everything in it by heart, but I haven't had time to.'

'I don't think I can let you keep this piece of paper. Burn it.'

'Hedgehog, I accept all your orders, but I beg you, let me keep this. It's so complicated. I'll learn it in the train.'

I called Magpie back in and repeated my strict instructions in his presence. Damm was going to Toulouse only to fetch his wife. They would separate at the station.

After they had gone, the cosiness and comfort of Castel Lolita struck me as a strange anachronism, a decor that some pretentious theatrical producer had adapted as the setting for a pure, classical tragedy.

I took the night watch, listening to the melodious murmur of the Lot, accompanied by the faint stirring of sleeping nature and punctuated by the shrill whistling of the trains.

The day of 29 January; 0900 hours. Magpie arrived on the first train, seething with desperate indignation.

'I couldn't stop them. Zebra was waiting for us at the station and then we went to dine. After that they wanted to take me along to the Rue Clauzel. I reminded them of your strict instructions, but it was no good. They said: "Hedgehog fusses too much, there's no hurry, we're going to clear up a few matters and we'll go on tomorrow."'

Magpie had gone to spend the night at the headquarters run by the policeman Guillot and used for the Pyrenees crossing, and had checked and logged the frequency on his set. In the morning, before starting back, he had prowled around in the Rue Clauzel. He saw a number of suspicious comings and goings and quickly cleared off.

At midday, Grasshopper appeared to say that Griffin and Zebra had been arrested at the Rue Clauzel at dawn. I told her to leave the city with Dromedary. Two hours later, Hummingbird (Michèle Goldschmidt), who had come on a liaison visit, returned to Lyons to give the alarm.

At four o'clock Edme Bichon, the Sarlat sector's liaison agent, turned up. 'By a miracle I met Cricket at Toulouse station,' he said, 'and in view of the urgency of what I have to tell you, he gave me your address.' Bichon had come back from Monaco and Nice and was nearly caught in a trap at Gazelle's house. He had time only to see that the OVRA, the Italian Secret Police, were there and to take cover in the Casino gardens.

'My God! If Gazelle has been captured, then Spaniel has certainly been arrested.'

'Nice must be decimated, too. The Bishop didn't turn up at the rendezvous we'd arranged. I thought the right thing to do was not to hang about. I'm sorry, madame.'

I told him to return to Sarlat and, whatever he did, not to move out of his house until he received fresh orders.

At seven in the evening Inspector Moudenc, Basset's adjutant, telephoned. In veiled, carefully chosen words he confirmed that Griffin and Zebra had been captured. He informed me of the arrest of several local agents.

Ten o'clock came and another phone call from Moudenc: 'I have very bad news for you. Your little basset hound has just been impounded. The rabies epidemic is so bad that the colt will also have to leave the stable.' Basset had been caught and the Colt was Moudenc himself.

An hour before midnight, Cricket phoned. 'Rabbit and Gavarni have been carried off by the fox,' he reported. That meant: Jean Broqua has been arrested in Pau, as well as the unfortunate Gavarni, who had not done a thing for months.

Midnight. In the large dining room with its crystal glass and its sparkling chandeliers I coded a message to London, anxiously watched by Ermine and Magpie. 'We can't stay in this house,' I told them when I had finished. 'Some of the arrested agents know it and the Gestapo's methods are such that the very best of our people may talk. Magpie, send this on your night frequencies.'

He began to strum. 'Great Scott, I've got them first go!'

I heard my message go out in Morse to the British. I informed them of the catastrophe and I begged them to pass on the alert via all our transmitters still functioning. I implored them to send this sentence out on the BBC: 'Marie-Madeleine has arrived safely in London and sends you her affectionate greetings.' I told them to send Faye back by Lysander Operation Pluto, which had been scheduled for February.

Magpie finished. He grabbed his set, Tuba, and a suitcase. Ermine saw to the clothes while I seized my own double-bottomed case and the bag containing the network's money. We marched off into the cold night and its army of hostile shadows, burdened like asses, to catch the dawn train.

We need not have left. None of those who knew Castel Lolita revealed its whereabouts to the Germans, even under torture.

We did not get to Tulle, about sixty miles north of Cahors by rail, until late in the evening of 30 January. Setter (Lemaire) who was head of the sector, got us into an old-fashioned hotel with big, ebony-coloured furniture, without our having to register our names. Outside my window flowed the turbulent waters of the River Corrèze. Hot and feverish, I flopped fully dressed between the spotless sheets, and burying my head under them, I relived all the horror of the new disaster that was overtaking us.

A council of war the following day with the main regional agents, Setter, Barbet and Cocker, brought me a few gleams of hope.

'We thought you had deserted us,' they all told me. 'We heard on the BBC yesterday that you had arrived in London. But why did you reveal your name since you're still with us?'

Revealing my name did not matter; the important thing was that the Gestapo should stop their interrogation of the unfortunate people who were being tortured to discover my whereabouts. My subterfuge was proving effective—but would it convince the Germans until Eagle came back?

Two men, Basset's bodyguards, had passed through Tulle and left me a letter that I nervously read and re-read over and over again.

'The six breaks in the chain have been crossed easily by the Gestapo, who know all the passwords, and Basset was beaten to death while he was trying to defend himself with a gun; we managed to get away by a miracle and want to escape through Spain. Colt has given us Panda's address in Marseilles. Apparently he can help us. We're sorry to be abandoning you, but the ruthless way the Nazis are destroying the network makes us think that *nothing more can now be done. . . .*'

Poor Basset, caught in spite of his knowledge of the police. Effective precautions were therefore impossible. Our fluidity was what counted, I thought. I must continue to foster the belief that I was in London, and I must move and keep on the move all the time. . . .

Another mystery: how did Moudenc get to know about the new escape route via Spain? News travelled fast in the network. It was impossible to prevent the boys from talking among themselves, from telling one another about their discoveries. Since they had been working together, all those men had come to regard the rules about strict separation as a joke. Had they really ever known those rules? We were not spies formed and trained in peacetime in the cocoon of specialized schools. I was not one of those big intelligence chiefs operating under remote control, manipulated by scientific 'centres' and protected by compartments so watertight that they were paralysed, or else compelled deliberately to surrender their living 'circuit-breakers'. I felt that I knew exactly what an ant must feel when the heel of a boot comes down on the nest.

'Nothing more can now be done,' the letter said. I took a grip on myself again. No, that was untrue. There was nothing that could not be achieved with men like Schaerrer, Vallet, Tiger and a whole army of volunteer fighters springing from a people ready for sacrifice.

On the evening of 31 January Magpie succeeded in establishing contact with London from the belfry of Tulle cathedral, while the Abbé Lair kept watch. He came back with gloomy and depressing messages: the Nice, Toulouse and Pau transmitters had fallen silent, like the one in Marseilles. It was not known what was happening in Lyons: VAL was transmitting irregularly and it would take a few days to locate. On the other hand there had been no break in Bordeaux or the northern zone. As for Eagle, he was in Algiers and could not return to France before the March moon.

Richards added: '*If you persist undoubtedly be arrested stop take the February Lysander stop awaiting you impatiently.*'

'You can't remain in the centre of Tulle,' Setter warned me. 'I've found you a safe hideout not far away, in the Chateau de Bra, but you shouldn't let the owners know who you are. We'll find some excuse. They adore the army.'

And so at the Chateau de Bra, a sort of poor relation of Malfonds, we passed for a military family whose menfolk were on the run.

'That's not everything, but I must get things sorted out and be ready for the contact with London,' Magpie whispered before we sat down for the evening meal. 'How can I put up my aerial? Our hosts will see through us in the end.'

'And the noise from the Morse key!' I called Ermine: 'Say that I've got a splitting headache and am staying in my room. When you get to the dessert, Magpie will come and join me on the pretext of bringing me an infusion. When you hear *ti-ti-ti-ta-ta* start up, you must begin making a noise, anything you like, but a lot of noise and really loud.'

As the time to establish contact approached, Magpie came up with a tray. He had soon twisted his aerial round all the picture hooks from which hung the old family portraits. 'It's the first time I've tried to transmit indoors,' he said anxiously. 'We were told it was O K at the training school. I'll try a few call signs.'

We immediately heard a shrill volley of vocal exercises coming up from the dining room, but they soon changed to a recital of patriotic songs sung by Ermine's pretty voice.

Contact was established. I informed British Intelligence that I was going to Lyons and consequently I would not be heard of for a few days.

'Colonel, calm yourself! Colonel!'

I suddenly recovered consciousness after a night bedevilled by nightmares that still haunted me. Where was I? From their ornate frames my host's forbears smiled condescendingly down at me. Other exclamations, even more heartrending, dragged me from my bed.

The Colonel could only be Cricket. I went into the room to see the masters of the house, Magpie, Ermine and a number of regional agents standing round the faithful Cricket, who had collapsed into a chair. When he saw me he began to shout: 'They've all been caught. Do you understand? My wife, my brothers, my liaison agents, my radio operator. All caught, you understand! All taken away by the Gestapo!'

His teeth were chattering and his eyes were blinded by tears. Upset but sympathetic, the friendly owners of the chateau at last knew what we were. I sent everyone except Magpie and Ermine out of the room and, kneeling down by Cricket, I managed to get hold of his hands, which he was wringing in despair.

'Explain, Cricket, you must explain.'

'It was those wonderful Delpechs, my "letterbox", who saved me. Forgive me, I'm exhausted. My family, all my friends. They won't release my wife unless I give myself up.'

'No, Cricket! Not that! You have no right to do that.' We were not the only ones involved. Nor were our own families the only ones. Our duty was to face up to our responsibilities, to save the network.

Eagle was in Algiers. Cricket must take his place. He was touched by my faith in him. Composed again at last, he dismissed all thought of surrendering to the Nazis. Then, drawing himself up to his full height, and wrapping his grey overcoat round himself, he said in a voice that was now steady: 'Very good, madame. We'll all go to Lyons.'

Our hosts came hurrying in to tell us that a car would enable us to catch the night train. We piled in with our luggage and the transmitting set. Before we started off, a courier from Tulle told us that the Gestapo had descended on Setter's house in the afternoon. But the Abbé Lair had stirred up the local inhabitants, who had besieged the shop, and the Nazi police had retreated. Undoubtedly a unique example of popular revolt. Setter had been able to escape, but I was afraid that the Nazis would wreak vengeance on the Abbé.

'Tell him to leave, too,' I urged the courier. He did not. A soldier does not desert his post, nor does a priest desert his priestly office.

Travelling by the local train that took hours to convey us to Lyons gave us all the time in the world to plan what to do on arrival. Cricket wanted to rush off to Mouse, Wolf's adjutant. I was dead against this: the Monaco, Nice, Toulouse, Pau, Sarlat, and now the Tulle sectors had been besieged practically simultaneously. The Marseilles transmitter no longer answered. We were beyond the shadow of a doubt the object of a concerted Gestapo operation. How, in these circumstances, could anyone imagine that Lyons would still be intact?

'Right!' Cricket admitted. 'So there's really not much point in going to Lyons!'

But we had a lot of friends in the city, who must still be at liberty. He could start by going to see Mlle Connorton, a nurse. When we stopped in the station, Ermine and I would get out at the front of the train, Magpie in the middle and Cricket at the back. He would go to Mlle Connorton and we to our friend the Baroness de Mareuil. Before meeting again we would, separately, make enquiries about what was happening at Mouse's.

Mouse, dainty, fair Madeleine Crozet, had lunched that day with Wolf and Gulliver (Ram). Then she had gone back home, to 15 Rue Neuve, to wait for a liaison agent, a new one, and probably not very bright, she suspected. When someone knocked at her door at five o'clock she never for a moment doubted that it was the young man in question and opened the door without giving it a second thought. A woman she had never seen before was there.

'Is Mlle Crozet in? A friend of hers is waiting for her downstairs. He's very tired.'

'Mlle Crozet will not be back until tomorrow,' replied Mouse immediately, suspecting a trap. And she shut the door again, without any obvious show of haste. Then she rushed to burn anything that might be compromising, in particular the schedule of the VAL radio and my last letter giving general instructions for the sector.

There was another knock. This time it was the agent she was expecting. She explained her position and handed him his orders. She told him to wait for her downstairs to cover her get-away, for she had decided to flee immediately with the papers she had not had time to destroy.

The agent went out into the street first. He could see nothing abnormal and gave her the green light. Mouse rushed out. She had not taken more than a couple of steps when the strange woman appeared out of a nearby gateway. She was accompanied by a tall, powerful man with a dog.

'The Gestapo,' Mouse whispered to the agent. 'Take my bag and run.'

She began to run, but the Gestapo man caught up with her at once and gripped her tightly by her coat sleeve. With her free hand Mouse grabbed the long hat pin that kept her turban in place and gave the man a sharp jab. He cursed and let go.

She started to run again. The dog leaped at her and seized her shoulder in his mouth. Instead of taking advantage of the scuffle to run for it, the agent continued to walk along beside her. Again Mouse hissed to him: 'Take my bag.' He never answered. It was only when they came in sight of the Grand-Hotel Terminus, the Gestapo headquarters, that he ran off. He did not take the bag. 'What a coward!' she thought.

While the Gestapo was moving into the flat in the Rue Neuve, the girl's interrogation began in the Grand-Hotel Terminus. She was beaten up, but she denied the Gestapo's accusations. She said she only knew the people they asked her about very vaguely; she knew nothing whatever about their activities. The sealed envelope found in her bag? She did not know what it was about, but she could try to decipher what was in it. The Germans gave her the letter and Mouse took the opportunity to make it unintelligible.

Her interrogation continued, interspersed with physical violence: she was punched, beaten with riding crops and given electric shocks. But Mouse did not talk. One day she was taken to see a man who had just had his eyes put out. Blood was streaming down his face and onto his manacled hands. But he was still on his feet and never even groaned. Mouse still refused to talk. And that went on for three solid weeks.

The trap set up in the house in the Rue Neuve proved fatal. On 3 February the enchanting Hummingbird was caught; on the 5th Pelican (Pierre Giovaccini), who reported on the Italian air squadrons, and Jean Zeiller (one of the chief agents in the Lyons area); and on the 6th Jean Pelletier (Bullfinch), the radio operator.

On 7 February, Mouren, the engineer, appeared with a bunch of flowers. 'Where is my friend, Mlle Crozet?' he asked, not looking at all put out.

'Who are these gentlemen?' he added, pointing his flowers at the two Nazis on duty.

One of the Gestapo men shouted: 'She's a dangerous spy. We've arrested her and you're her accomplice. I arrest you.'

'Good Heavens!' exclaimed Mouren. 'I thought she was just a very sweet girl. What will my great protector Marshal Pétain say when he hears that I'm mixed up in such a sordid business?'

And with a great flourish he produced cards, safe-conducts bearing dozens of official French Government seals, out of his double-bottomed briefcase, which also contained a report about the Japanese supply ships on the high seas.

'You're a friend of Pétain and of the young lady?' the Gestapo thug asked in amazement, as he examined the genuine Vichy papers.

'Yes, as I told you. But now it's all over between me and that young lady,' said Mouren sadly, affecting a superb sigh. 'Long live the Marshal!'

Although he was shattered at leaving Mouse to a hideous fate, he was pleased with himself. The alibi he had thought up in 1941—a girl in every port—worked. He would be released. After six months in Fresnes. There, the Germans failed to identify him with the network, or discover that he was the man who made the plan of the U-boat pens in Saint-Nazaire.

The bell rang again. A sort of Hercules, to whom the door was opened, grasped the situation in a flash. He turned on his heel, dashed for the stairs and went down all five flights in a terrifying tumble. Shouts. Shots. The Gestapo men fired at him through the hand rail but missed. They could not capture him as they had orders not to leave the flat. It was Ram who, in the end, had not left France, but continued to keep an eye on his wife's virtue.

Finally, Mlle Connorton climbed the stairs, knocking on every door. She was bent on a very worthy mission, collecting for Chinese children. When she got to the fifth floor she held out her wooden begging bowl to the two Nazis, who abused her roundly and held her for an identity check.

Hummingbird, too, was tortured at the same time as Mouse. Klaus Barbie, the head of the Gestapo in Lyons, was assisted by his mistress, who urged him to intensify the torture the two young women were enduring. Burning cigarettes were pressed into their breasts and electric shocks were applied all over their naked bodies. They said nothing, either then or ever. They refused to say where Petrel was, or Hedgehog, or where all those mysterious animals, Wolf, Ram, Cricket and Magpie, who dared to attack the Third Reich, were. At the end of their prison martyrdom they once more met Ewe, Moufflon's wife. And so Mouse, Hummingbird and Ewe went, erect and unflinching, to the military tribunal that was to condemn them to death, while paying homage to them at the same time. The German officers understood that these great Frenchwomen had accepted martyrdom to preserve the secrets that meant life and liberty to their comrades. They were themselves to submit to Hitler an appeal for mercy that the women had refused to sign.

The Baroness de Mareuil (Wasp) welcomed us with her inimitable graciousness. We took refuge in her tiny apartment in the very centre of Lyons where Magpie, bedding down on cushions on the floor, guarded the room where the three women shared the bed and the settee.

Cricket appeared the following morning, on the verge of a relapse into his nervous collapse. Mlle Connorton had almost been arrested at Mouse's. The Boche had gone home with her to check up on her story of the Chinese children and he himself only just had time to escape across the rooftops.

'But why did you send your friend into the wolf's lair?'

'I didn't think it was.'

'There's someone else who believes it now—Ram. He also went to the Rue Neuve. He had to dive headlong down the stairs and now he's got a head like a pumpkin.'

Cricket was telling me about his plans for living in Lyons when there was a knock on my door. He recoiled in horror when Wasp admitted Petrel (Georges Lamarque), whom Magpie had gone to fetch. Even I had difficulty in recognizing him. The healthy, well-built young man with the handsome, regular features, who had been full of drive and energy, brimming over with intelligence and sparkling with wit, now looked like some doped hobo. His eyes were red and swollen from strain.

He embraced me without a word and then muttered, as though talking to himself: 'Hummingbird and Mouse are being tortured, the Gestapo are burning their breasts with cigarettes.'

'Have you been able to get in touch with them, Petrel?'

'No, I got the news from the chaplain of the prison. He knows everything that goes on. I wanted to organize their escape. But nothing can be done against the Boche prisons, nothing can be done,' he repeated, gnawing the knuckles of his clenched fists.

'And that's not all,' he went on. 'All the Marseilles people have been captured: Panda (Jean Grappin), Jaguar (Camille Schneider), Eaglet (Robert Lynen), Pony (Jean Denis-Burel), Georges Zeppini, Badger (Gilbert Savon), and two young liaison agents, Emile Rocher and Georges Talon, they've all been caught! And Rivière's wife. And Basset's two bodyguards, who wanted to flee to Spain; and lots more whose names I couldn't discover.'

'How did you learn this?'

'Since Hummingbird's arrest—not that I'm afraid she'll talk, poor kid— I sleep only in the train. The work must go on and so I take a different train each night. I've been to Marseilles and Nice three times. They've all been caught in Nice, too. In Marseilles. . . .'

His voice was hoarse, the voice of a man unable to weep. 'There was a trap at Panda's,' he went on implacably, 'and it was my fault that Armand

Siffert, the irreplaceable Oriole, and Alexandre Lazard fell into it. To think that I, who am suspicious of everything, wasn't suspicious that day. Be careful, Hedgehog, we're walking in a minefield.'

My mind seemed to be reeling and in a mad, giddy whirl I saw all of them, from Spaniel to Rabbit, from Gazelle to Hummingbird, from Jaguar to Basset, the Bishop and Eaglet and poor little Zebra, all stepping upon mines, all beaten and bludgeoned, in chains and lost forever. I felt I was collapsing, going under, perishing. I would give up. It was all too difficult.

The reserved, phlegmatic Magpie never even noticed my despair and he called me back to reason. 'Are you thinking of letting London know that we're still alive, madame?'

I looked at him. I looked at Ermine, Wasp, Petrel and Cricket standing close together before me, joined like the five fingers of my hand. The second wave had also been smashed. To survive was not enough. The sacrifice must serve to bring victory. We must carry on.

19   *THE FINGERS OF MY HAND*

The Nazis had not blown up everything, but their mines had devastated the southern zone. Except for Grenoble, Vichy and central France, all the sectors had been destroyed. Being independent, our actual intelligence services had been more skilful and eluded the Gestapo's tentacles, but they were disintegrating.

I could count the principal survivors on the fingers of my hand. For the most part hunted, and perhaps destined to martyrdom, not one of them wanted to give up. Wolf, Petrel, Cricket, Sheepdog, Ram, Mahout, Elephant, Seagull, Magpie and Ermine would enable me to rebuild the organization.

The northern and the Atlantic zones had not, it seemed, suffered any sort of upheaval. As they ran their own autonomous radio transmissions, I told them to carry on as usual until they received fresh orders. But I needed a headquarters.

'I've found one,' Cricket told me, 'at Mme Berne-Churchill's. The name's a good omen.'

Our underground existence was organized in the large flat where Mme Berne-Churchill, 'Ladybird', lived. Dynamic, thorough, phlegmatic, and with the Lyons virtues of order and method, Ladybird was born to run a headquarters. Thanks to her I had two couriers in no time, Stann and Missou Berne, her own children; and four lieutenants, Louis Payen, Etienne Pelletier, Jean Parrache, and Jean-Philippe Sneyers. Their leader —an industrialist, the courageous Percy, called 'Etienne the Scarface'— was cut off from a network that had just perished in the eastern part of the south-west. He placed himself wholly at my disposal, together with a number of letter-boxes and places from which to transmit.

Undaunted by the prospect of trailing across the hilltops, Ladybird took Magpie up to the surrounding heights and contact with London was instantly resumed. I received a telegram of rejoicing from Richards. British Intelligence thought I had perished without trace.

Meanwhile, Cricket had found a job as a night watchman. He came to see me about six o'clock every evening and we got accustomed to his way of ringing the kitchen doorbell and then disappearing into the upper floors like a ghost until he was convinced that whoever opened a crack in the door was genuine. 'I've got a strong heart,' Ladybird then said, giving a snort.

Cricket, my new chief of staff, arranged our rendezvous out of doors on the Lyons bridges. He walked there every day at the appointed times, his face buried in a collaborationist newspaper. Too bad if the agents were late. He had learned never to wait.

In the beautiful room—her own—that Ladybird had given me I worked night and day to rebuild the organization as fast as I could.

Johannès Ambre (Gibbon), Eagle's lawyer, had introduced me to a Lyons businessman, Henri Battu, a tall, handsome, energetic, aggressive young man. I christened him Opossum and gave him the job of organizing a circuit of secondary command posts for setting up our own intelligence service. Magpie became the organization's chief radio operator. I had had plenty of opportunities to appreciate his tireless efficiency.

The Avia team was split up. Mahout, who no longer had Heron—tracked down in Nice and a prisoner of the OVRA—would confine his attention to the Lysanders, and Seagull would deal with the parachute drops. Dromedary would make sure that the transmitting sites and the headquarters were safe. Elephant would perfect his own particular line—providing forged papers.

Petrel (Lamarque) was a twenty-eight-year-old mathematics graduate. That was perhaps why he could solve the difficult and arduous problems of secret warfare more easily than anyone else.

'The only thing that counts is a sense of mission,' he said. 'The Nazis only understand a direct hit. I'm going to see they're not disappointed.' As it happened, the Compagnons de France, to which he belonged, had just been dissolved by Vichy and consequently their leader, Colonel de Tourhemire, had at his disposal a large number of picked, highly-trained men and cadres. I asked Petrel to recruit from among them sector leaders who could be sent urgently to the devastated southern zone. Their sole concern would be the search for intelligence information. To reduce risks to the minimum, equipment and money would be provided by me, thus enabling the new organization to operate completely independently. And so, at a single stroke, there sprang up in Lyons, Nice, Toulon, Vichy, Clermont-Ferrand, and Toulouse a trained and fully operational organization with units that were conjured into life as though by magic under the iron fist of an indomitable Petrel. He swore to me that he would achieve the feat of preparing a complete report for the March moon.

After he had gone, I looked with emotion at the little programme that we had drawn up together, then I burned it. Learning by heart was no longer a faculty, it was absolute necessity, like smoking.

The only name he had not given me was that of a girl of whom he had a very high opinion and whom he called Amniarix.

Richards continually asked for information about shipping. God knows, shipping had always been one of our major preoccupations, but now it became our top priority. With General Paulus defeated at Stalingrad and Rommel driven right back to Tunisia it was essential to reinforce Britain so that the Anglo-Saxon armada could sail to conquer the fortress of Europe. Simultaneously a hundred U-boats infested the Atlantic daily.

I summoned Sheepdog's (Raynal's) 'God of the sea' and at last one evening the famous Joël Lemoigne (Triton) arrived. He immediately produced a paper covered with information about the Keroman base. It showed the exact number of U-boats based there, with their fleet numbers and individual signs—a fish, a siren, an iron cross and so on—as well as their operational rosters and the losses sustained.

'It's monumental! Who did this for you?' I asked.

'I can't tell you,' he replied.

'Then, my dear chap, your agent's work is useless. I must be able to vouch for this. At least tell me what he represents.'

Triton looked hard at Magpie.

'Don't worry,' said Magpie, 'I only remember figures.'

'He's a naval engineer,' Triton explained, 'an Alsatian who speaks fluent German. He's gained the Nazis' confidence so completely that he's hated by the whole staff at the Lorient base, where he has held a key post since the Germans marched in. Everything passes through his hands—operational orders, U-boat movements and the results of their activity. He's noticed that, on returning to the pens, the U-boats run up small coloured flags to indicate their victories: white means a cargo ship, white edged with red means an auxiliary cruiser, red means a warship. He's the only Frenchman who's been able to get into the colossal Keroman base built by the Todt organization. He debriefs the U-boat commanders on their return from operations. A young Breton friend of ours takes him out in a launch and together they photograph the various units in their lairs.'

Triton also handed me information about Toulon: the observations to do with the unfortunate fleet sunk there were scrupulously reproduced by the brilliant engineer Jean-Claude Thorel (Shad) from Marseilles port and his friends.

And so the 'Sea Star' sub-network was born. Magpie was already drawing up a list of new transmitters to be brought into action.

'Of course, I'm giving them the names of fish,' said Triton. I took notes feverishly. For Brittany and the North Sea: Narwhal, Dab, Bleak, Conger, Medusa, Smelt. For Bordeaux-La Rochelle: Cariama, Cod, Lobster, Turbot, Loach. For Marseilles-Toulon: Shad, Sole, Beluga, Halibut, Murena. . . .

'I've a communications centre in Vichy, too,' Triton added. 'Pierre Magnat, divisional head of the merchant navy. We'll call him Scallop.'

Ladybird came in with a tray of tea and buttered toast, as in England. 'It's enough to make one pass out,' she said, sniffing the cigarette smoke. 'You've gone completely mad! Hedgehog, Magpie, go to bed, it's eight o'clock in the morning!'

'I'll sleep in the train,' said Triton, as lively as his mythical namesake. 'If your delicious tea will let me, madame,' he added.

As he shook my hand when he was leaving, he slipped me a final scrap of paper. I read: 'The naval engineer at Keroman is Jacques Stosskopf.'

Triton had hardly left before Seagull (Pierre Berthomier), whom I imagined was busy looking for suitable sites for his parachute drops, burst into my fortress-like room.

'Whom would you rather kidnap,' he asked, 'Pétain or Laval?'

Suppressing a gasp, I looked at the tall young man standing before me: 'My poor Seagull, don't you think we've had enough of that sort of thing with Giraud?'

'It's the chance of a lifetime. I'm very friendly with the chief pilot of the plane doing the regular shuttle service between Vichy and Paris. If we'll fix things for him, he's ready to fly off course and land in Britain. The plane's range makes it possible.'

'How can you pull off a coup like that?'

'There are two ways. Either one tricks Pétain—and it seems that it's simple to kidnap him when he's walking in the country round Vichy. . . .'

'Dreams!'

'Not at all. He always falls in with any suggestion made by anyone who's alone with him.'

'You also mentioned the possibility of kidnapping Laval.'

'Yes, that's easier. Laval intends to use the plane to avoid attempts on his life when he's travelling around. When we know the day he's going to fly, I can stow away on the plane, and if the passengers notice we're changing course when we're in the air I'll see that they keep quiet. Can't you imagine Hitler foaming at the mouth when he hears about it?'

So we decided to have a go, and at our next radio contact with London I asked Richards what he thought of the advisability of kidnapping Pétain or Laval, or if not that, then capturing the presidential plane.

They would undoubtedly think we were pulling their legs. To my great surprise, a few days later, I received a number of messages from British Intelligence indicating, without comment, an airfield on the southeast coast of England. Here the plane could land after coming in from the sea at low altitude and performing a whole series of acrobatics while its lights flashed the recognition letter P—for Pétain? Quite imperturbable, British Intelligence asked us to let them know the approximate time of arrival.

Félix Cros (Aurochs) had meanwhile come from Vichy to confirm Seagull's statements. He asked if he could have the honour of supervising the operation and he himself was rather inclined to favour kidnapping the head of the so-called French State. 'What a relief it would be and what good riddance!' he said.

I was annoyed that he had meddled in this particular business. His official position on the Air Force General Staff at Vichy was extremely useful to us and, in addition, I had just entrusted him with Bishop's job, the management and distribution of our funds. Almost accusing me of pro-Vichy sentiments, the two airmen returned to the attack and pressed me to make up my mind.

I waved Richards' messages: 'Look here! I'm the only one who's made any really practical contribution to your cloak-and-dagger scheme.'

'You're only going through the motions, taking two steps backward and one step forward!' exclaimed Aurochs.

'Infantile,' said Seagull with great emphasis. He and Aurochs withdrew, dragging their feet along the floor and flapping their great arms to give an idea of the fugitive plane winging into sight off the Sussex coast.

I could not indulge in the luxury of such dreams, and I was driven to rethink the security aspect of our activities. The time had arrived to form a protection team, of which Cricket could assume command. He was once more a marked man in Lyons because of a stupid muddle involving identity photos; and the loyal Tomboy, already entrenched in the impregnable Massif Central, had successfully regrouped the survivors from the Dordogne, who were demanding their leader. He was therefore to become the 'Great Manitou' of our new tribe, the Apaches. The security agents would be Sioux, Commanche, Iroquois, Algonquin. . . .

'It's an excellent idea, madame, we've had more than enough people getting caught, and then I thought we had too many animals. That's why I gave our four Lyons lieutenants quite different names: Basher, Convict, Buccaneer, Bumpkin. . . .'

'There will never be enough animals, Cricket! But the services we create must be differentiated from one another.'

Cricket would also have to shoulder a further task. Eagle was to arrange with our Algiers friends to attach one of our sets directly to French Military Intelligence. France-Algiers radio station was also to be isolated and used for nothing else but that.

I had let the February moon come and go, but now the flood of reports justified the re-establishment of the air link. Eagle informed me that he would land willy-nilly by the March moon. There was no question of letting him take a chance.

The RAF preferred the Thalamy landing ground, and Great Dane had sent me word that in spite of the police raids on Tulle—where the Gestapo, returning in force, had seized the intrepid Abbé Lair and many members of the sector—Ussel, thirty miles northeast of Tulle, was still intact. I decided to go there to make preparations for the operation with Magpie, whom I sent on ahead as an advanced echelon; but first I had to help Sheepdog, who had run against a dreadful snag in connection with Navarre's escape.

For some mysterious reason the scheme to rescue him in a van had come to nothing and he implored me to see Chambon, the van driver, who had promised to reconsider the whole matter. It was vital that this rapacious creature should not get to know any of my headquarters and so I arranged to meet him at Eygurande, near Tulle, where two devoted agents, a couple of railway platelayers, welcomed me in their little hut. Chambon appeared —a hideous-looking man with a bloated, ape-like face. Sly, glib and far too garrulous, he claimed that Navarre had not had sufficient confidence in him and that he preferred to get himself out of his own difficulties. This sounded highly dubious. Why had Navarre been suspicious? Chambon, sensing my disbelief, described his new escape plan at great length.

I had to call his bluff, as at poker. I had made up a bundle of twenty halved 5,000 franc notes, which I handed to him. He looked thoroughly annoyed: 'Couldn't you let me have fifty per cent in whole notes? I've got to tip some people first.'

'You told us you were working on your own so as not to risk raising the alarm.'

He turned pale. 'Well, there's also a woman in on this. She tells me about the Germans' habits.'

'A woman who's friendly with the Boche? What's her name?'

'Lébé,' he muttered, taken off his guard. 'She's very beautiful and very cunning. She's my mistress.'

This fat, pretentious wretch admitted quite cynically that he was living with a woman who, more likely than not, was a Gestapo informer. I must gain time and inform Sheepdog as soon as possible of the hornet's nest into which he had been thrust.

'Chambon, in the Intelligence Service it's the practice to cut the notes in two. You'll get the other halves when the rescue's been pulled off.'

Apparently flattered by this sudden promotion, he counted his money, hid it in the lining of his filthy old jacket and, loudly protesting his honesty and devotion to our cause, he swore that everything would be OK. I felt increasingly sceptical.

I located Magpie at the mountain hut near Ussel run by Cicada (Mme Dumont). Jean Vinzant (Great Dane) was not there, but our chief operator had installed his 'Tuba' set in the house where the old servant, Marie, was keeping a look-out. Roland Creel (Labrador) was on watch.

The prospects for Operation Pluto seemed good. It would take place at the new moon. I immediately sent for the passengers waiting in Lyons. There were three to go: Mahout, whom I wanted to release for a month, was going to take a special course on landing bombing planes; our old friend Dr Zimmern, and a Colonel whom I called Yoyo. He had invented a new type of parachute which, as it opened, adjusted itself to the natural pendulum movement that occurred during a drop. He was obsessed with the idea of making the British a gift of his discovery. In exchange for the trip to Britain he offered us an enormous stock of military petrol and tyres, which delighted Gulliver.

Suddenly I heard that the Germans were driving stakes into the Thalamy landing ground to render it unusable. Would it be possible to pull up the stakes and replace them the same night? 'Yes,' said some, 'you only need to detail a squad from the secret army.' 'No,' others objected, 'the marks made by tyres and feet will stay visible in the wet ground and the whole population will be shot.'

I had to make a decision, and quickly at that.

'The Gestapo have surrounded Great Dane's house!' Magpie panted, rushing in.

'What about your transmitter?'

'It's hidden in the attic. Labrador prevented me from going in.'

'Quickly,' I shouted. 'Quickly, give the alert in town. Send somebody to the station to warn the liaison agents bringing the reports for Britain. They'll all walk into the trap.'

'And my Tuba?' asked Magpie, looking shame-faced, as though the whole thing were his fault.

'Gone for good, I should think. How d'you expect to get a set out under the noses of the Boches?'

Nevertheless he returned a few hours later bearing his beloved Tuba in triumph. It was old Marie herself who had thought about the strange object that she sometimes heard making a disturbing hum. She told herself that it would undoubtedly be dangerous if it were discovered by the sinister men who were busily ejecting the masters of the house. And concealing it in the folds of her big apron, under a pile of haricot beans that had to be shelled, she had calmly come down from the attic, stumbling down the winding stairs and, proud and dignified, had walked out of the house under the very eyes of the Gestapo, who were too busy searching the rooms to pay any attention to an old peasant. She had then handed it to her little friend Labrador, who happened to be around at the time. All we had to do was to erect Tuba's aerial in Cicada's hut.

In a laconic radio message I informed London that I was postponing operation Pluto indefinitely.

I also learned that the Germans had completely invested Ussel. The railways were being checked by the military police and road blocks set up everywhere. It looked as though Magpie and I had had it, now that we, too, were encircled and trapped. And what of the passengers for London who were arriving by the noon train next day carrying my magnificent report, the fruit of Petrel's and Triton's hard work? I told Dr Syriex (Fox) of my dilemma. He, who knew everything there was to know about clandestine movement and transport, who doctored the poor and the outlawed, and who had proved his inexhaustible devotion, would undoubtedly have an idea.

'Be ready when it gets dark,' he said. 'I've an *Ausweis* that allows me to transport sick people in my car at any hour of the day or night. I'll take you to Clermont-Ferrand for an operation. Magpie will be your anxious and attentive husband. Actually I'll drop you at the first station, where you can take the night train and, with a bit of luck, you'll be at the junction for the branch line before your passengers catch the connection for Ussel.'

The optimistic doctor later sent us two local identity cards. 'That'll keep the Feldgendarmerie quiet,' he assured us. If by any chance it did not keep them quiet they were hardly likely to be satisfied by the discovery of the transmitter and the reports in the car. . . .

I had no difficulty in acting the invalid when we were pulled up by warning flashlights at the check-point on the road leading out of the town. My face was bathed in huge beads of perspiration when the torchlights swept over it. Fox, quite unperturbed, explained to the military police why he was travelling, and produced his papers and his *Ausweis*.

'Quickly, doctor, quickly, she's losing consciousness,' Magpie said in a distressed voice, sitting on Tuba at the back of the car and dabbing my temples with ether, the smell of which I loathe.

The road block was finally removed and Fox drove off full speed. In the icy night the moon, although in fact our accomplice, appeared to me as bright and hostile as the blade of the guillotine.

The train had just left the first station. Fox decided to catch up with it. 'We'll get it! We'll get it!' he shouted, crouching over the wheel.

We caught the train. Standing in the crowded corridor, Magpie and I made frenzied calculations as to our chances of reaching the junction in time. 'If we're late they've had it,' we thought, listening anxiously to the screech of the axles and the laboured chuffing from the engine. After an eternity the junction came into sight.

We raced to the buffet where we were now certain to find Mahout, Zimmern and Yoyo. As soon as I flung open the door I saw them through the thick fug, sitting close together round a table among soldiers going on leave and swarming about like colorado beetles, commercial travellers weighed down with suitcases, peasants in smocks carrying clucking hens, half-asleep and howling children. Poor, weird, foul-smelling creatures of the occupation!

As my passengers looked up at me in surprise I walked past without giving a sign of recognition and muttered under my breath: 'Back to Lyons.'

'Bloody hell!' said Mahout.

20 ENCIRCLEMENT

'You *must* see a doctor, Hedgehog!'

Ladybird (Mme Berne-Churchill) put me to bed, with a cup of boiling hot tea within reach, and called in Robert Worms, the famous Jewish practitioner whom she was also hiding. He made me describe my trouble.

'Nothing very unusual, doctor, except that I now get nightmares whenever I go to sleep and pains in the stomach whenever I eat.'

'How long have you been doing this job?' he enquired.

'It's hard to remember . . . twenty-seven or twenty-eight months. . . .'

He felt and sounded me. 'You can thank your lucky stars it's nothing serious. Mainly nervous. Put your whole heart and soul into things, eh? If you want to carry on you must listen to me. Get plenty of sleep and take a tonic. Live right away from the general hurly-burly.'

But despite the catastrophe at Ussel, I could not let the March moon go by without getting Eagle to come back. So, as soon as Worms' back was turned I sent a number of telegrams to say why nothing could be done during the February moon and the RAF finally agreed to land on the banks of the Saône. Operation Pluto was fixed for the night of 11 to 12 March.

Ladybird, impatient to make Eagle's acquaintance, prepared a very special breakfast. We had been waiting since first light, seated before the steaming coffee pot, the little grilled patés and pure pork sausage.

'It'll make a change from toast and marmalade,' Ladybird prophesied.

We pricked up our ears when we heard the sound of hurrying footsteps. It was Mahout, who should have been in Britain by then, who entered. The Lysander had not come. 'We watched for it all night,' he said. 'The weather was perfectly good. . . . I met Gulliver as I was coming along, chief. Can he come in?'

I had a dreadful ache in my heart. The plane had confirmed that it had left at ten o'clock in the evening. Had it been shot down? Had it. . . . ?

Gulliver (Ram) appeared, scarlet in the face and in a state of great tension: 'Moufflon's been murdered!'

We leaped to our feet, frozen with horror. Shouting and hammering out his words in the way one does when addressing the deaf, he repeated: 'Moufflon's been murdered by the Gestapo at Gannat station. The Boches surrounded him, he drew his revolver and they fired. A bullet got him in the throat.'

'Where was he going?' asked Mahout, after a painful struggle for words.
'Somewhere or other with that bloody van driver, Chambon. God knows where!'
'When did it happen?'
'On 8 March, chief. Ewe, his poor wife, was arrested the same day at her home.'
The Gestapo offensive had been resumed on all fronts. March 8 was the day Ussel had been invested. We were not clear of the minefield. 'Ram,' I said, 'it's now obvious that van driver's a dirty double-crosser. Get everyone he knows away, especially Sheepdog.'
'The General won't leave his home.'
'Try to make him. Find Chambon and hand him over to Cricket.'
'I get you,' said Ram, swooping on the coffee pot. 'May I, Ladybird?'
Like a mother she made the two men eat something. She began to pack my suitcase. But who was informing the Gestapo? I asked myself desperately. Chambon did not know enough to cause such terrible havoc. Then suddenly I was assailed by dreadful suspicions; the Nazis had undoubtedly found a lead and if anything had happened to Eagle, what was I going to do alone, with all my secrets . . . ?

On arrival at the Sussex airfield, Eagle had found his pilot already at the controls. The squadron commander speeded up their take-off because the mist came up at night at that time of the year and the plane therefore had to be back early. There was a brilliant moon and they were able to see as though it were broad daylight. Eagle tried to speak to the pilot, but the intercom was not working. Apart from this disturbing discovery, time went by uneventfully. By the landmarks on the ground and the stars above Eagle could clearly follow the course they were taking, and its choice struck him as strange. The pilot was obviously making a mistake in veering too far east.

They had been flying for hours. Eagle was furious at not being able to shake the pilot sitting just a few feet behind him. He thumped on the reserve petrol tank separating them; he yelled at the top of his voice. The noise of the engine drowned everything. The pilot at last began to show signs of anxiety. He circled low above the Saône, but then resumed his easterly course. Then, suddenly, they saw deep, dark valleys and large areas of snow on the mountaintops. They were over Switzerland!

Then the plane turned, but the pilot made the same mistake as on the outward journey. The course he now took was certainly not towards England but Orleans. To cap everything, the mist came on. Eagle saw that the poor fellow was completely lost; he flew on in the cottonwool-like mist, skimming the ground and hedge-hopping over the chateaux of the Loire.

They were now heading straight for the sea. They would soon be out of fuel, and Eagle thought of the icy water and the terrible, grotesque end that awaited them. Suddenly, a voice could be heard, very far away. The pilot answered and abruptly changed course 100°. Eagle thought he was dreaming but it was true—the intercom had, by some miracle, begun to work. It was the airfield, now guiding the plane, like a shepherd leading home the stray sheep.

The Lysander continued on its course, drawn by the soft female voice that grew clearer and clearer—but how much fuel was there left after so many hours? Eagle held his breath to make sure that the engine was still functioning. The pilot put the nose down and went into a long dive. Suddenly he emerged from the cloud ceiling, in the middle of a dazzling. fairy-like display of sweeping searchlights and ground lights. Then, h:s tank dry, he glided gently down and landed.

The RAF gave orders that Operation Pluto should be resumed that evening. British Intelligence informed me and the passengers were brought from their hideout for the third time. The gloomy, exhausted but un-daunted men comprising the reception committee set off once again on their bicycles for the open country round Villefranche-sur-Saône.

Just when the Avia team was bringing Eagle and his baggage back across the interminable, frosty, sparkling fields on the banks of the Saône, agents of the Paris Gestapo, escorted by armed SS men, leaped into their black Citroëns and drove off on a fatal mission.

One car came to an old and slumbering quarter of the city, turned into the Rue Saint-Sabin, jolted over the bumpy road and drew up in front of No. 54. A guard, sub-machine gun at the ready, took up position at the entrance. Two men entered the old house, climbed the steep stairs, stopped on the first floor landing and looked at their watches. Their deadline was five o'clock. It struck.

Robert Bernadac (Robin), the chief Paris radio operator, had gone to bed late that night. After coming off duty at the police station in the third *arrondissement* he had, in the absence of his wife, to look after his old army friend, Jean Kiffer (Asp) from Mandrill's sector.

A meeting of regional representatives under Armadillo had been arranged for the following day, 14 March, at the intelligence headquarters. Robin and Asp had spent the whole evening drawing up plans to submit to Armadillo, then they had got bored and had gone to bed at one in the morning, but not before hiding all compromising papers in the gas stove.

A ring on the doorbell roused Robin from a deep sleep. He went to the door like a sleep-walker. 'Who's that?'

'German police.'

A quick glance through the window showed Robin that they were surrounded. He opened the door.

'Get dressed, we're taking you along with us.'

'But I'm a policeman.'

'So are we.'

Ermine and *Magpie* after the war

The Army pays homage to the Alliance in Strasbourg after the liberation

Reichskriegsgericht
3. Senat.

Beilage zum Urteil in der Strafsache

. . . .

wegen Spionage

StPL. (3.Sen.) . . ./44.

Das französische Spionagenetz "L'Alliance".
======================================

A.
====

I.) 1.) Der französische Major [L o u s t a u n a u - L a c a u]
hatte etwa i.J. 1937 unter der Volksfront-Regierung aus dem Dienst
ausscheiden müssen, weil er sich in der französischen Wehrmacht sehr
rührig für den Kampf gegen den Kommunismus eingesetzt hatte. Er gab
nach seinem Ausscheiden eine Zeitschrift "Barrage" (=Schlagbaum,Wehr)
gegen den Kommunismus heraus. Sein Name hatte unter den französischen
Offizieren, soweit sie rechts eingestellt waren, einen sehr guten poli-
tischen Klang.
          Nach dem Zusammenbruch Frankreichs beauftragte der französische
Staatschef Pétain Loustaunau-Lacau, die französischen Frontkämpfer in
einer "Légion des Combattants" zusammenzufassen. Loustaunau-Lacau nütz-
te diesen Auftrag dazu aus, um vom Herbst 1940 an unter dem Deckmantel
einer Arbeitsvermittlung oder Auskunftsstelle ein Nachrichtennetz aufzu-
bauen. Zweck dieses Netzes war es, vor allem politische und wirtschaft-
liche Nachrichten über Frankreich selbst, insbesondere über die Vichy-
Regierung, zusammenzutragen. Nebenher richtete sich die Tätigkeit aller-
dings auch gegen die deutsche Besatzungsmacht. So wurden Personen vom
besetzten in's unbesetzte Gebiet und umgekehrt geschmuggelt, Agenten,
Kuriere und Sender über die Abgrenzungslinie verbracht, deutschen Fah-
nenflüchtigen wurde zur Flucht verholfen u.dgl.m.
          Schon frühzeitig nahm Loustaunau-Lacau Fühlung mit dem englischen
Nachrichtendienst auf. Um sich die Mittel für den Betrieb seines Netzes
zu verschaffen, leitete er in der Folgezeit seine Nachrichten an England weiter. Die von de Gaulle geforderte Unterstellung lehnte er ab.
          Als Mitarbeiterin in der Leitung des Nachrichtennetzes stand
[Marie Madeleine] zur Seite dem Loustaunau-Lacau. Sie stammte aus französischen Offizierskreisen und verfügte über außergewöhnlich gute und
weitreichende Beziehungen, besonders im französischen Offizierskorps.
          Wegen seiner Zusammensetzung führte das Netz Loustaunaus die Be-
zeichnung ["A r c h e   N o a h"]. Sein Sitz war zunächst in Vichy, dann
in Pau.
2.) Im Mai 1941 befand sich Loustaunau-Lacau in Nordafrika. Zu Ehren
seines Besuchs gab der Obstlt.i.G. der Luftwaffe [F a y e] ein Essen.
Faye hatte während des Kriegs eine Aufklärungsstaffel geführt. Nach dem
Waffenstillstand war er als Leiter der Operationsabteilung des Luftwaf-
fenbefehlshabers nach Algier versetzt worden. Bei diesem Essen kam es
zu Äußerungen gegen die Regierung in Vichy. Diese wurden durch einen teil-
nehmenden Oberstleutnant gemeldet. Bei einer daraufhin vorgenommenen
Haussuchung wurde bei Faye eine Denkschrift gefunden,die sich mit Maßnah-
gegen die damals erwartete Landung der Achsenmächte in Französich Nord-

Alger, le 2 1 août 1943

LE GENERAL

905/cab/

SECRET

-:- DECISION DU COMMANDANT EN CHEF -:-

I.) L'organisation **Alliance** travaillant en **FRANCE**
sous la direction du **Commandant PAYE** et faisant l'objet
de ma note secrète du 15 Juin 1943 est entièrement mili-
tarisée.

  a) Le personnel militaire de carrière sera considéré
     comme en service actif.

  b) Le personnel civil sera considéré comme rappelé
     ou requis chacun servant dans son arme et avec
     son grade.

  Les rappels nécessaires (solde, ancienneté, retraite),
  les propositions d'avancement et de décoration ainsi que
  celles destinées à régulariser les situations individuel-
  les feront l'objet en temps et lieu d'une décision du
  Commandant en Chef sur proposition du Chef de l'association

2.) Un représentant de l'association, désigné par ailleurs,
assurera à ALGER les liaisons nécessaires avec le Commandant en Chef et la D.S.R.

  Les modalités de coopération entre la D.S.R. et l'association feront l'objet d'un texte particulier.

11   General Giraud's formal militarization of the Alliance

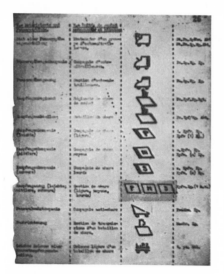

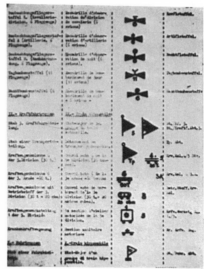

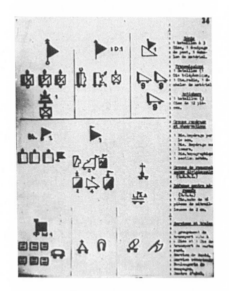

12   Four specimen questionnaires of the Intelligence Service. (For their own security, agents could only keep these for a brief period; they were then destroyed. Specimens are therefore rare.)

ations: probablement juillet 43

ARY TECHNICAL

(renseignements communiqués par un capitaine d'active attaché au cent
d'essai dont il sera question)

; Dans l'île de Usedon (nord de Stettin) se trouve concentré les
laboratoires et services de recherches scientifiques qui améliorent
armes existantes ou mettent au point les nouvelles armes. Le terri.
re de l'île est gardé de très près. Il faut pour y pénétrer, en plus
livret militaire, 3 autorisations spéciales:

- Sondergenehmigung   papier filigrané
- Zusatz   carton orange
4 Vorläufigergenehmigung   papier blanc.

Les services administratifs sont à Peenemünde et à .....

Les recherches sont axées:

a) sur les bombes et obus dirigés indépendamment des lois de la balisti
   que,

b) sur un obus stratosphérique,

j) sur les bactéries employées comme arme.

uppe K.G. 100 expérimenterait actuellement des bombes dirigées de l'avi.
par le bombardier. Ces bombes pourraient être dirigées d'une distanc
telle que l'avion pourrait se maintenir en dehors des limites de la
D.C.A. La précision serait parfaite lorsque l'avion n'a pas à se déf
dre contre les chasseurs (ce qui n'est pas le cas en Sicile)

it à la période des dernières mises au point d'une bombe stratosphérique
d'un type tout à fait nouveau. Cette bombe aurait un volume de 10
(dix) mètres cubes et remplie d'explosif. Elle serait envoyée presqu
à la verticale pour atteindre le plus vite possible la stratosphère.
L'informateur parle de 80 km à la verticale. La vitesse de départ xx
serait maintenue par des explosions successives. La bombe serait
pourvue de "Raeketten" (ailettes ?) et dirigée sur des buts précis.
bombe serait chargée de 800 litres d'essence nécessaires même en péri
de d'essai où les obus ne sont pas chargés pour permettre la progres
sion. La portée horizontale serait de 500 km. Des essais auraient ét
faits sans charge d'explosif de Usedon en direction de la Baltique et
auraient atteint la hauteur de Koenigsberg. Le bruit serait aussi as-

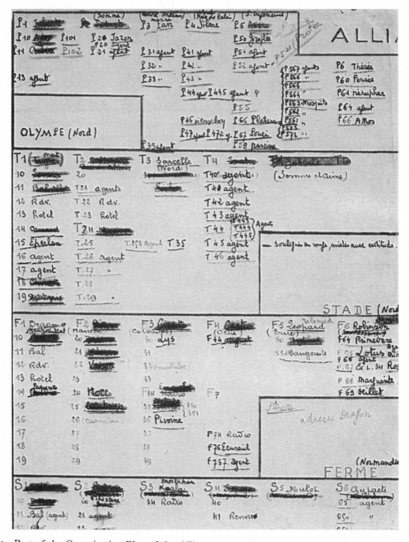

14 Part of the Organization Plan of the Alliance network

15 Commandant Léon Faye (*Eagle*)

16 Léon Faye addressed this letter from prison "to my friends of the Alliance." It was the letter he was allowed to write after being sentenced to death. In it he conveyed in code (later deciphered as shown) that his real testament was hidden behind the radiator grille in his cell ("*papiers . . . cas . . . chez [cachés] . . . derrière . . . radiateur*).

'Who are *you*?' they asked Asp, whom they found waking up on the sofa in the lounge.

'An old regimental friend paying him a visit.'

The Nazis had obviously not expected to make two arrests and, searching everywhere to no purpose, they began to show signs of impatience. Robin was ready. He asked if he might go to the lavatory.

'Yes,' said one of the Gestapo men, who followed him. Turning his back on the man, Robin dropped his only dangerous possession—his notebook—into the bowl. 'We must hurry,' the Nazis said.

Nothing could have suited the radio operator better: he had just spotted the little case with his DAN transmitter sitting in the corner where the brushes were kept. He had forgotten it. However, he merely asked if he might shut the windows. He did so, leaving one shutter in the way that gave warning of danger. A little later Armadillo, anxious because they had not appeared for the meeting, sent someone who slipped cautiously into the apartment, removed the set and recovered the papers hidden in the gas stove.

Once he was in the Gestapo headquarters Robin soon realized that the Germans did not know the network's new structure. They interrogated him about the service as it had existed before the previous November. He was horrified when he remembered that of the people arrested then only one had had his address. That one was Verteré.

To each photograph that he was shown Robin replied without fail: 'No, I don't know the Duke of Magenta. No, I don't know Marie-Madeleine. No, I don't know Fawn, or Jack Tar.' Patiently, at Fresnes that night, using the point of a pin dipped in his own blood, he wrote messages to his wife so that she might warn his chiefs. His endurance, his courage and his self-control were his salvation. He escaped being brought before the military tribunal. He was not shot, but he was deported—an almost equally terrible fate.

Asp, whom he was able to cover up by repeating over and over again 'He's an old army friend,' was released. But not for long, alas!

The same day, 14 March, three women, who were among the most important contact points in the network, were arrested. Saluki, the Duke of Magenta, head of the northern region, escaped the Gestapo's clutches by the skin of his teeth.

I gave in to Dr Worms and Ladybird and left the crowded place we were staying in to go with Ermine to live with Christiane Battu, Opossum's wife, where life would be quieter. Her beautiful, grave face, with its huge periwinkle eyes, and a lithe, slender body—I can see her bent over the cradle of the tiny baby daughter she had had after many years of marriage and whose smile was to her a perpetual source of astonishment.

We tore ourselves away from this pretty picture and went into the next room to begin the wait for the Lysander. Ermine and I talked about our underground life. Christiane listened, surprised and dismayed. 'I didn't know that anyone could do all that. . . . Take me on too. . . .' she said, quite unaware of what she was, in fact, already doing—sheltering a powder magazine.

'Marie-Madeleine, there's nothing left of you!' said Eagle's kind, reassuring voice. 'I don't recognize you any more.'

I broke down, my body shaken convulsively by the sobs I had been suppressing for so many days. I looked up at him, my eyes screened by the horrible locks of my badly dyed red hair. Suddenly I went off into a fit of wild laughter. I knew it was Eagle who stood before me, but what I actually saw was an old hunchback with snow-white hair and eyes hidden behind steel-framed spectacles.

'Who made you up like this?'

'The chief make-up man at British Intelligence.'

'Tell me, Eagle, d'you make a habit of making two return trips in a Lysander instead of one, just to give me a heart attack?'

'I'm not the only one it happens to! It's strange, you might say the plane refuses to bring me back . . . but what wouldn't I have done to come to your help. The network's in a mess, isn't it?'

'Did you see the huge bag of reports that was loaded into your seat to go back to England? The network's fantastic.'

'Richards said so. I didn't dare believe it, after all the disasters it's suffered. So it's really deserved its name,' he said, taking off his hunchback coat to be able to stand more comfortably. 'I have the honour of informing you that it's called "The Alliance".'

For two and a half years I had been fighting off all attempts to give us a definite, generally recognized title, as I considered that any linking up by name of the successive waves of our members was the thing that would be most damaging to them in the event of arrest.

'Eagle, you let yourself be talked into it. It's sheer madness.'

'The Resistance organizations have always had a name. Anything does for us: The Crusade, the Navarre Network, the Hedgehog Network. . . . We're such a mixed bag. No one will ever recognize our people.'

'I recognize them; that's enough. So much the better if the Germans are at sea.'

'I've got another big piece of news for you: we're militarized.'

This time I really blew up: 'That's the last straw. Now we leap out of the trenches, sound the charge and we all get ourselves shot up shouting: "Forward, the Alliance!"'

Eagle was utterly taken aback: 'The Alliance is such a glorious name and describes perfectly the oneness of soul and heart that exists in the network.'

'Yes, it'll be a glorious name . . . after the war. But underground work means self-sacrifice. To fox the enemy we should have to change our name all the time.'

'There's also the political angle,' said Eagle.

I leaped to my feet: 'You also want us to go political. Why not the "Alliance Party" while you're about it?'

'Take it easy, Marie-Madeleine, you're overwrought. I don't want to go in for politics any more than you do. What I see is that others do, and some who call themselves resistance fighters do just that and nothing else.'

During the two months he had been away Eagle had first settled with British Intelligence all details concerning the administration of 'The Alliance', then he had gone to Algiers. General Giraud had treated him like a son. Eagle had taken advantage of this kindness to request the militarization of the network. The Alliance would become a military unit, a proper regiment operating underground. We would send permanent representatives to Algiers and would establish a France-North Africa radio link. When the time was ripe arms would be parachuted to us from Algeria, which would allow us to go over to direct action.

'In the meantime, I imagine that Giraud will give us lists of his intelligence requirements, transmitters and money too?' I asked.

'Giraud hasn't any equipment or any money and his Intelligence services struck me as being very poor. That's why he needs us.'

He threw up his arms in despair. The situation in Algiers was dreadful. Bitter feuds had broken out between Vichyists, Giraudists and Gaullists. The expedient of sending Admiral Darlan to take command in Algiers, on 11 November, under the aegis of the Star Spangled Banner had really messed things up.

'Now, Marie-Madeleine! First, what's your opinion of this Gestapo swoop?'

'It's not easy, Eagle, as you very well know, to carry on espionage and counter-espionage simultaneously. Chronologically, they came to look for me at Malfonds first. They want to strike at the head.'

'How were they able to find out about Malfonds?'

'I'm afraid someone was shadowed, probably Jaguar. On 14 January he came to tell me they'd happened to pick up a deserter from the Kriegsmarine by chance in the bar where your brother-in-law, Lamasson, goes every evening.'

'They did that? They must be mental!'

'I told Jaguar to throw the fellow into the Old Port. It was undoubtedly too late. I'm certain, d'you understand, certain that's where the trouble started. Infiltration by the Abwehr. But infiltration doesn't happen by chance. To have swooped simultaneously in Nice, Marseilles, Toulouse, Pau and Lyons, the Germans undoubtedly have a lead. They even went to the old addresses of agents no longer active.'

'Yes, Marie-Madeleine, first infiltration, then capture. That way they get the maximum advantage from the traps in which people, running terrified from pillar to post, get caught, from the confessions extorted by torture and from the compromising papers they seize. They go for every-one, wholesale,' he said sadly. 'We shall also have to suspect those who've been left free of acting as a bait.'

'What makes you say that?'

'A piece of information from the British that weighs heavily on my mind. Hyena is at liberty, and his collaborator and girl friend, Gertrude, as well. They describe themselves as "escaped prisoners".'

I tried to fight the horrible suspicion that had been taking shape in my mind for some weeks. Eagle continued: 'He wrote to de Gaulle to ask his help to create a network. Unfortunately for him and fortunately for us the Abwehr sent the letter by one of their Lisbon channels that are well known to British Intelligence.'

'It's appalling! If Hyena is creating a false Alliance network for the Abwehr with the elements that it leaves free, our days are numbered.'

'Yes, Marie-Madeleine! This man is more dangerous than Bla. We're completely encircled. But we must make sure that the work goes on.'

In the meantime the Lille Abwehr was sending a telescript to the rest of the Abwehr based in France (19 March 1943):

'*III F Lille had requested by telescript that people marked on the attached list should in no event be arrested. Concerning this, the following important observation must be made:*

'*Certain persons enumerated on the attached list A can, if left free, lead to the discovery of the whole strength of the organization, something more valu-able than any benefit that would accrue from their arrest or interrogation.*

'*A certain number of them are already definitely beyond reach by reason of the arrests made in Marseilles.*

'*Several of them can be incriminated only by Verteré's statement. Their arrest would therefore expose the latter, who meanwhile has become a valuable German agent.*

'*According to Verteré, of particular importance in list A is X . . . , a former courier. At the moment inactive. She must on no account be taken. May provide an excellent starting point for Verteré.*'

The essential precaution was taken—to divide the headquarters into two. I took cover in the Clinique des Cedres, a private hospital in the high-lying part of Lyons, where a great-hearted nurse, Mme Prudon-Guénard, agreed to hide me and throw a protective shield round my activity. The Abwehr thought I was in London. Eagle went to stay in the Rue du Docteur-Mouisset with Bee and Ermine, who came regularly every day to contact me. I met Eagle either at Wasp's or in town, but always in a different café. The other centres sheltered the Avia team and the office, where Elephant produced his forged identity papers. Ladybird provided the cover for Magpie who transmitted to all points of the compass to keep the Nazi detector vans on the hop.

In spite of these measures I remained acutely aware of the precariousness of our position in the city of Lyons, which I had called 'Viva Villa' because of the warm, friendly welcome it had given us when we first arrived. Each day now brought us its quota of bad news, alas, but always much too late for us to be able to do anything about it.

After the Paris arrests of 14 March my sister had been arrested in Nice by the OVRA and my brother-in-law, Georges-Picot, was compelled to flee by way of Spain. The great, admirable, tenacious General Raynal (Sheepdog), who had refused to escape, fell victim to the wretched van driver, Chambon. I was so fond of him that it was like losing my father for the second time. After him, one by one, almost the whole Vichy sector collapsed—thirty-five people. Gulliver and a few survivors fell back on Cricket's new region in the mountains of the Massif Central.

What was the point of continuing if I did not ensure that the torch we had lit would be kept alive in the event of my own capture? It became a matter of the utmost urgency to acquaint a potential successor with the running of our service. Paul Bernard (Swift), who had been a volunteer in the organization since 1940, was the obvious choice. I had told him then that the important position that he held in the world of great affairs would make him more useful to us later. Later was now. So I wrote to him.

One afternoon Eagle summoned me to see him urgently. He was waiting for me in Wasp's little apartment and the dismay on his face immediately told me that we were confronted with another disaster. In his hand was a message that he kept screwing up, folding and unfolding: 'Navarre. . . .

Poor Navarre. . . .' he stammered.

'They've killed him.'

'Something much worse, they've handed him over to the Nazis.'

I straightened up, furious. 'It's the Marshal's doing.'

'Yes, along with a whole bunch of pre-war politicians. They have been flown to Germany. Navarre is being kept prisoner secretly in the German dungeons in Vichy.'

'They've separated Navarre from the politicians, so they're going to charge him with complicity in the network and they'll shoot him. I'm going to attack the Germans.'

'You're crazy, you're doing that all day long.'

'I'm going to write to them. I'm going to tell them that Major Loustaunau-Lacau has been imprisoned by Vichy for political reasons that have absolutely nothing to do with the Alliance of which I am the responsible head and that if they shoot him, they and their families will be liquidated within the hour.'

'You're signing your own death warrant!'

'Can you tell me what difference that will make in my case?'

'Who are you going to send your threats to?'

I got Ermine to buy some interzonal cards and addressed them to Dubidon, who had provided me with a marked *Ausweis*, and to some of Navarre's former friends who I knew stood in a privileged position *vis-à-vis* the Nazis. I was convinced that my move would intimidate them sufficiently to make them throw all the weight of their authority into an attempt to save Navarre from the firing squad, at least as long as I was at liberty.

'That isn't everything, alas,' said Eagle who I felt was very near to breaking point. 'A message from Tiger, transmitted via London, says that our principal agents in Lille were shot on 30 March at the fortress of Bondues. Others, more than ten in this case, have been deported.'

'How ghastly! Poor, poor devils; and Verteré, the chief whom we sent to them, is walking about freely and peacefully under the protection of the Abwehr!'

'I could die with shame,' said Eagle. 'That man is surely worse than Bla.'

The April moon brought us once more face to face with the problems of parachute drops and landing aircraft. Eagle had strengthened his Squadron by taking on a new recruit, Lt. Henri Cormouls, whom I christened Pegasus as soon as I saw his vital, vibrant body, that put me in mind of a winged horse. It was a simple matter to initiate such an experienced pilot into the art of handling flashlights and landing lights.

There remained the question of choosing the passengers. This, alas, was easy. Commandant Cros (Aurochs) was a write-off because of his stupid involvement in the plan to kidnap Pétain or Laval. There having been a leak, the Germans launched a big hunt for the audacious would-be kidnappers. Since we were to send a permanent representative to General

Giraud, I suggested that Aurochs should be appointed to the job. Seagull was also involved in the same affair and I thought it high time to send him to London. They would be joined by Robert Rivat (Finch), a young radio operator who was to undergo special training for the Alsace-Lorraine region.

The Lysander Operation Ulysses was carried out on the Villefranche site, where Pegasus performed brilliantly in bringing down Mahout and our delightful Fawn, the poet, the passengers who were returning to France while Aurochs, Seagull and Finch were flying away. A parachute drop brought us Boussard (Cockerel), a radio operator intended for the Avia team, to replace the luckless Heron, who had been captured in Nice.

I began to find Lyons untenable. One had the impression that the place was teeming with agents in disguise. Abwehr, Gestapo, resistance fighters of every kind made up an explosive mixture, and the British themselves gave vent to their uneasiness in the messages we received: '... *Why persist remaining in Lyons stop everyone is in Lyons stop advise you move....*'

I would begin with a half-measure. Why not move my headquarters somewhere outside the city? I had been told of a quiet and unobtrusive little house and I took a taxi to reconnoitre the district. The country was enchanting; the trees were in full blossom and the fields were wonderfully fresh in their first spring green. I began to forget the war and to dream of a rural retreat when the driver, a pleasant, talkative man, showed me a huge meadow, thick with daisies, on the banks of the Saône.

'That,' he said, 'is where the British parachutes come down.'

I looked at my Michelin map. 'How do you know?' I asked.

'Everyone knows, madame. You can see the flashlights a long way off,' he replied innocently.

It was the meadow we ourselves used. I went back with all speed and summoned Eagle. 'No more landings at Villefranche, Eagle,' I told him. 'It has been discovered. It's finished.'

'What beats me is that the Germans do nothing.'

'They know that all our men at a landing place are armed and that they'll be shot if they go near. They prefer to act before or after, using treason as their radar.'

'Preferably after,' added Eagle. 'In that way they get the latest news from London.'

The Germans' subtlety sometimes took a different form, as Magpie discovered to his cost one day, when he was transmitting from a small town out in the country. Leaving the house that he had been using with the case containing the transmitter that went with him everywhere, he bumped into the detector van which was already in the main square. Magpie escaped only by hurling the case at the head of the Gestapo thug who challenged him, dashing off like an Olympic sprinter, and dodging from side to side to avoid the Nazi bullets. The Nazis were still hunting high and low and we had to send our chief radio operator to Paris with the utmost urgency. This incident made a profound impression on me. What was I going to do without Magpie?

My children had also arrived in Lyons and I felt I had no right to see them. I had removed my son from the boarding school, where the enemy had demanded he be handed over and held as a hostage. The Jesuits had refused to give him up and they warned my mother to get him away at once; he had just spent some weeks in a mountain centre for Jewish children run by the Christian Friendship organization. Now my daughter, whom my poor hunted family no longer knew what to do with, had joined him. I decided to send them for safety to Villars-sur-Ollon in Switzerland, where my mother owned a chalet. Although Ermine had taken them out, given them good food to build up their strength, and generally spoiled them, the poor little things had not the slightest idea of what was happening to them. They thought I was in England! Could I disillusion them just in order to take them in my arms and kiss them and then let them go to their fate alone? One day Ermine had taken them past a window from which I could see them, thin and pale and looking utterly lost and helpless. As I watched them walk past me I had the feeling of being buried alive.

Their departure for Switzerland plunged me into the depths of despair. The escape route was blocked and the frontier bristled with incessant German patrols. Driven from pillar to post the children finally made their way across the frontier alone. At the last staging post the peasants to whom they had been entrusted had simply pointed out the direction in which the barbed wire ran, miles from their farm. My son, a future officer, came through the test with flying colours and saved his sister. He was twelve and she was ten.

During the May moon we were due to send London a special report for General Giraud, who had asked us for the intelligence he needed for planning his landings in Corsica and on the Mediterranean coast. In addition, we were expecting Armadillo (Michel Gaveau) with reports from the northern zone, Cricket with reports from central France, and Poodle, Mandrill's charming courier, with a report about the Atlantic zone.

René de Vitrolles, a member of the Squadron, would also be one of the party. Since the trouble in Marseilles he had performed prodigies. Eagle had given him the job of rebuilding the organization in the south-east region and he had discovered some very valuable recruits, including his nephew, des Isnards, also an airman, stationed in Aix-en-Provence with a sound civilian cover: called the Grand Duke, he promised to be a remarkable regional chief. Vitrolles could therefore take our reports to Algiers via London.

I was most apprehensive at having such a concentration of important people and information, and my heart turned over when Eagle arrived unexpectedly at the hospital with all the signs of bad news on his face.

'Eagle, has something happened to the reports?'

'No, it's last night's parachute operation, Operation Nestor. . . .'

'Have the Avia team been arrested?'

'Nearly. The boys who were on their way to the field we use near the village of Jonnage—Mahout, Wolf and Cockerel, the new radio operator —crashed into a wall in their car and smashed themselves up. They're all in the hospital. Pegasus has been to see them.'

'They must be got out at once.'

'I'm afraid it's too late, Marie-Madeleine. Cockerel talked about the Avia headquarters when he was delirious and the Vichy police are investigating.'

With my head ringing and my heart heavy with dreadful forebodings, I went to look for my marvellous nurse, now incorporated into the network under the name of Cat. I got her out of the room where she was preparing dressings and told her my latest worry.

'I thought something would go wrong,' she calmly told me in her lovely Burgundian accent and rolling her rs. 'Something always goes wrong. But don't worry, I'll find you another room on the ground floor, overlooking the garden. You'll be able to get away if necessary.'

I spent the night sorting out my records, burning the copies of my radio messages and keeping only indecipherable notes.

The next day the couriers were due to meet at Eagle's headquarters. Ermine did not come in the morning, which dragged drearily by. I merely picked at my lunch.

Just before three o'clock the phone rang. 'It's your little friend,' Cat said, alert and watchful.

I leaped to the phone: 'Hello, you're late.'

'The fact is, I've hurt my foot badly. I won't be able to come out today . . . nor tomorrow . . . nor the following days. Nor will the others either,' whispered Ermine in a heartbroken little voice and then rang off.

There could be no doubt: they had all been caught. Eagle, poor Eagle, arrested for the third time, and Vitrolles, Cricket, Armadillo, Ermine, Bee . . . the Avia team in the hospital, Magpie in Paris. To whom could I turn now? I wanted to go out, to find anyone at all. Cat took me back to my room. 'Sit quite still,' she said, 'and tell me what to do.'

'Go and alert Ladybird and Wasp. They'll warn the network. Their place will become a trap. Get them to send Elephant to me.'

I listened desperately for hours to the slightest sounds made in the hospital or out in the garden, and to the muffled roar of the city down below. At last came a heavy footstep. I opened the door a crack and saw Eagle appear. He flopped down on the bed like a log. 'I've just escaped, Marie-Madeleine,' he said, 'I've been running as hard as I could.'

The blood flowed to my heart again. I fetched some water from the tap in the wash basin and he drank as though he would never stop.

They had been having their lunch in the Rue du Docteur-Mouisset when a Vichy police superintendent burst in together with a crowd of inspectors. The four officers—Eagle, Vitrolles, Cricket and Armadillo—were taken to a police station at once. Ermine, who had remained in the flat with Bee, under police guard, had seized the opportunity—what extraordinary presence of mind the girl had!—to telephone me and then hide Armadillo's reports from the northern zone in the rubbish bin.

After their arrest Eagle and Vitrolles had taken a strong line. They bamboozled the superintendent by claiming they had the backing of the Deuxième Bureau. Impressed by Vitrolles' rank and puzzled by the ordinariness of the others' forged identity papers, the man equivocated and waited for orders. Meanwhile, Vitrolles, on the strength of the authority he had acquired in the man's eyes, had gone out to take a look at the court-yard. He soon came back and told Eagle that the main door was open and unguarded. The four men put their heads together, called out that they were just going out to get something to eat and walked out under the cow-like gaze of the guard, who had obviously been given no clear orders. Once round the corner of the street they split up like a flock of sparrows and disappeared in different streetcars.

Two days later Ermine re-appeared! She had given the inspectors on guard in the apartment the slip and run off across the courtyards, but not before asking the doorman, a really splendid fellow, to give the packet of reports that she had hidden in the rubbish bin to a messenger who would come for them later. A providential meeting with Elephant in the streetcar that was taking her to a safe hideout meant that she could send him to recover the stuff there and then.

Poor Bee had paid the penalty for everyone! She had been cast into prison, like Poodle coming from Bordeaux, who was the only one to fall into the trap.

But that was not the end of the affair. Alerted, it would seem, by the Vichy police, the Gestapo intensified their watch on the stations and set up road blocks.

We were blockaded in Lyons.

Thanks to Cat I had found refuge in a shady sort of hotel. There at least it was possible to go in and out without being spied on.

Eagle, who was hiding at his lawyer's office, had taken to his white-haired hunchback outfit again. I reckoned that even in this disguise it was too dangerous for him to go near a station or try to get through a road block. Fortunately, Ladybird was well in with the Red Cross. As Red Cross cars were rarely searched, they would evacuate our friends. Once again it meant collecting as many as possible together.

First we must rescue Bee. One of the inspectors involved in the Rue du Docteur-Mouisset affair, Fernand Clément, had discreetly suggested he should go and fetch her from her cell on the pretext that she was wanted for interrogation, then bring her to us. In return, he asked to go to Britain. We agreed, and I named this providential policeman Ferret. Bee was rescued according to plan. She and Ermine were soon driven away to the Massif Central by the ladies of the Red Cross.

The next thing was to get the Avia team out of the hospital. Disguised as a male nurse, the irrepressible Pegasus (Lieutenant Henri-Cormouls) had been able to talk to our friends. At first their state of health—in Mahout's case it was so bad that he was given extreme unction—had been against any real action; but the Lord helps those who help themselves and Pegasus staked everything on one bold throw. Having got on very friendly terms with the Sisters of Saint Vincent de Paul, whom he showered with gifts, he got permission to take our three injured friends out in their pyjamas. 'The air outside will strengthen them,' he argued. The open air did indeed prove highly invigorating and none of them went back to bed. But we lost the radio operator Cockerel as a result. In spite of a long and fruitless search, it proved impossible to trace him. He must simply have taken to his heels.

The car crash had really been the cause of the whole disaster. In going to investigate at the address that Cockerel had exposed while he was delirious, the police had learned that a fair girl—Ermine—who was often in the house in question, lived just outside the town. By checking up with one tradesman after another the police had tracked her down to the Rue du Docteur-Mouisset. Another twelve hours and they followed her to the hospital where I was. Once again I had had a fantastic stroke of luck.

In spite of the fact that the Avia team was smashed, Operation Nestor a failure, the command posts out of action, and the Lyons headquarters under siege, I could not allow the moon to come and go without any aerial liaison with British Intelligence.

We went ahead with Operation Gauguin. Taking the place of Mahout, who was still very shaky, Pegasus had carefully selected a site in the country near Chateauroux, northwest of Vichy, in the direction of Tours. Leaving for Britain were Vitrolles and Ferret but there were no passengers for France. To spread the risks of evacaution, our new treasurer, Gilbert Beaujolin, was to fetch the reports and the money by car while Pegasus was to take charge of the important equipment due to have been dropped in Operation Nestor and of which part would now be transported by the Lysander.

Moderately reassured by the precautions that had been taken, I waited forty-eight hours, at the end of which Eagle appeared in a rage. The first Gauguin night operation had been wrecked by a misunderstanding over signals. The consequences were shattering.

In looking for a suitable site, Pegasus had happened upon a gentleman farmer who had straightway put his house at the disposal of our friends, lavished hospitality on them and let the champagne flow in their honour.

When the aircraft's arrival was reported, the treasurer had gone off on another mission and, as he did not return for a long time, Pegasus had told his kind host in confidence that he was going to receive a consignment of arms and 'a large sum of money'. The man immediately suggested the money should be put in his own safe. The landing at last took place, with everyone in the best of spirits, and more champagne was drunk while waiting for the treasurer to arrive. He appeared next morning and asked for the envelope that had been entrusted to their charming host's tender care.

'What envelope?' asked the man.

'You know, the money.'

'What money?'

A conversation that started off like this was bound to end badly. Our men fled before a volley of sarcastic comments and insults from the gentleman farmer, who threatened to call in the Gestapo.

'And the reports?' I asked in consternation.

Eagle fairly foamed at the mouth: 'In the safe as well.'

Pegasus had returned to Lyons ready almost to commit suicide and explained that his one thought had been to save the sacks containing the weapons and the transmitting sets. Scared that he might be pursued, he had rushed off to give them into the safekeeping of the first village priest he happened to meet, who had said to him: 'My son, put them in the confessional.' It would be easy to recover them and take them straight to Paris.

'Pegasus did well, but now we must get the rest back.' I said. Eagle looked at me and whistled.

'Look, Eagle, this man isn't a traitor, otherwise he wouldn't have let the arms and the cases go. He's a rogue. He undoubtedly thinks that we're scared stiff and will lie low. Well, we didn't found the honourable tribe of the Apaches just for fun.'

'The Apaches!' Eagle tapped his forehead. 'You're absolutely right, the Apaches.'

Led by Pegasus, the Apaches surrounded the farm at night. They cut the telephone wires and broke into the house by forcing the doors. The servants were terrified at first and did not move. Pegasus, triumphant, hauled the gentleman farmer out of his bed, where he was nicely settled with a delicious little girl friend. 'I've come to make you cough up,' Pegasus said. 'You can't warn your Gestapo friends now, the phone's cut.'

The man jumped to it, trembling from head to foot. The open safe revealed our millions of francs. As the envelopes had been opened, Pegasus was afraid some had been taken and he soon spotted further piles of notes.

'Don't touch that, don't touch that, it's my men's wages,' moaned the rogue.

'How am I to know that?' Pegasus asked and grabbed the lot. As he went out he gave the old family governess a hefty advance. She had never seen so much money in her life. 'That's the way to do social work,' was his parting shot.

I was now alone in Lyons. Eagle and Armadillo, in workmen's clothes and with workmen's identity papers, had also been smuggled out by the ladies of the Red Cross. For a last time I saw Elephant busy reforging the cards of all the captured agents. He was not going to Paris until later.

'The Germans are furious,' he told me. 'A car crash, a Vichy police investigation, six arrests—all to no purpose: the suspects had escaped, a police inspector had disappeared, the injured had finally gone "to get some air", and the road barriers had been about as effective as a sieve for holding water.'

Taking over the investigation, the Gestapo, faithful to its methods, had at first tortured and deported the superintendent of the sixth *arrondissement* responsible for the Rue du Docteur-Mouisset affair. Afterwards it had taken its revenge by compelling the Vichy police to arrest two teenagers, Inspector Clement's son and Ladybird's daughter, the charming Missou Berne, and my dear Wasp. Ladybird was not at home at the time, but for some reason she had telephoned twice. The second time she realized the police were at the end of the line. So Ladybird had gone to Paris to continue the fight.

Elephant's story left us no room for hope. The German police had even gone to the Guillots' (Dromedary's) house. Dromedary and Grasshopper were shelling peas in the courtyard when they knocked. The Gestapo men had, very politely, asked to speak to 'Mr and Mrs Dromedary'. 'They live on the fourth floor,' replied Guillot no less politely. Once the Gestapo men's backs were turned, the two of them promptly bolted.

'It's a real explosion,' said Elephant. 'In Marseilles alone the headquarters and staff had gone west and here the services are taking a beating. I no longer feel safe. Get me out of it quickly, chief.' His big ears quivered anxiously like those of a hunted animal.

And so, after four months, everything I had laboriously built up again in Lyons had collapsed like a house of cards. Would the lives of underground fighters now and in the future be as short-lived as the life of a may-fly?

I determined to try again—this time in Paris.

22 BARRICADE

The vast grey suburbs rolled past in the early morning. Barricade was the code name I had given to Paris, and the Gare de Lyon looked to me as forbidding as fortified battlements. And it was Magpie, *not* Tiger, whom I saw waiting for me at the approaches to the barrier. The harsh truth shook me. What I had dreaded had happened. Tiger was in hospital, laid low by the illness that had long been undermining his health and which he had consistently neglected. The only thing I could now do for my dear Tiger was to see that he lacked for nothing.

'Where is he?' I asked.

'In the Massif Central. Josette's with him,' said Magpie, marching Cat and me off to an apartment under the roof of a quiet house nearby, normally reserved for the use of the radio operators.

Since he had been forced to flee from Lyons by the relentless hounding of the German detector vans, Magpie had become extremely careful. He had established a fantastic radio circuit. All the transmitting sets that had been parachuted to us in the last few weeks were operating. For the headquarters staff alone we had Harp, Flute, Flageolet, Ocarina, Guzla and Banjo—a real orchestra. Magpie's adjutants were André Riss (Lapwing) and Jean Portenard (Widgeon), two splendid young men who obeyed his slightest sign, and Gabriel Romon (Swan), an eminent Army engineer, who was going to find him a whole string of operators and mechanics.

Cat took a touching farewell of me. Lapwing and Widgeon saw to my luggage and took it to the headquarters where I was to go later. But first I had to see how contact with London was established in Paris and I accompanied Magpie on his transmission round.

The chief radio operator had put his radios in several different places, as far from one another as possible, and he carried with him only sets of crystals and the microphotographed operating schedules. He took caution to the extreme of never using the same plan twice running at the same location. Transmissions went out on a chromatic scale of frequencies. That was necessary as British Intelligence had warned me that enemy detection operations were being intensified. If a transmission went out from the same site and lasted more than twenty minutes the general position of the secret transmitter was located during the first session; the district was localized during the second transmission, and during the third the street itself was ringed by three detector cars cunningly camouflaged and placed in a triangle.

To speed detection the Nazis cut off the electricity supply to the area where they thought there was a transmitter. If a transmission broke off and, more especially, if it started up again when the current was restored, it meant that they were on the right trail. The cars approached the house. A man got out and a concealed portable detector would lead him unerringly to the apartment in use. 'Concierge-detection' was how British Intelligence had described it in a letter. 'It can be recognized by the wire hanging from the man's earphone.' I knew from experience that it was extremely unhealthy to let things get to the on-the-spot check.

While I kept a lookout on the street from the balcony of the various houses we went to, taking the utmost care to ensure that the fatal twentieth minute was not exceeded, I heard Magpie cursing his contacts under his breath—a thing he rarely did. 'This time it took me ten minutes to get London,' he said. 'It's now the nineteenth minute. Stop the message and move on to the next set,' I replied.

In the bicycle-taxi that took us to the next house with a set, I thought anxiously of Magpie's orchestration—Adagio at Rennes, Harmonium at Carentan, Fugue at Caen, Horn at Cherbourg, Ukulele at Louviers, Crotchet and Rondo and Clarinet at Nantes, Fife and Guitar in the north, Saxophone and Scherzo at Autun, Sharp at Pau, quite apart from Mandrill's radios in Bordeaux, La Rochelle and Poitiers, Cricket's in the Massif Central, and those used by the Avia team and the Druids sub-network. Others would have to be brought to Lyons, Aix-en-Provence and Toulon. We would have to keep all these supplied with spare parts, recruit enough operators and, above all, train them not to get caught. The survival of our orchestra, in fact, was due to the observance of the twenty minutes grace, after which the enemy always won.

We had arranged to meet Eagle for dinner. The black market restaurant —offering a menu of blackmarket beefsteak and chips, caviar at that time—was full of Nazis in uniform, which made any real conversation impossible.

'It's the best way to fortify the inner man in peace,' whispered Eagle, who had now recovered all his old spirit. 'Who would ever think we three were hunted by the Gestapo? Your health, gentlemen!' he said, raising his glass of Beaujolais in the direction of the Germans.

I thought of Tiger. 'It's not daring or carelessness that will be our undoing. . . .' He had said that more than two years ago. I also raised my glass. 'The King,' I whispered to Magpie, our English radio operator.

The new headquarters in the Rue Raynouard was a luxury apartment. We were again joined by the ever-busy Ermine. She had arrived from the Massif Central with her hair dyed black, and had already organized our camp.

What a pleasure it was to know that our little group had emerged unscathed from the recent alarms and excursions in Lyons. But one incident still had to be cleared up. Ermine had stuffed all the reports and documents and rolls of film into the rubbish bin. But the people sent to collect them from the doorkeeper had brought back the films only.

'Look here,' I said, 'Elephant sent someone there, but who?'

'Bumpkin,' replied Eagle. Bumpkin, as Cricket's first lieutenant, was in charge of the Apaches.

'Who went with him? Basher? Convict? Buccaneer?' I inquired, determined to get to the bottom of the affair.

'I think it was Lanky,' said Eagle. 'He's an Alsatian student. He and Bumpkin are apparently inseparable.'

Paris now resembled Shanghai, with its thoroughfares thick with bicycles, tandems and bicycle-taxis whose drivers, like Chinese coolies, got out of the way of the fast, powerful enemy cars with an enigmatic expression on the faces of their drivers.

Pierre Dayné (Ant) made himself responsible for my protection. The intense determination to serve that he had shown for two and a half years had now fully matured and I had christened him Ant, as a tribute to his unceasing activity. Ant was still attached to the Paris police vice squad and was still entitled to carry a gun. When we went out together it was understood that at the least sign of danger I would become his prisoner, as that was the only way to escape the checks and street blocks that were suddenly imposed. In anticipation of such a role, I had got Elephant to provide me with a complete set of identity papers for a person with the poetic-sounding name of Pamela Trotaing.

One afternoon, when we were sitting together in the Metro, I tugged Ant's sleeve. He looked at me, then saw that I was staring at the person opposite me—a well-built man with a brown moustache and thin, brushed-back hair, and wearing a suit of exaggerated elegance. It was the collaborator Dubidon, the man who had once given me a marked *Ausweis* and whose life I had threatened in order to save Navarre. He looked at me in utter amazement, scrutinizing my face with an intensity I found difficult to sustain.

'Come on, this is where we get out, sweetie,' said Ant brusquely, just as the doors were about to close at the Opera station. With a quick flick of the hand, like a conjurer, he yanked me out of my seat and catapulted me on to the platform. The train started, taking Dubidon, who was by now standing and looking back with his nose glued to the window. 'Quick, madame, he'll pull the emergency brake,' said Ant, and dragged me off at a wild, nightmarish speed.

Eagle did not like that at all. He urged me to go to London. I refused, arguing that I would not leave the network until my successor, Martin, was really able to take my place and that I had already promised Petrel and Great Dane that they would be taken to Britain in Operation Degas.

That brilliant student Bumpkin, arrived from Lyons in a great state. Elephant (Siegrist) had just been arrested.

'Elephant? But your only job, Bumpkin, was to hide him somewhere safe.'

'I know,' he admitted miserably. 'It happened when he was actually moving.' The capture of the man who ran our forgery service, together with his stock and equipment, was a terrible catastrophe.

Eagle sprang to his feet in a towering rage: 'How very appropriate! The security chief, protected by the security service, gets nabbed with all his security stuff and a collection of secret files. Can you beat it? And you? Where were you in this magnificent tactical plan?'

'In Nice, sir.'

'In Nice! What were you up to in Nice?'

I pitied him in his obvious distress. But he had considered the risks. What better solution could he think of than to offer his own house as a hideout for Elephant? Buccaneer was to escort him while Lanky, the Alsatian student, was to keep a look-out, having already made sure that the way was clear. It was so simple that he had not thought his presence in Lyons was necessary. Alas, while going to the carefully timed rendezvous, Lanky had noticed that the Germans had surrounded the house. In a panic, since it was too late to warn Elephant, who was already on his way, he had rushed to the tram stop.

'Did Lanky think Elephant was coming by trolley-car? With three transmitting sets, a parcel of crystals, a hundred-and-fifty seals, twenty pounds of identity forms, two revolvers, a dagger and a large amount of high explosives?' I asked.

Bumpkin buried his head in his hands. 'Lanky is an Alsatian revanchist by family tradition. He's given me a thousand proofs of his loyalty and courage.'

'Then what was he doing at the streetcar stop?' asked Eagle in exasperation.

'He was looking out for Elephant. When he saw Buccanneer's car appear it was too late.'

'So Buccaneer has been caught too?' I asked sorrowfully. 'Poor kid!'

'Your courageous Alsatian couldn't shout and warn them, of course.' Bumpkin's nerves went completely to pieces and he could no longer choke back a sob.

'Bumpkin,' I said gently, 'you made a grave mistake in deserting your post that evening. You can't pass a job on to someone else. You're the one who has our confidence and you in turn manage the men you yourself choose, but under your own control.'

'Lanky would like to see you, madame, to apologize and explain why he acted as he did.'

'No! Your man's a fool or a traitor. Now listen, Bumpkin, I forbid you to send him anywhere near headquarters. Does he know Cricket?'

'The Great Manitou is our superior officer; I introduced him.'

'All right, then take Lanky back home. Eagle is going to ask Cricket to clear the whole business up.'

The poor wretches! I was to blame. They were far too young. One would need to be everywhere at once to save these young men from their impetuousness, from themselves. Bumpkin had thought it was a simple routine move and his error of judgement worried me. One dare not play with fire.

Then Eagle suddenly remembered his notebook. While he was on the run in Lyons, Eagle had given Elephant his duplicate notebook, in code, that he always carried with him in case he had to get rid of the original. Elephant was to look after it, because writing down the hundreds of addresses, passwords and codes again was such a long job.

'Don't worry, Eagle,' I consoled him. 'You're the only one who can decipher your dreadful scrawl.'

'It isn't only that. They won't believe poor Elephant; they'll torture him to get the key. . . .'

'Yes, it means torture for us now, Eagle. I'm afraid our organization has become too big.'

Eagle, who had been pacing up and down the room, suddenly stopped dead in his tracks as though petrified. 'What do you mean?' he asked.

'It isn't adapted to today's conditions. I'd rather we curled up into a ball.'

'Like a hedgehog?'

'Our agents run to one another far too much on the pretext of helping one another. I beg you, Eagle, to send out a general order telling people to stay put and work on their own. We mustn't be dazzled by success.'

The 'wonderful show' put on for the June moon saw the exit of Petrel and Great Dane, and the reappearance of Seagull. The RAF were ecstatic about our latest landing site, called Degas. The approaches for the run in were exceptionally open, among wide cornfields, and its position, near the village of Nantheuil-le-Haudouin, north-east of Paris, reduced the Lysander's double trip to less than three hours.

Before leaving for London, Petrel (Lamarque) had given me a long memo. 'I'll try,' he said, 'to find out what the chances of arming our people are. The total strength of the Compagnons de France is about 17,000 men, a powerful secret division. It would be a great mistake not to reactivate them. I therefore count on you to impress on the Allies the importance of my offer, for you alone can discuss the terms.'

'That's a very far cry from your hedgehogs,' said Eagle. 'And what do you think about this?'

He handed me a report from Jean Carayon (Phoenix), a member of the Squadron who had just been appointed to the post of Secretary-General of Air Defence. Eagle had encouraged him to accept this promotion, which would put him in a position to give us and the whole Resistance movement tremendous help. That was how the Pompiers de l'Air came into being. It was, in fact, a vast plan of action designed to prepare for the return of Air Force personnel, including the reserve, in its entirety; to prevent airmen from going to Germany in the STO[1]; to obstruct the pursuit or search for those who had disappeared into the maquis; and to study, under an official cover, the effects of Allied bombing. All the intelligence obtained in this way came to the Alliance. We were informed of the names of airmen volunteering for service in North Africa so that we could help them to get there.

Phoenix pointed out in his report that the anti-aircraft platforms on the enemy rail transports would in future be manned by personnel from the Pompiers de l'Air, which Vichy had odiously pressurized them into doing. The poor wretches were to play the part of shields for the Nazis. Phoenix wanted secretly to arm his 'Air' personnel, who were to be joined by members of the Jeunesse et Montagne (Youth and Mountain), another Pétainist organization.

'Phoenix and Petrel have infiltrated Vichy marvellously,' I remarked admiringly. 'But why do they all want to be armed to the teeth?'

'Operation Torch, so splendidly led by the Americans, leads them to think that the landing in France will take place this summer.'

'The Compagnons de France, the Pompiers de l'Air, Jeunesse et Montagne—that means supplying at least 30,000 men. Some parachute drop for that lot, Eagle! You can't really be contemplating that!'

'But it would be magnificent, Marie-Madeleine. I beg you, *do* go to London and convince our friends.'

I felt increasingly loath to go. I was haunted by the fear of expanding the network to frightening dimensions. Eagle stood before me, tense, anxious and consumed by the desire to help his own particular service. I recalled his unbroken succession of disappointments: the abortive Algiers plot, the German invasion of the free zone and his failure to get the armistice army to act.

'You win, Eagle. I'll go to London at the next moon and plead the airmen's case.'

'Thank you, Marie-Madeleine. But above all, I'm so afraid for you. They've just arrested Bertie Albrecht. It's rumoured that she was beheaded. My God, that must never happen to you.'

They had arrested Bertie Albrecht, the inspiration of the 'Combat' movement, Jean Moulin, the founder of the 'National Council of the Resistance,' and General Delestraint, the first head of the 'Secret Army'. I thought sadly that the Resistance had received a mortal blow. Without this woman and these men, nothing of what they had created would have

[1] The *Service du Travail Obligatoire*, the German organization for recruiting forced labour in France to be employed in the German war effort.

the same power or the same inspiration. There were gaps, too, in our own ranks; some of our people who had disappeared or had been hunted down were irreplaceable. Since arriving in Paris, in addition to Tiger's absence, I had not been able to discover Saluki either, nor his wife, Firefly. The Gestapo had appeared at the Chateau de Sully to arrest him; Firefly had stood up to them, taking the Nazis through the house with a superb show of indifference, knowing that her husband was ahead of them, dodging from room to room, using the secret doors and odd recesses known only to him. In this way she had forced them to inspect the huge chateau from bottom to top. After hours spent marching round and round, they gave up in a daze, saying they were convinced that the Duke was not there but that they would return. Eagle had then ordered Saluki to go out of circulation and withdraw to Switzerland. Firefly, who was expecting a fourth child, had joined him, crawling under the barbed wire with her children.

Then Jack Tar (Poulard) came and described his 'arrest'. He had come from Brest with his usual cargo—orders of battle, the location of naval units, coastal defence plans. 'I had time only to hide with neighbours across the road,' he said. 'The Fritzes surrounded my parents' house. Then they forced their way in and I heard shouts of "Jack Tar" and "Poulard". There was I watching, but no one squealed on me, though everyone knew where I was.'

'Somebody must have given them your address and your alias.'

'Undoubtedly. From the questions the Gestapo asked it was clear that I was the only one they were after. The Fritzes don't know a thing about my sector.'

'Jack Tar, I'm taking you to London. You need to disappear for a bit.'

He blushed with pleasure. 'That's marvellous, chief, but I swear I haven't made the story up in order to take it easy for a bit.'

Arrests like those, coming when we were least expecting them, became a nightmare. I now knew what the real dangers were: overconfidence and excessive daring, as in Schaerrer's case, and getting caught red-handed. Radio detection was another danger, but we could not stop transmitting and our radio operators were the real frontliners, the first to sacrifice their lives. But the greatest danger of all was treachery, which led to infiltration by the Abwehr and left us almost completely defenceless.

So far my fears had been sporadic only. I had known fear in action on street corners and in the long hours spent waiting or watching at crossroads; but confidence, compounded of faith and hope, had very quickly prevailed. Now, even though my faith was unshaken, hope was ebbing. I was afraid I should be unable to carry my mission through to the end. I was deeply afraid of what lay ahead.

Awakening with a start, I stared at the darkness in my room, trying to conjure up again the nightmarish vision that had shattered my sleep. The scene was a great stretch of country, bounded by drifts of heather, where a

Lysander had landed; Eagle and Magpie climbed out of the plane, to be welcomed by a group whose faces I could not identify. The plane veered sideways and flew away. Suddenly a ring of Germans closed in on the travellers until it touched them: 'We have arrested Faye, we are delighted.' And where was I, the spectator? I probed the darkness again and again in my effort to reconstruct my dream, so that I could absorb the minutest details. The heather, the plane that took off again undamaged, the two men, the Gestapo and—always one predominant feature—the pink heather, the sumptuous masses of heather.

As soon as it was daylight I telephoned Mahout. 'Tell me, Mahout, which of our landing places has heather in bloom?'

'Heather?' He searched his memory. 'None, madame. May I ask why?'

'You're sure?'

'Absolutely.'

'Then Mahout, listen carefully. Never suggest anywhere where there's heather as a landing ground. Never, give me your word.'

'I give you my word, chief, if it gives you pleasure.'

He was bound to think, she's gone completely cuckoo. And, to cheer me up, he explained how my own pick-up would be done. It was Operation Renoir, fixed for 18 July, the first feasible day of the moon.

'It'll go off splendidly and I bet you won't have to wait either. The British'll be at the rendezvous strictly on time and on the first day, too. But you're coming back?'

'Of course I'm coming back. Can you see me stagnating in England until the end of the war?'

Swift (Paul Bernard) had been absolutely delighted to accept the suggestion that he should eventually be my successor. The legacy he would accept from us was now a vast machine, the mysteries of which were still unknown to him; but since receiving my letter from Lyons he had shouldered admirably all his new and unfamiliar responsibilities. The intelligence bureau for which he was responsible was a hive of activity. I loved to go and stay there for hours on end. It was headed by Jean Bouyat (Caviar), a young man from the Polytechnique; he collected, sorted and catalogued the documents along the lines that Armadillo had worked out and introduced more than a year ago, and which were now general practice in the network. Micheline Grimprel (Scarab), wearing a cyclamen satin blouse, typed the report so that a duplicate could be kept until the mail bag arrived in London. As soon as the code phrase indicating that it had arrived safely was broadcast by the BBC on the day after the Lysander operations, we burned our copy. It was a great drawback not to be able to keep these reports, but it would have led to accumulating tons of paper that we could not possibly have moved in an emergency. 'It's lucky I use special memory techniques,' Caviar gaily remarked. His handsome, calm, balanced face reassured me.

Eagle and Swift arrived at the bureau deep in a conversation that struck me as very animated, although carried on in a whisper. As soon as he saw me, Swift explained: 'I've got Jean Laurent to work for us. D'you remember my old friend from the Bank of Indochina? We'll call him Benteng, an Indochinese animal. A banker becomes rather like a father confessor and many of his clients unburden themselves to him. That's how he came to discover something quite fantastic.'

'A war treasure?'

'Much better,' said Eagle. 'A plot against Hitler.'

A number of Wehrmacht officers had apparently decided to bring the war in the West to an end. They were asking for a separate peace with the Allies and, using Jean Laurent as an intermediary, had proposed two negotiators whose names I was asked to give to the British, neither more nor less.

'And what about Hitler?'

'They're going to neutralize him or, more likely, kill him.'

'When they've actually done that, Swift, we'll see. For the moment Rudolf Hess has gone to Scotland, the high dignitaries of the Wehrmacht are parachuting down on Jean Laurent, and I shall be told that Hitler's pulling the strings . . . and what about the Russian front in this plot?'

'The fighting will go on.'

I was appalled. 'If I understand you correctly, we're joining the Wehrmacht against the wicked bolsheviks? Meanwhile the Nazis are tearing our guts out. The whole thing's utterly fantastic. The British will just laugh at me if I talk about it.'

'It must be easy to confirm how much truth there is in the story of these "plenipotentiaries",' Eagle commented.

'I'm convinced there's a genuine plot,' Swift insisted. I told them I would think about it. Hitler killed by his own officers! If only it could be true!

'You can't go to London without saying goodbye,' Eagle said to me a little later, when our bureaucrats had gone to lunch and we were sharing a snack while we worked on the machinery I wanted to leave for running the network during my absence.

Eagle anticipated a rather solemn session, for a disturbing rivalry was beginning to emerge among Resistance groups and our friends wanted to assure themselves that the road along which we had led them was the right one.

'They want to work against the Nazis and we give them the chance. What more do they want?' I asked, thoroughly annoyed.

'They're thinking of the future.'

'With all these rumours of a separate peace going around, I'm not in the least surprised. Horses start running when they scent the stable. I'm perfectly willing to give assurances, but you'll have to tighten up on security, Eagle, if people want to have a future.'

'It's high time you took a rest, Marie-Madeleine. You look on the black side of everything these days.'

The future? Which of the actors in this tragedy would see its aftermath, I thought bitterly. All those who had already gone beyond recall, all those who had been ensnared and had vanished in the enemy's traps were certainly not asking themselves questions.

The gnawing anxiety aroused by the dream gripped me again. I hoped with all my heart that Eagle was right, that it was I who was exaggerating.

On 16 July, two days before I was due to leave, about a dozen of us were sitting round the big table in the headquarters. It looked for all the world like an American film set: white walls, thick pile carpets, comfortable chairs, and—as in a film—greyish people had arrived one by one, escorted by shadowy figures who were subsequently seen coming and going past the ground floor window. I recognized them as they walked by, trying hard to look nonchalant and unconcerned. All the old guard—Wolf, Jassaud, Ant, Beaver, Jack Tar. Bumpkin was standing at the entrance with Magpie. Eagle had organized things splendidly and relays of armed sentries extended to the corners of all the adjoining streets.

We launched into a discussion about 'the Generals' conflict', a subject viciously played up by the Nazi radio. Eagle described his interviews with Giraud in Algiers and de Gaulle in London, and he expressed the opinion that de Gaulle would head the provisional government and therefore handle political matters, while Giraud would remain Commander-in-Chief of the French army, which was really his only ambition. In that case, once our network had been militarized by him, the natural thing for us was to be at the disposal of the French military command while being loyally Gaullist in everything that involved politics.

'What about the British in all this?' asked Cricket, unable to suppress his anti-British bias.

'In Britain the Gaullist bodies are necessarily integrated into the Allied machinery and therefore automatically come under the Allied command,' I said. 'That's the status we must acquire—to be officially detached, and then our activities will continue as before but to everybody's benefit.'

'We do a lot,' sighed Colonel Morraglia. 'We talk a lot, but our French friends don't often give any real help. Have you had the network's militarization papers yet?'

'It's a slow business, a slow business,' Eagle admitted. 'That's one reason why Marie-Madeleine is going to London.'

I spoke again and explained what I was going to do in London: assure our lines of communication, obtain a proper status for our agents and their families, secure financial help, and put the Alliance on an official road that would allow it to emerge from this conflict with its head high. But I had to fight to get our friends to give their unanimous approval.

Those who sat around the table addressed one another quite naturally by their animal names: Eagle, Swift, Sparrowhawk, Cricket, Bat, Triton, Dragon, Cayman, Argus, Gibbon. . . . And they were, in fact, all extraordinarily different. Eagle was the one remaining link with the original Crusade. Cricket represented the second wave and Swift the third. Three periods in the network's life. How many others would there be before the end? Those men were perhaps right to think about the future; but the present was still there, implacable, with death lurking beyond the door. I thought of the old saying 'action speaks louder than words', but how in hell was one to stop a Frenchman from talking? By making him draft a motion, and that was what Eagle did. Intentions were expressed: 'To remain united and to work as a group to defend the interests of those of us who would come to an unhappy end', 'to continue our intelligence activities for the benefit of the Allied troops until the end of hostilities.'

Each man signed with his alias, after the text had been agreed. Three copies were set aside for Saluki, Tiger and Petrel, all of whom were absent, but I had insisted that they should be associated with the conference.

Once unity had been established we went on to deal with constructive measures. The first was to announce that Swift would take over from Eagle and myself in due course. The third wave agreed there and then, but I saw the second wave look rather sour. No one said a word, however, and the motion was adopted. Then Eagle produced his new security plan to the effect that contact would henceforth be made from top to bottom of the ladder only, which was the reverse of current practice, with its incessant comings and goings. As each sector possessed one or more transmitters, London would warn the headquarters in the event of a disaster and vice versa.

I was then monopolized by all those comrades who had some special request to make. Cricket took me into the hall, where he introduced me to his new adjutant, Corsair (Lieutenant Pradelle), who was dressed in white from head to foot and who had been waiting outside, unknown to us. He had been running a very efficient local network in Vichy and for some time had been sending the Americans information. He explained his work to me. I was amazed by the lucidity, detail and length of the document he handed to me. It covered all aspects of Vichy's plans and intentions on the subject of collaboration. I thanked him warmly and gave him Sheepdog's (Raynal's) sector, which had been completely wiped out.

'As a matter of courtesy, madame, warn the Americans that I'm no longer working with them.'

'Your information goes to the common command and so they'll get the benefit of it.'

'Why did you criticize Lanky so severely,' Cricket then asked me.

'Because the way he acted when Elephant was arrested is suspicious.'

'I interrogated him at length. He was genuinely cut up at having botched his mission. He must be given a chance.'

'You must go on questioning the fellow, Cricket. And what about Chambon, that nasty little van driver?'

'He's a slug, but nothing's lost by waiting. You've given me a terrible job to do. I haven't got a prison where I can hold suspects and yet I can't just kill them at sight, as I shall run the risk of making a mistake.'

'Obviously,' I said, thinking of the dangers we had run to interrogate and judge Bla. 'I leave it entirely to your judgement as an old and experienced soldier.'

'Then why did you choose Swift, a newcomer, to take over? Do you think the old hands like that?'

'My successor mustn't be someone who's already known to the enemy.'

'He isn't yet. That's the only difference.'

There was no convincing him and, sad at heart, I watched him walk off along the Rue Raynouard muttering into his grey overcoat, followed by Corsair, his white suit sparkling in the sunlight of the beautiful summer afternoon.

The following day passed in a fever of preparations and goodbyes. I went to the agents' headquarters, to give my dear Ladybird final instructions about help for the families of the arrested agents. She and her sister, whose house in the Rue de l'Assomption was used as another hideout, arranged in which houses the transmitting sets should be kept, which places should be the letterboxes, checked on the various visitors and kept watch night and day—both of them vigilant, indefatigable, compassionate. In that thankless task, without which a network could never survive, the Churchill sisters displayed the same tenacity as their illustrious namesake.

As I went out I bumped into Chinchilla, Swift's pretty young wife. 'You must wear something elegant to make the British sit up!' she said. I had not given the matter a thought, but I accepted, not without a certain long-forgotten pleasure, a tailored suit and a black Maggy Rouff ensemble, as well as a brown batik dress.

A small farewell party was held in a smart bar run by Bernard de Billy. We sat there with drinks impossible to get except with special coupons, surrounded by the stuffiest, most affected of Germans, monocles screwed tightly in their eyes. Jean Sainteny, our proud Dragon, arrived with his pockets bursting with messages. Chinchilla, who was the headquarters despatch rider, pedalled off on her bicycle to take them to the radio operators; then Magpie turned up and confirmed that operation Renoir was on.

Eagle and I walked down the Champs-Elysées in the golden haze at the end of the lovely day. The air, no longer polluted by traffic, was sweet with the good smell of leaves on the trees. The unaccustomed drinks had induced a state of euphoria. We stopped at the Arc de Triomphe to look at the most beautiful view in the world. I gave the capital a big, conspiratorial, goodbye smile: it answered with a scowl—the swastika flags cracking like whips in the twilight breeze.

On the morning of 18 July I did some shopping, packed my case and burned some useless papers. In the afternoon Eagle came to tell me that Operation Renoir was definitely on. The plane would probably arrive at midnight GMT.

He was in a great state: he had discovered that Armadillo had two unknown women, who had no connection with the Resistance, living in his house. There had been a dramatic scene between him and Jack Tar. I could scarcely believe it. For a year he had worked for us in a strictly methodical and disciplined way; his role as instructor could easily finish, for his job was genuinely completed.

'Tell him I'm taking him with me,' I told Eagle.

'Good. I'll go back and send him along. You'll leave at 17.00 hours; you'll find Ant at the corner of the Rue François-1er; you'll get with him into the bicycle-taxi that he's hired. Don't worry about anything; I've arranged it all down to the last detail. See you again soon, Marie-Madeleine. Be brave, you know perfectly well that you must go.'

I could not bear to cut the cord between the Alliance and myself, but the risks the British took in coming to pick us up had to be paid for. War is selfish.

16.55 hours. I donned my trench coat, pulled my hat right down to my eyes, grabbed my case and set off to meet Ant. He was standing at the corner of the Rue François-1er, chatting to the tennis-shirted cyclist. We got into the ridiculous contraption that went by the name of bicycle-taxi, so reminiscent of the East. Progress is a wonderful thing, I thought, as the poor wretch pedalled his heart out to speed us through the streets.

At the Rond-Point in the Champs-Elysées I saw Eagle's hunchback figure waiting. His glittering eyes wished me bon voyage.

At the Gare de l'Est I sighted Mahout carrying the suitcases containing the reports, followed by his aide, dear old Bison. In the queue waiting at the booking office was Jack Tar, smiling all over his face, along with a pale, drawn-looking Armadillo.

Our tickets had been bought in advance and we went onto the platform. The train was already in the station with steam up. I dived into a first class carriage with Ant, the others splitting up and occupying nearby compartments. We got out at Nanteuil-le-Haudouin and walked some distance behind Mahout. Once we were beyond the range of prying eyes he stopped and we all joined him.

We had to wait for Dr Gilbert's car, which was not due until dark. Bison went to the Trumel family's farm, where the equipment for the operation was kept, to let them know that we had arrived.

The wait in the ditch was an anxious one, and the snack provided by Mahout was scanty. When night fell we set off again towards the landing ground. Then we heard a car. The wheezing and spluttering that went on could only come from one that belonged to a country doctor. It stopped when it drew level with our shadows and we piled in without a word.

Gilbert drove for a few more miles, then turned down a side road and suddenly halted in a newly-cut cornfield, the stubble gleaming faintly in the starlight. He switched off his engine beside a rick and asked us to get out.

'There are shadows at night, too,' he told me. 'I'll put my car up against the rick; seen from a distance they merge into one. It's less conspicuous than parking on the main road.'

I squatted beside him in the warm and friendly straw. Jean Trumel (Muskrat), the little, twenty-year-old plumber in charge of the equipment, had arrived before us. The men were silently marking out the landing strip. A large L, pointing to windward, would be formed on the ground by their flashlights. Mahout's, placed at the actual point where the plane would stop, would be recognized by its signals, which the plane would answer with the lights on its wing tips.

It was 22.00 hours, and with the preparations completed, the Avia squad disappeared against other ricks. Nothing could be seen from the main road. Alfred Jassaud prowled around, ready to fire a warning shot in the event of any untoward encounter.

'How lovely and peaceful it all is,' whispered Gilbert, looking up at the brilliant moon. I could see his face at last, a face in which could be read the long story of the weary, exhausted doctor who had devoted his life to tending the poor. Shell-rimmed spectacles, a large moustache, bushy eyebrows and a mane of grey hair still gave him an intellectual appearance, but his skin was lined like a peasant's. His clothes were simple and threadbare, but his manner was aristocratic. How old could he be? He told me: sixty-eight.

'Why haven't you been given an alias, doctor?' I asked him.

'I'm less than nothing in your network, I don't presume to compare myself to your big birds and wild beasts,' he replied.

'What can I do for you, doctor? Mahout says you never accept anything, not even for the cost of the petrol you use helping us.'

'Well, I must confess I'd love to have some toilet soap from London. You can't imagine how dreadful it is, going to see the sick without really clean hands. . . .'

Once again the figures of the Avia squad glided across the landing ground. At the head of the L, Muskrat; at the heel, Ant; at the toe, Mahout. I looked at my watch. It was 00.59 GMT. A few seconds later and a hum could be heard in the distance. Mahout's trained ear was not mistaken. He flashed his electric torch, aiming it in the direction from which the sound, now like a large, spluttering motorcycle, was coming, and his two helpers did the same. Soon, to the north-east, we could make out an approaching shape. Then Mahout began to send his signals M–M–M. Soon the Lysander blinked an answering R–R–R–R with its position lights. As arranged, I walked over to Mahout and watched him operating, fascinated by the elegance of his gestures. In the moonlight his gipsy personality took on a touch of the sorcerer. He literally attracted the plane towards himself.

The signalling stopped and the docile Lysander touched down level with Muskrat, taxied along the ground to Ant, turned towards Mahout, who swung it round and steadied it ready for take-off. There was no wind. The rear cockpit suddenly opened and three men shot out, then pulled their luggage after them. They grabbed our bags and bundles in accordance with the usual ceremonial and placed them side by side in a special little compartment. The three men were Petrel, back from his course, and our radio operators, Nightingale and Stork, who had come from Algiers to rejoin the fray. There was just time to hug them all and I was hoisted up into the cockpit, into which Jack Tar and Armadillo also slipped. Mahout, clinging on to the front of the plane, exchanged a few cheery words and some small presents with the RAF pilot, a friend he had made in London. The door closed again and the plane began to move.

We were already airborne when I observed that less than seven minutes had elapsed from start to finish of this magical performance—landing and taking off within twenty-five miles of Paris in the middle of the German occupation.

Seated facing backwards, we were separated from the pilot by the bulky extra fuel tank. The pilot, therefore, could only see ahead. All we could possibly do to help him as he headed back for England was to let him know about any bird of prey that might dive upon him. So we began to watch and search the sky conscientiously. The panorama of France that slipped past beneath us made me feel very miserable: we flew over dead, smokeless, unlighted cities, the very image of my own despair.

A conversation started on the intercom. The pilot had made contact with his base. We saw the cliffs of England, and then a great sweep of searchlights, a flood of beacons, a festival of lights. The pilot picked up his airfield, circled, touched down and stopped beside a group of officers in khaki or blue uniforms, who solemnly greeted us. The lights went out and the blackout was complete.

'Did you have a good trip? Wonderful night, wasn't it? Come and have something.'

I spotted Richards at once. 'Here you are at last, Poz!' he said. 'We were terribly worried about you. Why didn't you come before?' And he took me off to the mess, where a cheerful buzz of conversation could be heard through the carefully screened doors.

No one stopped talking or playing or drinking when we entered. The arrival of three wayfarers at two o'clock in the morning did not cause a single person there to give us a glance. In Britain questions were not asked. But in the cheerful, smokey fug we were offered all sorts of drinks and many different brands of cigarettes. My greatest pleasure was to see Jack Tar sprawling in an easy chair, tucking into a ham sandwich, made with white bread, and watching his brothers-in-arms, the RAF officers, with affectionate admiration.

I expected to be caught up in a military machine, complete with barracks and staff officers, whereas the cottage that came into view, buried in a garden, flower-filled, looked like something from the nursery rhymes of my childhood.

We were at Major Bertram's house near Chichester. His wife, Barbara, had auburn hair and a very graceful figure. Soon we were sitting down to another meal in spite of the lateness of the hour—three or four o'clock in the morning; I'd lost track. Bertram went to listen at the door that opened into the hall, where I could hear voices whispering and many feet on the stairs. He came back, lit his pipe and turned round.

'We're not the only ones here, then?' I asked Richards eventually.

'Of course not, Poz. There are others who come and go like you. The important thing is that you don't meet. By the way,' he added, hastily swallowing his tea, 'before I forget, give me a false identity so that I can get your papers made out. What name will you choose while you're here?'

'What for? My real name, of course.'

'Out of the question. No one must be able to identify you.'

I was completely bowled over. 'What have I possibly got to be afraid of in England?'

'Nothing in particular, but you never know: a spy from Germany, an ill-disposed rival agent.'

'You're not logical in this country. In France I get the BBC to put out messages to make people think that I'm in England and once I'm here you want to make people think I'm someone else.'

'That's the way it is,' he said laconically.

From his pocket he took a visiting card and a fountain pen. Another name, the twelfth, thirteenth, fourteenth. . . . What name would I assume? 'Villeneuve,' I decided. 'That's where my father was born. Marie de Villeneuve.'

We finished breakfast to the first pink flush of sunrise and the first twittering of the birds.

It was very late when I woke up, still fully dressed, in a strange room. Someone was banging on my door. The Gestapo, I thought, and jumped up.

'Marie, Marie, it's time to go to London,' Richards shouted.

Yes, I was in England, the England to which all my thoughts and all my work had been directed for over three and a quarter years. And the network? I burst into tears. Nothing could console me, neither the journey through the English countryside, nor the fact that I was going to the wartime London that I was so eager to see. I continued to weep, although I was perfectly well aware that I was being utterly ridiculous.

Richards' face was the picture of consternation. At first, with his natural delicacy, he had looked out at the countryside; then, as the suburbs became denser, he tried to reason with me: 'Come on, Poz. Aren't you pleased to be here?'

'I'd be very pleased if all my friends could be here too. I should never have left them. I feel that I'm not going to see them again. . . ,' and I burst into even greater floods of tears.

My Lysander companions had left separately. Armadillo had resumed his career as a British officer; Jack Tar had gone to the training school. I was soon alone in a service flat in London with my new treasures: my case and my secrets. Feverishly, I began to write out all the names that I could remember, to draw up charts showing the organization: it was wonderful to be able to do all that without having to hide.

The afternoon had nearly gone when Richards reappeared with a doctor, who soon prescribed bromide, vitamins, a dentist, rest, food. Richards took the prescription from me.

'I'll go and get the medicine,' he said, obviously relieved. 'Have a good rest, you're going to have a visitor. Sir Claude is coming here tomorrow, at eleven o'clock.'

'I'm beginning to understand,' said Sir Claude Dansey, who had arrived at eleven o'clock precisely. He had taken both my hands in his own. 'So this is the terrible woman who has had us all scared!' he exclaimed. 'I've often wondered what you were like, Poz. It's good to have you safely here.'

'Not for very long.' My haunting fear of not being able to return to France had begun to quicken again at sight of the man who could do everything.

'We'll see, we'll see. You've gone on long past the safety limits. According to the law of averages, an underground leader can't last more than six months. You've lasted over two and a half years. It's sheer witchcraft.'

'You mean you're not going to let me go back?'

'Not immediately, Poz! We've lots of things to fix up together, but more than anything else I wanted to thank you from the bottom of my heart for everything you've done. We're deeply grateful and greatly indebted to you. What can I do for you in return?'

'I don't know what to say. I've had a lot of luck, my friends have been absolutely wonderful. . . .'

Encouraged by his kind words I asked him to allow me to get in touch with my children in Switzerland. Then I told him all the information that I had learned by heart. But when I came to the anti-Hitler plot his face clouded.

'Your sources are obviously serious, but the affair lies outside my sphere. Nevertheless, I can tell you that the day we do make peace it will be an unconditional peace, a peace that will owe nothing to the enemy. Those people are diabolical. They're capable of doing anything to gain their ends. It isn't the first time they've tried to confuse us with this kind of proposal.'

'All the same, don't you think there may be some sincere anti-Nazis who deserve to be helped?'

'How can they be helped? You'll only compromise yourself by approaching them. The Hitler machine is still too powerful. Our only possible tactics are to pound harder and harder at it until it cracks.' He pressed his hands together as though he were cracking a nut. 'In the meantime, relax. I shall be very angry if I hear that you're working. Goodbye.'

The secretary who had been specially assigned to our organization showed me round London, and I experienced the heady joy of pillaging the shops for my friends: soap for Dr Gilbert, and surprises of every possible kind that Jack Tar (whom I saw from time to time) would take back to France come the next moon.

'Jack Tar,' I said to him on one occasion, 'I'd like to give you some decent clothes. What d'you want?'

'A dressing gown, chief. I've never had a dressing gown in all my life. . . .'

Under the astonished but discreet eyes of the salesgirls, and after endless tryings-on, he finally chose the longest, biggest and most English-looking of dressing gowns. A year later that dressing gown became his shroud, pierced by a dozen Nazi bullets.

I was taken to a building devoted entirely to broadcasts—a veritable Tower of Babel into which flowed, in all languages, the coded messages from the world that was occupied by Hitler, where hundreds of men and women picked up the clandestine messages which were decoded by linguists, and security checked. The chief of this establishment, I felt, was completely hostile, when I suggested it, to Magpie's theory that the British should call first.

'You'll avoid detection by changing frequency. It's out of the question for London to call first,' the obstinate man replied.

'You know radio operators,' I replied. 'When they've got onto a wavelength that works they don't stop until they've put out the whole message, and to hell with security.'

'Exactly! It's for *your* safety that we ask *you* to call. The detection squads locate *your* sets by listening to *my* central station. *Here* is where the trouble starts.'

'But the harder we struggle to make contact with you the more we catch it in the neck.'

He refused to listen. The unnecessary risks run by our operators, crouching in the front line, seemed to me utterly cruel. I had so often heard them sending out their desperate calls and saying 'They don't answer, the sods!' On the other hand, I realized the tremendous difficulties facing the London listening post, which had to pick up thousands of code groups in the Fortress of Europe to definite schedules. Nevertheless I was determined, and I asked for Magpie to be brought over for a large-scale demonstration. This was agreed to. Magpie would come in the August Lysander that took Jack Tar back to France.

In London my compatriots were useful people, but an encumbrance. But such as they were, they fascinated Londoners, who had not yet fully digested the fall of France and understood even less about the subsequent quarrels between French leaders. Only a few days after my arrival I was trying to explain a complicated address to a taxi driver who finally asked me, 'Are you French? Which side, Gaullist or Giraudist?' I was flabbergasted. At that time the two generals were in Algiers and delegations representing both in London looked at each other like a pair of china dogs. I made contact with the Giraudist delegation. Colonel Gonzales de Linares offered me his support. It was with him that Saluki had, the year before, organized General Giraud's departure. I asked him to put us at the disposal of the British, like other units of the Free French Forces under French command. Unfortunately, Giraud was just leaving for the United States and once again we had to wait for our famous militarization.

Eagle's daily messages thrilled me. He asked me to suggest innumerable operations and I would have felt even more enthusiastic about planning them with British Intelligence if Richards had not mysteriously disappeared. His replacement, Tom, was very much the British SOE agent. He ruthlessly cut short any questions, ignored my advice, and in the end I saw that he kept from me much of the information sent by the Alliance. Suddenly the spectre of the 'Gibbet' reappeared among the messages. 'Gibbet' was our sinister code name for the Nazi police service, representing the Abwehr and the Gestapo. My faithful Ant and Caviar were arrested; the OVRA had smashed the Grenoble sector; Fawn was caught in the general round-up.

The situation that had confronted me in Madrid had risen again, like a Phoenix from its ashes. Eagle regarded these arrests as the result of Elephant's capture in Lyons. As he had had reason to fear, the notebook that was found on him had been partly deciphered after two months and had yielded the three names. I asked Eagle to come back with Magpie in the next Lysander, so that we might together work out how to tighten up the network's security on the basis of complete decentralization approved in London.

The August moon was growing steadily bigger, and Jack Tar, fresh from his course, was itching to get back to France. He was a new man altogether, including a false identity, and we spent an exciting evening going into all the details of his mission in Brittany. He was taking back a big caseful of gifts, and more important, the first decoration awarded to a member of the network—the Military Medal, which Colonel de Linares had given me for Tiger. I only hoped that it would not arrive too late.

Rivat (Finch), a native of Verdun who had been on a course in London since May, was also returning, and Operation Dürer was due to take place on the excellent landing ground at Bouilhancy. On 15 August, Tom and I went down to Bertram's cottage to wait for Eagle and Magpie. Barbara did her best to cheer me up by chatting away gaily, but the memory of the hayrick, Gilbert and the Avia team—minus Ant—haunted me. My mind and my thoughts were in a turmoil when Bertram phoned from the airfield to say that 'it was time to put the kettle on for tea'. That meant all was well, and at last our passengers appeared. Eagle had brought Gibbon, his young lawyer, Johannes Ambre, who had become known to the Gestapo and had been on the run since the trouble in Lyons.

Eagle and I pored over the intelligence maps, the plans, the various samples stolen from the German stocks at the request of British Intelligence, and the intelligence notebooks. Among the latter an item sent by Petrel immediately riveted my attention. It was completely out of the ordinary run of what I had been digesting for so many years.

'*Information communicated by a captain (active list) attached to the experimental centre in question.*

'Concentrated on the island of Usedon (north of Stettin) are the laboratories and scientific research services for the improvement of existing weapons and the perfecting of new weapons. The island itself is very closely guarded. To gain admittance, in addition to the military identity book, three special permits are needed:

'*Sondergenehmigung*   watermarked paper.
'*Zusatz*   orange card.
'*Vorläufigergenehmigung*   white paper.

'The administrative services are at Peenemünde and . . . (an illegible name).

'Research is centred on:

'(a) bombs and shells guided independently of the laws of ballistics.

'(b) a stratospheric shell.

'(c) bacteria employed as a weapon.

'Kampfgruppe KG 100 is reported to be experimenting at present with bombs guided by the bomb aimer from the aircraft. These bombs could be guided from such a distance that the plane could remain out of range of AA fire. Accuracy is said to be perfect if the plane does not have to defend itself against fighters.

'The final stage in the development of a stratospheric bomb of an entirely new type is said to have been reached. This bomb is reported to be 10 cubic metres in volume and to be filled with explosive. It is said to be launched almost vertically to reach the stratosphere as rapidly as possible. The source speaks of 50 mph vertically. The initial velocity is said to be maintained by successive explosions. The bomb is said to be provided with *Raketten* (vanes?) and guided to specific targets. The bomb is said to be fuelled with 800 litres of petrol, necessary even in the experimental stage, in which the shell is not filled with explosive, to enable it to carry. The horizontal range is 300 miles. Trials are said to have been made, without explosive charge, from Usedon towards the Baltic and to have reached Königsberg. The noise is said to be as deafening as a Flying Fortress. The trials are reported to have given at first excellent results as regards accuracy. Hitler is understood to have alluded to the success of these trials when he spoke of "new weapons that will change the face of the war when the Germans use them."

'Difficulties are said to have developed quite recently, only half the bombs hitting the selected targets accurately. It is reported that this recent fault is expected to be remedied towards the end of the month.

'Colonel Wachtel and the officers that he has collected are reported to form the cadres of an anti-aircraft regiment (16 batteries of 220 men, the 155 W, that is going to be stationed in France, end of October or beginning of November, HQ in the vicinity of Amiens, the batteries between Amiens, Abbeville, Dunkirk).

'The regiment is said to dispose 108 (one hundred and eight) catapults able to fire a bomb every twenty minutes. The army artillery is said to have more than 400 catapults sited from Brittany to Holland.

'The artillery regiments would be supplied with these devices as and when there is a sufficient production of ammunition.

'The expert Sommerfeld is said to estimate that 50–100 of these bombs would suffice to destroy London. (Major Sommerfeld is Colonel Wachtel's technical adviser.)

'The batteries are said to be so sited that they would methodically destroy most of Britain's large cities during the winter.

'Reinforced concrete platforms are reported to be already under construction. It is thought they will be fully operational in November.

'The German experts are said to be aware that British experts are working on the same problem. They think they are sure of a three to four months lead.'

Eagle looked at me from the corner of his eye: 'I see it makes the same impact on you as on me,' he murmured. 'We're holding the secret weapon.'

'Who was Petrel's source?'

'Amniarix, the young Druidess whose real name he has refused to divulge. An extraordinary girl who speaks five languages. She has the information at first hand.'

The rumours of our presence in London had finally got around and, out of friendly curiosity, we had a number of visitors. This caused some alarm so we were told that arrangements were being made for me to have a house to myself, somewhere out of the way, to avoid all the coming and going that was so detrimental to vital secrecy.

A house to myself! But that meant that I should not get my return ticket for a long time. 'I *must* go back,' I told Eagle in a rage.

'They are against your running pointless risks. It is thought that the network is functioning admirably and that, in the circumstances, it's more important to have you here than back in France.'

Sir Claude Dansey, who had in fact invited us to lunch with him at Brown's the same day, was utterly impervious to my complaints.

'Your organization has grown vast,' he replied. 'You're the only network covering the whole of France. You work regularly and systematically and have a remarkable *esprit de corps*. Only here, Poz, can you get the overall view essential for organizing the business as a whole. In France, as you French people say, "the wood hides the trees". I know this winter is going to be terribly tough. The enemy is stepping up his drive against the underground. Reserve yourself for the future. I'm afraid the moment will come, Poz, when your return will become imperative.'

'Will the Liberation take place this autumn?' asked Eagle, ever an optimist.

'We're not ready. Not yet ready,' the Chief replied, and his face suddenly clouded.

I intervened nervously: 'There's not much point in building up colossal forces if you expect Hitler to launch his secret weapon. If he does it'll be impossible to move or get away from here. Which reminds me. Tom has told me nothing about Petrel's document on Peenemünde. Is it all right?'

'It's not for Tom to judge,' I was told brusquely. 'All I ask of you, my dear friends, is to help me to the end and to follow the old fox's advice. . . .'

One night, after we had returned from a party, the dream reappeared: the landing ground, the Lysander touching down, Eagle and Magpie climbing out, the ring of Nazis closing in as the plane took off, the Teutonic voice saying: 'We have arrested Faye, we are delighted,' and, in the foreground, the heather.

I woke up feeling sick with anxiety. The telephone was ringing. It was Sir Claude, to say that he would be coming to see me later that morning.

'My dear,' he began the moment he came in, 'Eagle must not go back to France.'

His suggestion came at exactly the right moment, but I must not agree to it too quickly. I said to Sir Claude: 'It's becoming a mania. Have you sworn to cloister us up one by one?'

He laughed, settled himself comfortably in a chair and offered me a cigarette. 'I ought not to indulge your vices.' At last he coughed discreetly to clear his throat. 'I've seen underground fighters come and go for three years, my dear Poz, and I can assure you that our friend Eagle is someone for whom I have the highest respect and feel a personal affection. So, in Brown's the other day an idea took root in my mind. Both of you have given me glowing reports of your eventual successor . . . what's his name?'

'Paul Bernard—Swift.'

'That's right. So I said to myself, if we let this Swift fly on his own for a bit, for a couple of months say, it would be better than seeing him take up the job again if there should be any trouble.'

'It's undoubtedly an excellent idea. In that case I must go back to France to give our people an explanation.'

'Your job is to give orders, not explanations.'

'In the underground army imponderables are a major factor—people's good opinion of you, the voluntary acceptance of discipline. If Eagle and I should be arrested, the network would work for Paul Bernard, if only to avenge us. With us in England, I wouldn't like to say.'

'The French *are* complicated!'

'Why don't you want Eagle to leave now?'

'Because he's going to be captured. I've been through his file again with my specialists: three arrests, two escapes, three two-way Lysander trips. He's also very much in the red.'

'Your law of averages again! You're ruthless but you're right. There's also something more than statistics, there's premonition.'

'I know,' he said, giving a shudder. 'The sixth sense that's sharpened by war. In different ways we sense the same things.'

'Eagle won't agree. He's a man, a soldier.'

The Chief stood up. 'If you order him not to return, Poz, we won't provide him with a Lysander. I'm putting his fate into your hands.'

I later told Eagle all about my conversation and that I had agreed he should not return. He leaped to his feet. 'Never, do you understand,' he shouted. 'I'll never agree to fall down on my job. Damn their law of averages. If they want to know, tell them that I've also got fifty bombing missions to my credit, that I was a volunteer at the age of seventeen, in 1916, in the trenches. According to their calculations I should have been dead long ago. I am dead. This ghost's going!'

'Only if I say so.'

'You can't do this to me! Look, Marie-Madeleine, I can't let all the airmen I've got to work for us get caught in place of me.'

'Well, I can't force you to stay in London, but you can't stop me from being worried about your going back. Swift hasn't got your experience and the Nazi vice is getting tighter every day. I insist on your taking special care as soon as you get on to the landing ground.'

'But it's been used three times already by the Avia team. They've got everything taped, absolutely taped.'

'Technically, yes; but from the point of view of morale, no. This is the first landing that neither you nor I have organized on the spot. I'm letting you go back, but you must promise me you'll slip away from the reception committee, go to Paris under your own steam and thoroughly investigate what has been happening while you've been away before you make the slightest move.'

'As you say, Chief,' he said in his light-hearted way. 'And then?'

'Then you'll put into effect everything we've agreed to do in the last few days to decentralize the sectors and you'll take the October Lysander back from a different place. *I* shall go back in November. In this way we'll divide the job up between us while we're waiting for D-Day.'

Eagle accepted my conditions and solemnly swore that 'my neurotic and womanish plan' would be scrupulously carried out. I phoned Sir Claude to say that, understanding Eagle's scruples, I had agreed to his going back to France, but for one month only and with the proviso that he must take exceptional precautions.

'It's up to you, my dear,' he replied. 'You've made a very grave decision.'

Transcript from the files of the Abwehr at Dijon:

'*Thanks to an agent attached to the German counter-espionage service, the essential facts about the resistance and terrorist Alliance organization are now known. According to information received, Faye is to return from London with new instructions on the 11th of this month. . . . Faye and his complete headquarters staff, the radio station, as well as the organization in the Clermont-Ferrand region should now fall into our hands. . . . We request 50 gallons of petrol for the various movements of the officers ordered to make the arrests and the transport of the infiltration agent E 7226. . . . Oberleutnant Merck is in charge of the operation.*'

24 OPERATION INGRES

Operation Ingres was on. During the afternoon of 13 September Tom, the officer who had replaced Richards, came to tell us that the weather conditions were favourable and that the car was outside. We piled the cases into the boot. Those containing equipment had already been sent to the airfield and the bulk of the rest of the stuff would have to be parachuted in an endless stream on to our 'Greuze' landing ground in Normandy. We set off for the Bertrams' cottage, picking Magpie up on the way.

Suddenly I saw the heather that had appeared in my dream. The rolling, wooded English countryside flashed before my eyes, the sunset creating a dazzling scene with its own pink hues mingling with the pale purple of thousands of heather bushes, stretching as far as the eye could see. My mind was in a turmoil, my thoughts racing and clashing in my head like maybugs against a window. Could I order the driver to turn back? Could I plead the excuse of a dream to prevent these men from carrying out their mission? And if they were going to their deaths, how could I be so base as not to stop them?

Nobody did justice to poor Barbara's dinner and as 22.00 hours approached the men left for the camp.

The dreadful wait began. I was expecting the Lysander to bring Saluki and Mandrill back. Saluki, who had been dying of boredom in Switzerland, where he had joined his family, had finally returned to France and we intended to get him over to England as quickly as possible. And the Royal Navy was anxious to see Mandrill, as direct questioning about the Atlantic submarine bases that he knew like the back of his hand would be invaluable. I had been told that he was physically exhausted and I had seized this heaven-sent opportunity to give him a rest.

At 02.00 hours the phone crackled: 'Tea for the same guests,' Major Bertram said laconically. So the Lysander had been unable to land. A few minutes later, Eagle and Magpie, famished and dead beat, pounced on the whisky and buns.

'I've never seen anything like it,' said Eagle, in a fury. 'The moon was as bright as the sun, we came right down three times, flew off again, came back, but the Avia team was not there.' That's a good start, I thought.

'There may be some explanation,' suggested Bertram. 'The brilliance of the moonlight on the ground makes the flashlights more difficult to see.'

On the 15th we knew by a message from Mahout that the major's theory was correct.

Mahout to Hedgehog: '*Sorry about contretemps night 13/14 September stop were at landing place stop saw Lysander coming from east at 22.30 hours gmt stop had already identified sound stop made pre-arranged signal morse letter G without reply and lit ground lights stop plane continued towards west stop after interval of more than ten minutes returned via east stop as soon as sounds of engine heard relit ground lights and new ones and flashed letter G stop new swoop and plane left for last time.*'

I went into a sort of ecstatic trance. 'You see, Eagle,' I said, 'for the third time the plane, your best friend, refuses to take you back. It's saved you so many times. I implore you to obey its warning; let it go back without you.'

'The RAF is going to repeat Ingres tonight,' he said. The abortive sortie had whetted his appetite for danger. He was straining at the leash and laughed at me politely.

The weather continued to hold and the code phrase 'Whale fishing is a dangerous occupation,' broadcast by the BBC, told Mahout that Ingres was again on. This time I watched Eagle go in the absolute conviction that it would be for ever, and my heart filled with the appalling knowledge that there was nothing more that I could do. In the friendly but now deserted lounge I sat for hours listening to Barbara's knitting needles clicking away in time with the ticking of the clock.

The telephone rang a little earlier than expected and startled me. 'Tea for our new friends,' said Major Bertram briefly.

Eagle and Magpie had landed and the Lysander had returned to the fold with its new passengers.

Saluki walked in. I ran and threw my arms round his neck. 'How did the operation go, d'you think, Saluki?'

'Very badly. I've never been so anxious in all my life. Waiting for three days and three nights in such uncertainty is more than I can bear.'

Mandrill came in dressed like a tramp and unrecognizable, his hair far too long and his face and body showing all the signs of his having gone through hell. 'The operation?' he said. 'It was dreadful. We had the feeling that we were being watched. It was sheer chaos on the ground.'

'Saluki, were you able to warn Eagle?'

'You know how little time there is to exchange confidences! As soon as he got out I tapped him on the shoulder and said: "Scram, old boy, don't stay here a second, this stinks." I hope he understood.'

Barbara begged us to go in and eat. Saluki found the way to cheer me up—by telling me about his 'prisons'. He had been arrested after he had crossed the Swiss frontier and as he had a magnificent tiger's head with bared teeth tattooed on his forearm, the local lads with whom he had been parked took him for a big shot in the underworld and had offered to help him escape. Mandrill, over-excited and a mass of nerves, talked on and on, non-stop. Saluki whispered: 'Marie-Madeleine, do make him go to bed and then nurse him.' I had the greatest difficulty in getting Mandrill to do so.

I asked Saluki if he had noticed anything in particular during the operation. 'Nothing in particular,' he replied. 'Just the old airman's intuition, as Tiger says. The Avia team wasn't the same as usual. But there's nothing more unreliable than your famous premonition, Marie-Madeleine. One of my comrades once caused me a hell of a lot of trouble because he had dreamed that he saw his best friend crash. We didn't sleep a wink in the squadron that night. Well, this friend came back cock-a-hoop with a fine bag of victories. Don't worry, Marie-Madeleine, I know Eagle. He'll get away with it.'

I was no longer listening. My one thought now was centred on Magpie's first message, due at the contact scheduled for 13.00 hours GMT next day, 16 September.

It was ten o'clock and the Alliance headquarters staff were beginning to feel worried. Eagle and Magpie had been expected at 08.30 but had not yet arrived. Ladybird, Mme Berne-Churchill, the ever-faithful priestess tending the headquarters, could do nothing to reassure her friends and decided to go shopping. When she opened the side door she found herself face to face with two strange men with revolvers in their hands.

'Who are you?' they asked.

Ladybird slammed the door behind her and gave the owner's name, Mme Badinon. Then she waded into them. 'What right have you to ask these questions?' she stormed. 'Let me pass, I'm going to get my ration cards.'

'*Ach so?*' the men said, producing their papers. 'Gestapo.'

She looked at them dumbfounded, fully expecting to have her bag searched, but she heard them say to one another in German that they had got the wrong floor. While they went down the stairs, she went back and announced: 'The house is surrounded by Gibbet. You've got two minutes to do something about it.'

Swift, Dragon, Triton, Jack Tar and Alain de Villeneuve, the headquarters liaison agent, snatched up the files. Jack Tar leapt through the window, grasped the drain-pipe and slid from the fourth floor down into the courtyard. Not a German to be seen. Swift threw the secret papers down to him.

Then, followed by Triton and Villeneuve, he also climbed down the pipe under the terrified eyes of the people in the house opposite. From the courtyard they climbed up to the first floor of another house, got through the window in spite of the owner's angry protests, jumped onto a roof and reached a deserted and unguarded street. Dragon preferred to go out in the normal way. He knew someone who lived opposite. His alibi worked.

Meanwhile, from force of habit, Ladybird had pushed anything at all suspicious into the refuse bin, picked it up and this time used the service stairs. At the bottom she ran into a German policeman—luckily not the one she had met a short time before. The man flung her into the caretaker's room, but immediately rushed off towards another innocent but terrified tenant. Ladybird seized her chance, climbed out of the open window, slipped through the little garden door and ran off to raise the alarm.

Then Superintendent Raison (Moth), Elephant's successor as head of our security department, suddenly appeared. He was saved by the caretaker, who threw her arms round his neck and called him 'nephew'. He grasped what was happening and escaped.

The headquarters was out of danger for the moment, but the hellish day, a day of Gestapo traps and ambushes, went on.

Until the curfew began Swift and Jack Tar took turns to loiter near the Metro exit closest to the headquarters in the Rue Charles-Laffitte, to prevent people from walking into the trap. Another team, consisting of Seagull and his adjutant Jean Fontaine, took turns to watch at the Gare du Nord. When he was not on guard at the Metro, Jack Tar ran to warn the radio operators. He found the Gestapo at their place. Once again he miraculously escaped their clutches. Magpie's faithful operators had been arrested.

Having escaped the morning round-up, the courier, Villeneuve, went to raise the alarm at a house where a set was actually transmitting. Another liaison agent, Mero, Swift's nephew, hurried off to Sainteny's headquarters. The Gestapo were there. He escaped and rushed to the Apache's head-quarters. The Gestapo were there too. This time he was not so lucky.

Deprived of all their resources, the leaders of the Alliance, now without identity papers and with nowhere to go, hunted and adrift, wandered aimlessly around Paris looking everywhere for Eagle.

By 13.00 hours GMT on 16 September I still had had no contact with Magpie. All the Paris transmitters were silent.

For two days Saluki, Ambre and I had examined the problem from all angles. The crew of the aircraft that had dropped the rest of the material of operation Ingres on the Greuze landing ground had reported everything normal there. The fact that Magpie had not yet been able to establish contact did not necessarily mean anything; but what had happened to the Avia radio and the four headquarters operators?

At last the black briefcase arrived and the day's messages were laid out on my desk. They came from Le Mans.

'*18/9—Swift informs me: three passengers operation Ingres plus Bumpkin, Lanky, Mahout arrested by the Gestapo Paris train stop all radio operators arrested stop headquarters all escaped records saved except Triton's stop seven set sites captured stop with Dragon and Jack Tar studying ways to repair damage stop Greuze parachuting successful.*'

There was no mention of Eagle or Magpie. And why did he speak of 'three passengers' when there were only two? There may have been some confusion with the men of the reception committee. If Eagle had obeyed my instructions and kept clear of the Avia team, then for him at least all hope was not lost. I sent a reply to Swift, asking him to let me know the aliases of the passengers who had been arrested. Tom dashed off to see to this.

'Poor Marie-Madeleine, what are you going to do?' Saluki asked.

'Try to get a clear picture by radio. Try to send someone to France to help them. Try to go back myself.'

I had had practically no sleep for a week and the reflection of my face in the bathroom mirror frightened me. My own eyes stared back at me like a fakir's. I said out loud: 'I'm going mad. I have no right to go mad.' I noticed the bottle of bromide prescribed by Richards' doctor standing on the little table. I picked it up and gulped it straight down.

The phone must have been ringing for a long time before I finally managed to lift the receiver with a hand as heavy as a block of stone.

'Hello, Poz, what's the matter? We were about to break your door down.'

It was Sir Claude. 'The London air doesn't suit you, my dear child,' was his comment when he appeared a few moments later.

'What I really need is French air. I want to go back. I *must* go back.'

'What has happened is obviously dreadful, Poz, but you must realize that I will never agree to let you set foot in such a hornets' nest.'

'Are you sure that Eagle has been arrested?'

'If he obeyed you he hasn't. Do you want us to get the BBC to broadcast the record he made before he went, so as to make people believe he's here?'

'No. If he is in the enemy's hands it will simply make him look silly. And I believe he did disobey me. What were they all doing on the same train? Those are not our evacuation methods. It looks as if the enemy organized the whole thing.'

He looked me straight in the eye: 'You know how fond I am of Eagle. I should regard it as a personal loss. We'll avenge him.'

The moment he set foot on the ground Eagle had been horrified to see so many people about. Dr Gilbert's car was so crowded that he could not move even an arm. When Mahout was asked the reason he replied that the region was unsafe but he had allowed for all eventualities. His team had been reinforced, they would sleep at the Trumels' farm and catch the early morning train which, he said, was perfectly safe.

The Ingres operation had been organized so grotesquely that Eagle had but one thought in mind—to manage his own affairs. When they reached the farm he was surprised to see that Mahout's 'reinforcements' consisted of Bumpkin and Lanky, who had no connection with the place, as the principle of keeping the different services quite distinct ruled out any kind of overlapping. He was particularly worried to see Lanky, whose responsibility for Elephant's capture came back to his mind.

He did not sleep a wink that night. When the time to take the train approached, Eagle, Magpie and the two Apaches, Bumpkin and Lanky, set off in Indian file behind Mahout for Nanteuil-le-Haudouin station, but they were trailed by a car that had switched off all its lights. The men hid in a ditch while Mahout sent Lanky to find out who they were. They turned out to be perfectly innocent travellers, wanting to know their way, and the car drove off towards Paris at full speed.

The first train of the day steamed in and Eagle was again appalled at Mahout's arrangements. He chose a carriage and the whole lot of them piled in. 'In this way,' he said, 'the Apaches will be able to protect you more easily.'

At Aulnay-sous-Bois, the last station before the capital, the compartment was rushed by a party of civilians with revolvers drawn. The Apaches were neutralized in an instant. Eagle, who was immediately recognized, did not even have time to draw his revolver. He was immediately bound hand and foot and separated from the rest. The Germans, who were delirious with joy at their success, took him to the Avenue Foch, where he was searched, tied to a chair and interrogated until the interrogator himself was exhausted.

25 GIBBET[1]

On the evening of 16 September, while the Gestapo were questioning the members of the Alliance network arrested during the day, Oberleutnant Merck, known as Kayser, was holding a celebration dinner in the Lido restaurant to mark his success. He had invited his right-hand man, Feldwebel Hertz, who had just been promoted to officer rank; Elizabeth Kuhn, his personal secretary; Wagner, his chauffeur and, of course, the V-Mann, confidential agent E 7226.

The orchestra was playing 'Lili Marlene' and 'Je suis seule ce soir', but a splendid champagne dinner was no reason for not planning the next move. If Oberleutnant Merck was glad to be free of the haunting fear of being sent to the Russian front—the fate with which he had been threatened in the event of failure—he was not resting on his laurels. He had, in fact, failed to gain one objective in the course of the day: the network's headquarters staff had slipped through the meshes of the net spread for them in the Rue Charles-Laffitte by his Gestapo colleagues in Paris.

They had, however, been hard at work for a month on all the addresses submitted by V-Mann E 7226, as is clear from the triumphant telegram from the Abwehr in Dijon who, in June 1943, had been ordered by the German High Command to take over the 'Verteré affair', now the 'Alliance affair', from the Lille-Belgium Abwehr:

'*Ast Dijon to Abwehrstelle Berlin-Paris-Brussels-Lyons-Lille 16/9/43*'. '*At 8 o'clock this morning the following arrests were made: 1. Squadron-Leader Faye—2. Radio operator Magpie (British)—3. Dallas 'Mahout' head of operations—4. Sneyers 'Bumpkin' head of security service—5. Marc Bernard 'Mero' command courier—6. Four radio operators attached to the HQ—7. Seven other persons from whose premises transmissions had been made—arms, ammunition, a large sum of money in French francs were seized—the two German officers responsible for the arrests are Merck and Von Feldmann—the success of the operation is due to the infiltration of confidential agents. . . .*'

At 16.00 hours the same day Navarre was suddenly deported to Mauthausen camp. The Gestapo had at last found an effective way of cutting him off from the network by whisking him away at dead of night in spite of the fact that no charges had been made against him.

[1] The Alliance's code-name for the Gestapo.

From Hedgehog to all sectors: '*Do not try to contact any member of our group stop examine ways of parachuting and rendezvous at sea stop will receive adequate independent means end.*'

From Hedgehog to Swift via Le Mans: '*First unmasked agents must be safe if indispensable your service taken out of circulation and hidden until new instructions second have contact our sets in north south Bordeaux Brest Rennes and Nantes which have received decentralization order stop use them sparingly stop you will all be given assistance and help stop love end.*'

On 19 September the Gestapo pounced in Paris. As a result of the information gained from the interrogations and the documents seized on the day of the great swoop, Wolf and Bison were arrested at the Intelligence headquarters. They had always sworn they would stick together, whatever happened.

The attack on the province as a whole was now launched. Under the direction of Oberleutnant Merck, the Vichy Gestapo struck first. Cricket's HQ at Volvic in the Massif Central was surrounded on 21 September. Colonel Kauffmann (Cricket), Lieutenant Pradelle (the gay Corsair), and Henriette Amable (the lovely Tomboy) were arrested with the radio operators, the agents, the Apaches and the young lieutenants from Lyons, Pelletier and Perrache.

The next move was against the headquarters of the parachute team in the area. The Gestapo besieged Seagull and his adjutant, Lynx (Jean Fontaine); they opened fire but were shot dead.

The Gestapo torturers got to work on Cricket to force him to divulge where the weapons were hidden. They hurled him to the ground and broke his arms and legs. Sickened by the bloody sight, Oberleutnant Merck thought it better to leave.

The whole central region was smashed.

From Hedgehog to Martin via Le Mans: '*Warning do not contact Cricket's sector any more stop all captured stop Seagull and Lynx reported killed stop have learned new disaster through Grand Duke courage end.*'

Oberleutnant Merck was driving towards Autun, where he had given orders that the sector run by the engineer Bat, and his adjutant, Raymond Pader, a banker, should be surrounded that same day, 21 September. The two men had been called to Paris by Swift. Siren, Bat's wife, was on the look-out, waiting impatiently for them to come back. Instead she saw the Gestapo arrive in force. She attempted to throw the transmitting set out of the window and escape. Too late; she was surrounded. A few seconds later Bat and Pader were brought in handcuffed by the Feldgendarmerie guarding the roads.

The first morning brought fresh arrests. Fourteen others were to be captured in the following days. Drunk with power, the Gestapo took

Pader into Autun in chains, with two machine pistols that had been found in his bank hanging round his neck. The pistols had belonged to the Apaches, now annihilated.

Oberleutnant Merck appeared on the scene with his squad and found that the job had been done. There was now no question of his being sent to the Russian front. His skill in the art of infiltration and in the exploitation of documents had put him among the counter-espionage aces in occupied France.

From Hedgehog to Unicorn (Brest): '*First warn you we have not heard Deer's set at Rennes used by Goldfinch since September 21 secondly can you arrange immediately rendezvous with Royal Navy launch Rapide off Brittany coast stop according to plan operation Vulcan organized with Jack Tar stop with Avia teams captured only solution to send someone to bring you help stop love end.*'

From Unicorn (Brest) to Hedgehog: '*First thanks Rennes information secondly if operation Vulcan plan seized by Paris Gibbet can change venue thirdly if Vulcan plan not seized operation possible beginning October stop on embarkation place being approved by Royal Navy stop end.*'

That message on 24 September was Unicorn's last. The same day Jack Tar was mysteriously arrested in Paris in the middle of the Champs-Elysées, and his magnificent region went under at the same time. The Rennes sector, run for six months by Inspector Le Tullier—'friend Pierre', who had been so efficient at the Villa la Pinède—had fallen first, then Unicorn's miraculous naval sector went down and with it Triton, leader of Sea Star, who had gone into hiding in Brest. After Paris, central France and the east, Brittany was now dead. These death throes affected certain sectors in Normandy, where the transmitters also fell silent.

The main architects of the Gestapo's triumph were the guests at a private banquet given by Oberst Ehringer, head of the Abwehr III F in Dijon.

'The Alliance', Ehringer announced, 'the Noah's Ark that we have been fighting since 1940, has been destroyed.'

Merck looked down in mock modesty, E 7226 sat smug and self-important. But Feldwebel Hertz timidly ventured an opinion:

'I consider Faye to be the most extraordinary person I have ever met. I asked him if he would work for us and he replied proudly, like an officer. Don't forget, Herr Oberst, that the network covered the whole of France. In spite of the vast number of interrogation reports, I don't believe we shall learn anything of real value from Faye's statements. He's leading us up the garden path.'

Ehringer turned to V-Mann, E 7226, the guest of honour. He presented him with the Iron Cross with Sword. With this distinction went a packet, elegantly tied up with ribbon, containing the sum of two million francs. Nor were the Gestapo's stooges forgotten in the distribution of the treason money. They were all Frenchmen, alas, traitors who came for the most part from the collaborationist parties. For their courage in infiltrating the various channels of communication and escape routes, for the attack on the train at Aulnay-sous-Bois and the various headquarters each received 100,000 francs.

From Swift to Hedgehog via Aix-en-Provence: '*Disaster extends regions east Brittany Normandy stop obliged to withdraw to transmitters in south stop parachute drop to me urgent material and money stop possible via Finch on Lilas landing ground stop all survivors loyal we are carrying on stop love end.*'

From Hedgehog to Swift: '*Implore seek cause of disaster stop undoubtedly due to treason stop we are trying to send you messenger stop congratulations to all for admirable sang froid thanks loyalty stop forward the Alliance stop much love.*'

From Swift to Hedgehog: '*I do not suspect anybody stop Eagle and Magpie tragedy due to fact that London sent an inexperienced pilot who drew attention to the operation.*'

The new head of the network did not suspect anyone. Yes indeed, 'in France the wood hides the trees', and I, in England, was instinctively using the expression I had rejected with such scorn in Lyons only a few months before—'Forward the Alliance!', as if I were on the spot to sound the charge. It was horrible, humiliating, and childish as well. Had I the right to tell them to carry on without actually sharing their fate?

Since 16 September Eagle, my magnificent Eagle, had fallen and with him more than 150 members of my beloved network, including the veterans. How many of them were now in the Gestapo's clutches? Three hundred, perhaps 400? There was no end to the list of names that I had to erase on my network chart as I learned of the casualties from the messages of the few who had escaped—the sinister transcripts passed on from the London listening post. In spite of the deeply moving loyalty of these men and women, in spite of their insane desire to carry on, the Gestapo had won.

Each time I crossed out the name of a friend I experienced the feeling of having wielded the executioner's axe: Eagle, Wolf, Alfred Jassaud, Seagull, Triton, Mahout, Jack Tar, Cricket, Magpie. . . . I saw their imploring hands stretched towards me, their twisted, agonized mouths crying out for help. I was dying of grief.

Within the network I had given London the code name 'Stronghold'. The re-establishment of a direct link with Britain and myself was a matter of life or death for the network, but the October moon came and went without any Lysander landing on the Lilas landing ground. Finch, who had gone back to France in August, after his training for the Avia team, had discovered this near Verdun. The weather was good, but Swift waited in vain, night after night. Accustomed to the extreme regularity that normally marked our aerial links, he thought I had deserted him. I could not, alas, tell him the sad truth. The Lysander squadron had suffered heavy casualties and its pilots could not be replaced at a moment's notice.

'M. l'Abbé, has your training reached the point where you can be parachuted into France during the November moon?'

As no actual Lysander landing was possible, I was forced to appeal to the first two volunteers that Algiers had sent us, now that we had finally been recognized as a military unit: the Abbé Chevalier and Lieutenant Pierre Gallois, two airmen of steel-like morale. They were unaware of the extent of the network's casualties. Saluki and I had decided to observe the strictest silence about our losses in case the cause of the disaster was in London itself.

I was dumbfounded by the Abbé's reply: 'Don't take offence at what I'm going to say,' he replied, somewhat embarrassed. 'My friend and I are not going to accept the mission you've given us. We've done everything we could to train for the job, but, sad to say, we've both come to the conclusion that neither of us is cut out for the underground. I think it only honest to tell you.'

'Has someone offended you?'

'Yes. Oh, not you! It's the British. We're living with Tom, but last night he searched our cases again. If we're not completely trusted the whole thing's pointless.'

'It doesn't mean a thing. Tom always overdoes it. Think of Eagle and of our friends waiting for us to send them help.'

'Well, we'll still help them. Gallois and I have just joined a bombing group. God bless you, madame.'

What an unrewarding task it was endeavouring to throw into the hell of the underground people who did not know what it was like. The Abbé was in fact destined to disappear during a bombing raid in the mission that he chose in preference to fighting in the underground.

I had not wanted to reveal my feelings but I was incensed by Tom's conduct. Saluki exploded when I told him: 'What does this chap think he's doing? He keeps coming and asking me whether I'm for the King, the Emperor or the Republic. He's holding up my departure for Algiers. I'm getting fed up with him.'

I went to Sir Claude at once and demanded Tom's replacement. A few days later the very prototype of the British officer was sent to me: he wore an immaculate, perfectly cut khaki uniform, belt and cross-belt polished mirror-bright; beneath his cap were eyes as blue as the sky, a splendid moustache and shining teeth. He clicked his heels together as he introduced himself. We adopted him on sight. And we called him 'Ham', an abridgement of his real name.

Our last chance of establishing any direct contact with Swift was to send Mandrill to France. His course was coming to an end, and 'playing at submarines' with the Admiralty experts had restored his strength and enthusiasm. One evening, when I felt he was his old self again, I decided to put him in the picture about what had actually happened, but what he told me made me hesitate. I now knew that he was a Jew and that his name was Philippe Koenigswerther. His parents were refugees, living in New York under the name of King.

'An extraordinary thing has happened. Mitsi (the name he gave his mother) has just written and told me that my sister and I have been left a lot of money by a fabulously rich uncle. She wants me to go and see her in New York to deal with the formalities.'

'But you must go, Philippe. You haven't the right to do nothing about this windfall.'

He scratched his nose, a familiar habit of his. 'Money doesn't interest me. If I survive the war I'm going to Tibet to become a monk. I won't go to America, I'll go back to France and resume command of my Bordeaux sector. When will you send me?'

In view of his determination, I could not possibly hide from him the havoc that had struck the network. He listened to me in dead silence then asked: 'Why didn't you say anything to me, Hedgehog? Lanky's the traitor, I'm sure it's Lanky.'

'What makes you think that? He was arrested with the rest.'

'Pure comedy. While we were waiting for the Lysander, Lanky never stopped questioning me. So I told him a lot of lies. They can go into my sector, but they'll find they're on a wild goose chase. Don't you see? Bordeaux is still going strong. The south is still going strong. Those are the places where Lanky has never set foot. If I only had my hands on him, the swine. I'm going back and I'll get to the bottom of the mystery,' he said fiercely.

From the bitterness of their messages I knew that my friends no longer believed that all their troubles were purely accidental. I made my decision. 'Thanks, Mandrill. We'll see Ham and examine ways of setting up a sea link, because if we have to wait for the RAF at the moment. . . .'

However, two beacons still shone forth in the ocean of misery: Grand Duke, head of the south-east, whom the British called 'Post Office' because his transmissions were so regular, and André Coindeau, alias Urus, head of the Nantes sector, whom they called Nero because he carried on oblivious of all the flames burning round him in Brittany.

Urus was given the job of organizing the sea operation. After an unbroken exchange of messages a landing place was fixed near Cape Frehel. The whole coast of Brittany was closed to traffic, and since Urus did not have the proper papers for the heavily guarded zone, Operation Duck was not possible until the beginning of November. It would be the first direct contact that the Alliance would have had since 15 August.

Thirty-six hours later Mandrill came back to me with his eyes popping out of his head: 'What fools! They missed the landing place. I kept telling them, but it was no good. I know all the creeks and inlets by heart, but Ham was with me and he didn't want me to land unless we saw the reception committee's signals.'

'Nero is as safe and sound as ever,' said Ham, who had now arrived and looked all in. 'He's just radioed to say he's ready to start again whenever we want to, but yesterday's failure was due to hideous weather conditions. It'll mean waiting a bit. There's a new moon and the navy says they can't risk being seen by the lookouts.'

'A lot of good your navy having all that marvellous equipment,' Mandrill burst out. 'If only you could see it, Hedgehog, extraordinary launches, armed to the teeth, versatile, supple, responsive, real thoroughbreds; and what crews! As for the navigational error, I admit you couldn't see a thing and I was quite wrong to insult them. Too bad, it was a wonderful trip. The only thing now is for me to be parachuted.'

Ham and I feverishly explored other possibilities of making contact. We put five operations in hand for November. We were determined to get someone into France by one means or another.

As always on my birthday I received a lovely present. On 8 November one of our five schemes, 'Marius', the parachute operation for Grand Duke had been a big success and the containers we dropped were safe. Sir Claude had proclaimed the good news first thing in the morning by sending me a great bunch of roses. He invited me to lunch at the Ivy, and, when taking me back home, he asked me what my views were on the disaster that had overtaken the network.

'I should have to go and see my friends and question them myself. I feel they're in a bad state of nerves and yet the Alliance is picking up again. Let me go back, please.'

'Patience, Poz, patience. As for giving help, we're doing everything we can. All the networks have suffered heavy casualties. But it's not the moment to stop,' he said, looking worried. 'In this connection I must tell you that we're very pleased with Petrel's information about the secret weapon. It's been of the greatest use.'

'Splendid! As I'd heard nothing more I concluded that it was of no value.'

The Chief gave me a quizzical look. 'Did you really think the information was no good?'

'You know how it's been ever since people started talking about the secret weapons. It's like the Loch Ness Monster!'

'They exist, Poz. I wanted to confirm your information first. That place is really where the secret weapons originate. Now we're looking somewhere else—in the field.'

The ground sank from under my feet. 'What is this new weapon? When are they going to use it?'

'A sort of robot, undoubtedly radio-guided bombs. We must see that they never use them, or at least as little as possible, otherwise. . . .'

'Otherwise?'

'Well, if they were to employ them as they intend, it would become very, very difficult to land in France.'

I went back to my rooms depressed and worried. How could I engage the Alliance in this new phase of the struggle?

However, the network's pulse was beginning to beat regularly again and signals that were no longer simply SOS calls crackled over the air.

From Sea Lion (Bordeaux): '*Dresden Tannenfels and another torpedo boat left morning 2nd stop Dresden returned on 6th for repairs according crews but without apparent damage and torpedo boat returned on 8th stop ship III left on 8th stop ship IV returned yesterday stop Nantes shipyards on strike that day stop remember 11 November 1918 today 11 November 1943 general strike stop Gestapo on rampage arrests and restrictions in full swing.*'

From Grand Duke: '*New infantry division stationed three days now mouth of Rhone stop coming from Italy delayed by destruction of lines Genoa Marseilles stop explosions grouped 600 yards east Agay viaduct stop searchlight and AA battery destroyed Agay village damaged.*'

From Urus: '*Made contact with Hesse, general commanding airforce in France stop tours airfield 30000 gallons petrol 109 aircraft AA 12 Stukas BB 43 Heinkel CC 20 training fighters DD 33 Fockewulf EE 3 reconnaissance aircraft FF 1 Messerschmitt.*'

From Alosa: '*Toulon bombing today success stop 1500 Germans killed electricity station paralysed for 48 hours stop Aude and Impetueux sunk stop Chamois and Captain le Prieur hit stop Jeanne de Vienne on fire stop port AA pulverized.*'

From Sea Lion: '*Bagnanelli left Thursday 11th stop Dresden definitely damaged aft by mines has discharged at Bassens to enter dry dock stop Fujiyama and another blockade runner being loaded stop all at Bassens stop from La Palice two submarines ready to leave beginning of week.*'

From Urus: '*Situation submarine base Saint-Nazaire 14 submarines AA August BB Delphin CC Werner DD Buffet EE Satan FF Kehlen-Klau GG Rabauk HH Florian II Amigo JJ Krieghan KK Pai LL Dragve MM U-boat sign black cross with white SW in middle NN submarine name unknown.*'

From Grand Duke: '*Submarine base Janet now worth urgent bombing because covering shelters beginning stop Lons bombing 12 Aircraft hit stop AA battery destroyed 100 Germans killed.*'

Every corner of the fortress of Europe had to be examined under the magnifying glass, every enemy movement watched, every position evaluated. After which, British air reconnaissance planes went on regular photographic missions. Any changes that appeared on the photographs were analysed and cross-checked.

Then the whole business began all over again: 'Please confirm . . . , please amplify . . . , please find out.'

Stronghold to Osprey: '*AA we are particularly interested in the names of commanders of warships whose bases are between Calais and Brest BB 25th Panzer Division at Hesdin CC give details formations between Rheims and Chalons-sur-Marne DD give details about telephone cables between Lille and Halluin.*'

Stronghold to Shad: '*Subject evacuation Fayence and Saint-Raphael aerodrome announced by you please send details about destination of units that were there stop please repeat names and complete lists ships Marseilles.*'

Stronghold to Grand Duke: '*Urgent need details concerning Nice La Turbie Monaco—1—situation fortified points—2—organization defences—3—minefields and observation posts.*'

Stronghold to Osprey: '*Have you source able to inform on activity at Dollmard near Le Havre to the east stop Boches have made earthworks about 100 yards that they are now demolishing to replace by trenches stop why.*'

Stronghold to Opossum: '*Have reason to believe long-range bomber planes may be in Lyons region stop aerodromes Lyons Bron Dijon Clermont-Ferrand Avord Bourges stop information requested urgently activity and preparations stop numbers identifications types for new squadrons.*'

As though there were no tragedies involving people, the war waged at a distance, the war waged without contact between the adversaries, the intelligence war went on. Mercilessly.

There was something sacred about each scrap of paper. Each bit of information, as my dear old friend Spaniel (Colonel Bernis) liked to say, represented such a wealth of suffering. To hit the target. That was the aim of the Resistance. But while the Gestapo were hunting us down in France, in London everyone was laboriously trying to normalize the existence of the networks and the various movements by written statements and hierarchical structures—which certainly had no effect on the resistance fighters' spirit nor, especially, on their melancholy position under the Nazi jackboot. At this stage of the war the pure criteria of productivity and efficiency were greatly exceeded. It was no good the British being astonished by the fact that the little embryos they had hatched so quickly had developed into tentacle-like patriotic organizations that were difficult to control rather than remaining neatly within the normal channels of communication and administrative constraints. The Resistance needed an *esprit de corps* and that spirit was instinctively Gaullist.

Maurice Schumann, the mouthpiece of la France Combattante, often used to say to me: 'Without de Gaulle there would be resistance fighters but there would be no Resistance.'

But the sharp rivalry between the secret services compromised this indispensable unity: the BCRA[1] criticized me more bitterly than ever for giving directly to the British the information that it could have used to help the accredited Gaullist organization; and Giraud's intelligence service no longer wanted to give me material support because it obtained my information through the British anyway. When questioned about this, the British replied that they did in fact have an intelligence exchange agreement with the French Army Intelligence Service, and therefore with Giraud's. They said that the information supplied by the Alliance and the BCRA was automatically included.

Never in my life had I felt so hurt. To use our information as part of the continuing struggle for power seemed to me to be quite inhuman.

Wrestling alone with my radio messages I was compelled to confine my efforts to maintaining our independence, now that we were officially labelled a fighting unit. This status embodied, on the whole, the intentions expressed by our July council. Nevertheless incessant requests poured in from our Algiers bureau, firmly controlled by Commandant Cros (Aurochs). He had managed to get out of Spain those members of the network who had escaped the great round-up. I was overjoyed to hear that my brother Jacques had just got back to North Africa after eight months internment in the French camps. My brother-in-law, Georges Picot, was also there, as well as Great Dane, a few Ussel agents and Pegasus. They had met the submarine passengers and the 'Canadians' who had arrived before them. Their affectionate letters gave me courage to face the depressing battle of our increasingly special services.

'What I'm doing isn't pleasant, madame, but I felt I must. This is what I found when I was filing.' Ferret, who had saved Bee in Lyons, now

[1] *Bureau de Contrôle de Renseignement et Action.*

in charge of the BCRA archives, handed me a radio message: 'Eagle was arrested with Mahout and a British radio operator in a train after he had been parachuted, along with Bumpkin, the head of parachute operations, on the landing ground where he had landed, as well as Bumpkin's lieutenant, Jean-Claude. The latter, an informer, was imprisoned with the others and was released by the Boches.'

'What was the date of this message?'

'About mid-October.'

I felt a chill run down my spine. 'And now it's 24 November. This wretch has been continuing his devastating work since 16 September and nobody said a thing to me? Who sent this to the BCRA?'

'A small Lyons network, *France d'Abord.*'

This was terrible. Brave and splendid people were facing the risk of detection to send warnings to their leaders and the wonderful secret services were doing absolutely nothing. I combed my records. Jean-Claude? Who was this Jean-Claude? There was only a Jean-Paul on the landing ground. I was getting warm. The name of Sneyers' lieutenant mentioned by *France d'Abord* was Jean-Paul, Jean-Paul Lien.

Jean-Paul Lien was Lanky.

'This time I *will* land,' shouted Mandrill, brandishing a huge revolver. 'I *must* go and help Swift, even if I have to blow the launch commander's brains out.'

Apart from the Marius parachute drop in the south, no other air operation had been possible during the November moon and we had to fall back on the sea links. As the night was sufficiently dark, Operation Duck II took place on the evening of 25 November. Ham returned the next day looking pale and drawn.

'What a dreadful night! We had come as far inshore as we could and Mandrill began to argue with the commander. He reckoned it was not the right place. The commander refused to budge and we scanned all the rocks in the hope of seeing the flash of the pre-arranged signals. Suddenly Mandrill said: "I've had enough of this, I'm going ashore." He had drawn his revolver and threatened us like some lunatic. I begged him to wait. I promised we would come back as many times as was necessary. But he jumped overboard, found the bottom and splashed off into the darkness. There was no point in hanging around.'

'I quite understand, Ham. D'you believe he would have fired if you'd gone for him?'

'Without the slightest doubt! Imagine what it would have been like then. All the coastguards would have appeared, the launch would have been sunk and we should have looked complete fools. As soon as he blew his top it was better to let him get on with it.'

We waited for news from Urus in a fever of impatience. It came the same evening:

'*41 of the 26th from Urus: Your ship touched coast 1000 yards to north of agreed spot stop crew did not see jetty stop Mandrill came ashore in mine-infested zone and contacted committee stop agreed about new operation night 29 to 30 stop my set Clarinette very sick contact becoming risky.*'

'Good old Mandrill,' I thought. The file sent for Swift contained two and a half million francs, my long report in code about everything that had happened in London since 16 September, questionnaires, new codes, instructions for everybody. Mandrill would go personally and give all the details of Lanky's treachery. He would contact *France d'Abord* to see whether those well-informed comrades might not be able to find the traitor. He would be captured. Perhaps it would be possible to force him to secure our friends' release? Perhaps Eagle could be saved? They must all be saved.

The top Gestapo were housed at 84 Avenue Foch. It was there that the *Sicherheitsdienst* organized its great destructive operations. The SS kept distinguished prisoners there so that they could be available at any moment.

Since 16 September, the day of his arrest, Eagle had been incarcerated in a cell immediately below the roof, in what had once been a tiny maid's room, containing nothing but a bed and a chair. Air and light came in through a large skylight that opened onto the roof: this was protected by a kind of square ventilation shaft about six feet high that was itself sealed off at the bottom by strong, firmly-fixed bars. During the first few days Eagle was tempted to hang himself. He fully expected to be subjected to torture and he was determined at all costs not to go back on his decision to say nothing that could implicate or lead to the capture of a single individual inside or outside the network.

Eagle was aghast at the extent of the enemy's knowledge of the network, but in spite of the wealth of information displayed by his interrogators, he soon realized that they had not discovered everything. The Gestapo had, however, more than 300 prisoners on hand, vast numbers of documents, damning, long-prepared dossiers. There had not been just one traitor, there had been several.

Eagle's interrogators were at great pains to convince him that his arrest was due to a leak from London, but he realized at once that it was Lanky who had been behind the operation on 16 September. He recalled everything, Elephant's capture, the easy reputation that Lanky had acquired for courage and dash, even with old and experienced officers like Mahout, who had left him to organize Operation Ingres.

The moment he landed, Eagle had made up his mind to get rid of the suspect. That was why he had not fled: he could not desert the network in midstream, in what he sensed to be a mortal crisis.

For the moment the Germans had won, and Eagle could only try to alleviate his men's fate and save what still existed. Under interrogation he made a great point of the network's militarization, of the high quality of its members—with the result that the Gestapo merely considered it more dangerous. The Alliance, 'the animal network', was the main enemy to be crushed. Sarcasm was a constant gambit:

'You refuse to talk? Too bad. At the rate arrests are going and people are talking, along with all the things we are discovering in our searches, we shall be able to destroy your network without your help. Then everyone will die.'

The German police continually produced confessions made by some members of the network. Why be tortured to death when the enemy knows everything? That was how they argued. Others had stupidly fallen for an old trick such as 'Your leader has told us everything, so why pretend that you know nothing?' Or, infuriated by such a heroic attitude, the Nazis told the same lies about Bison, whose real identity they failed to discover, the radio operator Peewit, who rejected the evidence with a laugh, and Magpie, who remained completely calm and unruffled.

At night, alone in his room, Eagle thought up new ways to thwart his interrogators, but he had no illusions about the grimness of his plight; in his heart he felt he was lost. So he decided to goad the enemy by insisting that Germany was on the brink of a crushing defeat: 'The end of the war is imminent, the military situation of the Reich desperate and the German army would have been better advised to reverse its alliances and join the Anglo-Saxon camp.'

The effect was magical. The interrogators now wanted to find out the truth about their own position. They asked a thousand questions that all too clearly revealed their underlying anxiety. Eagle soon became convinced that they felt certain Germany would be defeated and wanted to save their own skins. The tension dropped. Soon Eagle received the assurances that he had asked for: the Alliance was recognized by the enemy as part of the French army, no-one would be put on trial or executed and all members would be regarded as prisoners of war until the end of the conflict.

His main interrogator was a certain Scherer, a former professor, shrewd and intelligent. Through him Eagle eventually learned everything that the Gestapo knew. The man showed him all the interrogations that had been carried out since the 1941 incidents. He helped him to avoid traps and counter-threats. Obviously he was not doing this for nothing. This unexpected complicity roused a wild hope in Eagle's breast. He could see himself already fleeing with Scherer, reversing his present situation and confounding the traitors.

One day in November, Scherer failed to appear for the interrogation. The other Gestapo men were grim-faced. Eagle finally discovered that his only possible accomplice had been killed by the Resistance while an arrest was being made. Two months of superhuman effort to save his friends had come to nought. From that moment he came to the conclusion that his duty was to make every conceivable effort to send me the secrets that he had discovered and which weighed heavily on his heart and spirit.

At first sight escape seemed out of the question. His cell was permanently guarded and all possible exits were blocked. Against these obstacles Eagle pitted his faith and an uncommon physical strength that had been nurtured and tempered by the ordeal of years of war and underground fighting. By the end of October he had already succeeded in communicating with the occupant of a neighbouring cell by tapping out Morse on the wall. This person was Inayat Kahn, the young British SOE heroine. She was of Indian origin and seemed to be remarkably athletic and brave. She told Eagle that she herself was in communication with a young British officer, 'Bob' Star, both of them leaving messages on pieces of paper that they hid in a special place in the lavatories. Bob was a prisoner, too, but he agreed to 'work for the house'—as a 'draughtsman', he claimed—which meant that he could move around freely. He was therefore admirably placed to know everything.

Eagle suggested to Inayat that she should sound Bob out. The British officer's first reaction was unfavourable. He said that the SS guards kept such close watch that he could see no chance of escape. Inayat badgered him again and told him about Eagle and the possibilities of being evacuated by Lysander. This time Bob took the matter seriously and gave her details about the roofs of the houses in the Avenue Foch: 'You can reach the Rue Pergolèse through the adjoining houses,' he told her. 'Someone escaped that way at the beginning of the occupation, which is why there are bars across the skylights in the cells on the top floor.'

Eagle decided that all three of them would escape. He explained to them how to loosen the bars across the skylight—a task requiring time and extreme caution. It meant filling the hole patiently made at the end of the bar with crumbs from their bread ration. The rope that was essential for getting down from the roofs would be made out of their bedspreads. These preliminaries took weeks in exchanges that were carried on by Morse tapping and messages left in the lavatories.

Finally Bob sent a message to say his bar was ready. Inayat said that she was ready too. Eagle fixed their escape for that same night, Thursday, 24 November, at 22.30 hours for Inayat and himself, and at 01.30 hours on Friday for Bob, the time when the latter returned to his cell.

Eagle had kept himself fit by doing exercises and felt in splendid shape. As Bob had promised to bring some tools, a flashlight and a real rope, Eagle decided to take only the sixty feet that he had already made by cutting up the bedspread with his razor blades.

When the deadline came, Eagle carried out his operation in complete silence. He found it more difficult than he had expected to get out along the ventilation shaft against the skylight. He was afraid that Bob and particularly Inayat might prove unable to do so unaided. His anxiety melted away when he saw the sky and the stars—a sight that he gazed at in rapture. In spite of the shock at finding that the roofs and the houses around them were quite unlike those on Bob's plan, the view of the Arc de Triomphe in the distance and the night-time sounds of Paris were like a draught of wine. He felt drunk with joy. He was free.

As he approached the charming Indian girl's cell he heard her scraping at the bar across her skylight. Not realizing the situation he opened it. Horror! The girl was going at it in a frenzy as the bar was still firmly embedded and it would take several hours before it came loose, longer than what remained of the night. Eagle advised her to put everything back, to lie down and, if need be, to deny everything. He also told her that he was going to reconnoitre, because Bob's plan was useless, and he leapt on to the narrow roof, his one aim to reach the side away from the Avenue Foch.

There was not a ledge, not even any sort of roughness to give him a hold and save him from crashing down six floors into the black hole of the inner courtyard. Sliding and scrambling, the airman reached a wider roof. It was the end one. He now looked onto the terrace of a neighbouring house—one or two floors lower—but he could not see any Rue Pergolèse. Bob's information was worthless. Should he then go back or wait for Bob, who would at least be able to say what houses these were? He decided to play for safety and had another dizzy scramble back to his starting point. Once again he heard Inayat scraping fiercely at her bar.

It was only just 23.00 hours and the weather conditions were perfect. Eagle spent a few minutes recovering his breath. Once in the street he knew exactly where to go—to friends whom he had kept out of the network despite their wish to help. Now their big chance was coming. He would send them into the unaffected sectors and he could already imagine the wonderful thrill it would give the network.

Two hours went by in this way while he was waiting for Bob. To curb his impatience Eagle went back into the ventilation shaft outside Inayat's cell; with touching courage she was still scraping at the bar, at the full extent of her arms. He begged her to work quietly, but she scraped away implacably, with never a moment's rest, in the hope of finishing the job in time.

Gradually the sounds of the traffic and the city died. There was complete calm outside, the only sounds now coming from inside the building itself—Inayat scraping away and Bob in the guard room talking loudly and turning on the radio to cover the noise she was making.

At 01.30 hours Bob went back to his cell. Eagle was already at the skylight, which he lifted up cautiously. The bars had been well and truly loosened and a few seconds later he hauled Bob up. They then set off without Inayat. From the few words they had exchanged, Eagle realized that his companion was in a blue funk. To give him fresh heart he took him to have a look at the terrace below, but when Bob saw it he was no longer positive about anything. Was the house occupied by the Gestapo? Was it inhabited or not? Was the Rue Pergolèse clear or guarded by sentries? But Eagle assumed that the parcel Bob was carrying contained the things they had agreed they needed—rope, tools, flashlight and master-key.

They could do nothing until the curfew ended at five o'clock in the morning. The wait in the darkness and the cold grew increasingly trying. Not a sound was to be heard except Inayat's persistent scraping, fortunately now muffled, and the movement of the guards nearby, who were still awake. It was 03.30 hours by the time she had finished. Eagle hauled her up onto the roof.

Moving one behind the other the fugitives set off for the Rue Pergolèse. It was Eagle's third trip and he hardly appreciated the noise Inayat made clambering over the slippery roofs. He hurriedly organized the first rope down to the terrace below and he jumped, followed by his companions, whom he caught in his arms. Eagle was horrified to see that the luminous dial on the girl's watch shone like a torch.

The terrace door was locked. However, they could make out—one floor lower—a French window that opened onto another little terrace. This led into a yard that was in fact directly above the Rue Pergolèse. Eagle left it to Bob to decide whether to climb straight down the five storeys or go across the small terrace and down inside the building. The Englishman said he would rather go down through the house, but confessed that he had not brought any of the promised articles. Unfolding his bedspread—the only thing in his bundle—he began to tear it into strips, making an infernal noise. In dismay Eagle told them they must climb down direct and finished making the rope by using the razor blades he had brought with him.

It was about half past four. Suddenly the night was rent by the roar of aircraft engines and the opening burst of an anti-aircraft barrage. It was a large force of American Flying Fortresses flying directly overhead on their way back from a raid on Germany.

Half an hour passed and then, to their horror, a shrill voice rang out through the darkness. It cursed in German about a light, and an electric torch beam was directed towards the terrace. It came from a nearby window, but Eagle thought they could not be seen in the corner where they were crouching. An SS man may have seen Inayat's watch from the window. The only thing to do was to keep still and let things settle down. They had until six o'clock, when the guards would go into their cells.

The gunfire and the luminous caterpillar-like tracer shells followed one another in a terrifying tattoo. Below, in the Rue Pergolèse, a soldier walked along the street. The man at the window watched suspiciously. He thought it might be spies signalling to the British planes to let them know they were above the Gestapo headquarters.

Another quarter of an hour passed. Provided they kept absolutely still the fugitives would be safe. Suddenly, literally losing his reason, Bob stood up, saying that it was late and he intended to get going. Before Eagle could stop him, he went back to the part of the terrace that could be seen from the Gestapo windows. Eagle went after him to try to quiet him down, and Inayat could think of nothing better than to follow suit. Disaster loomed. This time they were caught for a few seconds in the beam from the torch.

Eagle dashed forward with the other two at his heels and jumped onto the terrace below. He fixed the rope for the climb down into the courtyard; but the sentry in the Rue Pergolèse turned round and also shone his torch.

Realizing that it would now be impossible to climb straight down, Eagle made for the French window, which he fortunately found easy to smash. The three fugitives groped their way alone until they came to a corridor and then ran hard down the service stairs. Several times they were caught in the torch beams flashed from the windows and they could hear the sound of guards in hot pursuit. They finally reached the hall on the ground floor. Eagle tried the knob of the door leading into the street. It opened. The sentry was on patrol and very near. As soon as his footsteps died away, Eagle made a dash for the other end of the street. But he was in for a dreadful shock. The street ended in a cul-de-sac and he was compelled to rush back into the house because the SS man was returning.

Bob was all in and as limp as a rag and bewailing their foul luck; Inayat was shattered. As soon as the sentry's footsteps had died away again, Eagle once more opened the door. He could see no sign of the man. Taking off his shoes, he sprinted across the pitch black street. If the sentry was still about, he would run into a hail of fire. He must trust in Providence. He made another dash and almost bumped into the man, who was crouching in the shadows. The sentry let out a howl and opened fire, discharging the whole of his magazine.

Eagle did not realize what had happened. The blast had hurled him to the ground and, thinking he was wounded, he was surprised not to feel any sort of pain. Then he got up, summoned all his energy in an effort to leap away and get to the next street. But a second SS man appeared, followed by civilians, all armed with revolvers. They came at him from every direction. Eagle was forced back against a wall, where his attackers clubbed him unmercifully with the butts of their revolvers, smashing his jaw. The Eagle sank to the ground vanquished.

The convoy that took Eagle into Germany drew up before the drawbridge at the entrance to the fortress of Bruchsal. The gaoler was given special orders: '*Ein wichtiger Terrorist, ein Spezialist des Entfliehens*'.[1] Eagle's twitching body was tossed roughly into a vault. He was chained by the ankles to the leg of an iron bedstead and the handcuffs that were biting deep into his wrists were not removed. He was told that he would get only half the normal food ration—to teach him a lesson. He believed he was in hell: the constant hum of the machines in a factory adjoining his underground cell was the only sound that broke the silence of the Nazi tomb where he was to begin his fight against death.

[1] An important terrorist, an expert escapist.

When the Chief had spoken to me about the secret weapons, I had wondered how the Alliance could make its contribution to this decisive battle. Even though it was disabled and hounded, the old network still had the strength to go instinctively into action.

From Grand Duke: '*Boches on point of completing between Calais and Boulogne installations under bomb-proof cupolas firing rocket-shells range 100 miles stop one thousand guns concentrated on London stop.*'

From Shad: '*Big excavation in progress at Nesles 8 to 12 miles from Le Treport stop probably launching base self-propelled rockets intended for bombardment southern England stop information comes from reliable sources.*'

From Urus: '*Pierre head security Boches works Nantes indicates Boches will make massive raid on England at Christmas or New Year with special bombs.*'

From Osprey: '*Official information obtained from Colonel von Kolbe stop fearing allied landing and wishing to forestall same and also as reprisal Boches planning and preparing attack on Britain by long-range guns stop range about 200 miles firing 1 round every 15 minutes type Bertha stop they are reported to be sited between 20 and 25 miles from the coast and to be invulnerable to navy stop attack starting towards Christmas stop shell blast has great destructive power stop four months pounding would break British morale stop that would confirm that the works in Watten Forest Eperlecques 7 miles north north east Saint-Omer are sites for these guns stop two guns have passed through Cives station stop one 140 foot gun by train stop more follows.*'

'Your friends are getting very near the truth,' was Ham's comment when we analysed these strange cross references. 'These are the messages that our experts are sending back to your network. Should the enemy happen to capture our messages their most difficult job will be to ask questions without themselves appearing to be in the know.'

Stronghold to all sectors: '*AA information urgently requested region Cherbourg Valognes Briquebec BB curious new constructions in reinforced concrete either platforms or tunnels CC give locations and construction details and use DD constructions reported to be linked by railway stop give exact line EE plans and sketches would be much appreciated stop the marks and inscriptions on the German aerial bombs are of great interest.*'

'I'm not the enemy, Ham, but I get the impression that you know that the secret weapon is already installed. What are you going to do to spare us the Happy Christmas they're talking about?'

'As soon as the information is received the RAF goes and takes photographs. Then, as these strange constructions are pinpointed, they'll start bombing.'

'A pity the poor French have to be bombed to be liberated.'

'It'll be done as efficiently as possible. I think the Lorraine group will be given the job and they'll go in at ground level to spare French lives.'

'More follows. . . .' Osprey's radio message of 26 November had promised. The London listening post had strained to catch the transmissions of the man who knew where the secret weapon was sited, but every day they told me that his radio remained silent. He was based in Lille, a forbidden zone, and we had come to expect periods of silence in that region where to transmit at all was something like witchcraft. I nursed a wild hope; Osprey's team had been in action since Tiger's time and was extremely careful, but in the middle of such an important series of messages this silence made us more anxious with every day that passed.

'More follows. . . .' But nothing more ever came.

'Mandrill's silent as well,' said Ham, looking drawn and pale. 'It's not like him at all.'

We delved feverishly into his last messages:

'*17 of 3 December from Mandrill: Bordeaux Himalaya completely reloaded left on the 30th stop Ida and Balduc left empty on the 30th stop submarine reported ready to leave in my No. 13 left on morning of the 3rd.*'

'*18 of 3 December: Request parachute drop at point of Michelin map 79 fold 2 21 MM east of 3 degree stop 45 MM from degree 49/600 west of Gourd 200 yards south of route 74.*'

'*19 of 5 December: View new situation due to intense radio detection campaign send 3 metal parachute transmitters with special transformers and buzzers stop 3 schedules and complete set of crystals stop 4 stenguns 4 large automatics 2 medium and 2 silencers daggers coshes and special papers stop my luggage baby clothes and provisions only if possible.*'

I thought of the clothes we had chosen together for Mandrill's agents' babies. I tried to find a reason for not believing the worst:

'If Mandrill is asking for arms it means that he's afraid of being encircled. Look, he's using Tap to transmit to Bordeaux, Violin for La Rochelle, Flat for Poitiers, that makes three WT sets. . . . He has three radio operators: Lanneret, Lory, Cariama. . . . He's a radio operator himself . . . and he's demanding more transmitters. . . .'

'Exactly, and they make a lot of noise,' said Ham.

Mandrill's message dated 5 December was his last. He had sent it five days after returning to France.

'And what about the operations, Ham?'

Ham shrugged his shoulders non-commitally. 'The answer's "bad weather, bad weather",' he said sadly. But I knew that was not always the only reason; the RAF operational squadrons were suffering tragic losses.

I looked at the great bundle of messages from our Urus, whose Clarinette and Rondo transmitters continued to spit out information with machine-gun regularity—294 messages in two months!

From Urus: '*Tours airfield camp strength since November 23 139 aircraft AA 35 fighters ex Liotard factories BB 10 two-seater training fighters CC 33 Junkers DD 49 Heinkels EE 9 Stukas FF 3 Condors GG 10 miscellaneous types.*'

'*Patrol boat 717 ex Alfred 3 leaves Nantes this day at 1400 hours stop believed heading for North Sea stop sign on middle roof red and black Penguin.*'

Urus' radio operator, whose alias was Penguin, must have chuckled to himself when he tapped out the last detail.

I looked up. 'Your damned shipping is always well covered, Ham, but have you warned Urus about Lille's silence. Tit, who operates Guitar, recently went to do a spell with Urus in Nantes. I've never liked this sort of general post.'

'Yes, madame. Urus tells me that he'll follow your security orders, but he'll take to the maquis only when we've successfully carried out the Seigle drop scheduled for his sector.'

By a sinister irony of fate the weather, for once, did not interfere with our plans. Operation Seigle took place. The RAF pilot reported that he had seen 'a lot of activity on the dropping zone.' Our one and only operation in December had resulted in everything falling into enemy hands. This time Urus, the invincible Nero, had not managed to escape the encircling flames.

The network was shrinking tragically. My only radio contacts were with Swift, Petrel (Georges Lamarque), Opossum (Henri Battu) in the north, and with Grand Duke and Shad (Jean-Claude Thorel) in the south.

In spite of Ham's friendly protestations and his insistence that every possible effort was being made on our behalf, in spite of the sea and air operations, which I could confirm to be a fact—some sixty messages about them were exchanged in ten days—I began to wonder if British Intelligence perhaps considered us finished. All the evidence went to show that our potential had dropped terribly and yet the Alliance was resilient and could revive quickly, provided it was given help.

A number of volunteers came to see me. The Abbé de Naurois, alias Palumbus, a naval padre; Robert Lorilleux, whose alias, Icarus, clearly showed him to be an airman; and the gay Félix Simon, known as Kite, a British Intelligence radio operator. These three would form a first-class operational team. But how could they get to France?

I was constantly reviewing our miserable plight. In France there was the tragedy of the seriously damaged network, whose survivors were beginning to doubt whether they would ever be saved. In Britain a sordid fight was going on for money within the French secret services. Had I the right to carry on? Having exhausted all the arguments and with a sense of death in my heart, I finally answered Swift, who bombarded me with protests against what he called British Intelligence's inefficiency: '*If I do not succeed in normalizing the situation will restore to everyone freedom of action from January 1. . . .*'

The house the Chief had long been wanting me to have was at last ready. I immediately christened it 'Alliance House'. It was No. 10 Carlyle Square and a typical English middle-class house, but the rooms had been attractively redecorated in shining pale green paint and flowery cretonnes. The basement consisted of a huge kitchen and a dining room; the ground floor comprised a drawing room and an office; and the first and second floors were bedrooms.

I had elected to live in the office, which contained a few chairs and a camp bed within reach of the large desk, where the telephone, directly connected with British Intelligence, had the place of honour. This one link with France meant more to me than all the other comforts.

Very late in the night when I moved into Carlyle Square the phone had rung: 'Major X, duty officer, speaking. I'm sorry to disturb you so late, Ma'am, but there are several urgent messages here and as the last one ends with SOS, I thought. . . .'

He dictated four messages of some sixty groups. In his haste to transmit them the agent had not signed his name. They reported plans for police raids on Communist resistance fighters. The source was a police commissioner in the north, who supplied all the names and addresses of the poor wretches who were in danger as well as the various dates when the Gestapo would strike.

'You did say, Major, that our radio operator had sent SOS calls at the end of the transmission?'

'Alas, yes, Ma'am, the poor devil had dangerously over-run his transmission time. Bad luck.'

I had immediately forwarded the messages to the responsible French Communist Party man in London. An Alliance operator had sacrificed himself to save his comrades but his sacrifice was in vain, for the Communists had no radio links with their members in France. How short we fell from representing the ideal Resistance, with all these cumbersome cliques and criminally childish antagonisms of the Secret Services! Cannon-fodder for the Intelligence, that's all we were. With SOS, SOS filling my brain, I spent the rest of the night in my chair, listening hopelessly to the calls from space.

FOURTH PERIOD
1944–1945

HOLY VICTORY

Thus the tide, receding,
suddenly revealed the
convulsed body of France.

Charles de Gaulle

In January 1944 London was wrapped in fog. It penetrated one like an intangible sandstorm. I imagined with horror the havoc that the secret weapon could cause, suddenly dropping into the pea-souper that enveloped this city, the brain centre of the war, where all kinds of services planning the assault on Hitler's mainland fortress were concentrating.

However, Alliance House was coming to life and my future chances of being able to use it for our own headquarters work prevented me from losing my nerve. All the rooms were now full and I spent many hours talking with Robert Philippe (Parrot) and Jacques Charles and reliving all the things we had been through.

Jacques Charles (Lizard), our railway expert, had managed to survive the September catastrophe and he had used the escape route across the Pyrenees to join me. His knowledge of the operational use of transport interested his British counterparts and, what never failed to amuse us, he was able to clear up certain features that puzzled them because they had been unaware that French trains kept to the left, as in England!

Parrot had arrived from Algiers, openly carrying the sector transmitter. He had not thought it necessary to declare it at the British check point. Scotland Yard had immediately spotted the case, shadowed him and then arrested him in the middle of Trafalgar Square. The British police were quite unaware of the need to bring back to Britain one of these radios whose parachuting to us had been so difficult. It had taken all Ham's powers of persuasion to make them realize that the set would be parachuted back into France.

The return of Kenneth Cohen—Crane of the Lisbon meeting with Navarre—solved a lot of difficulties. He had been out of Britain practically ever since that meeting and now held an important post in the highest Intelligence circles. He was a kind, just man and saved me from getting depressed by inviting me frequently to his home, where his family lavished affection on me. The terrible losses suffered by the network made a great impact on him and he personally saw that top priority was given to restoring the broken link, whatever the cost.

Actually, during the night of 6 to 7 January it was possible to make a second 'Matisse' parachute drop to des Isnards (Grand Duke); on the first attempt the RAF plane and crew had been lost. I wished I could have told my friends this so that they could temper their almost unbearable impatience in relation to the very great risks that were being taken to help them. In this way the south-east received transmitters and 'a litre of gin', our slang for a million francs.

I tried to imagine Henri Léopold's (Fawn's) state of mind as he languished behind his prison bars. He had been taken from Grenoble to Nice, which was occupied by the Italians. There he had met Spaniel, Gazelle, the Bishop, the British radio operator Heron and a dozen other members of the network. OVRA, which had, of course, been unable to get anything out of Spaniel, looked on Fawn as another important catch, likely to lead them to the head of the network. They used every trick they knew to make him talk.

One of their nicer touches was to make their prisoners spin round and round in an airless room that was lit day and night by powerful arc lamps. This was the *giro*. Fawn started to turn round and round and round and went on doing this for two whole days and a night, without food or drink. Then he was beaten savagely on the head until he lost consciousness. When he came round again, slumped on a chair, he was delighted to find that he was losing his memory. Sure that he owed this to the *giro* treatment, Fawn struggled painfully to his feet and started to spin round and round again deliberately. From time to time, to achieve greater effect, he lowered his head and charged against one of the walls of the macabre cell, after which he returned to his endless circling. The Italians were dumbfounded and gave up interrogating their strange client, who took such bizarre and perverse pleasure in his torture.

Unfortunately, Operation Velasquez, planned for the Lilas landing ground at Verdun, was also killed by the British fog.

'Never mind,' Kenneth Cohen said. 'I'm not a naval officer for nothing. Once the moon's over we'll pick up your reports from the Grand Duke by a new sea operation.'

For this operation, called Popeye, we had already suggested to Grand Duke two possible rendezvous on the Riviera near Saint-Raphael—a beach hidden by a screen of trees and a sheltered little creek. A first, tentative Popeye the month before had been a failure because of the frequency of the German patrols. Grand Duke had thought it better to change our tactics. He now wanted to use a rocky, thirty-foot jetty; but the British sailors had their doubts about it, thinking it was too exposed.

It was Count Elie de Dampierre, his brother-in-law, who was the real sufferer in all these mishaps. He had succeeded Mahout and was known as Shepherd. This brilliant airman, running to the four corners of the country with his reports, had vainly waited on the Lilas landing ground near Verdun for thirteen days and now he had to hang around on the Mediterranean coast. Every morning the disconsolate Ham would come out with the expression so dear to Jack Tar: 'What one must do to win the war!'

At last, on 27 January, he proclaimed triumphantly: 'Victory for Popeye. Shepherd's safe. We even had to pick up the reception committee. It seems to be particularly hot on the Riviera for the time of the year.'

Shepherd was short, slim and fair, with luminous blue eyes; Claude Descatoires (Roach), was stocky, muscular, with flaming red hair and not yet twenty. And what a tale they had to tell about Popeye!

The high-speed launch, due at 23.00 hours, was late, the rain that was pelting down probably prevented the British sailors from putting off in a dinghy and Shepherd had remained clinging to the rocky jetty for three and a half hours. The bag of mail, which he dared not let go, weighed ninety pounds, due to the photographic plates of the secret weapon sites that it contained.

The electric torches had been soaked by the downpour and no longer worked. After a lot of wiping they began to work again; but the mechanism was stiff and the signals they gave were no longer intelligible. He was afraid they might merely arouse the suspicions of the British. Although he did not feel very hopeful, Shepherd nevertheless continued to signal in a haphazard sort of way to show that he was there. At about half-past two in the morning he heard the sound of oars splashing through the water above the roar of the elements. The sound grew louder but, disastrously, with it came the sound of British voices. Shepherd immediately heard, coming from the road leading down to the jetty, another and far less agreeable sound that told him the enemy look-outs were getting jumpy.

A long time went by. By now there was a real uproar from the dinghy and panic started among the German patrols. They barked challenges at one another and began charging about in all directions.

But the British sailors won the race. As soon as they came alongside, Shepherd gave the password and asked them to take off the reception committee as well. The dinghy pulled away, but only with the greatest difficulty, almost turning turtle from the unexpected burden of two men and two huge cases, the mail from London obviously having to go back as well as the stuff coming from France.

Anyway, I had my mail, torn from the very marrow of France—a lot of it having magically been missed or overlooked in the Gestapo's searches. I read the letters from Swift, Petrel, Opossum and Grand Duke over and over again. There were other, very brief missives from agents who had been arrested in September. One was from Jack Tar, perhaps the last he ever wrote, dated a few days before his capture . . . 'as a reward for our stubbornness,' he concluded, 'the Alliance continues its forward march . . . the sky of our beloved France is beginning to clear, we are still going strong, why not hope?'

I found it almost impossible to re-read one of the letters, which told me of Coustenoble's (Tiger's) tragic death in the ambulance, on 17 October, taking him from Durtal hospital at a moment's notice so that he should escape the Gestapo. The Nazis overtook them just as Tiger was breathing his last. He had vowed to me: 'The Boches shall never get me alive,' but the Gestapo had taken a sordid revenge by deporting Josette, who was with him. His last earthly joy had been to receive the Military Medal. That clear-sighted, wonderful little Frenchman, the embodiment of French wisdom, hope and courage, had more than fulfilled his mission.

Shattered by this loss, I also discovered the autumn black list. There was so much that I had not known. The 'letterboxes', the 'hideouts' known only to the member of the network arrested and captured at the same time as Tiger, the new recruits, for whom I hardly had even a number, caught in the Gestapo traps; and the families helping them who were also arrested for good measure. It was clear, odiously clear. Who would ever repay the debt represented by all these sacrifices?

The reports that I received from Operation Popeye were at once the evidence of an agonizing disaster and of four months' desperate efforts to survive it. The men and women who had voluntarily gone aboard the Ark had never thought of abandoning ship. All had banded together, at the risk of their lives, to frustrate the enemy's plans.

The authority that Swift's outstanding qualities conferred on him, together with his peerless courage, had saved the network from annihilation. However, he intimated that certain rivalries were beginning to emerge and I decided to send him reinforcements at once. Shepherd would return with Commandant Lorilleux in a coming Lysander operation. And his 'reception committee', Roach, would be parachuted with Félix Simon, the gay and merry Kite, as soon as they had done their three regulation jumps. Unfortunately, I could not let Swift know about this programme, nor congratulate him on his brilliant reports because, once again, the Paris transmitters were silent.

At Chatillon, on the outskirts of Paris, Robert Caussin (Sea Hawk), the operator, put his aerial up in M. Ghyslain's house. With him was Henri Bonnard (Jay), picking up all the tips he could with a view to starting transmissions on battery sets, for it was now essential to plan against a lack of electricity during the landing period. In the Avenue de la Gare Jean, Swift's cyclist courier, and a liaison agent kept a look out. Pierre Neyrard (Yak), Magpie's successor as head of transmissions, watched the time.

It was 15.00. At 15.15 contact was established, Sea Hawk sent his message and received one. At 15.20 the transmission was over. Delighted at having got through it so quickly, the operator closed with 'OK! OK! OK!', which made Yak furious. The set, no bigger than a toilet bag, was camouflaged as a simple electric meter. Jay picked it up while Yak grabbed the leather briefcase containing the frequency crystals. Moving off in open order, they walked to the bus station in the square. They had hardly reached the staff room when a suspicious-looking car passed them and stopped fifty yards away. Yak immediately identified it as a camouflaged spotter car. Six policemen got out. Jay hid the radio in the spindle trees growing in the square and Jean, realizing the danger, leapt on his bicycle, taking the message that had been received from London. The others mingled quietly with the people waiting for the bus.

The six Gestapo men converged on the bus stop and drew their revolvers. Yak was shoved into the room where his friends had already been bundled. The radio was quickly retrieved from the spindles and the search began. The Nazis concentrated on Jay, a finely-built man whom they took to be the leader. While they were beating him about the face, Jay, whose hands were handcuffed behind his back, managed to take a wallet out of his revolver pocket and throw it behind the stove. (An employee of the bus company later took it to Jay's family.) Yak took advantage of this unpleasant interlude to drop his agenda and the transmission schedule into a hole in the floor.

More police cars were called up. All of them, and three innocent, scared and protesting passengers were chained and whisked off to the Nazi-occupied Ministry of the Interior in the Rue des Saussaies.

The torture began: the bath, in which Yak was held under until he nearly suffocated; the beating that went on until he lost consciousness; the ten-hour interrogations—all repeated at weekly intervals. This man who knew everything about the network thought up a strange dual personality: he presented himself as being his own, Yak's employee. 'I won't be the one to contradict myself,' he thought. The more he was beaten, half-drowned and starved, the more meeting points and false addresses he invented to send the SS and the Gestapo off hot-foot, only to come back empty-handed and beat him more viciously and hold him under the water more frequently.

Jay behaved in exactly the same way under torture. To keep everything as it was, Swift, alerted by Jean, the cyclist, switched to the transmitters under the control of Grand Duke who, with every passing day, showed how much he deserved the nickname the British had given him—'The Big Post Office'.

Sir Claude had invited me to dine with Kenneth Cohen on 29 February. They had a number of important things to tell me. The Chief went straight to the point: 'My dear, you've backed the wrong horse.'

'What horse?' I asked, nonplussed.

'General Giraud. He's lost the race.'

'And you have lost your memory,' I retorted. 'It was not *I* who backed General Giraud; it was *you*. Remember your messages of 1942. I was carefully steering clear of politics when you told me that the General would be of great value to the Allied cause if he joined you. In fact, I think he has been. What are you blaming me for now?'

I was quite wrong. The British had, for months, watched the two great men fight for power. The better man had won: Charles de Gaulle. Giraud no longer interested them. Nevertheless, in the Chief's mind General Giraud's elimination meant that the Alliance Intelligence Service would lose its protector. This possibility worried him greatly. I astonished him by saying that Eagle and I had long foreseen this development. It was vital for France that General de Gaulle should come out on top, but General Giraud's bitter and undeserved failure caused me infinite pain.

Since my network was now militarized I would have to await the decision of the future Commander-in-Chief. For the moment, with the Alliance Intelligence Service placed at the disposal of British Intelligence by the French High Command, there was no reason to worry.

'Should all your secret services come under BCRA, I'll help you to come to an arrangement with it. Poz has lost none of her pigheadedness,' the Chief added with a mischievous wink at his adjutant. These two men knew the inner workings of the network by heart. They declared themselves satisfied with the details that Shepherd had brought me about his new beaming technique.

'You were very wise to decentralize,' Sir Claude commented approvingly. 'The havoc caused by the Abwehr is terrifying. The emissaries that we send to France often find nobody at all. The more resistance fighters there are, the fewer there are at the crucial points.'

Shepherd (Elie de Dampierre) was back from the Avia training course and I summoned his team-mate Robert Lorilleux (Icarus) so that I could put him in the picture about the mission. The main object of their mission would be to get Deuxième Bureau agents in the Lyons region who were cut off from their base—Giraud's small delegation in London—working for us again. Although he was trained and ready and had an excellent report from British Intelligence instructors, Icarus nevertheless adopted a peculiar attitude. In his morning reports Lizard (Jacques Charles, the railway expert) gave me increasingly pessimistic accounts of his room-mate, whom he dubbed 'the ghost of Carlyle Square', because he was always seen hugging the wall.

Thinking that Lorilleux might be practising for the life of a secret agent, I decided to find out exactly why he was behaving in this way. No, he said, he wasn't afraid; he was just not the type to take a command in the Resistance. It was extraordinary to observe a further example of how the non-initiated thought about underground work. The more I tried to describe exactly what he could do for us the more determined he seemed to be to see only the worst side of the work.

'Icarus, you're going,' I finally said, thoroughly exasperated.

'Of course, madame. I simply wanted to put you on your guard.' On guard against what? Against himself? Against my wish to send him back at all costs, in spite of his apprehensions?

During the night of 3 March Shepherd and Icarus took off with an important assortment of equipment, mail and 'gin'. The Lysander operation, which was being organized by Kenneth Cohen personally, was to take them to the south-west, near Chateauroux, into very solid SOE territory, and I slept with one eye open, thinking of Swift's joy at receiving this monster consignment.

Early next morning Ham turned up in the depths of despair. 'The Lysander's not come back,' he muttered gloomily.

I felt the room begin to spin. 'Any hope?'

'We recover airmen every day, but a Lysander crash. . . .'

'Shut up, Ham. Our dear Shepherd. Poor Icarus. It explains his strange behaviour. He must have had a premonition of his approaching death.'

We now had to ensure the successful parachuting of Claude Descatoires (Roach) and Félix Simon (Kite, the radio man) into France within the next forty-eight hours. I made up more cases with the same equipment, and recopied the duplicates of the reports given to the luckless passengers of the lost Lysander.

After the disaster that had befallen Yak, I now pinned all my hopes on Kite being able to revive Swift's central radio station. A little Tangier Jew, who was only just twenty, Kite was endowed with a remarkably decisive mind. During his stay at Alliance House—a matter of several weeks—he had asked me an incredible number of questions about life in the underground. 'So that I shall never be surprised,' he explained, completely taken up with the importance of his mission. 'I can see myself there already.' And Roach fluttered like a real roach at the thought of his comrades' incredulity when they saw his new equipment—the first walkie-talkie to be sent for use in our operations.

The Lysander's engine had started to misfire when they were something like sixty miles from the landing ground: 'I shan't have enough power to take off again, we're going back,' the pilot announced over the intercom. Shepherd soon observed that things were no better after turning back: the machine constantly lost height and when they were thirty miles out over the sea the engine suddenly cut out completely. As skilfully as a homing pigeon the pilot started it again and returned to the French coast. The plane was flying as high as it could manage—250 feet only—when suddenly it dived and ploughed into a field.

Only Shepherd was unhurt. Icarus was flung out and suffered multiple bruises. The pilot was cut about the neck and cheek, and very deeply in the leg: his uniform was soaked with blood. To cap everything, he was six feet tall and had red hair. Shepherd thought anxiously that he would have the greatest difficulty in the world to conceal this. To hide the pilot's RAF battledress he gave him his own raincoat.

Although it was dark the men realized that they had crashed in the fortified German sector. Any thought of being able to save the Lysander or the cases containing the money and equipment, still less the presents, was out of the question. To set fire to the plane would instantly attract the attention of the enemy who, by some miracle, had not tumbled to what had happened. By means of an automatic detonator Bell destroyed the top secret guidance system. With Shepherd clasping the mail to his chest they set off to reconnoitre. Two miles to the south they came upon a woman farmer who lived on her own and proved co-operative. She gave them some clothing, so that they would not look as if they belonged to the underground, and pointed out the way to Caen. They would cover the seven miles before daybreak.

What could these poor devils, who were still bleeding and groaning with pain, do in a town where they were surrounded by Nazi soldiers? It occurred to Shepherd that the hotel used by the Gestapo was undoubtedly the last place where anyone would think they could hide. So they went there to rest for a few hours while waiting for a train.

Swift's message of 10 March was jubilant: '*AA Roach Kite parachuting successful already at work BB agree parachute operation Mignard on Lilas landing ground from the 12th CC agree operation Rubens on Signac landing ground from the 14th ground conditions satisfactory runways indicated without relief stop injured pilot will return by this operation.*'

Pressed to recover the pilot, the British had, in point of fact, planned the Lysander Operation Rubens for one of our landing grounds—Signac— in the Loire chateaux region during the same moon. A mass parachute drop on the Lilas ground was to make up Swift's lost equipment.

This time everything went off as in a fairy tale. Shepherd had, pedantically, made a point of himself putting his injured pilot on board and he arrived in Britain on 16 March, accompanied by Dragon and Scarab, the secretary of the Intelligence section. Contact had been re-established.

A fifty-five foot long map burst from our messengers' heavy cases. Dragon's (Jean Sainteny's) valiant old team of Normans had surpassed themselves. Their map showed all the Cotentin defences in detail. In addition there were thick files crammed with information, especially about the secret weapon sites. These reports seemed to me even more miraculous when Dragon and Scarab (Micheline Grimprel), the first actual eye-witnesses of the September disaster I had met, had explained their mysteries; but the thought that at that very minute Swift (Paul Bernard), in France, was co-operating with Alliance House and delighted to know that contact had been re-established, gave our conversation a peculiarly dizzy feeling.

Late that night I plunged into the network's correspondence, trying to read between the lines the anxiety of some of our members, the reticence of others, the pettiness that was sometimes born of so many fantastic dangers, but nevertheless had a common denominator of heroism.

The door opened and Scarab appeared. She was tall and dark, with a little fawn-like head of short, naturally curly hair. 'You must have been surprised to see me arrive?' she said.

'A little. I'd given priority to an emissary from Petrel (Lamarque), so that I could get an idea about the Druids sub-network.'

'Swift sent me.'

She held out a bit of paper on which was written in pencil: 'I am instructing Scarab to tell you verbally what I cannot put in writing. . . . I cannot tell you what joy it would give me to see you again.'

'Can't he manage?' I asked in dismay.

'It's not exactly that; he has command problems. He has replaced Petrel as his heir-apparent and they have practically quarrelled.'

'Well, who is his choice? With us it's a tradition to have a successor ready-made and on the spot. Swift suggests someone called Llama, but Dragon would seem to be the obvious choice.'

'Exactly. Swift also disagrees with Dragon about the organization of the network. He would like you to order him to stay in London.'

I thought of Normandy, which was Dragon's speciality. To go by the questionnaires that were being piled upon us, that zone would, beyond all possible doubt, soon be of major importance.

'Dragon must return, Scarab. In any case, neither you nor he can go back before the next moon. That gives me time to find a solution that will satisfy Swift and the rest.'

My gaze was drawn to the coloured glass in the window at the end of the room as it now began to glow in the dawn light. I went and flung the curtains wide. The first young, touching tulip shoots were piercing the mud in the little garden of Alliance House. It was 17 March 1944. There was one obvious solution—to return to France myself.

In Paris, Swift got up at the same time as usual to enjoy the manna that had at last fallen from heaven. Shepherd had just delivered the cargo from Operation Rubens. He eagerly began to draft orders for the sectors and gave them to Jean, his cyclist, whom he had arranged to meet in the Café Select just before 18.00. Before then he was to meet Inspector-General Michel, his alter ego, Llama.

Having done all his work, Swift left early to enjoy what was an almost spring day. He walked to a brasserie where Llama handed him a report about the port installations of the Gironde. He then headed for Montparnasse. The Café Select came into sight. Swift noticed that his courier was staring at him and came straight towards him, omitting the usual safety precautions. As he held out his hand, he suddenly found his shoulders seized by Gestapo agents, who shouted 'Swift' into his ears. In a flash he was handcuffed, bundled into a car and driven to 84 Avenue Foch, where he was dragged up to the fifth floor.

He was in an impossible position. His forged identity card, in the name of Barnon, merely made the Nazis laugh, since they found on him the orders, prepared in the morning, written in his own hand and signed Swift, as well as the information from Bordeaux that Llama had given him. But Swift never answered a single question. The Germans were completely unaware of his reserves of endurance. Nor had they any inkling of his ability to remain silent. His fierce power of abstraction was a byword among Parisians; he had the ability to go for whole evenings without speaking.

The Gestapo began to beat him and his nose streamed with blood. He was rushed down to a bathroom on the ground floor. All his clothes were stripped from him and he was left with his hands handcuffed and his feet chained. The bath was filled with cold water. He was immersed in it and his face kept under by an open palm that completely prevented him from breathing. Three other Nazis twisted his wrists and his ankles and punched him. As soon as he was beginning to suffocate his head was pulled out for a second and then he was pushed under again. Other men came in and joined in the sport until their victim lost consciousness.

When Swift recovered consciousness he noticed that his torturers looked anxious, but they did not stop the torture. Then came another round of questions, the water treatment and the beating. Swift sized up the situation and, feigning unconsciousness, tried not to react to the avalanche of blows that fell on him. '*Es ist genug,*' a voice said. Trembling, bloody, his body swollen and his brain numbed, Swift was dressed again and dragged back to the fifth floor. The Gestapo thugs disappeared, leaving him alone, face to face with the voice that had intervened to halt the torture. The voice apologized for the torture inflicted on him and began a further interrogation. In the SS man's hand was the list of Swift's rendezvous that Jean had kept for fear of forgetting them. The poor wretch had also been tortured and broken and had allowed himself to be taken out and used as a decoy.

How had Jean been captured? And the others that were paraded before Swift the next morning, among them the luckless Kite, captured so quickly. With him were his two personal radio operators. Then, in succession, they brought in the head of the northern sector, Moth, Elephant's successor; Sioux, the liaison agent who had so often escaped capture; the cartographer and stolid Norman, Sheldrake, and Spider, who had performed such prodigies in the forbidden Dunkirk zone; also Bee, the precious Maritou Brouillet. . . .

In a daze, Swift perceived through this lugubrious parade that such a haul was undoubtedly due to the seizing of a meeting place, because on the previous day they had all been due to receive the orders he was taking to Jean at the Café Select. The exceptional quality of the agents captured gave him reason to hope that they would defend themselves tooth and nail, but he must know what was still intact.

When the interrogators returned, Swift, who had been kept without sleep or food and who was frozen to his very marrow, launched into his story: 'You've made a mistake. These lads are only small fry and we can't know these women; they don't belong to our service. . . . Grand Duke? He's not at Aix-en-Provence, he's at Aix-les-Bains. . . . The code isn't taken from La Fontaine, it's from Victor Hugo. . . . Benteng? He isn't. . . . Llama? He isn't. . . .'

For once Swift talked and talked and talked. The interrogators meekly wrote down everything he said and sent the SS off on a wild goose chase.

To thank us for rescuing the pilot of the crashed Lysander, we were all invited to dinner. I had nearly cried off, but remembering what the Bishop had said—'In war, Marie-Madeleine, one must never talk about those who have disappeared'—I followed my friends.

A few hours earlier the radios in the south of France had transmitted news of the latest catastrophe:

From Shad: '*March 16, 17 and 18 nine people northern region were arrested one after another stop Swift disappeared since evening of the 17th stop do not expect any extension of the catastrophe which seems accidental stop following Swift's wish known to Chinchilla, Benteng, Shepherd and Shad interim command assured by Llama who accepts succession if you agree.*'

Around me people were dancing. I tried to join in but I no longer had any clear idea of where I was or where I stood. Dragon in no way seemed to share my agony of mind; he demanded to be parachuted into France as a matter of urgency. Whatever it might cost me, I must not act over-hastily in deciding on the network's continuity. The Chief was right: one must accept the evidence—an underground leader did not last more than six months.

When we eventually returned in the early hours, an air raid warning sounded. The men in Alliance House went down with Kid to the basement to play cards and drink beer until the raid was over.

Smouldering with thoughts of revenge against the bombs raining blindly down around me, I went through my bundle of messages. I re-read some of the daily reports from Jean-Claude Thorel (Shad) now head of Sea Star.

The British Admiralty continually asked him for exact details, and Shad replied imperturbably from his office at the port of Marseilles, where he was employed as an engineer. His information made it possible for the British to immobilize the enemy's military works.

The all-clear sounded. My heart turned over with horror at the thought of all the air raid warnings sounding in a world possessed by a mad frenzy of destruction. In order to survive it was still vital to let men like Shad continue to guide the blows against Hitler.

I would send Dragon back and give him command of the whole region north of the River Loire. Capitaine des Isnards (Grand Duke) would keep the south-east and the Mediterranean zone, Henri Battu (Opossum) would take the south-west. Petrel (Lamarque) and the Druids would also cover all the regions. Each of these young chiefs would have autonomy and his own funds and would keep personal control over his troops—the only way to safeguard unity was by sub-dividing it. And then, cost what it may, I would go and join these four men on whom I was pinning my last hope.

31 *D-DAY*

In his impatience to get back to France, Dragon looked just like those Chinese drawings depicting the Imperial emblem breathing fire from its nostrils. He was conscious of the vital importance of his mission, the secret weapon sites. Together with Michel Fourquet, who was now commanding the Lorraine group, we had been able to confirm that all the diagrams we had supplied had been or would be immediately destroyed by bombing. This category of intelligence was much more spectacular for us than the blind hunt for U-boats.

'When do you think they're going to land?' he asked me.

'Nobody, not even I, will know anything until D-Day. Unbelievable precautions have been taken to fox the enemy.'

'But it *will* be in France!'

'It can only be in France.'

Air Force General François d'Astier de la Vigerie had at last been given the task of reorganizing the secret services. Dragon and I went to meet him.

'The Americans refuse to believe or realize that the Resistance is Gaullist. Therefore it's necessary to prove to them that it is by getting everybody together in one organization. That's my aim,' he told us simply.

I was completely won over. The next day the lawyer Johannes Ambre drew up a legal document setting out the terms under which the Alliance Intelligence Service became part of the BCRA. The network's autonomy would be preserved; its air and radio links would remain independent; the money advanced by the British would be repaid. General d'Astier immediately called a larger conference with the BCRA headquarters staff. The present and the future of the Alliance were assured.

In this gigantic human duel the French, not content with fighting an implacable enemy, had engaged in a trial of strength among themselves, as in a medieval tourney, to attain the honour of being the strongest when facing adversity.

Now that our rear had been assured, Dragon, with complete contempt for the abyss into which he was destined to plunge, took off for our Signac landing ground on 11 April. Jean Godet, a captain in the reserve and the proprietor of an excellent brand of cognac, was the returning passenger: he was Antelope, Koenigswerther's right hand man in La Rochelle. He confirmed that Mandrill had been run to earth by the Nazi detector cars and that he had shot it out with them. He was believed dead. Within the space of a few weeks, the Gestapo's tentacles had closed round twenty-nine members of the network in the Atlantic region. The havoc had extended to the surrounding sectors; a whole band of fish, including Stickleback, Lobster and Turbot—also Kiffer, and Marco of the railway engine tender—had been captured.

'Stop, Antelope, it's dreadful. Why such a chain reaction from one piece of radio detection?'

'The Gestapo tortures have become much more sophisticated, Marie-Madeleine. They are now massive and scientific and extract more and more confessions. The slips that people always make, a notebook, some meeting that has been observed, do the rest.'

'And Paris?'

'Swift's arrest was due to the treachery of a newly recruited agent who led the Gestapo to the new headquarters letterbox. But that's not all, unfortunately; the sweep has now reached Normandy. All those who helped to produce that fantastic intelligence map have gone—twenty people.'

'Oh no! What can be done for them?'

'Nothing, absolutely nothing, Marie-Madeleine. We can only hope that we shall find them alive if the war really is coming to an end. Except in the forbidden zones, hardly anyone is being shot now—they're all being deported.'

'There's no doubt that the end of the war in France is near, Antelope, but these people all go back to the earliest days of the network—they're irreplaceable. Dragon will never be able to fill gaps like these.'

After these revelations I was kept going only by the hope that the BCRA would provide me with the *exeat* that the Chief had refused. Antelope tried to cheer me up: 'The Germans are describing us as "a chopped up worm whose bits always grow again." They're quite right. You'll see that everything continues as usual.'

The radio contact with Paris that was restored as soon as Dragon got back to France confirmed the enemy's statements. It was Pierre Bocher, Nightingale of the early days, who had got the main radio station at the northern headquarters going again. And the material sent in subsequent operations was safe, thanks to the indefatigable Emile Hédin (Beaver).

Dragon had established the expected contacts with the other regional chiefs. Even the forbidden zones had begun to resist, thanks to André Collard, a police inspector known by the curious name of Cactus. And Lorilleux (Icarus) had re-established contact with the Deuxième Bureau agents whom he had supplied with radio sets. A new batch of reports was even awaiting despatch to London.

As there was now a scarcity of pilots. British Intelligence opted for Operation Jeanneton, a naval operation. This was an extremely difficult sort of thing to carry out, as we had learned from the Duck and Popeye operations. This time it involved picking up three passengers and their reports. Bringing three passengers back in itself raised difficult problems; the intensive bombing of the railways had begun and it was no longer possible to rely on trains running according to schedule. The fortified sector was scrutinized by the enemy as under the microscope. Nevertheless Shepherd (Elie de Dampierre) was quite confident. The walkie-talkie that he would be using would allow him to keep in continual touch with the British launch and he would guide it in. Dispensing with light signals was a notable advance on his previous experience.

On this occasion I expected to bring over a fighter pilot, Raymond Pezet, who bore the pretty alias of Flying Fish and was coming to take the Avia training course; Amniarix, the young Druidess who had produced the sensational document about the secret weapon, and André Collard, the police officer 'Cactus', to whom we wanted to give important instructions for the forbidden zones.

Shepherd, aided by Beaver, had assembled his three passengers and their very large suitcases at an inn at Tréguier, a small town that was not far from the sea and parts of which went back to the fourteenth century. Operation Jeanneton was scheduled for midnight. Beaver went to fetch Yves Le Bitoux, a local veterinary surgeon, who drove them to the embarkation zone where one of his friends, François Margeau, was to take over and lead them through the minefields.

In spite of the pitch darkness, Le Bitoux easily found Margeau's house, down by the shore, and knocked cheerfully on the door. It opened to reveal the silhouette of a German officer against the bright light inside. Amniarix could speak fluent German and calmly asked the officer where Margeau was. 'Opposite', he barked, slamming the door.

Shepherd decided there and then to clear out of the village. He had the car stopped in a side road and left the mail with Flying Fish and Dr Le Bitoux, while he himself went off to find out whether there was a road by which he, Amniarix and Beaver could beat a retreat. He had scarcely gone forty yards in the thick darkness when he was surrounded by six German soldiers armed with machine pistols and grenades. They were all searched.

Amazed to find their papers in order, the officer who had opened the door to them a short time before asked to see the car. He motioned to Amniarix to lead the way. What could she, a frail, defenceless girl, do to avoid the trap that had closed on them? She decided to go as slowly as possible and to speak German at the top of her voice to warn Le Bitoux and Flying Fish in the hope that they would get away.

After twenty minutes of uncertainty, a scream of brakes signalled the capture of the car. The officer shouted triumphantly: 'They're all spies,' but he went back with Amniarix and Le Bitoux only. Warned by the girl's loud voice, Flying Fish had fled. The stoical veterinary surgeon had remained where he was. He was too well-known in the district and had no wish to escape and be responsible for bringing reprisals on the people whom he dearly loved.

The Germans now carted the little group off to a house in the town. Beaver then felt that this was his only chance. With a rush he scattered his guards and dashed towards a large courtyard enclosed by a wall some eight feet high. Bursts of fire sprayed from the automatics. Protected from them by the corner of the dilapidated old house, he scaled the wall, jumped down into the street and ran off at random. He came to a garden, went in through the iron gate, looked for the most suitable hiding place and found, buried away in a clump of trees, one of those wooden earth closets still commonly used in the country. It was just the place. He opened the door, lifted the seat, crouched inside and waited for the night to end, all the time listening to the shouts of the German squad who patrolled and terrorized the village until dawn.

As daylight broke the owner of the house walked towards the closet and Beaver was forced to come out: 'I'm the man they're after,' he explained. The worthy soul suppressed her surprise, but she refused to take him into her house; the Germans were continuing to search every house and altogether more than 100 inhabitants were arrested. Early in the afternoon she returned to say that the Boches were no longer keeping such a strict watch. She offered him clothes and her bicycle.

Beaver was to meet Flying Fish in Paris the next day. Meanwhile, Shepherd, André Collard, Yves le Bitoux and Amniarix—the big, frail Jeannie Rousseau—were taken away to their doom.

Dragon immediately asked me to arrange a Lysander operation. Flying Fish was keener than ever to take the Avia course in order to avenge Shepherd. Pierre Giraud (Teutatès), Petrel's No 1 agent, would accompany him to effect the link that poor Amniarix had been unable to establish.

Convinced of the imminence of fresh catastrophes, I speeded up arrangements for my own departure as much as I could. But the French seemed no more anxious to help me return to France than the British. Abandoning his frontal attack, the Chief adopted delaying tactics. Yes, I could go back. Yes, I could take the next Lysander. In the meantime I must pass a number of tests—the main one being to stop smoking.

Then British Intelligence experts insisted on giving me a cast-iron and genuine false identity. I was obviously not ready for Operation Michelangelo, which brought Teutatès and Flying Fish to Britain. However, their arrival provided me with one of the main conditions on which the Chief insisted: the genuine false identity. I would return to France as Mrs Flying Fish. The identity people took over this curious case with all the typical expert's professional keenness.

On the evening of 5 June, while I was finishing my preparations for departure, a sort of hum imperceptibly accompanied me in my work, although I did not notice it at first. In the end, the background of sound intrigued me. I opened the window and the noise became deafening, but not a single searchlight swept the sky nor had the air raid warning gone. It was impossible to see the aircraft flying in massed formation above the sleeping capital. They flew over in a never-ending stream.

Holding my breath and looking steadily in the direction of Nazi Germany, I could see, beyond the barbed wire sealing the frontiers, beyond the prisons, the dawn that was bringing to our enslaved friends the first glimmer of their victory.

Ham arrived, his face radiant:

'I've got de Gaulle's message to all the networks of Free France. Here it is: "*From General de Gaulle to the Alliance Network: at this moment when the forces of liberation are coming to drive the enemy from our country let me remind every intelligence agent that his first duty is to stay in the place he has gloriously chosen and to gather and transmit the information that is of vital importance to the progress of operations up to the very last minute stop only at that moment will he be authorized to join a combatant unit in the Maquis stop long live France end*".'

Kenneth Cohen had wanted me to go and dine at his home to celebrate the greatest event of the century. He had opened a bottle of claret, which we drank reverently.

'The hardest part is over,' said Kenneth. 'Once we have gained a foothold on the beaches, everything will go well. The enemy seems to have been surprised, thank God!'

I left early to go to Claude de Boislambert's farewell party. De Gaulle had given him the job of setting up a huge liaison organization to provide a link between the Allied troops and the French administration. He would soon be landing himself. Claude had not changed since the Ussel days, being still as dynamic and concentrated in action as ever. We did not dare talk about the future; the full, rich present was enough for us.

An air raid warning broke the spell of our desultory conversation and the anti-aircraft fire answered the clink of the ice in our whisky. We listened in a blasé way to a few dull bursts and then the all-clear went. Most of the guests took advantage of this to leave: I was about to do the same when the sirens started up again amid a great burst of tracer shells. Then they stopped and started again, and went on and on.

'That's odd,' said Boislambert. 'It's not the same as usual, Marie-Madeleine. I don't want you to go out in all this gunfire. You might easily get a piece of shrapnel in your skull.'

Outside the searchlights probed the heavens in all directions, the sirens kept wailing, going on and off so often that it was impossible to tell whether there was a raid on or not. The anti-aircraft guns seemed to be firing at random and, what was most remarkable, there was not a sound of an enemy plane. Just occasionally a sound like that of a powerful motor-bicycle pierced the darkness and suddenly cut out, to be followed by a terrible explosion.

'I know what it is,' I said, thinking aloud. 'It's the secret weapon.'

32 *FAREWELL*

Of course, our June Lysander operation had not taken place. Long waiting had made me resigned and I now believed that I would never catch up with the Allied armies that were liberating my native land. My longing to return changed to a kind of nervous weakness when, on 12 June, a message from Grand Duke informed us that Dragon and most of the Paris agents had been arrested the day after the landing. Pierre Bocher, Nightingale from Marseilles, was among those captured. It undoubtedly meant the end for them all.

The news of Dragon's arrest seemed, curiously, to give Sir Claude Dansey a new lease of life: 'You see, my dear child,' he insisted, 'there's absolutely no point in your going now.'

'But this is the third leader in the field to go in less than a year,' I replied. 'Your famous law of averages is all wrong. Paul Bernard lasted six months. Dragon only six weeks. I must go and take their place.'

'Unless security is cast-iron, Poz, you won't last six days.'

I now had two identities. First, I was Mme Germaine Pezet, Flying Fish's wife, apprised in detail of all her family connections, dates and places where she and her husband had been educated, spent their holidays and their honeymoon. Nothing escaped the cross-questioning of the security officer, a man of infinite cunning.

'And now let's have a look at your idea of a housewife,' he said sarcastically. 'Make yourself look like one, if you can. I'll get my camera ready.'

By using a net, I brought my hair forward to make my forehead a lot smaller, and my face heavier. But, to my great surprise, the proper effect was produced only when I had covered my own teeth with a dental masterpiece, a yellow plastic contraption as forbidding as you could ever wish to meet, which had been made for me by a dentist working for Intelligence. A pair of spectacles, clumsy make-up and a black scarf completed the picture. When I turned round, the officer burst out laughing.

He then took the identity photograph of Jeanne Lebrun, housewife, born in Caen on 14 August 1904.

'The Chief can't believe his eyes,' Ham told me a few days later, when he brought me the identity card complete with the photograph, the only thing still missing being my finger prints.

I had made provisions against Dragon's disappearance when dividing the network up again, but even so the only region that had miraculously remained intact after eighteen months was Grand Duke's in the south-east. I decided to go there direct. To reinforce this region to the maximum I arranged, with Ham's assistance, parachute drops, massive deliveries of transmitting sets, arms, money and all sorts of supplies. But how was I to join them? Our aerial infrastructure had been completely paralysed since the latest arrests.

'Don't worry,' Ham said, 'we'll deliver you safely. Anyway, a large-scale landing for the BCRA has been planned for the July moon. The security officer would like you to know,' he added in a mocking tone of voice, 'there's a serious omission in your civilian status as Mrs Flying Fish your grandparents' dates of birth!'

'You're a lot of maniacs! I don't even know my own grandparents' birthdays.'

'Our man maintains that people always know if the grandparents are old or still comparatively young, living or dead and, if so, in which cemetery they are buried, of course,' he insisted, quite unmoved by my outburst.

Chafing with impatience, I went through the chart showing the network organization. If things got no worse in the next few days, I knew that I was going to find a fighting force of seventy-five principal agents and, to judge by the signatures on the latest reports, about 800 secondary agents, quite apart from their helpers.

Seventeen transmitters had weathered the storm. Some of the radio operators had become so familiar to me that I might have known them always. Grand Duke's operator, Michel Lévêque, known as Weevil, held the record. British Intelligence had named him No 1 France Combattante operator and decided to award him the Military Cross. Michel Darnet (Bengali), who operated the Toulon radio, amazed the Americans. Every day at breakfast time, with the regularity of an alarm clock, he broadcast the results of the previous night's bombing raids. But the one who astounded me most was Emile Lorin (Sibelius), of Lyons. Ham showed me messages made up of 450 five-letter code groups; the average message contained only 60 groups!

While I was in the middle of all these preparations, I realized that I had given very little thought to my family and suddenly the idea that my children would not now see me was like a knife in my heart. Cut off from everything and everybody who had until now filled my universe, I was setting off again solitary and depersonalized. I had not even the right to confide in anyone outside the service.

'Don't tell your friends you're leaving,' advised Ham, who kept an eye on everything.

Other and more serious problems arose; for instance, those to do with counter-espionage. In the midst of all these disasters, agents could have been sent back and released by the enemy, then infiltrated to London or North Africa, and in this sphere the rivalry between the secret services was to our disadvantage.

I had been asked many times for reports on suspect members of the Alliance, in particular Verteré, who had turned up in North Africa with Gertrude, where he had proposed the Allies should join an anti-Hitler and anti-Communist pact. He admitted that he had been released by the Abwehr, which made his case extremely disturbing. Others had also reappeared. A certain Red, who gave Navarre's name as a reference, had reached Britain via Spain and was going back on an important mission for the BCRA. When he had been screened, his story of having escaped from Fresnes with forged discharge papers seemed brilliant. It was, indeed, but not brilliant enough to outweigh the facts I was able to produce about him and his doings in 1941. He collapsed.

During this period some terrible orders and counter-orders had brought about some tragic mistakes within the Resistance. When certain agreed messages were broadcast by the BBC, the Resistance had thought that D-Day was to be D-Day for them too, everywhere. They came out into the open and the Nazis fell upon them instantly. Consequently, London intensified the parachute drops and the despatch of specialists. All those who were in reserve in England were sent into action.

With a firm bridgehead now established in Normandy, the Continent was no longer isolated, but I began to feel uneasy. It was no longer anguish that I felt, but a profound nostalgia.

33 *EAGLE'S TRIAL*

On 28 June 1944, the Military Court of the Third Reich pronounced its verdict in the case of Eagle, Commandant Faye. To try the agents of the Alliance network, the Court had moved from its seat in Torgau to Freiburg-im-Breisgau. For Eagle it moved to the fortress of Bruchsal, the Gestapo having issued instructions that the prisoner was not to leave the prison where he had been secretly immured for six months.

By now Eagle was like a skeleton. In the damp vault where the radiator had long ceased to function, the water was permanently stagnant and the straw mattress on the floor oozed with it. Eagle rolled himself up in the sodden blankets. Although it was summer, his hands and feet were raw with chilblains.

The machine tools kept up a perpetual infernal growl in the nearby underground factory, aggravating the endemic buzzing in his ears. He stuffed paper into them. An abscess formed in one and nothing could relieve the lacerating pain. He found the sacrifice of physical cleanliness more trying than lack of food—his daily ration being one bowl of soup served with a wooden spoon. He was so wasted and listless that even hunger died. He was allowed to exercise for ten minutes a week, away from the other prisoners. He was never to know that there were a dozen other members of the Alliance in Bruchsal, dispersed throughout the various parts of the fortress. During one of these brief outings he chanced to see himself in a mirror, and failed to recognize the white-bearded old man reflected in it.

Not a single human being helped him. His thoughts were in a constant whirl. Painful, haunting, unbearable in the morning. Then, by dint of reason and prayer, his brain steeled itself to face the night. He was endlessly plagued by remorse about two things—the Lanky episode and the disastrous attempt to escape across the roofs of the Avenue Foch. He should have avoided capture. He could easily have escaped. He nursed one remaining hope: the Gestapo had assured him that they would treat the members of the Alliance as prisoners of war and not as 'terrorists'. His own fate, which he attributed to his attempt to escape, was of little moment.

On 10 June, his forty-fifth birthday, Eagle received a visit from a Freiburg-im-Breisgau lawyer, Dr Hermann. He learned that the High Court of the Reich had already condemned ten of his friends to death.

Some had already been shot. Eagle realized that he had been the victim of a vile trick. He never even reacted. He was 'glad to put an end to it'. Gradually, however, the sense of his responsibilities prevailed. The verdict awaiting him would decide not only his own fate but the fate of the whole of the Alliance. If true justice were meted out to him by the German military judges, those who came after him would be saved, the executions now going on would be stopped.

He decided to prepare a defence of the network. He applied all the brilliance of his intellect, brought all the remaining resources of his martyred body to bear in the pursuit of this supreme aim. At last he would be able to fight again. To answer the charge of espionage, he would prove the difference between the spy and the resistance fighter.

The Hague Convention had been drawn up for other times, for a different type of war. It could not be applied to the resistance of a whole people in its purest official and military form, which was the case with the Alliance. Five hundred and fifty soldiers captured on their own territory could not be condemned as spies; so many patriots could not be executed after months of torture and suffering. Eagle would recall the Gestapo's solemn pledges. He would make crystal clear that the only spy in the Alliance was Lanky, an infiltration spy in the enemy's pay.

His defending counsel, therefore, must be associated with this plea. The lawyer returned to see him on the 25th, the eve of the proceedings. He was not a Nazi. He agreed.

On 26 June, serene at heart, Eagle appeared before the tribunal, which was composed of three generals, two colonels and two interpreters, surrounded by a guard of soldiers, all in full uniform. The scene, which reminded him of the Clermont-Ferrand trial, did not over-awe him.

Alas, from the start, by his very first words, by the mere tone of his voice, the President made it clear that the proceedings were taking place under the sign of the Swastika. Terrible days followed, each of two court sessions. Except at the final session, it was only the President who spoke. He addressed his words to Eagle, who stood in front of him and, because his health was undermined, felt his strength ebb away. But he was determined not to collapse, not to faint, and he took a firm grip on himself.

Eagle was forced to stand for hours on end listening to the most violent, false and unjust vilification of the Allies, France and the French, of his friends and of himself, the accused. The President poured scorn on his officer status. The network's activities were besmirched, reviled, derided. Eagle was told that the French army did not exist, that it was a band of 'Moroccans' obeying either de Gaulle or other stupid generals. One grievance was brought up repeatedly—Giraud's escape. The President brandished innumerable newspaper articles that were quite meaningless to Eagle. He was accused of 'killings on the Normandy front'—which was how he learned of the Allied landing. At this the blood surged afresh through his veins and he tried to explain, to prove that the network was a military organization. The President replied: 'That is the very reason why we are going to shoot you.'

In the evening, when he was taken back to his cell, Eagle collapsed from fatigue and despair; but there was something that he still possessed. He had been given paper, a pencil, a pen and ink in order to prepare his defence. He began to write his will. At dawn he rolled up the messages he had inscribed with his manacled hand and threw them behind the thick grille of the defunct radiator.

At the end of the second session he was able to keep his word. He presented the defence in law of the Alliance and spoke of the Resistance. Germany did not know it. Nazi propaganda depicted it as a handful of terrorists who were murdering good Germans and broadcasting inflammatory speeches on the BBC. Eagle had the feeling, confirmed by his lawyer, that his speech impressed the judges. His confidence in the military members of the tribunal was reborn and he redoubled his efforts.

In the afternoon another figure appeared on the scene—the public prosecutor. Black. Cynical. Contemptible. Nazi. He produced faked documents, he quoted people and incidents of which Eagle knew nothing. He had but one desire: to send as many people as possible to their deaths.

Eagle's lawyer rose. His task was impossible. He nevertheless pursued the same line of argument as Eagle and asked for his acquittal.

Finally, the accused was allowed to speak. After proceedings conducted as they had been, there was no point in resuming his defence in law. It was then that Eagle discovered in the depths of his soul spiritual treasures of love and self-sacrifice. Rather than avenge his honour by launching into a stinging attack on the court, he appealed to the men who had insulted him. He endeavoured to strike a responsive chord of commonsense. He tried to awaken their humane feelings, stir their Christian feelings. He exhorted them to display some generosity to officers who were fighting men like them.

The President interrupted him brutally and Eagle knew that he was lost. His final words were an expression of hope for his native land: 'Long live France!'

The icy blast of the death sentence swept through the courtroom. The President felt a curious need to comment at length. Would he be overtaken by remorse as he faced the man who had been reduced to a wreck by his fellow men and who had done his duty to the very end? He gave orders that the soup ration should be doubled. 'A funny idea, fattening me up just to send me to the firing squad,' the condemned man murmured. He was no longer listening; his thoughts were elsewhere, with God, his family, his friends. . . .

Back in his cell Eagle was again manacled, but he found a bit of pencil that he had hidden and on odd scraps of paper he put down what he could remember and had witnessed. He wrote down everything that he still carried in his head and he found the strength to put into code what he dared not include in his messages. In an open letter addressed to 'his friends of the Alliance', a letter that every prisoner condemned to death has the right to write and which he was to leave with the clerk of the court, he informed me in the Corniche code that his real testament was hidden behind the radiator.

Time began to flow again, inexorably, but the Nazis were not to triumph; soaring on wings of faith, Eagle discovered the way of escaping in spirit from his concrete coffin.

It was Ham who suddenly told me that my return to France was imminent. I had a mere two hours in which to pack. Into the false bottom of a large, soft hold-all went some crystals, replacement codes, money, and the excellent false denture to transform me into a French housewife. No need for questionnaires; I knew them by heart. My clothes were in a light fibre suitcase. In my handbag were the identity card showing me to be Flying Fish's wife and the poison that looked like big aspirin tablets.

I wore a grey woollen costume, the old, broad-brimmed felt hat that best concealed my face and, as I was taking only one coat, I chose the navy blue gabardine, brother of the fawn one that had stood me in such good stead the year before.

Sir Claude came to see me. He was very upset: 'I want you to know that but for the BCRA I would never have allowed you to go back, Poz. It's sheer madness. We're sending you into the wolf's mouth and it's too stupid, so near the end.'

'You must understand my position,' I replied. 'I *must* go back before the war's over, otherwise my friends would never have any confidence in me again.'

He stood stock still, as he always did when he wanted to think, his whole body motionless. In the distance bursts of anti-aircraft fire and the racket made by the V.1s could be heard. 'Listen,' I continued. 'Things are pretty hot. You still need your French friends.'

He moved again: 'I wanted to say, my dear child, that should you be arrested you must make no attempt to defend yourself as head of the network, because then there is no way out except by taking the cyanide. And as I know you will not betray anyone, you must be quite cynical about the whole thing. Say that I sent you to France to report on the Communist Party. They know who I am. They'll be very interested indeed and they won't kill you.'

'And the network? And use your name?'

'As for the network, you'll say it's smashed and nothing's left, that your job now is not to gather information for use against the Nazis but simply to prepare for future action against the Russians. Believe me, they'll all put themselves under your orders when you mention my name, with all my titles, of course.'

'The Gestapo will never swallow a story like that.'

'If they don't believe you, you'll send a message on one of your transmitters and I'll answer them—in my own way. Believe me, Poz, I've never made this offer to anyone before.'

'Why make it to me? I'm not British.'

'You're a woman and I'm ashamed of seeing you all these years doing things I couldn't do myself. I also deeply pity you.'

He left, putting into my hands a little souvenir, the traditional mascot, a rabbit's foot.

I gazed at Alliance House for the last time, at the large-flowered cretonnes, the camp bed with its tearful night-time memories and the telephone that had so often been the direct bearer of appalling news. Kid was in tears, Captain Godet and Jacques Charles clasped me to their hearts—they were to stay in London as liaison between the Alliance and the BCRA—and the long black cars glided swiftly and silently towards the road to the airfield.

We drew up at dusk before the steps of a country house and were immediately taken to a huge dining room that had been converted into a mess, where waiters in white jackets above their service trousers were bustling about.

'So it's to be tonight?' Teutatès asked Ham, who had come back from the phone box.

'No, it's postponed until tomorrow.' My heart sank. After dinner I invited Ham to drink a last whisky with me.

'You're frightened about going back, Poz?' he asked.

'Yes, I'm frightened, I'm really in a blue funk. I'm going to be arrested and yet I've got a feeling I shall get away with it.'

We talked until dawn, going over all the ups and downs we had experienced together—the disastrous Lanky affair, Mandrill's launch episode, Operation Jeanneton, Dragon's arrest. Ham took things in his stride. His kindness and his tact were a great comfort.

I woke up very late, certainly not before the afternoon. The huge place felt like a haunted house. One sensed the presence of a lot of people lurking behind the partitions but, as at Major Bertram's, no one ever met anyone else. Kenneth Cohen appeared.

'It won't be long now, dear Poz,' he said, greatly moved. 'Mary asked me to give you her best love and we'd like you to have this little memento. It's an heirloom.' He handed me a charming ring with a heart-shaped stone. 'Take it with you. It'll bring you luck,' he said when I protested. 'That's why we're giving it you. And here's a luminous watch from British Intelligence. It's Swiss and keeps perfect time.'

'We must be at the airfield very soon,' he continued. 'Everything's fixed. Grand Duke's waiting for you in Aix-en-Provence.' And we drove off at top speed.

'Grand Duke hasn't told anyone of my return?'

'No-one, except Petrel, as we agreed.'

The airfield presented an extraordinary sight, with aircraft standing wing to wing as far as the eye could see, and in the middle a crowd of agile and athletic-looking RAF men moving about. 'You're not going to tell me that all these are off on secret missions?'

Kenneth Cohen laughed: 'No. They're bombers and will be taking off in waves from dusk to dawn. You're going in just behind them, so that the enemy radar won't be able to pick you out. They'll think you're one of the raiders.'

On arriving at the mess I saw my travelling companions sitting apart with Ham and, in another corner, half a dozen men of all ages and ranks. 'Those are the other passengers,' Kenneth said, going over to greet them, 'but I'm not making any introductions. Take no notice.'

'But we shall meet on the plane. Do you really imagine we will cold shoulder one another in these circumstances?'

The sun began to go down and waves of aircraft headed eastwards, disappearing into the oncoming darkness. An officer asked us to follow him. Another, with a poet's face, came over to us with a pile of little cages, each containing a white pigeon. I received one like the rest.

'You'll slip a message into the ring on its leg as soon as you land,' Kenneth told me.

'This seems very strange in the day of the V.1.'

'No, we do it for people who haven't any transmitters. That's not the case with you, but as you're with a lot of other people you're getting one as well, so that nobody's jealous.'

We were driven to the tarmac, where I could see the burly outline of a Hudson, its paintwork chipped by machine-gun fire. I fell for it at once. I had the honour of being first up the ladder into the fuselage, where I bumped into all kinds of containers piled up by the entrance and went sprawling.

Our party came in one by one and crouched down in any available corner, the sergeant making sure that the weight was equally distributed; then our luggage and the pigeon cages were passed to us and the door shut with a loud bang. I stood up to try to catch through the window a last glimpse of Kenneth Cohen's tall figure in naval uniform and Ham's familiar cap. They saw me, stood stiffly to attention and gave me a magnificent salute. I felt a terrible urge to cry.

The runway began to speed past under our wheels. Then the big machine heaved itself off the ground ponderously, while around us the bombers rose with a similar effort. The sergeant carefully drew the curtains across the windows.

'Why won't he let us see this extraordinary sight?' I asked Pierre Giraud, shattered not to see the sky any more.

'They don't want us to see the course they're taking. We're going into the battle zone.'

Flying Fish went to visit the navigators who were vaguely visible against the multi-coloured dials of their instruments. 'We've left England,' he said, rousing me out of a pleasant doze.

'Then we're nearly there?'

'Not exactly. To avoid the battle front we're going to fly round Brittany, follow the Loire and approach Paris from the east.'

'Come and see how beautiful it is,' Teutatès whispered. Eluding the sergeant's watchful eye, he had engineered a peephole in one of the curtains and I was amazed to see what looked like a firework display.

'It's the flak, look, we're climbing.'

The plane shuddered several times, then stoically resumed its course. I was fully awake now. I looked at France below and suddenly something extraordinarily moving happened. As we flew on, from each district, from fields and from clearings torchlights came on, their beams forming the letter L and flashing in Morse R for Robert, S for Simone, V for Victory. They were the identifying signals of secret landing grounds in the maquis.

The sergeant sprang on us. 'Not allowed,' he admonished us, pulling the curtains together. 'We shall be there in half an hour. Get ready.'

We moved away, straightened our clothes, sorted our luggage and pigeons.

The plane began to bank. The watchful sergeant was swaying about and seemed uneasy. I felt the machine bank first left, then right, describing endless figures of eight. The passengers were all lurching about with the constant tilting of the plane. I began to feel uneasy too. Pierre Giraud (Teutatès) had gone back to his seat to look through the peephole. 'No sign of a reception committee,' he observed.

At that moment the Hudson got back on an even keel and the sergeant removed his forage cap. 'We're going back, friends,' announced the unknown agents' leader.

The ribbon of the Loire unwound again. The maquis torches continued to flash all the letters of the alphabet.

We got back to the airfield as the bombers were returning from Germany. We saw them swooping down from all levels of the sky, like some gigantic farandole, and landing in an orderly way one by one. When eventually we landed, Kenneth and Ham were waiting at the foot of the ladder.

Asleep on my feet, I went back to my room. In the afternoon I discovered a piano and tried to loosen my fingers and my mind, but my fingers had lost all their agility and I could not even remember my favourite pieces. I felt very annoyed. The war had amputated a faculty that had so far been essential to my life—music.

'The operation's on,' Ham said when he returned from London next day. 'The Commander sends his apologies. He can't come because his desk is piled high with problems.'

'What happened yesterday?' I asked listlessly.

'The reception committee was afraid of a raid and thought it wiser to lie low.'

We went through the same routine as on the previous evening; the goodbyes, the take-off, the devious course, the flak and the Loire, the Seine and the forest of Fontainebleau and the torches. But there was a surprise in store when we arrived directly above the clandestine landing ground. We saw an extraordinary display of bright red ground lights. The Hudson took full advantage of them to make a majestic landing. The door opened and friendly hands stretched up.

'Where's the lady?' a voice asked.

An old crock of a lorry spluttered towards us over the dewy grass. The head of the reception committee helped me out of the plane and, looking at me in the moonlight, said: 'Hello, Marie-Madeleine.' Scarcely an *incognito* return! Shadowy figures were scurrying to and from the plane.

We eventually gathered around a huge dining table at a farmhouse in the middle of the village of Maisons-Rouges near Nangis. How many people were there, eating, drinking, gesticulating? Twenty, thirty, forty perhaps. Men dashed about, shouting odd pieces of news that sounded magnificent.

The Hudson had vanished. The sector was quiet. The containers were loaded on to lorries. I took the other two members of the network aside: 'We must get moving. These people are marvellous but we *must* get moving!'

'You're tired, madame,' said Flying Fish.

'Remember Eagle. If he'd left as soon as he landed he'd never have been caught. There's nothing for us to do here now, so let's get moving. You, Teutatès, go to Paris with one of those lorries and tell Petrel that I expect him at Aix as soon as he can get there. Don't forget, give priority to the V.1s. Flying Fish and I are going to hitchhike south.'

Flying Fish gave me a black look: 'D'you mean to tell me that we're going to walk?'

The bird cages were brought. The people round us cracked the usual joke: 'They'd be very tasty with green peas.' I took my pigeon and tied a message to its leg: 'With love and kisses from Poz.' It flew off.

We shook hands with the farm people and the reception committee and set off along the road. Flying Fish carried a case in each hand and I slung my bags over my shoulders, but they seemed dreadfully heavy. We walked something like three miles without a word. Not a car, not an animal, not a living creature did we see. Fields, market gardens, roads criss-crossing one another in a complicated network, none of the lights working because they had been suppressed since the occupation. At last I was back in France; I picked up a little earth and fondled it as I walked along.

A squeak of axles heralded the arrival of a cart. Flying Fish hailed the peasant, who pulled on his reins and looked at us suspiciously. He stared particularly hard at our cases. He evidently thought that we were returning from a fruitful black market trip. He agreed to give us a lift.

The big trees of the forest of Fontainebleau at last closed in on us as we jogged along behind the horse. Then at noon the driver put us down before a hotel, where the proprietor explained the situation: 'You can't count on the trains. The railway's being bombed all the time and the convoys machine-gunned. The whole area is infested with Germans, who are on the move in all directions.' She advised us to hitchhike. Yes, there was a taxi, but it was out on a job.

'Give us a room.'

Soldiers in grey-green uniforms kept coming in and out, far too numerous for my liking. They looked at us with curiosity; our looks were scarcely suited to this holiday hotel. The owner insisted that we fill in the usual registration forms, so Flying Fish gave the name of M and Mme Pezet and went off to look for the taxi.

I washed, changed my clothes, packed my raincoat and felt hat in the suitcase in exchange for a lighter jacket and a scarf, and lay down on the bed, thinking. It was going to take us a hell of a time to get to Aix-en-Provence at this pace. Moreover, it was impossible to let anyone know where we were. I felt painfully lost.

The taxi driver agreed to take us to Joigny, a station on the line to Marseilles. The waiting rooms were crammed with people, which seemed to indicate that there had not been a train for a long time, but that there was still hope. I pushed our cases towards a central pile of luggage and sat on a seat.

Suddenly the waiting room was invaded by a crowd of armed soldiers who swooped on the passengers shouting: 'Papers, papers.' I showed mine. 'Luggage?'—'No.' They left it at that and passed on. They took away three protesting young men and a woman. Other soldiers appeared and stood in a circle round the luggage, sub-machine guns at the ready. Flying Fish, who had managed to slip off down the track, beckoned to me to join him outside. But the cases! And the things hidden in the false bottoms! I walked over to my own case, opened it and under the sentries' eyes rummaged about for some underclothes. Then I closed it again and took it and my bag back to the seat. My things were safe. There were still Flying Fish's.

A little old man who was dozing beside me opened his eyes. 'The swine,' he hissed between the stumps of his teeth, 'the swine.'

'Grandad, I'm tired. You see that blue fibre case. Would you be very kind and go and get it for me?'

He got up, politely raised his cap and pushed the guards aside. 'Do you mind if I take it?' he asked with a grin. The German asked him to open it and the old man looked questioningly at me. When I nodded he clicked open the lock and the soldier rapidly inspected what was inside. '*Raus!*' he ordered.

'Thank you, grandad,' I said as I went up to an open steam lorry beside which Flying Fish was chatting.

'Are you from the maquis?' the old man whistled. 'I can see you're not a local.' To think that my father came from this *département*! How can you cease to be local in one generation!

'Yes, grandad, I am local. I come from Villeneuve-sur-Yonne.'

'Oh,' he said, disappointed. 'Well, goodbye! Oh, the swine,' he muttered, turning round, 'the swine.'

'You're crazy,' fumed Flying Fish, 'to let that old man into such secrets. If you're interrogated they'll find out the Pezet family has no connection with this place.'

'Get in, ladies and gentlemen,' the lorry driver shouted. 'The boiler's white hot, we can start.'

Flying Fish put his hands together to form a step for me. Trying to recover my balance I slipped, fell forward, crashed into the boiler and let out a howl. My right wrist remained glued to the red-hot surface like a cutlet stuck to a frying pan. The driver roughly grabbed me away and sent me packing on to the platform: 'Why couldn't you be careful?' he barked.

Flying Fish sprang to my side and tended to my burn with handkerchiefs soaked in eau de cologne. He passed me a cigarette, and absent-mindedly I began smoking again.

After wandering about for three days we finally took the Marseilles-Aix tram, our eleventh vehicle, and arrived at the Hotel Negre-Coste. We had travelled by freight trains and slow passenger trains, amid explosions and through gunfire. I was astonished to observe the scale of the general chaos. My mission, already well behind schedule, would hardly be helped by what I saw.

I begged Flying Fish to fetch Grand Duke (des Isnards). What would be his reactions to me? I had been corresponding with him for fifteen months without ever seeing him. And yet I felt that I had always known him. Suddenly a large figure in denim bent over me and kissed my hand.

'Did you get hurt, madame?'

'It's nothing serious, just a burn on an old lorry.'

'We were beginning to get worried. Why have you been so long?' He spoke in a low voice, making the point with a precision that was altogether military. 'I've got nearly sixty pounds of correspondence and reports waiting for you. The letter-box that you gave me for London letters is a goner. The agents running it were shot six days ago. Dragon has escaped. He must be evacuated. We're having trouble making proper radio contact. London's not listening to us. I'll take you to your hideout.'

So here we were, back in hot water with a vengeance! A furtive goodbye to Flying Fish and a few minutes later I found myself once again on the first floor of a small, old-fashioned house, in the flat occupied by Mlle de Weerdt, a nurse whose father had been shot in the 1914 war.

'We're the only three who know the place,' Grand Duke informed me. 'You're perfectly safe here.'

'Tell me about Dragon first, that's much more important.'

'He escaped by sawing through an iron bar. He's back with the network. He was tortured and at the moment is being nursed back to health. There's a big hunt going on for him. We must get him away as soon as possible.'

'Who told you all this?'

'Petrel. He went through Aix this morning, very disappointed that you hadn't arrived yet.'

From a cupboard on the wall he took piles of documents and papers written in all sorts of coloured ink. It was an immense mail.

'Good heavens! How did it get like this? We must send it by radio.'

'I'm all for that, but London has never been so bad. During his interrogation Dragon learned that the Gestapo knew all about the existence of my radios, but they haven't been able to pinpoint them. There are, sometimes, zones where it's impossible to pick up anything. Aix must be one of them.'

'Does your miraculous operator Weevil often move his set?'

'Never, he's been in the same place for months. In our Turtle Dove's home on Route Nationale 7. It's unique.' Grand Duke's face became serious. 'When will the landing in the south take place, madame?'

'Very soon now, I think, in three or four weeks at the most.'

'Then we'd do well to take every possible precaution. The Boche saw what was in store for them when the maquis began to act everywhere after the Normandy landing. It was disastrous here. They took ferocious reprisals.'

While I began to sort out the reports in order of urgency, I explained to Grand Duke the mechanism of the V.1s and the V.2s, and told him about the terrific job done by the Lorraine group. We talked in this vein until night fell; so many things had made us close friends in advance, particularly the tragedies of the past year. Grand Duke gave me some appalling details of the blood that had flowed in the room where Colonel Kauffmann (Cricket) had been captured, and of Pierre Berthomier (Seagull), who had been seriously wounded defending himself and was then treated worse than an animal. When he was in prison the guard put a bowl of soup in the corner of his cell and Seagull had to crawl over to it and lap it like a dog. Our friends arrested by the OVRA had been handed over to the Germans after the fall of Mussolini. Nothing was known of the rest. 'Except in the north only, hostages were shot on the spot,' Grand Duke reported. 'The prisons were emptied and train-loads were deported to Germany. Nobody knows what has happened beyond the Rhine.'

Nearly every day Grand Duke took me to dine with him at his little farm near Aix and I gradually fell again under the sweet spell of the Provençal way of life. Grand Duke was the centre of a constant stream of agents, coming and going between the various sectors, a traffic that he regulated with clockwork precision. And so I met once more all the fighting generations of the Alliance, from the first Patrol to Sea Star, as well as the Squadron and the Druids. Here, in Aix, the survivors of our decimated assault waves renewed the links in the chain of loyalty, restoring the Alliance to its old vitality.

Grand Duke, like a figure-head at the prow of a ship, was the man whom fate had chosen to save the Ark from sinking. In defiance of all statistics he had kept it afloat for fifteen months through the many typhoons, in the same place and using his real name.

Having organized things with a view to the coming landing in the south, all I was waiting for now was the parachute drop I had arranged with Ham in London; then I could transfer my efforts to the northern zone. The six tons of supplies of Operation Sergeant were dropped during the night of 15 and 16 July.

35   *THE BAR OF FREEDOM*

As always in July a heavy, humid heat hung over Aix, intensifying the smell of the plane trees and making the scent of the rioting roses infinitely precious. I gazed nostalgically at my narrow street through the closed shutters. It carefully treasured the shade through which busy housewives slipped in search of tomatoes and garlic to brighten the sad meals in the fifth year of German occupation. From the inner courtyard a vague sound of activity, of carpets being beaten and anvils struck, broke the wave of heat that pressed upon one's head and lulled one's mind. Another day of this and I would be off to Paris with Petrel. My conscience was clear: the huge pile of mail had been dealt with and despatched. Every item relating to the secret weapon, troop movements, the order of battle on the Normandy front, and railway traffic, had been transmitted according to its degree of urgency.

After indexing and classifying the reports, I sewed them into old pieces of carpeting I had found lying at the bottom of a broom cupboard. They looked like 1830 hassocks and, to make them look even more genuine, I sat down at the table in the middle of the drawing room and planted my feet on them.

Flies were dancing in the sunbeams slanting through the shutters and in the semi-darkness of the room I began to examine what I had kept as a titbit for London. Once again, it was a plot against Hitler. The source of this information was Llama, Swift's much valued general from the Military Academy. A devotee of Stendhal, he wrote his reports in a prose of unusual quality; but was he not perhaps allowing his imagination to run away with him under the influence of *La Chartreuse de Parme*?

Knowing the man only through his reports, I kept turning over the typewritten sheets. A Wehrmacht general commanding an armoured division was in touch with two friends of Llama, who gave me the names in his personal code, though I decided to camouflage them and to designate the German general by XXX and the other two by ZZZ. The gist was that XXX, who occupied a key position in the Wehrmacht, was shattered by the Führer's blindness and the German field-marshals' incompetence. Utterly incensed with the Nazis, XXX considered that Hitler must be killed. According to him the fall of the Third Reich was now only a matter of five or six weeks. XXX was therefore plotting with a number of generals (Llama supplied their names), who in this way intended to prevent the pointless slaughter of their troops. The plotters were thinking of provoking a military revolt, followed by a pure and simple withdrawal of their troops to Germany. ZZZ (Llama's friends) advised XXX first to hand over military authority in France to General Koenig, who was in command of the Fighting French Forces. They stated that the first condition put forward would be the saving of French political prisoners.

Indeed, while American and British soldiers were sacrificing their lives on the Normandy front in the cause of our liberation, the prisoners of the Gestapo were paying the same terrible price for the Allied advance. At Caen prison all the detainees had been massacred on 7 June, including those heroic Normans who had compiled the intelligence map that had made such a sterling contribution to the success of the landing the day before.

If that were to be the pattern of events throughout the ebbing of the Hitler tide, what chance would our friends have of surviving the long chain of prisons and camps that marked the road to Berlin? I trembled with fear. We must do something to ensure the success of the plot to kill Hitler, perhaps the one and only chance of curtailing their martyrdom.

The most striking feature of this story was that important personalities were implicated. The names mentioned by Llama revived memories of the old German army which in 1918 had remained loyal to the Kaiser until the final battle. The British had been suspicious of the propositions made to Benteng the previous year; now the situation was different.

Llama concluded his report by asking that his friends ZZZ be put into immediate contact with General Koenig. But I took a dim view of this part of the programme, which meant General de Gaulle authorizing the victor of Bir-Hakeim to receive the military command in France from the enemy's hands. Had they gone mad? The Nazis were all going mad. That was the intelligence fact that seemed most valuable to me. I began to code the report, my messages reading rather like the instalments of a detective novel.

The hours went by. A light scratch on the door heralded the arrival of a friend. I opened it to find Grand Duke there. He was in a great state. 'I've just seen the sub-prefect of Aix,' he said. 'The Germans are preparing to make a thorough search of the town tomorrow evening. They're out to get the men in the maquis.'

'Yes, they're expecting a landing in Provence. That means they must first mop up their rear. I've nothing to be afraid of. They're out for bigger fish than a woman travelling on her own.'

'With all the stuff you've got, I can't leave you here.'

He began to ferret around. 'Where's the "gin"?'

'The four million francs that were dropped by parachute are in the crate of potatoes under the sink.'

'And the mail?'

I pointed my foot at my pretty little hassocks.

'It's a hell of a lot,' he interrupted peremptorily. 'I'm going to take you home with me right away.'

'You can't be serious. How did you come here?'

'On my bike. You can use it. I'll walk and bring the cases.'

'But we've lots of time. The raid is not until tomorrow. Come and pick me up by car at eight o'clock in the morning. Now go back quickly and put Marie-Sol's mind at rest before the curfew begins.'

He walked towards the door with his lithe, nervous stride. I was suddenly filled with an inexplicable sense of fear. I called him back: 'Grand Duke, you might take the messages I've just finished.'

'About the plot against Hitler?'

'Yes.'

'Tell me, d'you really believe there's one?' He pocketed the sheets of squared paper as he bounded down the majestic, echoing staircase four steps at a time. In closing the door I forgot to shoot the bolt.

I suddenly felt hungry and went into the kitchen. I absent-mindedly peeled a few tomatoes and ate them, dipping them first in fresh olive oil, a royal gift from Turtle Dove's mother. Then I went back to the drawing room to tidy up. At that moment an infernal racket broke out at the main entrance and welled up the staircase. I leapt into the hall and, seeing the bolt drawn, rushed to close it. I was too late. The door was already opening. Exerting all my strength I pushed it, desperately trying to turn the key. If I succeeded I should gain the two minutes that were essential for escaping through the courtyard with the double exit. The banging on the door punctuated the orders that were being shouted in German, and mingled with the heavy breathing of a band of furious soldiers who were milling about on the other side.

'German police! Open!' I heard, just as my strength failed.

The wave surged in. There were two dozen of them, almost all in grey-green uniform. Among them were four civilians, one obviously a North African. 'Where's the man? Where's the man?' they screamed into my face, digging their revolvers into my chest. The soldiers carrying sub-machine guns gathered in a circle round me.

'What man?' I asked, putting on a bewildered look. 'I'm a woman and I'm on my own.'

'He went that way,' the North African said, pointing to the courtyard.

I flared up. 'There are other flats in the house. If you're looking for someone, why do you imagine he's in the first one you come to?'

'That's true,' said another civilian, who seemed to be in charge. 'We're wasting time. Let's go and see. You, watch her,' he said to a little soldier, who leaned against the mantelpiece and trained his gun on me. I heard the doors banging on the other landings and people shouting and protesting. In the half-light the grids of my messages glimmered on the table in the centre of the drawing room. It was a miracle that in their excitement they had noticed nothing. Under the watchdog's vigilant gaze I went back to the table and quickly piled up the papers spread over it. Then pretending to blow my nose noisily I backed towards the divan in the alcove and, slipping out of my guard's line of sight for a second, I threw the whole lot as far as possible underneath.

'What are you doing?' barked the watchdog.

'I'm blowing my nose,' I said gravely, walking over to him.

'In this heat!' he commiserated. Seeing that he was ready to chat, I asked him who they were looking for. 'A man who is causing us a lot of trouble, a terrorist.'

This was my cue and I picked it up at once. 'Someone from the maquis?' I asked, pretending to be frightened.

'*Jawohl!* Someone from the maquis. He came into this house about three-quarters of an hour ago. We were sent to get him.'

'What does he look like?' I asked in a dead voice.

'Tall and fair, apparently. The Gestapo chiefs call him Grand Duke.'

At that moment the Gestapo chiefs themselves came back, still shouting. 'He's not up there; he's got away. This woman is lying to us; she wanted to gain time,' they told the North African.

'Why did you push against the door when we wanted to come in?' shouted the leader, grabbing me by the shoulders.

'Put yourself in my place. You gave me a fine old fright. I thought you were terrorists from the maquis. I stopped as soon as I heard you shout "German police".'

'That's right,' he said, withdrawing his claws. 'What are you doing here by yourself?'

I let fly. I told them I was getting away from the bombing in Toulon, as the raids were driving me mad. I hated the war and I'd come to Aix to get some peace and quiet. It was a deliberate decision. 'Can't you go about things a bit more gently?' I added, going over to the offensive. 'I've always heard the Germans were courteous. If I'd known that you were the Gestapo I'd have opened the door right away.'

Meanwhile the soldiers and civilians had been searching the flat, turning up the mattresses and easy chairs, rummaging through the cupboards, the suitcases and the fireplaces. 'What are you hoping to find?' I went on, to keep the atmosphere relaxed.

The leader described Grand Duke, going into details about his importance, and a big network that they had not yet been able to smash, the 'Alliance'. My blood froze. So it was *us* they were after, not me. But what then? I must go on and spin out my yarn. I blundered on, making myself seem as stupid as I possibly could.

'You see how right I was to be afraid of the man from the maquis. I heartily approve of your hunting them down. Is there any way I can help?'

The ferrets returned empty-handed. 'Nothing suspicious, chief,' said the North African.

Now completely mollified, the leader lowered his revolver: 'Here's the address of our office. If the man I've described comes back here, let me know at once.'

'Are you sure he lives here? What's his name?'

'We don't know. We only know his alias. He may have come in under the porch to throw his pursuers off the scent and then got away while these idiots were raising the alarm instead of shooting him on sight.'

Once again they split up and looked through the flat. Suddenly they pointed to the pile of cigarettes on a corner of one of the pieces of furniture. 'I see you smoke Gauloises. You've got a lot. Cigarettes are rationed.'

I began to curse my vice. Why ever had I started smoking again? 'I made a swap on the black market,' I said brazening it out. 'Some people would rather have butter.'

I offered them the Made-in-England Gauloises and lit one myself. They seemed to be in no hurry and went on standing around and smoking. Then, after a few brief orders, the soldiers picked up their weapons and moved towards the door. My heart gave a leap. I had won, they *were* going. The civilians began to say goodbye, repeating their request. I gave a silent whoop of joy. Bells rang in my ears. 'They've gone, they've gone.'

Before passing through the drawing-room door, one of them suddenly went down on all fours and looked under the divan. I saw his arm shoot underneath. Carefully he pulled out the grids, looked at them and with a triumphant gesture thrust them under his colleagues' noses.

That was that. My turn had come. I tried to think only of those who had gone before me: Navarre, Eagle, Swift, Schaerrer. The glorious band gathered round me and sustained me. It was perfectly normal; it was bound to happen to me as well. Anything else would have been unfair.

Hurling abuse at me in a way that convinced me it would be better not to make a dash for it, the Gestapo began to smash the furniture with their rifle butts. They shoved me violently aside so that they could get at a pretty desk. I was swept by a terrible rage.

'Stop! Nothing here is mine, this isn't my home. The owner hasn't the least idea who I am and has locked her cupboards. Wait until tomorrow and she'll open them for you. Anyway, you're surely not going to smash up old furniture just for the sake of smashing it up!'

'But who are *you*?' asked the leader, shaking me like a plum tree.

I looked at him and his sweaty face with withering contempt. 'You're much too unimportant for me to tell you.'

'You're British?'

'No, French.'

'When did you arrive?'

'A few days ago, parachuted in the dark, not far away.'

'Who is the man who came here just now?'

'It was the first time I'd seen him. I don't know his name any more than you do.'

'What did he come for?'

'To arrange to meet me at noon tomorrow in the Place du Marché, to introduce me to someone who's to take me somewhere else.'

'Where?'

'I don't know. I do as I'm told. I just carry out orders.'

'Who is this person?'

'One of the network's agents.'

'How will you recognize him?'

'*He* will recognize *me*, by a scarf that I shall wear.' I must gain time, yes, gain time by saying anything false but plausible.

'What's your name?'

The North African had just discovered my bag and was brandishing my identity cards in the air. 'Her name is Germaine Pezet.'

I burst out laughing. 'But it's a false name, of course. We've all got false names. The identities manufactured in London are always fictitious.' Patiently, I set out to prove the opposite of what had been so carefully and solidly established to save me from any trouble on my trip.

'Come off it,' said the leader. 'Don't let's waste time. All this is obviously false; you all have the same tricks.'

I sighed with relief. Flying Fish and his real wife would be OK. In kicking up the carpets, the soldiers had burst open my little hassocks. The reports in them flew out like a swarm of butterflies, spread all over the room and were passed quickly from hand to hand. They had found some cognac, and they made the most of it. Their voices rose as anger overcame them. An NCO explained to the men the meaning of the plans and schedules at which they were goggling: '*Ach so! Geheim! Sehr geheim!*' ('So! Secret! Top Secret!') they growled. 'They're going to lynch me,' I thought. Giving way to indignation, several of them rushed at me, itching to shoot. 'Halt!' ordered the leader and, not without some difficulty and the help of his acolytes, he restored order by punching and threatening his men. Then he dragged me off sheepishly into a corner of the room.

'You don't look scared,' he said.

'I've nothing to reproach myself with.'

'Exactly!' he said and lowered his voice. 'That's what I'm beginning to think. If you're in the same business as I am we could both do ourselves a bit of good.'

'That takes the biscuit,' I thought to myself. Then it dawned on me. 'He takes me for a double agent and he's offering to go shares.'

'I don't understand what business you want to talk about,' I hedged.

'Mine only concerns me.'

'That's not helpful,' he insisted. 'At least tell me who you are.'

'I'll only tell the big Gestapo chief who I am. I haven't the right to tell you. Once again, you're too unimportant.'

He snapped an order to the North African, who ran off and then, trying his luck again, asked me about the rendezvous at the Place du Marché. 'If we take you to this rendezvous, will you be helpful and allow yourself to be accosted by your agent? God help you if you're lying. You've been leading us up the garden path for two hours. We have ways of making you talk and beg for mercy.'

'Tomorrow? Of course!'

I must gain time, I must gain time. The blood was pounding in my head. I saw the North African coming back, still running, like a figure in a nightmare. The civilians went into a huddle.

'You're lucky,' the leader said to me. 'The regional boss will be in Aix tomorrow at nine. He's willing to see you.'

'You bet he is,' I thought. 'Considering the time he's been after me, he's going to have a very pleasant surprise.'

'Meanwhile we're going to get you out of here. Pack your case.'

They were going to put me in prison. How could I raise the alarm? Grand Duke was going to arrive at eight next morning and would walk into the trap. 'I must escape tonight,' I thought, throwing a few toilet articles into my big bag. Toothbrush, toothpaste, soap, comb and a change of dress. 'I must escape to save Grand Duke, Weevil and the others. I haven't come back to France to be caught. I must save them.'

'Get a move on,' shouted the Gestapo man on guard outside the dressing room. I groped for and found the poison. If I had not discovered a solution by tomorrow. . . .

'I'm ready,' I said, and I was bundled down the stairs and into a black car that drove off with a strong escort.

I realized at once that we were heading for the prison on the Rue Rifle-Rafle near the Rue Granet, and this brought me a feeling of relief. As we drove along, the North African tried to take my hand.

'You certainly took us in, madame, you never betrayed the slightest sign of emotion, except perhaps a trembling of your fingertips; but we were quite convinced that we were on the wrong track.'

'Then why did you look under the bed?'

'An old professional reflex. But what about you? After all you're not the Queen of the Netherlands. I don't see why you refuse to tell us your name.'

'Perhaps I'm another queen,' I said, trying to put on a haughty voice.

The car had stopped and the driver had got out to inquire the way from a scared passer-by. The two Gestapo men flanking me in the back seat also got out and joined in and I was alone in the car. A man might have attempted to make a break for it through the right-hand door into the black night, or even a woman who was able to run; but I could not. They got back in and we set off again at top speed.

I had heard the words 'Miollis barracks'. So I was going to be put into a barracks. Would it be to shoot me at once? We did in fact draw up at the entrance to a barracks and I was taken through the guard room, at the back of which was the classic 'punishment cell' for recalcitrant soldiers. There were a few men in it, but they were promptly kicked out and I took their place in a suffocating fug of stale urine, sweat and German tobacco. The Gestapo man gallantly put my travelling bag at the foot of the bed, which was covered with a thick, greyish blanket.

'There you are. I'll be back at nine tomorrow to see the chief. Do you want me to leave the light on?'

'No, I mean to sleep.'

'A cigarette?'

'Why not, if it's one of mine.'

He laughed as he held out the packet. 'You're not going to commit suicide?' he asked, suddenly seized by suspicion.

'Why should I?'

'Because all British spies commit suicide as soon as they're left alone.'

'But I'm neither a spy nor British and I've no reason to commit suicide.'

'Then I needn't worry?' he asked stupidly.

'Not in the least.'

These people were incredible. They arrested you so that they could kill you and then they asked you to put their minds at rest!

The door was heavily bolted and the light hanging from the middle of the ceiling went out. I felt my way towards the right-hand corner of the window like a lost dog and was overtaken by a horrible fit of vomiting. If the oily Gestapo thugs had only known how mortally afraid I was! The tremendous effort I made to face up to this ordeal left me gasping, limp and exhausted and my head was as empty as a nutshell. 'You'd do better to go to sleep, old girl,' I chided myself, flopping onto the bed in spite of its stench, compounded of squashed bedbugs and leather badly maintained with ersatz soap. 'You'll have to sleep so as to stand up to tomorrow's interrogation.'

A Gestapo interrogation! Arrest, the possibility of being shot or of having my throat slit had been with me too long to cause me fear; but in a few hours they would open the door and they would say: 'Marie-Madeleine,'—for they would have discovered my real name during the night from the captured mail—'we've got you. Tell us what's going on in your network. Tell us what it did in the past, the inexplicable things still happening, because in spite of the hundreds of arrests, we can't wipe you out. Now we've got *you*, the most important one of all. Where is Grand Duke? Where are all the others?'

I would have no choice but to say nothing, grit my teeth, endure the beatings, the humiliations, the tortures. I should have to resist. Resisting torture was undoubtedly what Resistance meant.

The Chief's chivalrous offer came back to my mind: 'If they arrest you, my dear, tell them that I sent you to France to watch the Communist Party. They won't dare touch you.' How was I to tell them that and make them believe it when they had captured me with all that material! And the grids beneath the bed! They would read the first grid written out in clear and I should be implicated in the plot against Hitler: that was the only thing that would interest them. I knew them; they would want to drag the names of the conspirators out of me. Everything became as clear as day: their haste to get me away and out of sight, to bring in the head of the Gestapo, their pretence of friendliness. I was becoming the centre piece of a diabolical game of chess that could bring them great honour and great fortune.

To save Hitler! Better to die here and now. I sprang to my feet and rushed to find my bag. Where was it? It had fallen on the ground near the window. I opened it and felt for the pills. Should I take them now or tomorrow, when they came in? No! Before taking that irrevocable step I must try everything. . . . Escape! The idea that had been uppermost in my mind from the beginning took hold of me. Escape! Escape! Every other thought was paralysed.

I looked at my watch. It was midnight. Sounds came from the guardroom. Through the crack in the middle of the door I could make out the figures of soldiers going on duty and coming off and flopping down on their beds, eating, swigging great draughts of beer and swapping yarns. Moved by an uncontrollable impulse, I thumped on my door. The soldiers stopped talking and looked at one another. I went on hammering. A tall brute stood up and came and opened the door. I got him to understand that I wanted to go to the lavatory. He picked up his gun and went with me. We turned right as we went into the courtyard and he pointed the place out, keeping the door open with his foot. I studied the general layout, the vast courtyard embedded in the whole complex of the barracks. Not a hope. I quickly went back to my cell.

I must think of something else. I had five hours left in which to escape.

I lay down again on the bed. I was stupid; it was impossible; it would be better to go to sleep. I could not close my eyes. A faint gleam of light came from the window. I was suffocating. 'You must breathe, old girl, you're going mad.' I got up and went over to the window, a big, ordinary kind of opening, probably overlooking the street by which we had arrived. A thick wooden board screwed into the frame blocked four-fifths of it. It had undoubtedly been put there to prevent soldiers under punishment from communicating with the world outside while at the same time allowing the air, as well as a little light, to come in. But this meant that they must have removed the glass. There was, in fact, no proper window at all, only bars dimly outlined against the night.

I pushed the bed under the window, put the sanitary receptacle (a sort of big zinc washing-up bowl) upside down upon it, took off my shoes, climbed up and found I was level with the opening. I avidly gulped in the soft night air. I tried the bars with my forehead. They were not prison bars; simply the bars that are found on all ground floor windows the world over, strong and proud in their protective role. Without proper tools it was pointless to think of moving one from the uprights or of tearing down the wooden board. The problem was to slip somehow between the board and the bars and, once there, to push to get out.

I got down again. Behind my door the soldiers were playing cards. I reckoned that at three o'clock the guard would be changed and that those coming off duty would be only too glad to sleep. I carried on with my preparations. What a pity I hadn't brought Turtle Dove's olive oil. I would have smeared it all over my body like those Indo-Chinese burglars who, according to my father's stories, used to break into houses at night, their naked bodies covered with fat or grease so that they would slip more easily through the hands of anyone trying to catch them. They went about the job stark naked. I must go naked like them, to be as thin as possible. I took off my clothes and practised holding the little batik dress in my teeth and a few banknotes in my hand. The main thing was not to take anything that might make a noise if it dropped.

My watch showed three o'clock and, as I expected, there was a change of guard. The men coming in got into bed without a word and the light went out. Those men were really tired, as their snores immediately confirmed. I waited a few minutes, then got back into my batik dress and banged on my door. They were not the same men and so I could safely repeat the lavatory trick to test their vigilance. I banged on the door three separate times. No response but snores.

I undressed again and began my climb to freedom. Steadying myself at the top of the window opening and plunging feet first between the wooden plank and the bars was less difficult than I had feared; but I lost almost all my bank notes in the process. I immediately stopped trying to push my head between the bars that were set into the stonework on both sides of the frame, for only iron is likely to give. Methodically, I tried the rest of them. To my great surprise one gap seemed big enough to take my head provided I was prepared to push hard. I tried them all again. I was right; only one was big enough for me to get through. I returned to it and pushed with all my strength. My head went through.

At that precise moment a motor convoy swirled into the street from the left and drew up with a screech of brakes. It stopped opposite my window and I quickly withdrew my head, so sharply that I thought I had torn off my ears. The Gestapo were returning. They would find me, naked and pinned like a beetle against this board that scraped my back. What an idiot I was to have waited so long! The NCO in charge of the convoy began to shout: the raucous voice of a sentry posted a few yards to the right answered. I hadn't seen him! And I was counting on fleeing in that direction. . . . A dialogue started. The convoy had missed its way; it turned and went back. It was not the Gestapo. As it went by I saw that it was a unit that we had told London was being sent to reinforce the Normandy front. The trucks disappeared, their headlights glowing like cats' eyes, just above ground level.

Pushing my head through again was even more painful than the first time, but the pain and the fear of failure made me perspire profusely, which helped my skin to slip against the iron. After my neck I got one shoulder through, then my right leg. Squeezing my hips through was sheer agony. The pain was appalling but I knew that once the head is through the rest of the body will go, while the pain I felt would be nothing compared with what would be in store for me with the Gestapo.

I suddenly found myself down on the pavement, but the slight thud of my feet as I dropped to the ground had attracted the sentry's attention. I wrapped my dress round my neck and crouched down. '*Wer da?*' The soldier flashed his torch and its beam swept the darkness. I lay flat on the ground. I must get away quickly! Summoning up all my remaining energy I crossed the square on all fours and began to move as fast as my legs would let me, first straight ahead, then dodging from side to side, out into the vague open space that I could just make out. I ran on, stumbling into the potholes and tearing my skin on the brambles. At last, no longer hearing any sounds behind me, I put on my dress. I was free. Free! But if the sentry had raised the alarm, they would send dogs after me and I should be found in no time.

The whitish outlines of the stone crosses in a cemetery caught my eye. Here there was safety. I could hide in one of the chapels. In the morning I could be sure of finding a priest who would help me, or a grave digger who would take pity on me. I plunged into the cemetery and sat down on a tombstone to rest.

The thought of the dogs and how to escape them obsessed me. But an episode in a childhood book came back to mind; the story of an escaping officer who had put the dogs off the scent by washing his hands for a long time in a stream. But no river flowed through Aix, except a stream that skirted the city to the east—the Torse. The road that I was now following ran due east, so, rolling and tumbling down a stony bank, I eventually found the Torse—a thin thread of water, but big enough for me to wash in. I began with my feet and then washed my raw, badly skinned face for a long time.

Which direction must I take to get to Grand Duke's farm? It looked in fact as if I had to start all over again and go back through the town. The very idea terrified me. If need be I could go to the radio operator, Weevil, but would he have time to warn everybody? At half-past seven Grand Duke would leave his farm and go to pick me up at the flat on the Rue Granet and he would walk into the trap. I was ashamed of my hesitations.

So I retraced my steps. In the dawning light that in Provence spreads swiftly in an immense haze of gold and birdsong, I found myself close to the barracks once more. Everywhere was quiet; the sentry was lost in his own thoughts and saw me appear without interest. How could the German suspect that the person coming by was the prisoner who had escaped? I walked past him, proud and dignified, but panic seized me once I had turned the corner. I ran feverishly up a path that looked like an Arab street and went into a garden where I crouched down among the hollyhocks. It was too much; I could not move.

Then the thought of Grand Duke being arrested because of my cowardice drove me on. I dashed up to a very simple little house and began to hammer on the shutters. After a long delay a woman opened them. She was altogether unpleasant—dishevelled, rheumy-eyed and stinking of garlic. I mumbled that I was fleeing from the bombing and had lost my way in the curfew.

'Clear off! If you don't go away and let us sleep, I'll call the police,' she barked, threatening me with a broom. With that she barricaded herself in.

I set off again, my legs trembling. In the barracks the bugle would soon be sounding reveille. In ten minutes time they would be opening my cell to take in some food.

By a miracle I came out in the centre of the town. A woman in deep mourning was clearly on her way to mass. I went up to her and said: 'Madame, I lost my way during the curfew, I'm looking for the Vauvenargues road.'

'Come with me, I'm going that way.'

She started walking again, not too quickly, so that I could pad along barefoot behind her. 'Would you like to lean on me?' she asked. 'You seem to be in pain.'

I leaned on her arm. The city was awake and passers-by looked at me in surprise. The woman in mourning appeared to me like a marvellous bulwark against the dogs I could hear barking in the distance and the armoured cars dashing across the square. That was it! They had discovered my escape. They were going to close the roads out of the town. I saw with horror that we were heading for the very street where I had been staying. We crossed one square, then another, and when we reached the corner of the Sainte-Marie-Madeleine church, my protectress parted from me.

'Go straight on. Past the convent you'll find the Vauvenargues road. Cross the Torse.'

'Thank you. You've undoubtedly done me the greatest service any one has ever done me in my life.'

I left her standing there, looking intrigued, while I walked on and disappeared, a quarter of a mile further on, into the gardens running down to the wild little valley leading to Sainte-Victoire. I was back where I had started.

How was I going to cross the bridge over the Torse? It was bound to have been guarded since my escape had been discovered. I crept through terraces and leapt over piles of stones and found myself in a field in which some old peasant women were busy gleaning. I began to do the same, picking up ears of corn and bits of dandelion. Out of the corner of my eye I could see the German soldiers setting up road blocks, striding up and down the bridge, stopping all the women who went over it and checking their papers. But they paid not the slightest attention to the gleaners below. I moved forward, bending double and finally came out on the road a long way beyond the soldiers.

Seven o'clock. I should be in time to warn Grand Duke. One, two, three bends. Where was the farm? They all looked alike in their setting of olives and cypresses. At last I saw it, a cool oasis nestling among its geraniums. One more hill, a stream to cross, two bends. The front door was unlocked—how careless Grand Duke and Marie-Sol were! I went into the hall. I called out and pushed open their bedroom door. They were up and on their feet in a flash, naked, healthy and beautiful, their wide, staring eyes brimming over with loyalty as I heard myself saying: 'I've just escaped. I've saved your lives.' Then everything around me became confused and I collapsed.

Grand Duke took me off to a hideout, the place where he stored his arms and equipment further along the road to Vauvenargues. Turtle Dove was the first to visit me there. She brought me a new blouse and a peasant skirt. 'Well!' she exclaimed. 'They're turning the town upside down, but we haven't been touched. Weevil is bringing the radio by roads that are little used.'

I heard a rustle of leaves. Was it the enemy? No, it was Petrel, Georges Lamarque, punctual as ever, even when the rendezvous had suddenly been switched to a strange new place.

'Here you are at last!' he said, examining the marks of my escape with a grin. 'Not much point in having a nice long rest in England just to come and do that to us as soon as you get back.'

'Who told you, Petrel? I'm absolutely ashamed.'

'It's not your fault. Let's forget it. You must go to Paris right away. Our people are getting impatient.'

'Do you expect her to go to Paris in her bare feet?' said Grand Duke vehemently. 'You can see for yourself, she can hardly get into a pair of shoes. Wait until her feet have healed.'

'No,' I said. 'I must repair the damage that's been done here and order another parachute drop.' I arranged to meet Petrel in Marseilles in a few days.

Night descended on the hills round Aix. Grand Duke, Weevil and I were alone in the grassy, sweet-smelling, little garden.

'It's time to go back and get some rest,' said Grand Duke.

'I shall never be able to sleep in a house again. I'd rather listen for strange sounds out in the open. Then if anything at all happens I shall be ready.'

The two men distributed the sub-machine guns and, suddenly overcome by the events of the last thirty-six hours, I lay down and slept until dawn.

A loud humming roused me from my sleep. Through the pink rays flung out by the rising sun I saw Grand Duke, Sten gun at the ready, watching the Vauvenargues road that wound its way round the spur of the hill.

'Don't be afraid,' he said smiling, 'they're Messerschmitts out on patrol from the base nearby.'

'Why are you watching the road?'

'Because I'm expecting the Germans to come up to the maquis and because we must go there tonight! And just in case we have to make a forced march, I'm going to do something about your feet. Imagine that I'm the Gestapo,' he said in a fierce voice, dabbing my blisters with God knows what: 'Marie-Madeleine, where is Grand Duke? Who is the man who wants to kill Hitler?'

We were choking with laughter when Weevil emerged from his blankets. 'My contact,' he muttered. 'My contact. I'm going to miss my contact.' And he hitched his aerial to a cypress tree.

I was thrilled to watch the oft-repeated miracle of transmission. After receiving the thousands of coded messages on my desk in London, I was now seeing them again, but this time direct from the battlefield. I had had to code the story of my own adventure myself, taking great care not to omit the security check that meant 'I'm free.' I knew that I should get by return an innocent-seeming message that would mean 'Are you really free?' and that I should be obliged to reply in the affirmative by employing other phrases to indicate that I was indeed safe. That would involve a lot of risks for Weevil, but London needed to be absolutely certain before sending help.

Contact was made without a hitch. Then the agents began to come in, the brothers Descatoire (Roach I and II), Boar, White Stone, head of the Aix-en-Provence city sector, and Turtle Dove, her basket full of fresh food. They took it in turns to go to and fro to bring us the latest news.

It had been possible to warn Flying Fish, but since my escape the Gestapo had been on the rampage. Mlle de Weerdt had courageously gone to the *Kommandanture* to complain that her flat was being used as a trap.

'It's a very serious matter,' she was told. 'The woman captured at your house is a highly dangerous spy. When and to whom did you rent your flat?'

'A little more than a year ago, to a M. Pierre Delille. . . .'

'It's ridiculous. This man has been in the area for over a year and we didn't know. He's also a very important agent.'

'British agents! How dreadful! And who is the woman? I don't know her!'

'That's what she said too. She had hidden some documents of the greatest importance under your bed. We've taken her to prison.'

'That's splendid.'

'Yes, but unfortunately she has escaped, naked, naked, mark you, stark naked, leaving all her clothes behind.'

'You don't say! And have you also arrested the man?'

'We cornered him somewhere else.'

Quite certain that the truth was quite otherwise, Mlle de Weerdt agreed with alacrity to let them know if her wicked tenant put in an appearance again and she went away free.

What an extraordinary way to behave! On the one hand unusual obsequiousness, on the other outbursts of rage. And they had shot the NCO in charge of the guard at the Miollis Barracks. Something in the enemy's behaviour had changed.

'And no wonder,' roared Boar, arriving from Aix for the third time that day. 'A bomb has gone off between Hitler's legs. The Wehrmacht almost seized power.'

I was shaken to the core. 'The plot. My reports.'

'Forget them,' said Grand Duke. 'It's time we took to the maquis.'

So we took to the maquis. Night fell with its usual suddenness and soon we were three shadowy figures on the Vauvenargues road. Grand Duke, Roach and I were bowed down by the weight of our weapons and bags. Twelve miles uphill! Our footsteps echoed loudly on the rough surface of the road. We listened intently and dived into the prickly undergrowth at the slightest sound. We lay flat on our stomachs in the dusty ditches; again and again we set off, then dashed for cover when headlights appeared, only to pass on. They were German cars every time. The night seemed never-ending, and my two companions had soon to support my entire weight. I begged them to go ahead and leave me in some hollow, I was so terrified that they would be discovered by a patrol.

'No,' said Grand Duke stubbornly. 'We must first get within sight of Vauvenargues, where we have helpers.'

As the southern dawn broke the delicate turrets of the chateau came into sight, an unreal vision against the unforgettable backcloth of the Sainte-Victoire mountain. I collapsed; my torn feet refused to take another step and my legs were numb. My companions soon organized things and a strange-looking equipage quickly arrived, a squeaking cart drawn by a sturdy mule. The road became steeper and steeper as it wound up into the wild scrub. Sainte-Victoire sparkled and the hamlet of Claps appeared in the rising sun, a dazzle of ancestral stones and rural ruins. A few whispered passwords and an old, half-starved, scraggy-looking couple ventured out and came across to us. I felt myself lifted down, carried away and deposited in the safety of the only house still standing, rather like the decor of a romantic operetta. The woman offered me some hot coffee and suggested that I go to bed.

Grand Duke was busy organizing the place as a fortified camp. We had enough to withstand a siege. The parachute drop that I had arranged in London was laid out before my eyes. Boots, battledress, weapons and food, with the basic ingredients Spam and powdered coffee. The troops were dispersed. The outlying spur that overhung the road would shelter the lookouts in a nest of juniper trees. A special corner was set aside for the radio operator, Weevil, who would use batteries and an aerial slung from a twisted pine. I held my conference in a clearing a few hundred yards away, on the slopes of Cezanne's Sainte-Victoire. Grand Duke stayed in the ruins. I went back into the open at once to think about the day's messages.

A flood of information was pouring in, about the German troops' hurried dash to the Normandy front, the reinforcement of certain coastal areas, the results of the bombing raids. Boar arrived with a screech of weary wheels and left again, only to return two hours later.

'Another recruit for the maquis!' he shouted. 'I just missed being arrested on the way down. I prefer your chateau to theirs.' He told us what had happened: his address found on a courier, the trap spotted in the nick of time, his flight. In my clearing, with its moonlight shadows, we were gathered round a tiny wood fire, each of us buried in his own thoughts and turning over his own particular problems.

'But what about your cell bars, chief?' one of them asked me. 'Tell us how you hit upon the idea.'

'It just came into my head,' I replied. 'What astonished me was that, after trying them all, only one of the gaps held out any hope of getting my head through.'

A laugh burst from the throat of the *dinamitero* who was stirring his brushwood fire, a fire of embers that would be invisible from any real distance. How long would you have to live in the maquis before you could make one like that? Fascinated, I watched him keep it going, but his words pulled me up with a jerk.

'Ah, *señora*, I believe you. I'm a mason and I've put up bars in prisons and cells.' We all drew closer to the fire and into the sweet-smelling smoke. 'Yes, I've put bars up, so I can tell you how it happens. When the cement is still fresh, and after the officials have come in with their measures to check the gap, we always push one of the bars a bit with our thumb. That was the bar, *señora*, that allowed your head to go through. We call it the bar of freedom.'

Later, like shadows, the men slipped away to their lairs one by one. I remained alone in the shelter of a bush, huddled under my blankets, with the silhouette of the man on guard a score of yards away, outlined against a sky brilliant with beauty.

Each morning I slipped back to the house-that-was-still-standing to wash and dress for the day. I was able to do so because the enamel water jug was miraculously filled by the old revolutionary crone. Standing guard behind the porch while I washed and sponged down, she was as watchful as a snake. And so, when she whistled, I came up in a flash from the depths of the jug, knowing there was trouble. A glance through the shutters told me that the village was surrounded. One second to remember that Grand Duke was at the radio set, another to grab my gun, a third to decide to sacrifice my life by making as much noise as possible to warn the others and give them a chance to get away. I flung the window wide open and knocked down two startled men who were attempting to get in.

'Don't shoot, madame,' they implored. 'We're Puma and Pika.'

'That's a lie!'

'We swear we are, we've got the information from Montpellier. Turtle Dove told us to come here.' Their faces looked too kind for me to fire, but as they backed away I began to blame myself for being weak. I put my finger back on the trigger.

'Don't shoot!' yelled Grand Duke, who had been alerted by the lookout and arrived panting. 'They're agents of ours.'

Grand Duke was a real war leader. Here he was absolutely in his element and had foreseen everything in this maquis, even the patrol times of the Fieseler Storch, the German spotter plane that flew over us several times a day.

The alarm was raised. A line of trucks filled with men in uniform was coming up the hill. The awful fear of being recaptured seized me. With an agility that I thought I had lost for ever, I began to retreat, scrambling up the stony mountain tracks. Then, turning round, I saw Grand Duke making signs for me to stop. It was not long before he was beside me.

'The convoy has passed Claps. They're Senegalese prisoners of war the Germans are taking to work on the road over the mountain pass they need for withdrawing their troops from Toulon. I'm pleased to see, madame, that your feet are now all right! Thank God it'll soon be time for the rendezvous with Petrel.'

'And *you*, Grand Duke, must not go back to Aix. They'll get you the moment you arrive.'

'I won't go into hiding,' he retorted. 'The parachute drop you asked for has been agreed on. Let's take advantage of the fact that everything's going so smoothly and deal the final blows.'

I had had my photograph taken, with hair dyed and in a different style. The new forged identity card gave Vauvenargues as my birthplace. On 29 July, riding pillion and tightly pressed against the leather jacket of a member of the maquis, and trying to keep my balance, I watched the Claps *maquisards* gradually disappear from sight. Knowing they were there I could, for a long time, make out the slim figure of Grand Duke, the flamboyant Roaches, the black chiselled bust of the old Spanish woman, and the bodies of the old mason, Weevil, Boar, and of our couriers, Lion Cub and Sea Urchin, crawling in the grass and discreetly waving to console me and to wish me luck.

The motorcycle, obviously badly maintained, misfired dangerously as it chugged up the pass. We went through the cohort of black workmen and a Wehrmacht picket who glanced at our forged papers without showing the slightest interest: 'Peasants from Vauvenargues? You can go!' he said. To save petrol we free-wheeled down the wonderful hill that was taking me to the final phase—Liberation.

I turned my back on Sainte-Victoire, Cezanne's holy mountain, and upon the slopes where in the year 102 BC the Teuton hordes were defeated by the Roman general Marius. Shad, the head of Sea Star, was waiting for me at Saint-Maximin and I got into his official car while my comrade of the maquis disappeared, bound for new missions.

37 FLUCTUAT...

Marseilles looked very different in 1944. I had left on 11 November 1942, on the eve of the full German occupation, and I now found the city scarred by the ugly stigmata inflicted by the destruction of the Old Port and the blind bombing of certain allegedly strategic points that we had never mentioned as such because they were of no value to the enemy.

Ready for me was a set of full mourning: a dress and a black woollen coat, a bonnet and crepe veil that came down to the waist, jet black stockings and patent leather shoes—the ideal garb for the brilliant day at the end of a Mediterranean July, the sort of day one dreamed of swim suits and a cool sea. I donned my uniform. The shoes pinched and hurt my feet horribly. As quickly as I could, I left Petrel's HQ down south.

I had to go through the station barrier and find a seat in the train on my own this time. I did so with poignant memories of the earlier journeys with my former companions, now alas vanished from the scene—Eagle, Wolf, Jack Tar. When the train began to draw out of the station I saw first Georges Lamarque (our Petrel) his shirt unbuttoned and his whole chest bared; then, to my surprise, Henri Battu (Opossum), looking very smart, dressed as usual in a Lyons silk shirt and a suit of fine Scottish cloth, appear in the corridor. I rushed out and leaned against the window beside him. The train was puffing along by the Etang de Berre and we could see the oil tanks standing quite untouched.

'How do you come to be on the train, Opossum?' I whispered.

'I've come to keep an eye on you. As soon as Petrel told me the good news about your return, I felt I just had to escort you.'

'And Christiane, your sweet wife, who was so kind that evening when we were waiting for Eagle to come in the Lysander?'

He suppressed the grimace of pain that for a moment flashed over his face. 'Captured, like the rest, taken east, not a word. It's pointless working for the underground now. The Gestapo have us taped, they'll take us back with them. You wonder what they're waiting for.'

At Avignon the air raid sirens began wailing and it was already night by the time we reached Lyons. In the station itself the train shunted to and fro in a disturbing way for hours, then it finally decided to take shelter in the tunnel, where we spent the night. At dawn we emerged, only to stop again. I saw Petrel enjoying a shower on the platform with the help of buckets of water that some railwaymen were throwing over him. He had got to know them all since he'd been travelling around.

Another day passed, then a night in another tunnel. As we approached Paris the tracks, which had been hastily repaired after each raid, were very uneven, and finally, coming to a mountain of rubble, the locomotive gave up.

Petrel and Opossum walked past my compartment, beckoning me to get out. I followed them and we found ourselves in a devastated, blackened square with people milling around among cases and bags.

'Come on, we'll find the Dijon road.' I continued to trail after them, shambling along in my crippling shoes and wondering why on earth we were going back to Marseilles on foot.

'Will you explain why we're walking back?' I demanded.

'Fathead! We're going to stop the first lorry before it gets to the train, where there'll be a hell of a scramble.'

A large steam-driven lorry appeared, carrying a huge pile of charcoal in sacks. I was hauled to the top, where my crepe veils and the charcoal made one solid block and I could at last take the vices off my feet. Petrel and Opossum settled down beside me.

'They didn't make too many difficulties,' I murmured.

'Money talks. Give them the cash and you get the carry. That's real solidarity! It's more expensive than travelling by Pullman.'

The capital appeared, without a sign of smoke, like a dead city. The lorry stopped. We took a bicycle-taxi, crossed Paris and arrived at a cosy little flat—the Druids' headquarters—and a hot bath. I was back at last! But would I be able to do a useful job after so much time had been wasted?

In Paris I had to look like a Parisienne. I did my hair in the latest fashion, wore a tailored beige corduroy suit and the famous shoulder bag that all the women carried, like bus conductresses. I felt so unrecognizable that all my strength flooded back.

The first contact I made with the Alliance was with the tenacious Emile Hédin (Beaver). He was waiting for me on a seat near the Grenelle Metro station with a bunch of flowers, and when he presented them to me without a word I felt that it was bringing me the affection of all our brave people and the friendship of all the members of my old network.

'It's horrible, Beaver. Where are all our friends? And you? What a miracle it is to see you again!'

He was a ghost telling a story from beyond the tomb. The tragedies of Cricket, Seagull, Tiger, Mandrill. If I had but seen all the slaughter!

'It was enough to drive one mad at times,' he concluded. 'After Eagle's fall I thought we'd had it, that we were finished. Afterwards Swift made me run all over France and then he was caught. After that I travelled for Dragon and then he was caught.' Beaver suddenly seized my hands: 'They mustn't get you.'

'So you, too, have made the acquaintance of prison bars, Marie-Madeleine. I brought mine back with me,' Jean Sainteny (Dragon) said triumphantly, waving a piece of iron.

We both laughed. He told me about his arrest, due to a radio operator he had just taken on, who was a Gestapo agent; of how he had escaped; then his headlong flight into Paris and his return to the network, where they were at first terrified to see him reappear and finally convinced of the truth of his story.

'They're despicable. They tell you anything in order to confuse you after you're dazed from torture. You don't know what it's like to be in their clutches.'

'I made damned sure I didn't stay,' I said. 'Now we must see that you're not recaptured. You can be evacuated by bomber or by sea, whichever you like.'

'I'd rather cross the lines on a motorcycle.'

'Have you got someone to take you?'

'Yes, Bernard de Billy, the young fellow who runs the bar near the Arc de Triomphe. But I'd like to take the mail.'

'I'll get all the intelligence reports from the Paris region for you.'

Early the following morning I met Jacques Formery (Halibut), a member of Sea Star, who was the present head of the intelligence headquarters. A mass of papers revived unhappy memories of the Aix-en-Provence experience. Halibut was ploughing systematically through an almost impossible crop of reports, for we no longer had any very clear idea when the information would be sent. Only the radio messages were really vital and together we got down to sorting them out, leaving aside the documents that might be useful for Dragon's meeting with the Allied staff when he crossed the lines.

At the end of the morning Pierre Noal (Grouse) appeared, a young doctor attached to the blood transfusion centre. From now on he would handle our remaining agents in the entire northern zone. He was one of the bravest men one could meet. Indefatigable, and with iron nerves. I soon saw he was incredibly daring. He was delighted when I made use of his natural drive by giving him a few extra questionnaires, since he complained about the lack of material, and I co-opted him to help with the parachute drop I was expecting on 7 August on the Corot landing ground, ordered from Claps.

Broadcasts from London asked me to restart all possible activity in the Bordeaux-La Rochelle and Strasbourg-Nancy sectors. The system of broadcasting into the void was a great improvement and helped to settle the thorny question as to who should act first. At mutually agreed times, the main station in England twice transmitted the messages from London; all we had to do was to pick them up without ourselves transmitting. That allowed us to initiate the contact only when we had something of top priority.

The orders from London clearly implied that the liberation of Paris was imminent. I had naturally refused to take the Lysander during the last moon, as Kenneth Cohen had begged me to do. But was it right for me to expect to be picked up in the capital?

Since our job was not yet over and I was being asked to actuate distant strategic sectors, I organized the final patrols. On the 16th Dragon would cross the lines. On the 18th Halibut would leave Paris for the central south-west *départements* with all the directives affecting Bordeaux and La Rochelle, and if Hoplite (Zakovitch) succeeded in getting through he would go to Toulouse to give Petrel's train dynamiters a radio set. The northern sectors would be detached from Paris as soon as it was liberated and switched to the east, where I had decided to transfer my headquarters.

The decision to transfer to the east was one to which Lamarque, Noal (Grouse) and I had given much thought. Now that the liberation for which they had laboured so assiduously and suffered so sorely was as good as achieved, we no longer felt justified in thrusting our people into new ventures. And so we ourselves volunteered for Nancy and Strasbourg. For Grouse there was only one course open: 'I'm going with you!' he said. 'The war stops in Berlin!'

Moreover, to be honest, we were in the dark about the liberation of Paris. We received lots of reports, some of them contradictory. The bridges known to be mined would be blown up; nests of fierce resistance would be organized in the Bois de Boulogne and the Bois de Vincennes, where ammunition was being dumped; systematic destruction was planned, notably of various mains, pipelines and electric cables. Men between the ages of 16 and 45 had been conscripted to dig shelters six feet deep at the approaches to the capital, along the roads leading to the front, and vast numbers of anti-tank defences had been fixed. The stationing of a certain number of formations on the outskirts suggested to many that a defensive shock line was being established.

To intelligence veterans like ourselves the whole proceeding looked more like a manoeuvre intended to give enemy troops time to withdraw from central and southern France. What we had been witnessing for several days was the impressive rout of entire units that crossed Paris from west to east by Metro or the outer Paris railway to regroup in huge lines made up of any and every sort of vehicle, ranging from heavy lorries to push chairs, all requisitioned by the retreating Wehrmacht.

Other reports were extremely reassuring. General de Gaulle's chief commissioner of police had arrived secretly to occupy the police head-quarters building, still under Vichy control. An agreement was certainly going to be concluded between General von Choltitz, the new German commander, and the Swedish Consul, Raoul Nordling, that Paris should not be destroyed. Benteng, who saw Nordling every day, confirmed this. So, if Paris was to be left intact, why should these poor people be killed in the streets? I could hourly see more and more atrocities being perpetrated:

young boys caught in cross-fire from a couple of sub-machine guns at a crossroads, women dodging to escape the bullets, clutching their babies to their breasts. Such a sense of chaos was born of the tense atmosphere that my anguish was almost as intense as it had been at the time of the capitulation.

On 16 August, as planned, Dragon (Sainteny) left Paris carrying information and messages, riding pillion behind his friend Bernard de Billy. They had disguised themselves as telephone engineers. Two days later, when I was with my dear Ladybird (Mme Berne-Churchill), who was once again together with Chinchilla, Dragon phoned us from a neighbouring cafe. Why had he come back? It was tempting the Devil, all this coming and going through the lines.

He had sent my messages to London on General Patton's headquarters transmitter. The Americans were delighted with our information and with his personal observations in the course of his trip. They had thought there was nothing before them, but he had been able to point out the existence of several defence lines. In particular, the German Panzers from Picardy had taken up a position in the Chevreuse valley. Then the head of G2 branch had asked him to get as much more information as possible, especially about troop concentrations in the Bois de Boulogne and the Bois de Vincennes, the mining of bridges, and so on.

'It's becoming increasingly clear,' I said, 'that apart from this delaying line, the Germans have only one aim—to retreat with all speed to the Rhine and save what they can. They are obviously no longer able to stand a siege in Paris against both an uprising and the arrival of the Allied forces. The troops crossing the capital need the Paris bridges because those further downstream have been cut. They won't be blown up. The Allies can come.'

'How can we prove that to them? I believe it's essential to invest Paris as quickly as possible, if only to save it from epidemics and starvation.'

'The quicker the better, since Von Choltitz is no fool. He's saving the German army, make no mistake about that. What's more, he hasn't enough fuel to set Paris on fire, his vehicles badly need every drop he has. Take a look at the reports.'

'I'm as convinced as you are,' said Dragon. 'Hurry up and let me have your papers so that I can cross the lines again before dark.'

We all got busy, flattening the bits of paper, and Dragon hid them in the pocket of an old pair of trousers.

'Let's hope that the Americans let Leclerc's troops enter Paris first,' he said, going off to find Bernard de Billy, who was waiting for him at the corner of the street.

'Let's go,' said Dragon, having rolled the trousers up in the sweaters and shirts that were already bulging out of the motorcycle saddlebag. They took the road to the front again. Suddenly, four men in camouflage, their helmets covered with leaves, bounced out of a ditch, and, pointing their sub-machine guns at our men, ordered them to stop. Billy tried to explain that they had been sent to repair the telephone lines damaged in the battle. The Germans methodically searched the bag.

Not finding anything unusual—Dragon kept a close eye on the grey trousers—the four Germans took equally long putting the clothes back tidily. They consulted one another and finally pushed the two motor-cyclists over to a house near the side of the road and shut them up, leaving the motorcycle outside. Getting out was child's play.

After Billy had shown the GIs in the front line the safe conduct directing that he should be given all possible help, they reached Patton's headquarters without any further delays and handed over the papers. Two days later De Gaulle landed on an airfield in Normandy and took charge of the wounded body of France.

To be able to get through the German army in retreat was an undertaking that needed careful planning. Before I could leave I had to acquire a new false identity and a friendly police commissioner in the Paris suburbs offered to make me one immediately. To go out to his office I hired one of the tandem taxis to be found around the Madeleine district at prices that were grossly inflated because of the general scarcity of transport, and the driver, who demanded a thousand francs a trip plus three thousand for going to the suburbs, left me to do all the pedalling when we went uphill. But it was well worth the effort to get an excellent identity card in the name of Jeanne Imbert, nurse-secretary.

This identity was made out to fit in with the scheme devised by Grouse (Pierre Noal). He had borrowed a superb ambulance, the red cross being the only emblem that would still enable us to get through the roadblocks set up by the Germans at crossroads. And it was as an ambulance that we were going to make for Verdun, in eastern France, where Finch (Robert Rivat) was waiting for us.

Petrel (Lamarque) and his chief of staff, Louis de Clerq, would go by tandem to Nancy where Starling, the sector chief, had laid everything on for them. Once our Verdun and Nancy headquarters had been set up we would establish contact with one another and material to be parachuted would enable us to carry on in both places and then to advance to the Rhine and beyond. London was informed.

Before getting into the ambulance I asked Grouse to give me his word that there was nothing compromising on board. We had decided to pass ourselves off as collaborators—the only feasible alibi—and it was essential that our story should be watertight in case the ambulance was searched. 'Don't worry,' Grouse assured me. 'The cases you're eyeing so suspiciously contain medicines only.'

Night was falling by the time we reached La Ferté-sous-Jouarre, the small town that had been the GHQ in the phoney war. At every crossroads we were stopped and questioned, then warmly congratulated for remaining loyal collaborators. Our 'withdrawal' was guaranteed by the master race, who were going to reorganize their defence in their own country. We nodded our approval.

We overtook the main stream of the German army as day was breaking and arrived at Verdun well ahead of it. The shutters of Finch's little house were closed and I said I would like to breathe some pure air. 'Don't open them,' he said. 'The Paris Gestapo are in the hotel opposite.'

So staying there was out of the question and even more so any thought of using the transmitters. 'I'm sending you out into the country,' Finch explained. 'The schoolmaster, Emile Jacquemin (Lilac), who organizes the Lilas landing ground that you know about, is waiting for us in Brabant-en-Argonne.'

'Let's see what you're doing first.' Verdun possessed an excellent nursery of agents. 'As soon as we have our radio sets,' I began.

'But your sets are here,' said Grouse.

'What d'you mean, here?'

'With us in the ambulance.'

'Grouse, you swore. . . .'

'I'd put the crystals and the schedules in the medicine chest. A bird in the hand's worth two in the bush.'

'And there was I, feeling so easy in my mind at the German road blocks! Anyway, all this equipment is useless. As Finch is compelled to stay here, I don't see how we're going to be able to transmit from Lilac's house.'

'Lilac has just taken in a navigator-radio operator who parachuted down from an American Flying Fortress.'

'That's the last straw. The whole Feldgendarmerie will be out looking for him. And that's where you're sending us to?'

At Brabant-en-Argonne, Lilac's little house was as fresh as a lily and his wife and two daughters gave us the warmest of welcomes. At the bottom of the garden a low-browed young man, whose dark brown hair hung untidily down over his eyes, was lounging about disconsolately. The small cuffs of his shirt and the narrow trousers at once revealed his distant origin.

'Welcome, first liberator,' I said as soon as I saw him.

'At last someone who speaks American! When do I get away from here?'

'Take it easy. These brave people have saved your life. I don't imagine you want to get them shot by asking them to take you back to the States.'

'So I'm going to finish the war here?'

'If you want to get back to your bombers you must help us.'

'I can't help the underground! If I were captured I should be treated as a *franc-tireur*. I'm a soldier. I'm entitled to the protection of the Hague Convention. I benefit from the prisoner-of-war statute.'

'So we're not soldiers?'

'Such is war!'

'If war is that, you're going to stay here and rot.'

He changed his tune. 'What d'you want me to do?'

'You're a radio operator. Here's a set. You'll make contact with London; in the first message you send I'll announce that you're safe and sound. Is that OK?'

'OK! But I'll keep my identity discs.' He had one on each wrist, one on each ankle and a spare one round his neck.

Several dreary days went by. Radio contact with London was not established. A remarkable amount of information piled up. Grouse and I were furious not to be able to pass it on. The never-ending flight to Luxembourg and the Rhine bridges would soon leave the whole of Lorraine empty. Verdun was protected only by the mining of certain roads and a few machine-gun nests. Given full knowledge of the facts, the Allies could push ahead and liberate the eastern marches in one swoop. In a few days the war could be won in France. With such high stakes to play for, we decided to abandon the uncertainties of the radio and send our information across the lines. Groups of couriers were formed and our agents were despatched to meet General Patton's army.

One afternoon, Starling (Gaston Grosbety), head of the Nancy sector, appeared. Petrel (Lamarque) had arrived safely and had immediately made contact with London. Worried at no longer hearing from me, Stronghold asked him to make inquiries about my fate. In addition, Petrel wanted my permission to advance the planned parachute drop, as he was ready to push on. I handed Starling a message for London, giving details about my position. The following day Petrel arrived in person with Louis de Clerq on their tandem. I reproached him for being so careless.

'In our job,' he said, 'it isn't carelessness when it's justified. We had to work together.'

We walked to the edge of a little stream and, lying in the grass, reviewed history. The landing in the south had been successful. Paris was free. Petrel proposed to continue his advance so as to cross the Rhine before the Wehrmacht. He already saw himself in the Black Forest.

'D'you think we need to push on so far?'

'It's my duty. Besides there are those young women that I feel I've sent to their death—Humming Bird and Amniarix. If there's any hope of their still being alive, *I'm* the one who must open their prison doors, I and no one else.'

'Oh, Petrel, I'm afraid we shall have to wait another winter for the battle of Germany.'

'That would be monstrous! There's nothing ahead. Only a few service units protecting the general retreat. The bulk of Hitler's troops are pouring back across the Rhine. We must arrive hard on their heels to have any chance of finding our friends alive.'

'That's the fear that's haunting me. Only a lightning advance can make the Gestapo let go. If the Nazis are allowed time to turn round again there'll be a massacre. You know what they're like—no quarter, no mercy.'

'That's another reason for pushing on.'

'Just you, on your own? No, Petrel, believe me. The only thing we can do is to go on gathering information and with it to try to persuade our allies to advance as rapidly as possible. I'll wait here for Patton's army. You'll wait for Patch's army. Push them! Push them on as far as possible!'

'Count on me, Marie-Madeleine,' he said, getting up. 'Goodbye. I've got twelve miles to do but it'll be quicker with two pairs of legs.' He called Louis de Clerq over. 'Say goodbye to the lady,' he said.

'Petrel,' I tried again, 'don't go, stay here another day or two. We'll arrange a parachute drop together. This sector is much quieter than yours.' I could think of no other excuse to keep them.

'See you soon,' he called out as he set off, bending like a ballerina over his twin cyclist, who was also laughing with delight and pleasure at preceding such a leader on the warpath.

Streaming back, the retreating Wehrmacht began to choke every village, and one evening we learned that Brabant-en-Argonne, too, was going to be occupied. Would defences be organized around Verdun?

'My belief is that they're regrouping to count their numbers before crossing the Rhine,' said Grouse.

'But we can't stay on in Lilac's place with the transmitter and the American.'

'Of course not. Finch suggests we set up a maquis in the Hesse forest. It's almost impenetrable, and at least we shan't compromise anyone if we're discovered there.'

For greater safety we spent the night in a disused barn with Finch and the American. The ambulance was hidden in the entrance. We had to leave it there so that we could set off as soon as day broke in Musk Deer's cart. Musk Deer was a tall, craggy peasant, as solid as a rock.

Dawn broke to a multitude of sounds, with the village being commandeered. Dull thuds rang on the barn door.

'Open up, open up.' bawled an unpleasant voice.

'I'm going down,' I said to Grouse. 'When they see it's only a woman on her own they may not insist.'

'If they do. . . .' Grouse threatened grimly, loading his revolver. I got down just in time to see the door give way under the weight of three great louts in the black uniform of the SS.

'Car, garage, petrol,' they shouted.

'*Nein*, Red Cross here,' I said, pointing to the markings on the ambulance. 'You sick? I nurse you?'

They screwed up their faces in disgust. '*Ach so!* Sick? *Kaput* No! petrol?'

'*Nein!* Only oil, castor oil.' They went off shaking with laughter.

'We must get away before they come back,' said Grouse. 'I'll keep the set. You'll have your hands full with the Yank. We must reduce the risks. I'll walk.'

Musk Deer arrived with his cart. He brought me a voluminous skirt, a shawl and a peasant kerchief. 'And this is for you,' he said to the airman, handing him a magnificent hay rake.

I sat by the driver, who explained how to use the reins. He made our wretched parachutist sit at the back with his legs dangling over the road and put a rough hand through his hair to ruffle it. We started off, at the bottom of the hill, in Recicourt, the little country town on the main road. The traffic was heavy: unbroken queues of every kind of vehicle, crammed with troops, and a stream of infantry trudging alongside. How were we going to get through that mob? I glanced at the parachutist, sitting there deathly pale and pressing his rake against his chest, and I was horrified to see his identity discs flashing in the sunlight.

Quite unperturbed, Musk Deer climbed down, went to the horse's head and threaded his way to a group of officers busily directing the convoys. He raised his hat.

'We'd like to cross the road,' he said politely.

'*Raus*, no time,' replied a young SS lieutenant with a drawn and weary face.

'It's to get the hay over there. I—peasant,' insisted Musk Deer.

Heaving a sigh and cursing, the young lieutenant shouted out a few orders in a hoarse voice. The stream stopped abruptly. Musk Deer climbed slowly back into his seat and whipped up his horse. The inhabitants of Recicourt stood riveted to their doorsteps and held their breath. My eyes went from their agonized faces to our American's shining discs.

'They'll spot them, they'll spot them,' I muttered. Then, out of the blue, something quite incredible happened to divert their attention. With horn blaring and brakes screaming our ambulance appeared. Grouse, his grave, tense face thrust forward over the steering wheel, shouted: 'Doctor, make way, doctor, make way!'

And without further ado he accelerated hard, scattering the SS, skidded, slithered and scuttled like a crab, zig-zagged in a huge cloud of dust and dashed to the other side of the main road pursued by a few shouting military police whom he soon left standing and looking utterly dejected.

'We must make the most of it,' whispered Musk Deer, whipping up his horse with a zest worthy of Ben Hur.

We reached the forest that Finch had suggested. Transformed into members of the maquis, the people of Verdun were waiting for us. The ambulance was already there, camouflaged with splendid freshly-cut branches, as well as the radio set.

'Make contact, lad,' said Grouse in an encouraging voice to the poor parachutist who, convinced that he was dealing with a bunch of fools, began tapping. The birds' singing would cover the clandestine calls. The men were bustling around with mess tins and sacks of bread. They started to cool the wine in the stream. At the foot of the trees were their weapons—shotguns, various kinds of rifles, altogether an odd, rag-bag armoury.

'It's a bit too much like a picnic,' I said to Grouse. 'How will we be able to work?'

'After they've made contact with Patton, our couriers will come and join us here. They'll set off to cross the lines again with the information that our agents bring from Verdun. So all we can do is wait.'

I walked round the clearing to see for myself how quickly anyone melted away the moment he took to the thick undergrowth. It was a real forest, where all sense of time and distance was lost, the sort of forest where it was possible to lurk and watch unseen, like wild beasts. Here and there were traces of the 1914 war, places that echoed with the sounds of battles long ago. As night fell the noise from the road increased and soon we thought we heard other sounds, sounds of boots approaching and moving along the edge of the forest.

A courier appeared out of breath. 'You boys aren't easy to find. OK, we've made contact with the Americans. They were delighted. We gave them your messages, pointing out all the traps, and they've changed their route. They're asking for information before they move through the Argonne forest.'

'Are they as near as that?'

'Yes, they could be here by tomorrow, the day after at the latest. The Boches are decamping. It's great news. But I forgot to tell you, they're gradually leaving the main road and beginning to move along the edge of the forest, they're so scared of being taken in the rear.'

The men crowded round the hero-who-had-seen-the-Americans, bombarded him with questions and rapturously inhaled the cigarettes with which his pockets were bulging. Grouse and I scribbled out further messages for Patton's army and towards eleven o'clock a new patrol left to go westwards. The night passed, then a day, then another night began.

A dull growling started in the west, soon to swell until it was like millions of pebbles rolling down a beach. At the same time hurrying footsteps approached; we heard branches snapping and oaths muttered—German oaths. We glimpsed new shadows peopling the forest. We realized what had happened. With Patton thundering through Récicourt with all his tanks, Hitler's soldiers were diving helter-skelter and ingloriously into the forest.

Dawn broke. Grouse informed me that he was going off to reconnoitre. After an hour he returned, looking deathly pale. 'We're liberated,' he said simply. 'Patton's at Verdun. Why are you crying?'

'I think it's because the war is over.'

'Yes, that's what's called "Victory".'

'Victory is a meaningless word. What is victory to us when those who won it are missing?'

'Marie-Madeleine, we're going to Berlin to find them. For you and me Patton's advance is only an episode.'

'Not for them,' I said, pointing to the banners, the flags and the white cloths that had appeared as by magic at all the entrances to Récicourt. The villagers were drinking, singing, laughing, dancing, and as soon as they saw the ambulance they rushed up to us, kissed us, carried us in triumph and poured us out great draughts of wine, wine that had been kept for this occasion and now flowed in torrents, spilling out of the glasses and flooding our hearts.

It was quite impossible to adjust ourselves to the situation, to the American uniforms instead of the German. Was it really possible to tell people one's real name after suppressing it for years? Was it really possible to believe it was the postman knocking on one's door and not the Gestapo? How many months would it take to get rid of the virus of the occupation? No, the war was not over; we were even in the front line, but it was so much less frightening in spite of the tremendous bombing that marked the first night of the liberation of Verdun.

We returned to Finch's; on the door I put up our sign: ALLIANCE— BCRA-DGSR—INTELLIGENCE SERVICE and the agents streamed in from Paris and the north, eager to continue the fight and tickled pink to discover a social reason for their existence. So it was true? The phantom network was becoming reality. I had not lied to them; they were soldiers like the rest. Of course, they immediately put on uniform.

Finch warned me that I was expected at the *mairie*. No doubt they wanted to congratulate me. I went. A crowd of gesticulating, loud-mouthed toughs were sitting in an unimpressive, rather sordid, untidy room. I noticed that they wore tricolour armbands bearing the letters FFI. I was pushed towards a chair.

'Who are you?' barked a young colossus who seemed to be their leader. Who was I? It was funny, I was wondering that myself. What identity should I choose? My hesitation in answering heightened the suspicion that was plainly written all over his face.

'Aha, so you won't answer? And this, what's this?' He suddenly whisked my transmitting set from under a table. I reacted like a shot.

'That's mine. Who gave you permission?'

'Aha, so you admit it? And whom does madame contact with this thing?'

'London, of course.'

They burst into laughter. 'London? I ask you! As though anyone could get in touch with London! You're a dirty German spy. It was you who got us bombed. You'll see what that'll cost you.'

I heard an ominous clatter of weapons, then hasty knocks on the door and the leader disappeared for a few minutes leaving me facing the hostile gaze of his cronies. I suddenly thought: 'They're going to shoot me, the fools.' A fierce rage seized me and I gave them a piece of my mind.

The leader returned looking far less cocky. He was followed by Finch, who took me away, mopping his brow. 'What a beast,' he muttered, 'I had a job to convince them. . . .'

Grouse was itching with impatience to take me to Paris so that I could get him the help he needed to move on to Berlin. We had made contact with Patton's headquarters, and every day we sent Colonel Bilbane, the French liaison officer with the division, the reports from our agents around Verdun. Nothing—there was nothing between them and the Rhine. What were the Allies waiting for? They were short of petrol! Anyway, that was the reason I was given. To come all the way from America and then stop through shortage of petrol!

'The landing, the drive to the east are several weeks ahead of schedule, you know; the supply people can't keep up the pace. So we shall have to winter here.'

'But the Germans will come back!'

'Nonsense, they're finished, they're far too scared.'

This was anything but true. There were already rumours circulating about the re-occupation of places that had put out the victory flags.

We raced to Paris. Euphoria. Uniforms everywhere. I dug out mine— why not?—from the cases brought from London by Lizard, Antelope and Kid. Reunions, hugging and swapping stories. The animals of the Ark were becoming people again, visible in the sumptuous premises that we requisitioned in the Champs Elysées. Ham was there, still at our disposal, and Kenneth Cohen too. As soon as I arrived, they wanted to organize a grand ceremony without more ado.

To the circular office above the avenue that was the scene of all the triumphant processions, they all came from the British Embassy, magnificently dressed—some in Royal Navy uniforms, some in kilts, some in that sumptuous khaki cloth and shining leather. I was pushed into the middle of the circle and Kenneth Cohen read a long and wonderful citation, then pinned on me a vermilion cross, bearing the royal profiles, surmounted by a graceful rosette of pink ribbon. With a huge bouquet of red roses in my arms, the dreadful sobs in my throat stopped me from replying.

'And now, what can we do for you, Poz dear?' Kenneth asked amid the buzz of congratulations and the clink of champagne glasses.

'I ought to have an immediate parachute drop at Verdun, on the Lilas field, and another for Petrel. We must supply our patrols in the east. I'm very much afraid they'll be going to and fro across the lines the whole winter. And then I think you might get my children back from Switzerland.'

'She's incorrigible! You shall have your parachute drops and we'll go and receive yours with you and at last see for ourselves what it looks like.'

Beaver went back with us to Verdun. Patrols that we consulted on arrival told us that things were now much more difficult further east, and Grouse and I resolved to test the ground ourselves so that our consciences would be clear.

We passed the Douaumont charnel house, which I saw for the first time, wire-entanglements and road blocks, and encampments of GIs who could not understand why we were so bent on running up against the Boches. They examined our American papers and we had to explain why they had been issued. 'Intelligence! Intelligence!' they repeated. 'Fine.'

Gravelotte, the site of a famous battle in 1870, finally came into sight. The last Americans were at the first houses in a completely deserted and seemingly mummified village. Grouse stopped the car in the main square and began to crawl towards the road leading out of the place. The minutes dragged by in silence. A far-off sound warned me that Grouse had stirred up something, and when I started the engine again, expecting to see him come running back with the enemy in hot pursuit, I was astonished to see a magnificent flock of geese march out, loudly complaining of the hard times and advancing with the Teutonic army's notorious step. Grouse herded them towards me, signalling to me to open the door. When he was level with the car he whispered: 'They're there, packed tight in the last houses. They're watching us and undoubtedly thinking that we're laying a trap to draw them into no-man's-land.'

'It's time we went,' I replied, helping him to get the geese into the car. The astounded Americans saw us coming back in a white feather eiderdown. I offered the GIs some of the succulent birds to give them a change from their ordinary rations, but to my intense surprise they refused. Why go to all the bother of plucking, trussing and roasting a gosling when there were such good ones in tins!

Ever faithful to his promises, Kenneth Cohen came to Verdun on 7 September. I immediately tackled him about our growing anxiety to see the Germans across the Luxembourg frontier. 'They're regrouping. They know that Patton is stuck. They also know that he's badly protected.'

As soon as dawn broke, Grouse had sent out two of our agents, who were to beat through the region from south to north and then report back at dusk so that we could give Kenneth the latest information.

The parachute drop took place in the afternoon and the bombers released dozens of parachutes of all conceivable colours. Whooping with joy, our men hurled themselves upon the containers, and at that very moment a swarm of GIs, who had been hiding in the undergrowth, popped out to seize them. They thought it was a German drop. But for the Commander's presence we should never have seen our stuff again: battledress, nailed boots, Sten guns, grenades, revolvers, provisions, radios—an excellent stock of things to keep us going through the winter.

In the evening Kenneth asked if he could go with us to meet the agents who had gone off in the morning. One of them returned. The other, Jean-Pierre Pineau, never did: he was twenty-one and he disappeared without a trace. He was a volunteer who had been eager to carry on to the bitter end and his tragic disappearance confirmed the fact that danger still existed in France. The Commander left us, grieving. He had had his wish and seen us at work in the field. The picture we had shown him was still one of death.

We spent the rest of the night stacking and distributing the contents of the parachute drop that transformed our little troop into an operational unit, happy to think that Petrel was also being set up. His drop had been due to take place at the same time as mine—in the dark, obviously, since his region was still occupied.

During the night of the 8th, Finch brought me a message from London: *'Our planes circled above the dropping zone indicated by Petrel last night and saw nothing but villages in flames stop dropping impossible stop we can no longer hear Petrel's transmitter end.'*

We never heard of Petrel again. He had been surrounded by the SS in the village of Luz and had refused to flee. He could not give the Nazis an excuse to massacre the inhabitants who had given him such a friendly welcome. He had been captured with his operator and adjutant, and after four hours' interrogation they had been seen going off into an orchard surrounded by armed men.

Petrel (Georges Lamarque) had been shot. Shot with Louis de Clerq and Clement Defer. Summary execution, without trial. Shipwrecked at the very entrance to the harbour. The flames seen by the RAF were from the farms set on fire as a reprisal.

I then remembered that Petrel's father had fallen on 7 September 1914, on the border marches of Lorraine, and that thirty years, almost to a day, separated the sacrifice of the father and the son who had been born after his death and had fallen on 8 September 1944.

For Petrel I wept bitterly. Petrel, who always used to say, 'The only important thing is a sense of mission', was dead and I could no longer believe in a mission that took life from the purest, the noblest and the finest among us.

Then began what was for us the longest winter. Sick at heart, I wondered how many more lives the war would cost; and I was afraid that, as our advance to free them from their chains progressed, my friends on the other side of the Rhine would have to suffer the most murderous months of all.

Nevertheless the mission continued. I had christened our special operational unit 'Antenne Lyautey'. Based in Verdun and in regular contact with General Patton's headquarters, it probed the terrain for him in every direction. Since our warning, which had alerted his advanced posts just in time to escape a counter-offensive in the Longuyon-Spincourt area by German armour from Luxembourg, and after we had guided the US Army Air Force and enabled it to create havoc among the German tanks at Merry, destroying some that had belonged to the Afrika Korps, the Americans multiplied their questions. But they still refused to move.

Grouse and I pushed on to Luxembourg, to Mondorf-les-Bains, to operate up front as we did at Gravelotte. From there, after organizing a crossing to the Saar, we were able to establish that there was no armour east of the Moselle. Only an anti-tank ditch defended by a few guns. What was that compared with the massed might of the United States Army? And yet the weeks followed one another in vain while all the possibilities of tactical, close-contact intelligence were exhausted. Heavy reinforcements of network volunteers were called in from all the liberated regions and even a captured Fieseler Storch was used, piloted by Grand Duke and Saluki in turn.

As a last, desperate resort we sent out missions to probe as far as the German frontier itself.

On 3 November Starling (Gaston Grosbety) left for Delle, near Belfort. On the 5th, at 22.00, Operation Walton—consisting of Grouse, Beaver, Pierre Schohn and Paul Plouel, a radio operator, packed together along with radio equipment and baggage in an inflatable dinghy supplied by Patton's G2—crossed the Moselle. I watched them leave under fire from the patrols on both sides of the river, wondering whether they would even manage to make the enemy bank.

The following day I received the first message transmitted by the expedition's set, poetically named 'Joan Pearl': '*The Alliance is speaking from occupied France stop Beaver mission in good shape at Bass Yutz stop advancing stop Grouse end.*'

The Walton mission's advance was to last forty-eight days. Fifty-four messages, giving tactical information about the enemy lines between Thionville and the German frontier, were the basis for the offensive finally launched by General Patton's Third Army and General Patch's Seventh Army about Christmas. The old network, conscious of its vocation, had remained in the vanguard of the liberation of France.

I had to make frequent trips between the eastern front and Paris. The west of France was not completely liberated and the members of the network still trapped in the Atlantic pockets carried on the fight. We who had talked so much about the 'Breton redoubt' were now witnessing the melancholy spectacle of German redoubts in Brittany. In Brittany, at Lorient, Robert le Louër (Elk), continued to slip in and out of the naval base that he had so often photographed to check on the anti-aircraft posts and the location of the troops still in the pocket.

In La Rochelle, Captain Godet (Antelope) had smuggled equipment to Mandrill's admirable successors. Until the capitulation of Admiral Schirlitz on 7 May 1945 their sector was a model of its type, sending fifty batches of reports by land, leaving them in special places in the marshy no-man's-land, and 300 radio messages, sometimes necessitating six transmissions a day, giving the French command timely warning of any planned German attacks. We were also asked to cross the Alps. Three people volunteered to carry out the mission that I called 'Mona Lisa': I went to Nice several times to organize their operation, which, very satisfactorily, established first contact with the Italian partisans.

Each time I went to Paris, always in fear and trepidation of what I might learn, I did not, fortunately, hear only depressing news. First, my children returned, miraculously unaffected, bigger, of course, but above all enriched by a flame that would make them for ever different from many others. And then my beloved mother, alas, ill and exhausted. My brother Jacques had been badly injured by a mine on 18 July 1944, during the Italian campaign, and it was not known whether he would recover. He had become a casualty the very day that I had myself fallen into the hands of the Gestapo at Aix.

Then, arriving one evening at the office in the building in the Champs Elysées that housed the Alliance, I had to rub my eyes. I was looking at the back of a man who was not really very tall but looked it because he was slimly built, a man with cropped grey hair, his arm arched over little flags placed on the map of the Alsace front, his white, elegant hand inscribing cabalistic signs on the roads, and arrows that pointed to the spire of Strasbourg cathedral.

'Colonel Bernis,' I murmured.

Spaniel, 'the dedicated man' turned round: 'It's my finest intelligence map, my dear. Thank you.'

They were there, alive: Spaniel, the Bishop, Gazelle, Fawn, Peccary! They had been handed over to the Gestapo by OVRA after the downfall of Mussolini and owed their lives to the fact that their police dossiers had not followed them to Belfort, where they had finally landed after twenty-two months in prison. Spaniel, in great form in spite of the ordeal he had undergone, had played his cards superbly. 'Those Fascist fools had committed a major legal error,' he explained. Lacking proper incriminating evidence on which to prosecute the group, and only too pleased to hit back at the renegades of the Berlin-Rome axis, the Gestapo had released them. Bernis and his fellow prisoners immediately fled across the lines. I never wearied of listening to the story of their terrible experiences.

And the rest? The first dreadful scraps of information suggested stark tragedy. The Struthof camp in Alsace, the only concentration camp in France to have gas chambers, had just yielded up its ghastly secrets: the slow death of its prisoners by cold, forced labour and privation; the systematic destruction of the human species by brutality and experiment. It was rumoured that many of our members had perished there, in that wild and beautiful setting. During the night of 1 September 1944, following the sudden transfer of a hundred of our friends from the Schirmeck camp, the crematorium chimney had never stopped smoking. I clung desperately to hope when, some time later, a voice came over the phone:

'Some very good news for you, Poz. Magpie's been exchanged.'

'Good heavens, is it really possible? Where is he?'

'Somewhere on the way back. They're doing everything they can for him. He needed attention badly.'

He looked like a ghost! He was appallingly thin and gaunt. There was a glassy look about his light blue eyes. His wrists still bore the marks of the manacles that he had worn unceasingly for fifteen months. He refused to talk about it and it was a very long time before I could drag out the story of what had happened to him. His only thought was for the others:

'Miraculously, Eagle and I met on 3 January 1945, on the stairs of Schwäbisch-Hall prison. We were both being transferred to Sonnenburg fortress. There I left him on the 15th, in the dungeon next to mine. He was convinced that I would get out alive. Because I am British, he thought I would be exchanged. But we must act with all speed if we're to save him.'

'I know, Magpie. The German radio announced that Faye was alive and that the Germans would agree to release him as well as Captain Pimont, head of BCRA counter-espionage, in exchange for Angelo Chiappe, a collaborator under sentence of death.'

'Then it'll be easy,' he said, his face lighting up.

'Don't you believe it! Although Jacques Soustelle, the present head of our special services, did his utmost, Angelo Chiappe was executed. Only Britain could do a deal for you. . . . Your country hasn't been conquered or occupied.'

'It's ghastly to be here and to think. . . .'

'That all our friends are dead, Magpie?'

He had not the strength to weep, and I had not the heart to ask him what he really knew. Gradually, bit by bit, he told me about the trial in June 1944, the military tribunal of the Greater Reich, that had gone specially from Torgau to Freiburg-im-Breisgau to try the Alliance. All, or almost all, had been sentenced to death. Many had been shot even before he himself was tried. In the prison of Schwäbisch-Hall, besides Eagle and Magpie, twenty-four of our members had been imprisoned, too.

On the night of 20 August 1944 Magpie had picked up their farewell messages, tapped out in Morse on the walls. He had heard them walk down the stairs, their footsteps ringing on the iron staircase. They had all gone.

He went on: 'Eagle gave me a message: he left his testament and papers for you behind the radiator in his underground cell in Bruchsal.'

What a deep abyss of pain! Other missions were attempted. Peter Morton (Lohengrin), a radio operator in Grouse's team, was killed on 9 March crossing the lines in eastern France. The last member of the Alliance to be killed was British.

However, the enemy was yielding everywhere. Hitler, the beast of the Apocalypse, died by his own hand and the cease-fire began. The first to come back was Professor Léon Mazeaud (Agami), the pride of the Law Faculty, then Robert Bernadac, then Elie de Dampierre (Shepherd). We knew through Sweden that our heroines Mouse, Hummingbird, Ewe and Amniarix were safe, and through Switzerland we learned that the founder of the network, Navarre, was alive. Whatever condition they might be in when we saw them, the hope still burning in our hearts was fed by this wonderful news. And the rest? Why not the rest. . . .?

As soon as possible after the armistice, I took to the road with Magpie and Beaver. We had Allied safe conducts and pockets bursting with revolvers. The revolvers were quite pointless, as all activity had ceased. Once across the Rhine, amid the ruins and the rubble already neatly arranged and scientifically laid out in piles ready for the rebuilding and reconstruction that was bound to start soon, the abominable stench of corpses got into our nostrils and stayed there.

We began by investigating the prisons in the Black Forest. In each one I asked for the register showing the entries. When I saw my friends' names and read against them the word 'left', with no destination, I knew that my quest would be short.

At Kehl prison a single name, Paul Bernard, had been shown as being transferred to Berlin, to the Moabit prison. The others who had 'left' were Urus (André Coindeau) and eight men from his region round Nantes. They had been executed in pairs, not far from a bunker, and dumped in the Rhine on 23 November 1944.

At Rastatt, on 24 November, twelve of Colonel Kauffmann's (Cricket's) men had been killed near a wooden bridge in the vicinity of Blittersdorf and thrown into the Rhine. At Bühl, on 28 November, Raymond Pader and seven men who had worked for Paul Mangel, head of the Autun sector, had been taken in a boat to the middle of the Rhine, shot in pairs in the back of the neck with a revolver, and thrown into the river. At Offenburg, on 27 November, four young women, each aged thirty, had been shot in pairs in the back of the neck in front of a gaping hole in the ground in the depths of Rommersweir Forest. They were Henriette Amable (Tomboy), Paul Mangel's wife (Siren), and two of her friends, Lucienne Barnet and Simone Pauchard.

When I reached Pforzheim I met one of our own people, now attached to the First Army. 'I'm living a nightmare,' he shouted as soon as he saw me. 'Yesterday I discovered twenty-six bodies in a mass grave filled with water. We gave them a solemn burial. All the troops were there, six German civilians and a wreath-bearer. Here's the prison register. The names may tell you something.'

They were all members of the Alliance: eight women included Marie Gillet (Unicorn's wife), and a young, seventeen-year-old girl, Alice Coudol. Among the eighteen men were my dear Ant (Pierre Dayné), and Buccaneer (Louis Payen), arrested with Elephant, and Turtle Dove's brother, Marcel Fontenaille. . . . All had been shot in the back of the neck and bundled headlong into a hole filled with water in the middle of the forest. On 30 November 1944 they had been taken from Pforzheim prison; they had been led to believe they were being freed, for they had each been given eighteen marks, as the register showed.

At Gaggenheim, in a camp this time, and in another mass grave in Ratenau Forest, nine men had been executed on the same day, 30 November: 'Mouchou' Damm and his son, the indomitable Zebra, and seven of Mandrill's men, including the venerable Canon Joseph Bordes, and Marco the railway engine driver, Pierre Audevie and André Soussotte (Lanneret), the radio operator. The latter had given a letter for his fiancée to Canon Hett, who had escaped the massacre because the Gestapo did not know that he belonged to the Alliance:

'. . . Don't grieve for me. I'm the happiest of men. We could certainly have had a good life together but I had to give all that up to serve my country. . . . I often told you what would happen to me if I were captured. I find comfort in telling myself that they will never be able to do as much to me as I have done to them. If they shoot me, what is the life of a man compared with all the ships I have helped to sink. . . . Not much. I am even proud to be able to die for my country and knowing I can hold my head high. . . .'

He was twenty-one.

We reached Freiburg-im-Breisgau, the city where on three occasions, in December 1943, in April and June 1944, the tribunal of the Greater German Reich had passed sentence on the Alliance Intelligence Service. Magpie had some difficulty in finding the lawyers in the ruined town. They had lost their archives in the bombing and no longer remembered the names of all their 'clients'. There had been so many. One of them, Doktor Hermann, told me that, in twenty years of defending criminal cases, he and his colleagues had never seen anything as moving as these trials. They admired the attitude of the accused. They had the greatest respect for the patriotism and the remarkable bearing of the members of the Alliance.

'I must mention Commandant Faye in particular,' the German lawyer insisted. 'He declared over and over again that he and he alone bore the whole responsibility for the acts of all the members of the network. And I must also mention the British captain, Magpie. But those remarkable personalities must not be allowed to overshadow the worth of their comrades in the Alliance.'

'What were the main charges?'

'General Giraud's flight was often brought up. Your extensive "broadcasting" service. It was repeated several times that the Alliance organization, which the tribunal called "Noah's Ark", achieved quite remarkable successes, especially in anti-submarine warfare. The court also regretted that it was unable to institute proceedings against you, Marie-Madeleine.'

'What defence argument were you able to submit?'

'In the course of the trial I came to learn of two laws of whose existence I was completely ignorant. Two decrees issued personally by Hitler. First, the *Nacht und Nebel* decree, that laid down that arrested persons were to disappear "at night and in the fog"; their kin would never be able to learn what had happened to them, and all trace of the person was to be obliterated. The second decree stated that the execution of officers could be authorized only by the Führer himself. Since Commandant Faye had declared that all his agents were officers, I protested after the death sentence had been pronounced. I insisted that Hitler should be asked to decide. I tried to delay the executions, but the officers commanding the execution squads always refused my request for a stay.'

We made our way to the huge fortress of Freiburg-im-Breisgau. On every floor drawings and messages written on the walls marked the *via dolorosa* trodden by my friends: Mahout, Wolf, Jack Tar, Triton. . . . Their names had been cut in the walls and sometimes, carved in the tables, I read the words 'The Alliance', or 'Long live the Alliance'.

Bending over the register, Magpie said: 'Someone escaped during the bombing. It was Inspector Le Tullier's wife! The others are shown as going to several different places: Schwäbisch-Hall prison, I know that—Bruchsal fortress, that's where Eagle was—Ludwigsburg prison. There are also the names of camps, but for very few of them. For three, no destination is shown.'

'Who were they?'

He gave me a despairing look: 'Cricket, Corsair, and one of their agents.'

'They can't be far away,' shouted Beaver, and grasping hold of the warder following us he demanded: 'Where are they? Where is *Oberst* Kauffmann? Where is *Hauptmann* Pradelle?'

The warder trembled from head to foot.

'Tell us,' the lawyer said. 'These people won't hurt you.'

'I know,' the warder said. 'They are here.'

'How do you mean, here?' We stared distraught at the porch, the drawbridge and the moats.

'Down there,' he repeated, tapping his foot. 'In that bomb crater. A bullet in the back of the neck. Gehrum came for them.'

And so the war crime bore the signature of Gehrum. *Obersturmführer* Gehrum. Gehrum who, during the bloody week in the Black Forest, had given orders for the 'liquidation' of fifty-nine people, old men, priests, young men and twelve women, none of them sentenced to death. They had all been killed solely and simply to prevent their release. Thus neither Gehrum nor any of the assistant executioners had at any moment felt a gleam of pity, even when it came to the four frail little women who had fought so hard to live free. None had relented or thought of bestowing any favour on them, in spite of the suffering, the torture and the agony of mind they had endured. Life must be denied them at all cost. No remission. The Nazis spoke only one language: a bullet in the back of the neck.

On entering Schwäbisch-Hall prison, Magpie's waxen look suddenly returned and he dropped into something like the attitude of a person under sentence. We climbed the iron stairs and went into his cell. The prison was in the American sector and the servile warder did us the honours. He had paid no attention to the officer in British uniform with me. Reaching the foot of the bed, Magpie could no longer contain himself.

'Where are the manacles, eh? What about the chains for the feet?'

The gaoler stared at him aghast: 'You? You're not dead?'

'No, not dead. And the others?'

'I've kept the suitcases. I'll show you the suitcases.'

'That's enough, you bastard,' said Beaver, sending him sprawling, and closing and bolting the door on him.

Going on without him, we discovered the poor, bashed and battered little cases from the time of the occupation, full of blood-stained underclothes and precious little treasures—tattered old wallets, dog-eared photos, crossword puzzles, brief notes revealing the state of mind of those who had been sentenced to death.

Magpie had not been the victim of an hallucination. They had indeed left by the iron stairs for the rifle range attached to Heilbronn barracks, where they had been shot on 21 August 1944. Gabriel Rivière (Wolf), Lucien Poulard (Jack Tar), Pierre Dallas (Mahout), Alfred Jassaud (Bison), Joël Lemoigne (Triton), Ernest Siegrist (Elephant), Jean Bouyat and five radio operators; little Marcel Trumel from the Bouillancy landing ground and Jean-Philippe Sneyers (the unfortunate Bumpkin), doubly betrayed by Lanky, and the remarkable sector leaders and helpers, nine in all. We found the place of execution—a field full of apple trees where the grass was green.

And we found the bodies!

'Are you looking for a lot of people like this?' asked the American officer accompanying us.

'Yes, a lot, far too many. We should like to go to the fortress of Sonnenburg.'

'There were nearly a thousand of us in that prison near Küstrin on the Oder,' said Magpie. 'On 3 January the Nazis transferred me there with Eagle. I want to go back. You must help us.'

'It's in the Russian zone. You won't get in, but there's a warder here who was there. He left on 1 February 1945 with a column of prisoners.'

The man was fetched. He told us that on 30 January the SS had received orders to kill everybody before the Red Army arrived. He and a few other guards had succeeded in saving about 500 prisoners, mostly Germans, from the hands of the SS executioners.

The others? They had all been massacred. More than 800. Made to line up. Then a burst of fire in the back of the neck. The bodies were burned with flame-throwers. . . . We could not bear to listen to any more. Eagle's ghastly end paralysed us with its horror.

'I can't believe it,' said Beaver. 'Perhaps he left with the column.'

'Perhaps he escaped to Russia,' said Magpie, hoping with all his soul that this was so. I let them hope against hope and imagine the impossible. I had known for a long time: by insisting on returning to France on 15 September 1943, Eagle—Commandant Faye—had died in my stead.

Ludwigsburg was the only place where we saw proper graves. They were well kept and bore the names of those who had been shot. Everywhere else they had been buried outside the cemeteries.

'Your friends won our admiration,' we were told by the pastor who, with a Roman Catholic priest, had ministered to them. As they were bound to the execution posts they kept one another's hearts high by shouting: '*A bientôt au ciel.*'

Magpie knelt down on the grave of his great friend, the Abbé Lair, with whom he had transmitted his messages from the belfry of Tulle cathedral. I looked hard at the grassy, flower-covered mounds, at the crosses on which I read the names: Armand Siffert, Petrel's chief radio operator, Alexandre Lazard, Jean-Pierre Chanliau and Pierre Chanliau, his son, Eugène Mazillier and four men from Vichy. With them a man from Marseilles and three from the north whom I did not know. One name that I had seen in the register was missing: General Raynal.

'He was reprieved at the last minute because of his age,' the governor of the prison told me. 'Try the fortress of Ebrach.'

I did. General Raynal (Sheepdog) had indeed been transferred there. He died a little later. The gaolers forced him to remain standing to attention naked, at night, in the snow.

Bruchsal was the most terrible of all the fortresses. At my request General Lechères had already gone there to collect the messages that Eagle had slipped behind the radiator in his cell and whose existence had been revealed to me by Magpie. In the subterranean dungeon I found the chains that had held Eagle lashed to the foot of his iron bed. The warder, a sort of gnome, complacently described the treatment the prisoner suffered: 'I was told to give him only a bowl of soup. They were afraid he might escape.'

I could guess the terror that Eagle, even chained, must have struck into the heart of this sinister Quasimodo. Beaver, driven to distraction by these reminiscences, hurled himself upon the man.

'You let him die of hunger, you chained him up like an animal!'

I intervened between them: 'Let him be, Beaver! He's just another without any sense of responsibility.' The man dragged himself to our feet sobbing: 'Forgive me, *Oberst* Faye. Forgive me, *Oberst* Faye.'

The Bruchsal register informed us that there was a grave in the prison garden. It was that of Jean Broqua, the faithful Rabbit. As he was already a dying man he had not been executed with his companions.

Not far away, in a hole outside the precincts of Karlsruhe cemetery, we found the bodies of the following, who had been shot on 1 April 1944: Jaguar (the conscientious Camille Schneider), Robert Lynen (the spirited and impetuous Eaglet), Badger (the veteran Gilbert Savon) and four people from the Marseilles sector; also Basset (Superintendent Philippe) and four of his agents. Like all the others we had found, each had a piece of red cloth sewn on his clothes to show where the heart was. Only one of the fifty-three had accepted the offer of a bandage to cover his eyes. They were all perfectly recognizable.

'Time will pass and soon no one will be able to recognize them; it will not even be known how they died,' said Magpie.

'We must return their bodies to their families, and above all we must bury them in French soil. . . .'

Beaver drew himself up: 'I claim this honour, Marie-Madeleine. I will bring them all back to France.'

At Strasbourg our local leaders confirmed the truth of the tragedy at Struthof. During the night of 1 to 2 September 1944, fifteen women and twenty-two men from the Brittany region, twenty-two men from the Bordeaux-La Rochelle region, four from Normandy, ten from the Autun region, nine from the Mediterranean and four from the northern regions, thirteen from the radio service and eight from the headquarters services and the Paris region, had been extradited from Schirmeck camp and killed at Struthof concentration camp—108 more victims to add to the account of SS Obersturmführer Gehrum's war crimes. 'The job,' he had admitted, 'will take two days.'

The massacre was terrible, like that at Küstrin, where Eagle had met his end; but at Struthof the killing on higher orders had struck only the members of the Alliance Intelligence Service.

How could we compile the terrible list with any accuracy? How could we give up hope that a few of them had escaped falling into the hands of the SS executioners who had performed the same movements and the same ritual for forty-eight hours on end—pushing them one by one onto the staircase in the execution chamber, shooting them in the back of the neck and then placing them one by one on the hoist that precipitated them into the oven so that no trace of the crime should remain.

There was a living witness, Dr Lacapère (Dolphin), from Le Lavandou. Isolated from the rest of the network and kept at Schirmeck to act as camp doctor, he had seen our friends driven off by the vanload. His statements were confirmed by the discovery of a bottle beneath the trodden earth that constituted the floor of Hut 10 in Schirmeck camp, where they had spent the last months of their lives; it contained sheets of paper showing the fatigues they had to carry out and, in the margin, cartoons and caricatures, notes—a frightening puzzle which, when it was put together, left us with no more hope.

Mandrill! No, Philip Koenigswerther had not in fact died in Bordeaux, defending himself against the Gestapo. He had finished up in this camp, after months of torture. Nor had Pierre Berthomier (Seagull) been favoured with a merciful death at Volvic, shooting it out with the Germans. Whole families and married couples had disappeared during those apocalyptic days. Unicorn—Maurice Gillet—and his family accounted for seven victims. And there was Colonel Delmas-Vieljeux, Mayor of La Rochelle, aged sixty-nine, and his step-brother and grandson. And so many other names that I had read so often in the glorious reports: Sealion, Cod, Stickleback, Lobster. . . . And Bee! And Christiane! The radiant Maritou Brouillet, the gentle Christiane Battu. They, too, had been murdered and cast into the flames. . . .

So many good Frenchmen! The senior male prisoner among them was nearly eighty, the senior woman, the heroic Spider from the Dunkirk region, was only just twenty-one; the baby of them all had only just turned twenty. Old men, sick and wounded, and a priest who was almost blind. It was appalling, almost beyond belief. Yet the lists of those poor lost souls were there in the bottle, signed 'Sioux', the liaison agent who had written down the name of each inmate of Schirmeck camp, sketched each face . . . the only trace now left of them, and of Sioux, who had vanished as well.

Navarre had languished in prisons and penal settlements for four and a half years, but he had returned to France, his 1940 wound still unhealed. Swift (Paul Bernard) was also back. He had not been thrown into the Rhine with his comrades from Kehl prison, and must have owed his life to the fact that the Gestapo had implicated him in the plot against Hitler. The grids discovered under my bed in the Rue Granet had been curiously to his advantage. Transferred from Kehl to the Moabit prison for interrogation, and put in with the German resistance fighters of the 20 July plot, who protected him, Swift had escaped during the bombing raids on Berlin and then from the German capital itself when it was attacked by the Red Army.

We met again in the Rue de Courty, the seat of The Crusade. Three of the leaders of the Alliance were reunited again for the first time since the days of the Hôtel des Sports, five years earlier. And the fourth?

On my table was a large envelope containing Eagle's will. One of our agents had been able to get as far as Küstrin and had confirmed the Sonnenburg warder's story: on arriving at the prison the day after the massacre, the Russians had found 819 charred, half-burned bodies. They had buried them in two mass graves. It had been impossible to identify Eagle's remains among them. We could not even bring him back to rest forever in French soil. A sentinel grandly isolated, he would continue his vigil on the most distant horizon of the gigantic front.

I asked Navarre and Swift what their plans for the future had been. During his long nights in prison Swift had dreamed of flying. He wanted to create an air navigation company and he eventually did so. Navarre wanted to go into politics, and he was elected deputy for the Basses-Pyrenees.

'And you, Marie-Madeleine?' they asked. I personally did not think that our mission was at an end. We had to ensure that the families of those who had died would receive help, pensions and rewards; and it was also essential to carry on the fight so that our children should never have to suffer the same martyrdom that our friends had endured. I affirmed my determination to devote myself to this task until the end of my life.

And what would Eagle have done? We opened the envelope from Bruchsal, releasing the sheets of paper covered with his impassioned words:

'. . . I ask you to serve our unhappy country so that it may enjoy peace again and happiness, songs, flowers, and flower-covered inns. Close the prisons. Drive out the executioners. . . . Like many other countries France will have to tend, cleanse and heal cruel wounds and rebuild vast numbers of ruined places. But she is the only one whose moral unity was broken. Pulled and torn in all directions, she is a dyke bursting under the weight of water. That is the most serious and urgent task. Everything must be done to get out of this impasse. Later, historians will judge. For the moment the important thing is union and not reprisal, work and not chaos. Act to this end, my dear friends, that is my last wish. . . .'

Eagle had written this letter with his manacled hand on 14 July 1944.

Swift, usually the most taciturn of men, was the first to break the silence that had descended on us: 'Eagle died sanctified by torture, but we have to face the sad realities.'

'You're right,' said Navarre. 'A watchdog never rests.'

They were so pale, haggard, emaciated, but I felt they were eager to do other things and impatient to give their all to plans that had matured in the days of their suffering. They had done their full share for the Resistance.

'Go and take up your men's responsibilities,' I said. 'I who have had the extraordinary luck to have come through everything. . . .'

Navarre smiled: 'Of course, you will carry on.'

Magpie came into my office and sat down facing me, visibly moved. I thought he was upset because of Jean-Paul Lien's (Lanky's) arrest. He had unmasked this man in the heart of Paris, parading in the uniform of a captain of the FFI. The traitor had confessed and would now pay his debt.

'We owe this to you, my dear Magpie. You're the sole survivor of the disastrous Operation Ingres. I don't know how to thank you.'

'You may be going to have the chance, madame,' he replied. And standing ceremoniously to attention he said: 'I have the honour to ask you for Ermine's hand in marriage.'

I called in the frail, fair young girl who had been my companion for so many painful hours, and left them together, taking with me the sight of their tender smiles. They were right. Faithful to memory, they were mapping out for us the way of hope.

I. THE MAIN CHARACTERS UNDER REAL NAMES

Albert, M.: *Mastiff*
Allibert, Fernand: *Barbet*
Amable, Henriette: *Tomboy*
Ambre, Johannès: *Gibbon*
Arbassier, Dr: *Snail*
Audoly, Emile: *Fox*

Barjot, Admiral Pierre: *Pluto*
Battu, Henri: *Opossum*
Battu, Mme Christiane: *Cricri*
Bernadac, Robert: *Robin*
Bernard, Paul: *Swift*
Bernard, Mme: *Chinchilla*
Berne-Churchill, Mme: *Ladybird*
Bernis, Colonel Charles: *Spaniel*
Berthomier, Jeanne: *Seamew*
Berthomier, Pierre: *Seagull*
Bichon, Edna: *Cat*
Blanc, Pierre: *Boar*
Bocher, Pierre: *Nightingale*
Bonnard, Henri: *Jay*
Bonnet, Armand: no cover name
Bontinck, Hermine: *Ermine*
Boussard, —. : *Cockerel*
Boutron, Jean: *Bull*
Bouyat, Jean: *Caviar*
Bridou, Jacques (the author's
   brother): no cover name
Broqua, Jean: *Rabbit*
Brouillet, Marguerite (Maritou): *Bee*

Carayon, Colonel Jean: *Phoenix*
Caussin, Robert: *Sea Hawk*
Centore, Denise: *Sable*
Champion, Henri: *Boa*
Charles, Jacques: *Lizard*
Clément, Fernand: *Ferret*
Cohen, Commander Kenneth: *Crane*
Coindeau, André: *Urus* (also *Nero*)
Collard, André: *Cactus*
Contrasty, Augustine: *Gazelle*
Cornouls, Capt. Henri: *Pegasus*
Cottoni, Superintendent: *Alpaca*
Coustenoble, Maurice: *Tiger*

Crawley, —. : *Heron*
Crémieu, Capt.: *Alligator*
Cros, Commandant Félix: *Aurochs*
Crozet, Madeleine: *Mouse*
Creel, Robert: *Labrador*

Dallas, Lt.-Pilote Pierre: *Mahout*
Damm, Sigismond: *Griffin*
Damm, Mme: *Vicuna*
Dampierre, Elie de: *Shepherd*
Darnel, Michel: *Bengali*
Dayné, Pierre: *Ant*
Denis-Burel, Jean: *Pony*
Descatoires, the Brothers: *Roach I
   and II*
Dor, Henri-Léopold: *Fawn*
Dumont, Germaine: *Cicada*

Erzberger, Else: *Adela*

Fabius, Odette: *Doe*
Faye, Commandant Léon: *Eagle*
Fontaine, Jean: *Lynx*
Fontenaille, Jeanne: *Turtle Dove*
Formery, Jacques: *Halibut*
Fourcade, Marie-Madeleine:
   Hedgehog
Fourcaud, Capt. Pierre:
   Bombshell
Freméndity, Henry: *Osprey*

Gartner, Arnold: *Zebra*
Gaveau, Michel: *Armadillo*
Georges-Picot, G.: *Giraffe*
Gillet, Maurice: *Unicorn*
Giovaccini, Pierre: *Pelican*
Giraud, Pierre: *Teutatès*
Godet, Jean: *Antelope*
Goldschmidt, Michèle: *Hummingbird*
Grappin, Jean: *Panda*
Grimprel, Marguerite: *Scarab*
Grosbety, Gaston: *Starling*
Guillebaud, Paul: *Moufflon*
Guillebaud, Rachelle: *Ewe*

Guillot, Georges: *Dromedary*
Guillot, Mme: *Grasshopper*

Hédin, Emile: *Beaver*
Hummel, Paul: *Cocker*

Isnards, Capt. le Comte Helen des:
  Grand Duke
Isnards, Comtesse des: *Marie-Sol*
  (her real names)

Jacquemin, Emile: *Lilac*
Jacquinot, Louis: *Tiger-Cat*
Jassaud, Alfred: no cover name
Jolly, Lucien: no cover name
Joyon, Victor: *Sea Lion*

Kapp, Antoine: *Peccary*
Kauffmann, Col. Edouard: *Cricket*
Kay: no cover name
Kiffer, Jean: *Asp*
Koenigswerther, Philippe: *Mandrill*

Lacapère, Dr: *Dolphin*
Lamarque, Georges: *Petrel*
Le Couteux, Philippe: *Valori*
Lefevre, Jean: *Gorilla*
Le Lorier, Robert: *Elk*
Lemaigne-Dubreuil, Jacques: *Tripe*
Lemaire, Louis: *Setter*
Lemoigne, Joël: *Triton*
Leveque, Michel: *Weevil*
Lien, Jean-Paul: *Lanky*
Liess, André: *Stork*
Lorilleux, Commandant Robert: *Icarus*
Lorin, Emile: *Sibelius*
Loustaunau-Lacau, Commandant
  Georges: *Navarre*
Lynen, Robert: *Eaglet*

Magenta, Maurice de MacMahon,
  Duke of: *Saluki*
Magenta, Duchess of: *Firefly*
Mahé, Commandant: *Pike*
Mareuil, Baroness de: *Wasp*
Marty, —. : *Hound*
Mengel, Paul: *Bat*
Mengel, Marie Thérèse: *Siren*
Mesnard, Marc: *The Bishop*
Michel, François: *Llama*

Nayrard, Pierre: *Yak*
Noal, Dr Pierre: *Grouse*

Payen, Louis: *Buccaneer*
Pelletier, Jean: *Bullfinch*
Pezet, Raymond: *Flying Fish*
Philippe, Commissaire Jean: *Basset*
Philippe, Robert: *Parrot*
Pinault, Lt.-Col. Lucien: *Dorado*
Portenard, Jean: *Widgeon*
Poulain, Edmond: no cover name
Poulard, Lt.-Pilote Lucien: *Jack Tar*
Pradelle, Capt. Emile: *Corsair*

Raison, Jean: *Moth*
Raynal, General Camille: *Sheepdog*
Richard, Daniel: *Blackbird*
Richard, Ulysse: *Lobster*
Riss, André: *Lapwing*
Rivat, Robert: *Finch*
Rivière, Gabriel: *Wolf*
Rodney, Frederick: *Magpie*
Romon, Gabriel: *Swan*
Rousseau, Jeannie: *Amniarix*

Sainteny, Jean: *Dragon*
Salmson, Georges: *The Knight*
Salmson, Mme Geneviève: *Mélisande*
Savon, Gilbert: *Badger*
Schaerrer, Henri: no cover name
Schneider, Camille: *Jaguar*
Siegrist, Ernest: *Elephant*
Siffret, Armand: *Oriole*
Simon, Félix: *Kite*
Sneyers, Jean-Philippe: *Bumpkin*
Stosskopf, Jacques: no cover name
Syriex, Dr: *Fox Terrier*

Thobois, Paul-René: *Pigeon*
Thorel, Jean-Claude: *Shad*
Trimel, Jean: *Muskrat*

Vallet, Lucien: no cover name
Verteré, Commandant: *Hyena*
Villedon, Lindley Williams de:
  Poodle
Vinzant, Jean: *Great Dane*

Zankovitch, Robert: *Hoplite*

II. THE MAIN CHARACTERS UNDER COVER NAMES

Adela: Else Erzberger
Agami: Professor Léon Mazeaud
Alligator: Capt. Crémieu
Alpaca: Superintendant Cottoni
Amniarix: Jeannie Rousseau,
  interpreter
Ant: Pierre Dayné
Antelope: Jean Godet, cognac
  merchant
Armadillo: Michel Gaveau, military
  intelligence expert
Asp: Jean Kiffer, company director
Aurochs: Commandant Félix Cros

Badger: Gilbert Savon
Barbet: Fernand Allibert,
  manufacturer
Basset: Commissaire Jean Philippe,
  police superintendant
Bat: Paul Mengel
Beaver: Emile Hédin
Bee: Marguerite (Maritou) Brouillet
Bengali: Michel Darnel
Bishop, The: Marc Mesnard,
  treasurer of the Network
Bison: Paris radio operator
Blackbird: Daniel Richard, radio
  operator
Boa: Henri Champion, industrialist
Boar: Pierre Blanc, engineer
Bombshell: Capt. Pierre Fourcaud
Buccaneer: Louis Payen
Bull: Jean Boutron, naval officer
Bullfinch: Jean Pelletier, electrician
Bumpkin: Jean-Philippe Sneyers

Cactus: André Collard, police
  inspector
Cat: Edna Bichon, student
Caviar: Jean Bouyat, naval engineer
Chinchilla: Mme Bernard
Cicada: Germaine Dumont, nurse
Cocker: Paul Hummel, public works
  contractor

Cockerel: —. Boussard
Cockroach: radio operator at
  Corniche CP
Corsair: Capt. Emile Pradelle
Crane: Commander Kenneth Cohen
  of the British Intelligence Service
Cricket: Colonel Edouard Kauffmann
Cricri: Christiane Battu

Doe: Odette Fabius, society woman
Dolphin: Dr Lacapère
Dorado: Lt.-Col. Lucien Pinault
Dragon: Jean Sainteny
Dromedary: Georges Guillot,
  policeman

Eagle: Commandant Léon Faye,
  military head of the Network
Eaglet: Robert Lynen, actor
Elephant: Ernest Siegrist, policeman
  and head of the Security Service
Elk: Robert le Lorier
Ermine: Hermine Bontinck, student
Ewe: Rachelle Guillebaud, dressmaker

Fawn: Henri-Léopold Dor
Ferret: Fernand Clément
Finch: Robert Rivat
Firefly: Marguerite, Duchess of
  Magenta
Flying Fish: Raymond Pezet,
  fighter pilot
Fox: Emile Audoly
Fox Terrier: Dr Syriex

Gavarni: patrol leader in the
  South-West
Gazelle: Augustine Contrasty,
  post office clerk
Gibbon: Johannès Ambre, lawyer
Giraffe: G. Georges-Picot
Gorilla: Jean Lefevre
Grand Duke: Capt. le Comte Helen
  des Isnards

Grasshopper: Mme Guillot
Great Dane: Jean Vinzant
Griffin: Sigismond Damm, Polish
manufacturer
Grouse: Dr Pierre Noal

Halibut: Jacques Formery
Hedgehog: the author, Marie-
Madeleine Fourcade
Heron: —. Crawley
Hoplite: Robert Zankovitch,
civil servant
Hound: —. Marty
Hummingbird: Michèle Goldschmidt
Hyena: Commandant Verteré

Icarus: Commandant Robert
Lorilleux

Jack Tar: Lt.-Pilote Lucien Poulard
Jaguar: Camille Schneider, engineer
Jay: Henri Bonnard, radio engineer

Kay: her true name
Kite: Félix Simon, student
Knight, The: Georges Salmson

Labrador: Robert Creel, student
Ladybird: Mme Berne-Churchill
Lanky: Jean-Paul Lien, student and
Sneyer's adjutant
Lapwing: André Riss, student
Lilac: Emile Jacquemin
Lizard: Jacques Charles, civil
servant
Llama: François Michel, civil
servant
Lobster: Ulysse Richard, treasury
official
Lynx: Jean Fontaine, fighter pilot

Magpie: Frederick Rodney, British
radio operator
Mahout: Lt.-Pilote Pierre Dallas,
head of the Avia Service
Mandrill: Philippe Koenigswerther
Marie-Sol: Comtesse des Isnards,
wife of Grand Duke

Mastiff: M. Albert, butler at the
Corniche command post
Mélisande: Mme Geneviève Salmson
Moth: Jean Raison, police
superintendent
Moufflon: Paul Guillebaud, civil
servant
Mouse: Madeleine Crozet, nurse
Muskrat: Jean Trimel

Navarre: Commandant Georges
Loustaunau-Lacau, founder of the
Alliance Network
Nightingale: Pierre Bocher, merchant

Opossum: Henri Battu
Oriole: Armand Siffret, airman
Osprey: Henry Freméndity

Panda: Jean Grappin
Parrot: Robert Philippe, head of the
radio service
Peccary: Antoine Kapp, civil servant
Pegasus: Capt. Henri Cornouls
Pelican: Pierre Giovaccini, Air Force
engineer
Petrel: Georges Lamarque, head of
the Druid sub-service
Phoenix: Colonel Jean Carayon
Pigeon: Paul-René Thobois, radio
operator
Pike: Commandant Mahé
Pluto: Admiral Pierre Barjot
Pony: Jean Denis-Burel
Poodle: Lindley Williams de Villedon,
student

Rabbit: Jean Broqua
Ram: also known as *Gulliver*
Roach I and II: the brothers
Descatoires
Robin: Robert Bernadac, policeman

Sable: Denise Centore, HQ
secretary, historian
Saluki: Maurice de McMahon,
Duke of Magenta
Scarab: Marguerite Grimprel,
society woman

Seagull: Pierre Berthomier, civilian
  pilot
Sea Hawk: Robert Caussin,
  electrician
Sea Lion: Victor Joyon, shipper
Seamew: Jeanne Berthomier
Setter: Louis Lemaire, merchant
Shad: Jean-Claude Thorel
Sheepdog: General Camille Raynal
Shepherd: Elie de Dampierre
Shrimp: net repairer at Brest
Sibelius: Emile Lorin
Siren: Marie Thérèse Mengel,
  wife of Paul Mengel
Snail: Dr Arbassier
Spaniel: Colonel Charles Bernis
Starling: Gaston Grosbety, merchant
Stork: André Liess, radio operator
Swan: Gabriel Romon, army
  engineer officer
Swift: Paul Bernard

Teutatès: Pierre Giraud, insurance
  agent
Tiger: Maurice Coustenoble,
  Air Force NCO
Tiger-Cat: Louis Jacquinot, former
  Minister of the Interior

Tomboy: Henriette Amable,
  housewife
Tringa: radio operator
Tripe: Jacques Lemaigne-Dubreuil,
  industrialist
Triton: Joël Lemoigne
Turtle Dove: Jeanne Fontenaille,
  student

Unicorn: Maurice Gillet
Urus (also *Nero*): André Coindeau

Valori: Philippe Le Couteux
Vicuna: Mme Damm

Wasp: Baroness de Mareuil,
  journalist
Weevil: Michel Leveque
Widgeon: Jean Portenard, electrician
Wolf: Gabriel Rivière

Yak: Pierre Nayrard, radio
  constructor

Zebra: Arnold Gartner, adopted son
  of M. and Mme Damm, factory
  foreman

Library of Congress Cataloging-in-Publication Data

Fourcade, Marie-Madeleine, 1909-
[Arche de Noé. English]
Noah's Ark / Marie-Madeleine Fourcade.
p. cm. — (Classics of World War II. The secret war)
Translation of: L'Arche de Noé.
Reprint. Previously published: New York : Dutton, 1974.
ISBN 0-8094-8587-7 — ISBN 0-8094-8588-5 (lib. bdg.)
1. World War, 1939-1945—Underground movements—France.
2. Fourcade, Marie-Madeleine, 1909-
3. World War, 1939-1945—Personal narratives, French.
4. Guerrillas—France—Biography.
5. France—History—German occupation, 1940-1945.
I. Title. II. Series.
[D802.F8F6313 1991]   940.53'44—dc20   91-16460 CIP

Published by arrangement with EDITIONS PLON, Paris

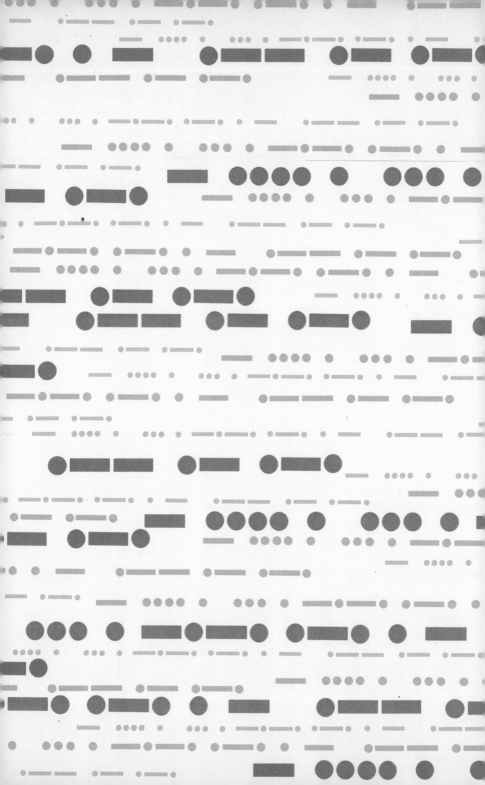